Also in the Variorum Collected Studies Series:

Ideas in the Medieval West

Professor Valerie I.J. Flint

Valerie I. J. Flint

Ideas in the Medieval West:
Texts and their Contexts

VARIORUM REPRINTS
London 1988

British Library CIP data

Flint, Valerie I. J.
   Ideas in the Medieval West: texts
   and their contexts. — (Collected
   studies series; CS268).
   1. Europe — Intellectual life
   2. Civilization, Medieval
   I. Title
   940.1'46   CB351

   ISBN 0–86078–216–6

270.41
H774Y
F625i

Published in Great Britain by   Variorum Reprints
                                   20 Pembridge Mews London W11 3EQ

Printed in Great Britain by   Galliard (Printers) Ltd
                                   Great Yarmouth Norfolk

                                   VARIORUM REPRINT CS268

CONTENTS

This volume contains xii + 322 pages.

PUBLISHER'S NOTE

The articles in this volume, as in all others in the Collected Studies Series, have not been given a new, continuous pagination. In order to avoid confusion, and to facilitate their use where these same studies have been referred to elsewhere, the original pagination has been maintained wherever possible.

Each article has been given a Roman number in order of appearance, as listed in the Contents. This number is repeated on each page and quoted in the index entries.

PREFACE

One conviction, which has grown in strength through the writing of these articles, now serves to unite them. It is that no text, and so no idea to which a text gave flight, can be properly understood unless it is placed firmly within its immediate historical context. This stricture applies even to those ideas and treatises which are undoubtedly the product of an individual genius. The publication of written work of any length, before the advent of printing, involved considerable expense of many kinds; it required also, therefore, powerful contemporary incentives. The pressures which brought a writer to the point of composition, and the immediate patrons, audience and purposes for which he wrote, demand, then, the most careful attention. I have attempted here to search out some of these pressures and purposes, and to trace their impress upon certain writers and certain types of text.

Many clues helpful to this search have become now a little buried; some by the passage of time, some by the fact that surviving evidence is indirect or in disguise, some, especially, by the ways in which scholars of literature and historians of ideas have been encouraged to approach their sources. There has in the past been a tendency to concentrate attention upon two chief ends: the completion of a definitive edition, replete with apparatus and analysis, often linguistic, and the placing of a treatise within a primarily chronological framework. Illumination is sought in the main, within a framework such as this, about the sources upon which the author relied, the tradition within which the text stood, the legacy it bequeathed to posterity. Without in the least meaning to belittle these two activities—indeed, we need far more such exercises, and quickly—these articles are an attempt at a third. Rather than look backwards to their literary ancestors, or forwards to their heirs, I have tried to look sideways from the texts, and so into the society which pressed upon them and their compilers. This 'lateral' view, of course, will alter the perspective through which we see the treatise; and this different perspective may, in its turn, lead to an opinion radically revised about the place of that treatise in the history of ideas. It has led me to many such revised opinions. In the *Historia Regum Britanniae* (article

II), for example, we have a work which has attracted much interest as part founder, part inheritor of a strong and purely literary tradition. I have felt bound to challenge this view, and to suggest instead that the work was in fact a work of propaganda, bound to its own period and directed in the first place at strictly contemporary institutional ambitions and parallel social anxieties. Later users of the treatise speedily lost sight of these its true pre-occupations. 'Tradition', and the adaptations of supposed heirs, can thus both inhibit our understanding of the immediate aims of a work, and mislead us as to its nature. This is the lesson also of article IV. This time I have tried to untangle, again by strict reference to their immediate contemporary contexts, interpretations distorted by the pressures of the seventeenth century, and visited backwards upon the eighth. Article XI, again, is an effort to modify a narrowly chronological approach, this time to biblical commentaries. I try to shew here that there is profit to be derived from placing certain such commentaries against a backcloth of differing contemporary scholarly and monastic communities.

When looking to and from written texts in this way, my attention has been attracted increasingly to the needs of the medieval christian pastorate, and to the influence upon writers exerted by these needs. By 'the pastorate' I mean those persons to whom the christian pastor hoped to bring his message, an area of action impossible demographically or geographically wholly to define at this period, but one bursting with energy and of the first importance. Bursting energy often shows itself in obduracy and I have, indeed, chosen those areas of the pastorate which have been thrown into relief by their resistances as the best point from which to begin. An obdurate resistance to his message confronted the christian pastor from many quarters. It might be expected, of course, to be found among Jews. It might remain among the remnants of the old religion, to be re-awakened when the new seemed to fail, or to make too great demands. It might even spring from forces within the christian church itself. It might come, for example, from persons who felt ill-equipped to bear the burdens of the pastorate as it stood, and yet were pressed to do so. It might come, on the contrary, from those who felt excluded from it, and so denied an influence they were sure was rightly theirs. Each of the remaining articles is concerned in some way with these resistances. Article XIV calls attention to the imprint left upon certain texts by the presence of Jewish communities. Articles III, IX and XIII uncover the traces of residual pagan superstition and try to shew that these left their mark upon both scientific treatises and histories.

Article X concerns primarily the pastorally ill-equipped, articles XII and I the pastorally ambitious. Article I is perhaps my favourite. It attempts to illustrate how easy it is to misunderstand the place in intellectual history of 'schools' if we neglect the ambitions of the excluded, or the needs of the pastorate as a whole.

Honorius Augustodunensis has a section all to himself. I have given him this for two reasons. Firstly, he is an outstanding example of an exceptionally prolific writer who was, in addition, subjected to a great variety of pressures; a microcosm, perhaps, of the larger considerations upon which I have dwelt so far. Secondly, an enormous amount of work remains to be done on him. Not even the outline of his career is as yet established beyond doubt, although (articles V and VI) I have tried to depict some of the influences attendant upon it, and to date some of its crucial moments. In article VII, I set out also a possible chronology for Honorius's works; indicate, in articles VIII and IX, some of the editorial difficulties and messages from the manuscripts we need still to take into account; place, in articles X, XI and XII, some of Honorius's efforts within their immediate contexts; and point, in articles XIII and XIV, to a few of the special stresses to which he may have been subject. My reconstruction of Honorius's life has developed progressively over, now, some twenty years. Rather than drag the reader chronologically through all the stages, I have put those articles which come closest to a conclusion at the head of the list (V and VI) and these will modify some of the observations made in some of the lower ones. These, in their turn, fall into two groups. Articles VIII–X treat works associated with his time in England, and articles XI–XIV set his works within their wider contexts. Even so, this is only a beginning, and some of my tentative conclusions have been called into question along the way. In a short addendum, therefore, I have given a little further bibliography and drawn attention to opinions which differ from my own.

I should here like to thank the original publishers of the articles reprinted in this volume, that is: the *Revue Bénédictine* and the Abbaye de Maredsous (V–VII, X–XII); *Scriptorium* (VIII, IX); *Recherches de Théologie ancienne et médiévale*, Abdij Keizersberg (I); *Speculum* and the Medieval Academy of America (II); *Viator* and the University of California Press (IV); the Oxford Universty Press (XIII); and the *Journal of Jewish Studies*, Oxford Centre for Postgraduate Hebrew Studies (XIV). Permission to reproduce was instantly and generously given by each one. Many of the additional debts I have incurred are acknowledged in the footnotes to the articles and in the bibliographical addendum. I wish especially to mention, however, the overwhelming ones I owe to Sir Richard and Lady Southern for guidance and friendship extending now over very many years, and to my friends and colleagues in Auckland, Miss Jean Silver and Dr Philip Rousseau. I wish also to thank the Interloans section of the Auckland University Library for their willing responses to often appalling demands, and Mrs Barbara Batt of the Auckland University History Department for her skilful help in the preparation of the manuscript.

VALERIE I. J. FLINT

Auckland, New Zealand
April 1987

I

The "School of Laon":
A Reconsideration

Trying to understand the history of the twelfth century schools of France is a little like picking one's way through an uncharted mine-field; and the charge lately detonated near the school of Chartres has done nothing to soothe the nerves [1]. The school at Laon, however, still remains in all its solidity of outline, reassuringly on its rock, apparently the foundation of all the rest. We owe its now familiar shape, and especially our belief in its solidity, to efforts made early in the present century by a small group of devoted scholars [2]. An exceptional amount of exertion uncovered the exegetical work of the brothers Anselm (d. 1117) and Ralph (d. 1131/33) and, with it, the numerous theological 'sententiae' to which this work, so characteristic of the school, seemed to have given rise [3]. It was a relatively painless step, at the end of these

1. R. W. SOUTHERN, *Humanism and the School of Chartres*, in *Medieval Humanism and Other Studies* (Oxford 1970), pp. 61-85. Again my debt to the help and inspiration of Dr. Southern is beyond measure. I should like to thank, too, Dr. Philip Rousseau for much helpful criticism.

2. Most notably F. BLIEMETZRIEDER, *Anselme von Laon Systematische Sentenzen*, in *Beiträge zur Geschichte der Philosophie des Mittelaters* (= BGPM) 18 (1919) 1-167, H. WEISWEILER, *L'École d'Anselme de Laon et de Guillaume de Champeaux. Nouveaux documents*, in *Recherches de théologie ancienne et médiévale* (= RTAM) 4 (1932) 237-269, 371-391; *La Summa Sententiarum, source de Pierre Lombard*, in RTAM 6 (1934) 131-148, and *Das Schrifttum der Schule Anselms von Laon und Wilhelms von Champeaux in deutschen Bibliotheken*, in BGPM 33 (1936) 1-415; R. SILVAIN, *La tradition des Sentences d'Anselme de Laon*, in *Archives d'histoire doctrinale et littéraire du moyen âge* (= AHDL) 16 (1948) 1-51. The most resolute of all, perhaps, has been Dom O. Lottin. The major part of his work on the school is collected together in *Psychologie et morale aux XIIe et XIIIe siècles*, V (Louvain 1959).

3. See especially F. BLIEMETZRIEDER, *L'œuvre d'Anselme de Laon et la littérature théologique contemporaine. I. Honorius d'Autun* and *II. Hugues de Rouen*, in RTAM 5 (1933) 277 and 7 (1935) 47.

'exertions, to the decision that the associations between this incipient theology of the twelfth century revival of learning, and the biblical exegesis of the school at Laon, were clear enough and close enough to enable all to be treated together under the general heading 'school of Laon'. This step was taken, and the decision has since gained wide acceptance.

This paper, it should be said immediately, has no charge to set against the school *at* Laon. The existence of the school of the brothers Anselm and Ralph in the late eleventh and early twelfth centuries is, unlike that of Chartres, unassailable. It does, however, seek to challenge the general heading 'school *of* Laon' and the equally general acceptance of it. To use the phrase 'school of Laon' to describe both the school *at* Laon and a whole phase of biblical and theological enquiry is, it will be argued, inadmissible. It is inadmissible in the first place because even the lightest use of the phrase inclines the mind to accept assumptions about the primary importance of Anselm's school which are not at all firmly based; and it is inadmissible in the second because this initial inclination may lead to a serious misunderstanding of the later history of the schools, including that of the school *at* Laon. The simpler steps are often the most dangerous in mine-fields; and this one was very dangerous indeed.

The first part of the discussion which follows will advise, therefore, a retreat to safer ground. The deceptions of the phrase will, it is hoped, be exposed, and with them the perils involved in its use. We may pursue then, however, a more positive end than this. Some evidence, up to now quite smothered by the description 'school of Laon', may be seen, once its grip is loosened, to be of a quite outstanding independent importance. The later parts of the discussion will concentrate upon this evidence, and will examine the bearing it may have upon the later history of the schools.

I

The school *at* Laon seems largely to have been created by a single master. Master Anselm taught there before 1100, and was dean in 1110, perhaps until 1115, when he became archdeacon[4]. It has so far proved impossible to compile an exact corpus of Anselm's biblical and theological writings, but we may attempt an approximate one. Anselm wanted to gloss the whole bible, but was prevented from carrying out his project, says Peter the Chanter, by the demands of administration[5]. He managed, however, to produce glosses and commentaries on the Epistles of St. Paul[6], perhaps a commentary on the first chapters of the Book of Genesis[7] and on St. Matthew[8], and, perhaps again, one on the Song of Songs[9]. He wrote a letter, also, to Abbot Heribrand of St. Laurence of Liège about the academic indiscretions of Rupert of Deutz, and this letter has survived[10]. Anselm made contributions

4. G. LEFÈVRE, *De Anselmo Laudunensi Scholastico (1050-1117)*, (Évreux 1895), pp. 16, 46. As Dom A. Wilmart pointed out (*Un Commentaire des Psaumes restitué à Anselme de Laon*, in RTAM 8 (1936) 341, n. 58), there is no proof that he studied at Bec under St. Anselm nor at Paris. This assumption continues nonetheless to be made; for example, by A. LANDGRAF, *Lexikon für Theologie und Kirche* (Freiburg i. Br. 1957), I, 595.

5. B. SMALLEY, *The Study of the Bible in the Middle Ages* (Oxford 1952), p. 50.

6. The gloss *Pro altercatione* seems now certainly to be his. LOTTIN, *op. cit.*, V, 31. This was to become the *Ordinaria*. One section of a commentary on the First Epistle to the Corinthians (ch. 10, v. 16) was long disguised under the name of Anselm of Canterbury as a letter on the eucharist. Doubt about this attribution was first expressed by A. WILMART, *Les Homélies attribuées à S. Anselme*, in AHDL 2 (1927) 9-10, taken up again in *La tradition des lettres de S. Anselme. Lettres inédites de S. Anselme et de ses correspondants*, in *Revue bénédictine* 43 (1931) 39, n. 4. The letter was found to be part of a commentary on the epistle by H. WEISWEILER, *Das Schrifttum der Schule Anselms von Laon und Wilhelms von Champeaux in deutschen Bibliotheken*, in BGPM 33 (1936-37) 192-198, and was finally attributed to Anselm of Laon by Dom LOTTIN, (*Anselme de Laon auteur de la « Lettre » de S. Anselme sur le Cène*, in RTAM 13 1946, 222-225). Dom Wilmart, again, suspecting the attribution of homily XVI (PL 158, 673-674) to St. Anselm prepared the way for the discovery that it too was part of a commentary by Anselm of Laon on Hebrews (II, 10). The so-called homily was contained in the *Liber Pancrisis* and printed as a sentence from it by Dom LOTTIN (*op. cit.*, V, 50-52), Dom Lottin does not refer to the fact that the sentence had been so disguised.

7. This seems probable because of the subject matter of some of the sentences attributed to him; for example, LOTTIN, *op. cit.*, V, pp. 30, 36-41, 44-45.

8. Most probably that found in Ms. *Alençon 26*. Lottin has argued most effectively against the attribution of the text printed in PL 162, 1227-1500 to Geoffrey Babion (LOTTIN, *op. cit.*, V, 153-169).

9. PL 162, 1187-1228. Discussed by J. LECLERCQ, *Le Commentaire du Cantique des Cantiques attribué à Anselme de Laon*, in RTAM 16 (1949) 29-39.

10. PL 162, 1587-1592, and in an amended edition in LOTTIN, *op. cit.*, V, 175-176.

I

too to the gloss, later to become the *Glossa ordinaria* in the form
of a gloss on the Epistles of St. Paul, one on the Psalter and
one on the Gospel of St. John [11]. To the sum may then be added
those of his opinions on matters of theology which have been
handed down as fragments in the sentence collections. The *Sententiae
divinae paginae* may have been largely based on his work [12].

These glosses and commentaries of Anselm upon specific books
of the bible can, I think, be described as characteristic of his
school at Laon. Laon was not, however, the only physical centre
for such efforts. There are some almost contemporary writings,
later ascribed to 'Master Manegold', which are very similar.
We are still very far from knowing whether these writings come
from the pen of one man, namely Master Manegold of Lautenbach,
or whether there were two masters of this name writing at this
time [13]. Fortunately the definitive resolution of this very difficult
question is not essential to the present argument. 'Manegold',
like Anselm, wrote glosses and commentaries, glosses most probably

That it was addressed to Heribrand is maintained most convincingly by H. SILVESTRE,
A propos de la Lettre d'Anselme de Laon à Héribrand de Saint-Laurent, in RTAM 28
(1961) 5-25.

11. B. SMALLEY, *op. cit.*, p. 60, and also *Les commentaires bibliques de l'époque
romane : glose ordinaire et gloses périmées*, in *Cahiers de civilisation médiévale* 4
(1961) 16. Dom Lottin argues against the opinion put forward by Wilmart that
the commentary on the Psalms attributed to Haymo of Halberstadt is really that
of Anselm of Laon and can find therefore no evidence of a continuous commentary
(*op. cit.*, V, 170-175). There is, however, much to be said for Wilmart's view;
V. I. J. FLINT, *Some Notes on the Early Twelfth Century Commentaries on the Psalms*,
in RTAM 37 (1971) 80-85. For the gloss on John, Anselm drew on distinguished
earlier work from Laon. E. JEAUNEAU, *Les écoles de Laon et d'Auxerre au
IXᵉ siècle*, in *Settimane di studio del Centro italiano di studi sull'alto medioevo* 19
(1972) 508-509.

12. F. BLIEMETZRIEDER, *art. cit.* (1933) 277-81. The *Sententiae Anselmi*, contained
in Ms. *Gonville and Caius College, Cambridge, 151*, seem, on the other hand,
to have been founded upon the work of Anselm's brother Ralph.

13. See F. CHATILLON, *Recherches critiques sur les différents personnages nommés
Manegold*, in *Revue du Moyen Âge latin* 9 (1953) 153-170. This article revives
the old problem of the two Manegolds. It is primarily a destructive one, aiming
simply to demonstrate that many of the attributions made to Manegold of Lautenbach
are not adequately proved. It does not, however, shew any of them to be beyond
doubt false, and it may still be that Manegold of Lautenbach is the single author.
The best recent treatment of Manegold of Lautenbach is that by W. HARTMANN,
Manegold von Lautenbach und die Anfänge der Frühscholastik, in *Deutsches Archiv
für Erforschung des Mittelalters* 26 (1970) 47-149,

on Isaiah and St. Matthew, and commentaries on the Psalter, the Song of Songs and perhaps on the Apocalypse[14]. A gloss later ascribed to 'Manegold' on the Pauline Epistles seems actually to have influenced Master Anselm's work on the same[15]. It is most unlikely, however, that 'Manegold' ever came to Laon[16]. All this work, in fact, is evidence of the strength neither of the 'School of Laon', nor even of the School *at* Laon, but of an exegetical interest in certain books of the bible, most notably the Psalter, the Epistles of St. Paul, the Gospel of St. Matthew, which spread far more widely than the school both in its origins and, indeed, in its ends.

The school physically situated at Laon, then, is at best only one manifestation of a much larger exegetical endeavour. The phrase 'school of Laon' is hardly adequate to describe this endeavour in all its breadth and depth. There are, however, more profound reasons for disquiet at the continued use of this phrase than these. When one turns from the contemplation of this large scale effort at exegesis to the theological sentence collections which supposedly emanated from it, two things become

14. It is as difficult to collect together 'Manegold's' writings as it is Anselm's. It is perhaps, however, possible to rely upon the so-called Anonymous of Melk for some information about the glosses and the commentary on the Psalter. E. ETTLINGER, *Der sogenannten Anonymus Mellicensis De scriptoribus ecclesiasticis*, (Karlsruhe 1896), p. 91. The commentary on the Song of Songs is mentioned in the exegesis of psalm 77 in an existing commentary on the Psalter which may be by Manegold of Lautenbach, V.I.J. FLINT, *art. cit.* 86-88. For a sympathetic discussion of the problems which still surround Manegold of Lautenbach's commentary on the Psalter see, W. HARTMANN, *Psalmenkommentare aus der Zeit der Reform und der Frühscholastik*, in *Studi Gregoriani* IX (1972) 319-327 and 354-366. For the 'stillae verborum Magistri Menegaudi in Apocalypsim' see CHATILLON, *art. cit.*, pp. 165-170.

15. O. LOTTIN, *Manegold de Lautenbach source d'Anselme de Laon*, in RTAM 14 (1947) 218-223. In his revision of this article in *Psychol. et morale* V, 146-153, Dom Lottin wondered about his earlier insistence that this Manegold was Manegold of Lautenbach.

16. And, of course, there were others likewise independent of Laon, engaged in work that was similar. Lanfranc of Bec and Canterbury is one of the more spectacular of these. His own commentary on the Epistles of St. Paul seems to have been built into the gloss *Pro altercatione*; M. GIBSON, *Lanfranc's Commentary on the Pauline Epistles*, in *Journal of Theological Studies* 22 (1971) 112. See also B. SMALLEY, *La Glossa ordinaria: quelques prédécesseurs d'Anselme de Laon*, in RTAM 9 (1937) 365-400.

apparent. The first is that it is difficult in the extreme to find among these collections any real unity. The second is that that little unity which can be found obstinately refuses to be linked firmly and finally with any recognisable body of biblical exegesis, including that body we have tentatively assigned to Laon.

The theological 'sententiae' generally known as of the 'school of Laon' are to be found scattered throughout the medieval libraries of Europe. Many of the larger collections, such as the *Sententiae divinae paginae*, the *Liber Pancrisis*, the *Sententiae Anselmi* ('Principium et causa omnium'), and the *Sententiae Atrebatenses* have been fully and carefully edited. They are found for the first time in manuscripts of the twelfth century, and so have been seen, rightly, as an important phenomenon in the twelfth century revival of learning. They have come down to us, however, in an appallingly tangled state. They vary in form from the relatively extended treatise to the occasional remark, and in substance from prolonged discussions on the economy of the redemption to bitter polemic against failed priests; and, unhappily, attempts to recognise a pattern *in* them have tended to degenerate very quickly into the imposition of a structure *on* them[17].

There is a species of unity to be found in the connections between the contents of the 'sententiae' and early twelfth century biblical exegesis. There are connections, certainly, between the 'sententiae' and precisely those books of the bible which the exegetes of the late eleventh and early twelfth centuries singled out for close attention. Of the two hundred and twenty eight sentences set out by Lottin as certainly, probably, and plausibly traceable to Anselm of Laon, at least ninety two are clearly drawn from the exegesis of the Epistles of St. Paul, thirty eight

---

17. An extended exercise in this form of artificiality may be found in R. SILVAIN, *art. cit.* In his efforts to shew 'que les textes de l'École de Laon répondent tous à une conception commune qui ne peut être que celle des sentences originales d'Anselme et qui a été reproduite par les disciples du maître sous forme de reportatio' (p. 3, n. 1), Silvain had recourse to a threefold division. This comprised 'textes modèles' (such as the *Sententiae divinae paginae* and the *Principium*), 'compilations', 'textes isolés'. Yet it is impossible to trace the 'textes modèles' back to an absolute model and we have no means of being sure that they are not also 'compilations'. It may also be that for the 'textes isolés' we simply lack the collections which contain them. All we have really is a tremendous multiplicity of 'sententiae' on a comparatively limited range of subjects.

I

from that on Genesis, six from the Psalms, five from St. Matthew, three from the Song of Songs, two each from Luke and John[18]. This correspondence of interest at so many points between the sentences and Anselm of Laon's exegetical work has been largely responsible for that determination to tie them all, once and for all, firmly together which has resulted in the ascriptions which have been made; and the geographical distribution of the collections, the state in which many of them are found, their anonymity and above all their detachment in this form from their exegetical roots must increase our admiration for these feats of identification. But still, after so many such labours, and so much energy spent, the sentence collections simply cannot as a whole be annexed to any course of commenting upon books of the bible which we can describe as a 'scholarly' one. They come from comments on these books, these books were, we know, those which most interested Anselm of Laon and his contemporaries, and some of the 'sententiae' are undoubtedly Anselm's. But the comments come, too, from other people, and from almost everywhere within these books; and when we look for the structure of any lesson in which any master might have let slip these remarks, information suddenly, and it seem inexplicably, fails. The best explanation which has been so far offered for the tantalisingly complicated condition of the 'sententiae' in the earliest manuscripts, is that they were based in the first place upon oral teaching. The master commented upon a section of the sacred page, and the further comments and discussions which followed this were written down. They were not, accordingly, ordered by the central course of exegetical exercises, but were subsidiary to it. Some evidence for such a process is provided by Abelard[19]. Yet we have no 'published', no magisterial version; and we lack this not for want of a will to find it[20]. If the 'sententiae' were, even though

18. LOTTIN, op. cit. V, 19-143. I have counted only those which actually quote a text of the bible. Far more could be fitted with a high degree of probability into these biblical categories. Very few fall outside them.

19. Historia calamitatum, ed. J. MONFRIN (Paris 1959), p. 68. And see LOTTIN's criticism of Silvain, op. cit. V, 178-183.

20. The loss is constantly acknowledged by SILVAIN, art. cit., pp. 2, 11, 20, 31, and his efforts to reconstruct them were very thorough if, according to LOTTIN (ubi supra p. 183), misguided.

loosely, associated with the teaching of an established school, this lack is strange. It is stranger still if they were associated with Laon, for we know, again from Abelard, that Anselm minded what went out from his school[21]. Here, then, is another enigma; but there are still more. We have no magisterial version, or versions, but we have a multiplicity of almost the opposite, that is, of interwoven, intermixed and usually anonymous theological opinions. To say the least, the sentence collections in their present state take us far from the school at Laon itself; and they begin to take on an appearance to which it is difficult to apply the term 'scholastic' or even the description 'of the schools'[22].

There has been found, so far, only one pattern which underlies the sentence collections, gives them some cohesion and allows them to be treated as an entity. It is neither a magisterial nor an exegetical one. It is based not on origins, formal or physical, but on order. For the most part, the 'sententiae' follow in their arrangement the order of creation. They take us through the attributes of God, his creative work, the fall and its results and remedies, the old law, the redemption and the sacraments, the moral life, the last ends, the after life. This 'common air', built of common concerns but above all of a shared arrangement of them, is their truly distinguishing feature[23]. Now, this order, this structure of the sentence books, is not at all the structure, as we have it so far, of the teaching of any of the schools. In other words, that which describes the 'sententiae' best as a genre is *precisely* that which divides them from the schools from which they are supposed to have come. It can certainly never be used to link them directly with Laon.

We may now see why there is profound reason for disquiet at the continued use of the phrase 'school of Laon' to describe

21. *Historia calamitatum, ed. cit.*, p. 69.

22. Silvain explains this by 'reportatio', that is, the recounting of oral lessons in theology by pupils in successive schools, *art. cit.*, pp. 17-19. Lottin prefers the idea that the sentences were written down from the first lessons, then formed the basis of further written collections. The difficulty in the way of the resolution of these points of practice is a reminder of the dangers of large assumptions.

23. LOTTIN, *op. cit.* V, 17. Valuable information about the order common to different sentence collections may also be gained from SILVAIN, *art. cit.*, pp. 6-7, 8-10, 38-52, provided one is wary of the conclusions he draws from it.

this phase of biblical and theological enquiry. The exegetical work of the period may not be confined to Laon, and the 'sententiae' shew themselves in the last resort unyielding even to the most fervent efforts to link them with Anselm's famous school. Thus the description is deceptive, and it should be relinquished. There are, however, unexpected advantages hidden in one aspect of the deception. The heroic efforts made to trace the 'sententiae' back to Laon have not been entirely without reward: for in the very difficulty of the search, in the very intractability, that is, of the 'sententiae' in particular to this form of enquiry, there are real clues to be found. It may be possible, on the basis of these, to make discoveries which will compensate, at least in some measure, for those efforts which seem at this moment to have been so unprofitable.

II

The theological questioning recounted in the collections of 'sententiae' may be, indeed has been, distinguished from both earlier and later types[24]. It may be distinguished by the fact that it dispenses with the philosophical background which a discussion of, for example, the hypostatic union or the problem of transsubstantiation would require. Scholarly enquiry of the profounder sort is, in other words, alien to this brand of literature, as it is indeed to the glosses and commentaries on the bible. It may now be said in addition that these questions and answers were, of all theological matters, those most pertinent to the moral concerns of every day life. They were answers to questions about, for example, the foundations of sin and happiness[25], about God's presence in places and in his creatures, about God's will, free will, justice, virtues and vices, the avoiding of scandals, the place of carnal affection, the sacraments of baptism and marriage, the

---

24. Notably by Dom LOTTIN in *Nouveaux fragments théologiques de l'école d'Anselme de Laon*, in RTAM 14 (1947) 158.
25. One interesting article which treats of the concern of the sentence books with sin is J. GOSS, *Die Ur- und Erbsunderlehre der Schule von Laon*, in *Zeitschrift für Kirchengeschichte* 76 (1965) 12-40. Unfortunately, however, this perpetuates the idea that all such concern sprang from Laon.

priesthood, the ultimate reward for honest labour. Much of this can be seen simply by taking the printed 'sententiae' and reading them. A good example is 'De temptatione'[26].

> "Temptatio nos non apprehendat nisi humana" (*I Cor.* 10, 13). Temptatio alia humana, alia demoniaca. Humana est quedam suggestio que est motus carnis, que ex humana fragilitate, <quam> homo non potest evitare, et per baptismum solvitur a reatu; remanet tamen ad agonem, ut dicit Iheronimus, et est fomes peccati, scilicet culpa descendens ex transgressione primi parentis, unde dicitur temptatio *humana*, quia homo primus fecit eam suam ex propria culpa et inde modo omnibus nobis communis est. Dicitur etiam eadem in nobis temptatio nature, quia est ex fomite peccati quem habet homo a prima sua origine, qui ita familiariter comitatur naturam humanam quasi humane conditionis a prima conditione, priori status Ade.
>
> Demoniaca temptatio dicitur motus carnis qui potest evitari; et dicitur diabolica, quia valde placet diabolo; per eam enim habet potestatem in hominibus, per humanam autem non. Que licet sit peccatum, excusatur per humanam infirmitatem et in baptismo sufficiens habet remedium. Demoniaca etiam dicitur temptatio voluntatis, quia ex propria voluntate et deliberatione hominis est. Itaque si dixerimus: temptatio sive suggestio alia humana, alia demoniaca, vel alia nature, alia voluntatis eamdem summam expressimus ...

Here is all the concern with sin and guilt and blame and their origins, with, in fact, the human condition, which so characterises the theology of the 'sententiae'.

These characteristics may be demonstrated even more clearly by looking directly at the manuscripts. Two 'sentence' manuscripts, of the twelfth century and at present in the Bodleian Library, Oxford, Mss. *Laud Misc. 277* and *Lat. Th. d. 35* are particularly good examples to take. *Laud Misc. 277* contains first of all (ff. 2-23ᵛ) the *Principium et causa omnium*. In the set of isolated 'sententiae' it then includes it shews a special concern with marriage (f. 23), frigidity, (ff. 27-28), with the place of corporal creation in God's scheme of creation, with the divinity of creatures, with the relations between soul and body, between God and the devil (ff. 28-29). It also has points to make (f. 28ᵛ) about the place of preaching and, in particular, about the fact that even false preachers may bring forth good fruit. *Lat. Th. d. 35* begins with the giving

---

26. No 134 in *Psychol. et morale*, and thought by Lottin to have come most probably from Anselm of Laon himself.

of the Lord's body to his disciples at the last supper (f. 167), and goes on to discuss the love exhibited at the crucifixion and mediated to man (f. 229^v), the ways of sinning, the affections and the gift of tears (f. 230), baptism, the soul, the meaning and place of marriage (f. 230^v), why God gave men bodies and souls, the corruption of nature through the sin of Adam (f. 231), the sacrament of the Eucharist (f. 231^v), the goodness of God (f. 232), the beatitudes and the commandments, sin, temptation and penance (ff. 276-83). The sentence quoted above appears also in this manuscript (f. 282^v).

The phrase 'school of Laon' has been allowed so to capture the 'sententiae' and so to contain them within the shadow of the schools that these characteristics have never been looked at for themselves. But when they are, when the 'sententiae', that is, are seem in isolation from the captive phrase, they have much to offer; for it becomes suddenly startlingly easy to see how the questions to which these 'sententiae' are the answers arose, and why the books that contain them were put together. The sentence collections, and indeed the endeavours of the exegetes, owe their existence as a genre to that in their content which bears upon the moral needs of Christians. They met a demand made, in short, not by professional scholars, and not originally by the schools, but by the pastoral clergy and, especially, the people who were in their care. The sentence collections themselves shewed some interest in exegesis of a scholarly kind, and many of the sentences, including those in the two Bodleian manuscripts, can be traced back to the exegesis of Anselm of Laon; but they had their roots in the pastoral needs of the world outside the schools[27]. It is this, and not the fact that they emanate from

---

27. The fragments themselves are, in addition, in the early manuscripts, to be found almost without exception in small and easily manageable practical pastoral handbooks; handbooks which contain in addition to them, for instance, texts of the creed, prayers, the *Breviarium*, *Passiones*, sermons, treatises on morals and on ecclesiastical offices and vestments, short commentaries on the Gospels, the Epistles of St. Paul, the Song of Songs and those other books of the Bible from which moral instruction is most easily to be drawn, for instance Proverbs and Ecclesiastes. I am deeply indebted to Dr. A.C. De la Mare of the Bodleian Library who, with her customary generosity, made available to me all the results of her own work on the two Bodleian manuscripts.

I

100

any one school, still less from any one master, which explains the order they follow, the interests they manifest, the anonymity of some of the earliest manuscripts and, above all, their unamenability to particular sorts or enquiry. The reasons for the recourse of both the exegetes and the 'sententiae' to certain books of the bible become clear immediately; for, if one wants scriptural answers to pastoral questions, where better to go than Genesis, the Gospels and the Epistles of St. Paul? And, if one wishes truly to reach the laity, then those books most familiar to them in their devotions, the Psalter, that is, especially, should be able to be shewn to have a bearing on their lives. The anonymity of many of the 'sententiae' may be accounted for, too, by the fact that we are now in a world in which scholarly pedigree is of less importance than pastoral efficacy, and where scholarly analysis is, though desirable, less so than 'relevance'. Lastly, the difficulties the 'sententiae' have interposed in the paths of earlier investigations suggest that, for an understanding of the history of the cathedral schools of the twelfth century, including that of the school *at* Laon, we should take a new path. We should cease for a while to scrutinise the schools themselves and look instead through the 'sententiae' to the world to which this theology speaks.

III

This world is far too large, of course, to fall within the compass of a single essay, but it is, in some of its contours, as familiar as the school at Laon. It is the world of the movement for ecclesiastical reform. Since the seminal essay of Z. N. Brooke, we have come to know how inapplicable is the description 'investiture contest' to this movement, and how passionately the true reformers espoused the more general, and so more difficult, cause of pastoral renewal[28]. We know little still, though, of the intellectual demands made by this cause and the ways in which they were met. We know little because fewer questions have been asked of the intellectual history of the eleventh century than of that of the twelfth; and because those which have, have been

28. Z. N. BROOKE, *Lay Investiture and its Relation to the Conflict of Empire and Papacy*, in *Proceedings of the British Academy* 25 (1939) 217-247.

confronted with intractable problems, such as that of the two Manegolds, whose solutions seem both vital to seek and impossible to find. We know little too because the cathedral schools, and with them the school at Laon, have been seen as things apart, as institutional phenomena as detached from the world in general as the intellectual life is sometimes detached. Here, however, the reconsideration of the 'school of Laon' has something positive to offer. The fact that the sentence material is so intractable to certain forms of enquiry is, we have seen, perhaps more of a help than a hindrance; and the corrective to detachment, in the form of those collections of theological opinions which reflect so clearly the general concerns of Christians, is now at hand. All that remains is the need, as it were, to change course. To move, that is, not from the schools to their supposed echoes in the sentence collections, but from these last and the features which give them that unity they have, to the anxieties and aspirations of the movement for reform. If we do this, then we may come close at last to the cathedral schools; for it becomes increasingly plausible to suppose that the anxieties of the reform, in their intellectual projections, gave the 'sententiae', the exegesis, the school *at* Laon and perhaps the schools in general the forms we seek to understand.

The movement for reform is too large, of course, in its more learned aspect too, to be handled confidently. The 'sententiae', however, divorced at last from the 'school of Laon', suggest two approaches which may be made. The first is through the intellectual choices demanded, and rejections involved, within the world of the clergy. The second is through the articulate concerns of christianity at large. The first approach may be taken now with mounting hopes. The second must be adopted with more caution and less immediate prospect of enlightenment; but even here the sentences offer guidance which may lead us eventually to a far deeper understanding of the whole.

We may begin with the world of the clergy. In that part of the work of 'Manegold' which can be firmly associated with the reformer, Manegold of Lautenbach, the *Liber contra Wolfelmum*, we can see some of the choices and, with them, some of the sacrifices, required of learned clerks in the cause of pastoral renewal. Manegold abandoned, for example, the type of philosophical enquiry into matters of theological concern which was later so to interest Abelard, and he substituted for it a deeper interest in the bible[29]. Such a substitution was doubtless in some respects painful to him, but Manegold was on the whole fortunate. The dilemma in which he found himself was one which could be contained by the Augustinians best, perhaps, of all the orders, and was one which he, it seems, could resolve. This dilemma had the seeds in it, however, of a far larger one which could not be so contained and so resolved. This type of intellectual sacrifice was not, we know, easy for all members of the clergy to make; nor, on the other hand, was this quality of biblical expertise attainable to all. Then, in addition, there was a whole galaxy of ancient and incipient institutions to be taken into account. On the one hand, at the extreme right we may say, there were those of the secular clergy whose habits required some adjustment to the new cause; on the other, there were the regulars, of rapidly proliferating enthusiasms for, and interpretations of, the reform. On the very edge of these, physically and institutionally, that is, although in the eyes of many at the centre, stood that remarkable late eleventh century phenomenon known as the eremitical movement[30]. The 'sententiae' shed light upon two aspects of this larger dilemma. They tell us more, firstly, about the new positions of eminence made available, as it were by compensation, to those able to profit of the new exegetical fervours. And, perhaps more importantly, they reveal the ambitions of some, at least, of the monks. This light should illuminate in turn the later history of the schools.

We have quite independent evidence, coming from the early twelfth century, of a series of encounters between one German champion of the pastoral rights of monks, Rupert, monk of St. Laurence of Liège and later abbot of Deutz, and no less a person than Master Anselm of Laon himself. These encounters

29. W. HARTMANN, *art. cit.* (1970) 77-85.
30. See, for an interesting study of this movement and for a summary of the sources J. BECQUET, *L'érémitisme clérical et laïc dans l'Ouest de la France*, and the discussion which follows it in *L'eremitismo in Occidente nei secoli XI e XII (Atti della seconda Settimana internazionale di studio, Mendola, 1962)*, 182-211.

culminated, moreover, in a fortuitously helpful piece of drama. At the climax, or rather the proposed climax, of the conflict, Rupert actually set out to meet the master, riding on a donkey; perhaps not the most refined criticism of pomp and intellectual glory, but one whose point would not have been lost upon a biblical scholar [31]. The master did not in fact live to suffer this demonstration, but an earlier letter, written to Rupert's abbot, Heribrand, may give us a foretaste of the sort of reception he might have provided if he had. In this letter, Anselm made a distinction between a 'sententia' and a mere battle of words. The word 'sententia' he reserved for that security of opinion which comes from a thorough grounding in the certainties of the faith. Discussion and, still worse, contradiction, has no part in a 'sententia'. Such discussion is the occupation of mere children and is beneath the dignity of grave men [32]. This grounding, he implies, is only obtainable through special means, and certainly some people are excluded from it. We have here, I think, an important indication of the attitude at least one famous master was proposing to take on behalf of the schools, and against some of the ranks of the clergy. Anselm was neither going to admit to this realm those who, in his view, could not profit from it, nor allow that the conditions which prevailed within could easily be re-created outside. Rupert's demonstration, we may suppose, would have been, with some scorn, ignored. A wedge, in other words, was being driven between the new world of the schools and the old one of the monastic orders, and it was given the name 'sententia'; the opinion of a grave man and one who, by implication, has access to the schools. This new world was to be continued, furthermore, at the cost, if need be, of those monastic orders which had until now been pre-eminent in the world of learning.

This somewhat theatrical confrontation tells us a great deal. It shews in an exaggerated way certain of the pressures to which the school *at* Laon was subject, and the rather singular stand a distinguished master could take; and it increases our comprehension of, and perhaps sympathy with, the reactions it could

31. *In Regulam S. Benedicti* (PL 170, 482-483).
32. LOTTIN, *op. cit.* V, 175-176.

provoke. The attitudes of Anselm and Rupert were the expression of visions so different that without such moments of dramatic intensity they perhaps could not be seen with the same eyes. Certainly they were not by contemporaries. The 'sententiae', however, as we have them and as we may now understand them, give to this momentary expression a more permanent and recognisable quality.

As early as 1936 H. Weisweiler drew attention to the amount of 'Laon' material which came from far away from the school at Laon; which came, in fact, from Germany, especially Southern Germany, and from monastic libraries there[33]. This discovery has so far troubled the dreams of the proponents of the 'school of Laon' hardly at all; but it should have done so, for it is likely to shatter them. We know that in the early part of the twelfth century, when many of these sentence collections were made, the monastic orders, and particularly those in South Germany were growing anxious about their place in the renewed pastoral life of the church[34]. This anxiety was certainly in part generated by their concern for the progress of the movement for reform as they understood it, and they attracted to their cause known reformers[35]. There were many levels to this debate, of course, but one of them was an intellectual one. It seems, indeed, that the 'sententiae' are here annexed to the aspirations of a particular section of the supporters of the reform, the monastic orders; and the monastic orders especially, though not, of course, exclusively, of Germany.

The 'sententiae', we may now see, have two guises. In one they are the last word, perhaps reluctantly uttered, of a man of the schools. We have known, though dimly, a little of this guise. In the other, the theological sentence collection, they are a weapon taken up by the monks in their cause. This last guise has been concealed but it is, for our understanding of the later history

33. H. WEISWEILER, art. cit., pp. 92-93.

34. U. BERLIÈRE, L'exercice du ministère paroissal par les moines dans le haut moyen âge, in Revue bénédictine 39 (1927) 246-250. For a revealing confrontation which took place in England, see R. FOREVILLE and J. LECLERCQ, Un débat sur le sacerdoce des moines au XIIᵉ siècle, in Analecta monastica 41 (1957) 8-118, especially pp. 22-24.

35. For example Bernold of St. Blaise, Gerhoh of Reichersberg, Hugh of St. Victor, cf. BERLIÈRE, art. cit.

of the schools, the most important. The 'sententiae' in this guise shew us that the answer of some sections of the clergy to some of the demands of the reform was also, in one respect, an answer to the demands of the schools. They were correctives to their restrictions and protests at their cost; and, in the last event, they were designed as a substitute for schools such as Laon. The fact that Anselm provided much of the material for them has in it a dramatic irony which should be appreciated to the full. The true position of the sentence collections of the twelfth century must be seen as almost the opposite of that previously ascribed to them; and they emerge, now, as evidence of some of the pressures which may have cast the later schools in the very roles we seek eventually to describe. They are a measure of the strength and purpose of some of the forces which reacted against the early schools and with which they, in their turn, would have to contend.

I have mentioned, in the context of the turmoil within the clergy, the rise of the eremitical movement in France. There is a dimension of some importance to be explored here, for it also bears upon the schools. The eremitical movement made reference to the schools but, interestingly, not to what they could do but to what they could, or would, not. Some of the early hermits, such men as Geoffrey du Chalard (who became a hermit in 1089), Bertrand de Griffeville (1080), and, of course, Robert of Arbroussel, had been to the schools and had reacted against them[36]. And the reaction, in some of its manifestations, took the form of somewhat threatening alternatives to them. Bernard of Tiron, for example, encouraged a relationship which was described as that of a master to his pupils, but which was in reality very different from any of the more 'scholarly' kinds we can describe[37]. Here we have a substitute which could be turned with only a very little ingenuity into a parody. We need only a slightly more talented and a shade more tenacious Rupert of Deutz to exploit it. This is a situation to which few persons of academic ambition could, and indeed

---

36. BECQUET, art. cit., pp. 187-188. In the discussion (p. 203) M. Dereine spoke of his suspicion that 'une espèce de dégoût intellectuel après un très grand enthousiasme' may have been a fundamental motive.
37. Vita Beati Bernardi, ch. 69 (PL 172, 1408-1409).

I

should, remain insensitive for long. The effects of the eremitical movement too, then must have a place in any description we may try to make of the contribution of the schools. We may look to this movement for another explanation of the anxieties which stood behind the collecting of the theological 'sententiae', and for more evidence, if more is needed, that these collections sprang primarily from the world outside the schools. The sentence collections defended the rights of their monastic copyists to a place in the pastorate, against the increasing claims of the men of the schools and against the evident effectiveness of many of those who eluded the grasp of both secular and regular clergy.

The second approach invited by the 'sententiae' to the intellectual projections of the reform is through the world of the christian people as a whole, clerical and lay; a world perhaps penetrated best, initially, by the eremitical movement. It is impossible to go far along this way, for it is long, confusing and largely unexplored; but it is signed again by the sentences and may, too, be exciting. When the content of the sentences is broken down, two particular pre-occupations stand out above all the others. The first preoccupation is with marriage and its failure, with affection and choice and the effects of original sin. This preoccupation we have seen. The second is with the Jews. Some of the 'sententiae' clearly bear upon the Jewish religion; sentences such as those, for instance, about the demands made by living under the Mosaic Law, on usury, on the need to avoid any fraternising which may cause scandal, on the validity or non-validity of Jewish marriages, on circumcision, betray a clear sense of the thoughts provoked by the existence of the Jewish communities[38].

We may add the first pre-occupation to the argument that the sentences sprang from the movement for reform, for great heart searchings were involved in the pursuit of clerical celibacy. It is, however, of a greater importance than this. It shews that the

38. LOTTIN, op. cit. V, nos. 7, 9, 12 (on the Mosaic Law), 14 (on usury), 125 (on fraternising), 130, 131, 208 (on the marriages of Jews and infidels), pp. 422-23 (on circumcision). See also the interesting opinion, ascribable apparently to Anselm, that whilst a Jew may be prayed for, his obduracy must prevent a Christian from bending the knee (no. 116).

I

sentences were primarily concerned with questions which were common to the world both of the clergy and of the laity, and which were, above all, adult. They give answers to adult problems, particularly to the problems of sexuality and choice. Far from lying, as their simplified form sometimes suggests, on the surface of life, these collections were designed to meet the urgent and deeply felt anxieties of mature and serious people; and they met them with that determination to relieve distress which seeks to do so by going back to the source, in this case not the childhood of man but that of the world, the creation itself. The nature of the questions and the lengths taken to answer them shews the power of these anxieties. They are an extraordinarily impressive monument to intellectual enquiry at its most forceful; and such force required one of at least equal magnitude to contain it. This power and this need acted upon the men and institutions of twelfth century learning and we should examine them in the future with this fact in mind. The second pre-occupation, too, takes us back to the reform; and again, and more importantly, beyond it and the early schools, especially in France. The Jewish communities of France, after a long and relatively untroubled residence there, were in the late eleventh century attracting hostile attention[39]. The crusading movement, especially, affected them in two particular ways. It constituted a public military enterprise in which they could not publicly participate, and it therefore made them, by that confusion of thought and emotion so liable to happen under pressure of war, subject to persecution and its rationalised condemnation. This too, like the rulings on clerical celibacy, produced a situation calculated to disturb the peace of mind of serious people. It finds a reflection in the sentences and we may hope that it may also find a reflection in the schools. At the very least, it must be looked for in any assessment of the later role they played.

39. N. GOLB, *New light on the persecution of French Jews at the time of the First Crusade*, in *Proceedings of the American Academy for Jewish Research* 34 (1966) 1-45.

IV

Those schools which prospered at first did so under men who could seize the practical advantages presented by these confusions and these agonies. Here is the place of the school *at* Laon; for Master Anselm was such a man par excellence. Abelard had harsh things to say of him as a teacher. The picture he gives us is not unlike that we have from the latter of Anselm to Heribrand although we have it, of course, now, from the other side :

> Accessi igitur ad hunc senem, cui magis longevus usus quam ingenium vel memoria nomen comparavit. Ad quem si quis de aliqua questione pulsandum accederet incertus, redibat incertior. Mirabilis quidem in oculis erat auscultantium, sed nullus in conspectu questionantium. Verborum usum habebat mirabilem, sed sensum contemtibilem et ratione vacuum. Cum ignem accenderet, domum suam fumo implebat, non luce illustrabat. Arbor eius tota in foliis aspicientibus a longe conspicua videbatur, sed proprinquantibus et diligentius intuentibus infructuosa reperiebatur[40].

Anselm could stand apart. He had a firm belief in instruction and he was not troubled by doubts. He had that instinct for survival which can fashion an intolerable situation into a form which can, after all, be accepted[41]; and he had a very strong streak of practicality[42]. Thus he gained adherents. As a master he could be trusted to provide for those sons, nephews and protégés of established dignitaries who wished for advancement in the new church. They could be sent to him for a firm grounding which gave every prospect of this and none of their imbibing confusing ideas. He gave answers which at least held out the hope of quietening questioners and which could therefore help those inclined to make a profession of it. He gave security, in short, both mental and material to those who could accept it in this form.

---

40. *Historia calamitatum*, ed. J. MONFRIN (Paris 1959), p. 68.

41. His behaviour towards Bishop Gaudrey seems to shew this. He had not liked his election, but once it had been carried out he acted loyally towards him. After his brutal murder it was Anselm who insisted on a proper burial. GUIBERT OF NOGENT, *De vita sua*, ed. G. BOURGIN (Paris 1907) III, x, 174-175.

42. To his practical sense Guibert also pays tribute (*op. cit.* III, xv, 207). When Anselm was asked whether a robber should be summarily punished or paid to tell where his hoard was, he had no hesitation in recommending the latter course.

But not all either could, or would. Abelard's flight and Rupert's attack were symptoms of a far deeper unease. The school *at* Laon appealed to only a part of the complicated articulate world of the reform, and that, perhaps a rather small one. To understand the place of this school one must look not so much to its achievements as to its limitations and, further, to the reactions these limitations could provoke. To understand the place of the cathedral schools in the twelfth century world of learning one must look to their capacity to transcend these limitations and to contain these reactions. We may not take the school at Laon as an archetype; it may in some ways been an unfortunate accident. To say these things is to advocate a drastic change of perspective; but there comes with it the prospect of a new understanding of the successes and failures of later masters and later schools.

The phrase 'school of Laon', then, should now be removed, for a time completely, from the vocabulary of historians of the twelfth century schools. Like 'feudalism', it arouses far more intellectual anguish than it can ever hope to allay; and it can lead to misdirection of a very far-reaching kind. It ascribes to the school *at* Laon, on the one hand, a pre-eminence which is, to put it at its mildest, beyond its deserts; and it fails, on the other to draw that distinction between this school, the later schools and the true origins and objectives of the exegesis and theology of this crucial period, which is so evidently required. At best the use of the phrase will lead to an incomplete description of what was really happening; at worst it can wholly obscure our understanding of that ferment in the world outside which was the true object of intellectual concern.

The world of the schools was the world of the reform; and by the end of the eleventh century it was in a state of articulate anxiety complicated enough to test the mettle of any educational institution. It was far beyond the grasp of that of Anselm; but the sentence collections and the efforts of the exegetes, so long thought to be in the penumbra of his school, may now be seen, in detachment from him, as a source of light. They are evidence both of learning and of the politics behind it; perhaps a political allegory in themselves. They shew the vulnerability of the earlier schools, of their critics and, above all, of the intellectual life at

I

110

the hands of both. The way to the later schools may begin to be sought through them in the world they reveal[43]. This route will be more varied and more difficult than the one by way of Laon; but it will, in the end, be surer.

Auckland, University.

43. It may even be that once we withdraw our gaze from both the 'School of Laon' and the School at Laon we may come full circle and begin to find in this anxious world the true reasons for that re-working and de-christianising of the myth of Genesis which was thought to give institutional form to the 'School of Chartres'. So much is still to be done.

II

THE *HISTORIA REGUM BRITANNIAE* OF GEOFFREY OF MONMOUTH: PARODY AND ITS PURPOSE. A SUGGESTION

THE *Historia Regum Britanniae* of Geoffrey of Monmouth has enjoyed an enormous amount of attention. In the first place, the work itself was extraordinarily popular. The most recent edition of the text, by Acton Griscom, lists almost 200 surviving Latin manuscripts, 48 of the twelfth century,[1] and more have been added and will be added.[2] In the second, it was and is a puzzle. It was found difficult to interpret as soon as it appeared. Henry of Huntingdon was frankly surprised by the work, which he found at Bec in 1139. Gerald of Wales claimed that it had been exposed as a fraud; William of Newburgh would have it so exposed. Alfred of Beverley thought it worthy of at least some serious attention by historians.[3] Gerald's claim is good-natured and softened by a story. William's is not; indeed his accusation that Geoffrey attempted to give historical falsehood the color of truth by turning it into Latin forms one of the most vitriolic of his passages.[4]

---

[1] Acton Griscom, *The Historia Regum Britanniae of Geoffrey of Monmouth* (New York, 1929), pp. 551–582. References in this paper are to the book and chapter divisions of this edition. This paper was completed with the help of a Visiting Fellowship at the Humanities Research Centre, ANU, Canberra, for which I am most grateful.

[2] J. Hammer, "Some Additional Manuscripts of Geoffrey of Monmouth's *Historia Regum Britanniae*," *Modern Language Quarterly* 3 (1942), 235–242. Hammer cites an additional four manuscripts of the thirteenth and fourteenth centuries in his edition of the variant version: Jacob Hammer, *Geoffrey of Monmouth's Historia Regum Britanniae: A Variant Version* (Cambridge, Mass., 1951), pp. 5–8. See also W. Levison, "A Combined Manuscript of Geoffrey of Monmouth and Henry of Huntingdon," *English Historical Review* 58 (1943), 41–51, H. D. Emanuel, "Geoffrey of Monmouth's *Historia Regum Britanniae:* A Second Variant Version," *Medium Aevum* 35 (1966), 103–110; D. Huws and B. F. Roberts, "Another Manuscript of the Variant Version of the 'Historia Regum Britanniae'," *Bibliographical Bulletin of the International Arthurian Society* 25 (1973), 147–153; and W. G. East, "Manuscripts of Geoffrey of Monmouth," *Notes and Queries* 220 (1975), 483–484.

[3] The relevant passages from their works are conveniently collected in Edmund K. Chambers, *Arthur of Britain* (Cambridge, 1927), pp. 251–2, 260, 268, 274–5.

[4] "Quidam nostris temporibus, pro expiandis his Britonum maculis, scriptor emersit, ridicula

This full range of responses, from bewilderment through amusement and exasperation to serious attention, is still to be found in the works of twentieth-century commentators. Griscom collects opinions on Geoffrey as a romancer.[5] Griscom is himself perhaps the most earnest modern defender of Geoffrey as a sober historian. Here the matter was for a long time allowed to stand. Those inclined to be indulgent saw Geoffrey's "romanticism" as forgivable by reason of artistic license and the popularity of the work. Those not so inclined, from William of Newburgh onwards, supported their indignation by reference to a veracity and moderation which are the foundations of all historical literature deserving of the name, foundations of which Geoffrey was ignorant, or for which, still worse, he did not care. Geoffrey was either an historian who fell short of a full expertise at his craft or a writer of fiction occasionally curiously mired in fact.

I say for a long time. The magisterial study of the *Historia* by J. S. P. Tatlock, published in 1950,[6] far from furnishing the last word on the subject became the herald of a new effort to understand Geoffrey's work. A few examples of this effort may be mentioned. In 1958, two scholars paid tribute to the skill and close knowledge, especially of contemporary writing and events, that went into the construction of the work.[7] In 1966, in a study of many aspects of historical writing in early Britain, a long chapter devoted to Geoffrey stressed the growing complexity of the histories produced in Anglo-Norman England and, in particular, the "secular strain" to be found in them.[8] The *Historia Regum Britanniae* emerged from this analysis as a heightened and artistic form of a developed historiographical movement. It gained in dignity accordingly. The anger of its opponents and the anxiety of its defenders began to dissolve before these demonstrations of the sophistication of the treatise. Geoffrey's *Historia* became a "superbly" audacious piece

---

de eisdam figmenta contexens, eosque longe supra virtutem Macedonum et Romanorum impudenti vanitate attollens. Gaufridus hic dictus est, agnomen habens Arturi, pro eo quod fabulas de Arturo, ex priscis Britonum figmentis sumptas et ex proprio auctas, per superductum Latini sermonis colorem honesto historiae nomine palliavit: qui etiam maiori ausu cuiusdam Merlini divinationes fallacissimas, quibus utique de proprio plurimum adiecit, dum eas in Latinum transfunderet, tanquam authenticas et immobili veritate subnixas prophetias, vulgavit . . ." (Chambers, *Arthur*, pp. 274–5). William of Newburgh's attitude to Geoffrey is discussed by N. Partner, *Serious Entertainments* (Chicago and London, 1977), pp. 62–68.

[5] Griscom, *Historia*, pp. 109–110. "Geoffrey's manipulation of his material, where its nature is apparent to us, makes it impossible to believe that he was a completely veracious chronicler, even where due allowance is made for what he might reasonably consider as legitimate rhetorical embroidery." Chambers, *Arthur*, p. 56. See also Robert W. Hanning, *The Vision of History in Early Britain* (New York, 1966), p. 122 and notes.

[6] John S. P. Tatlock, *The Legendary History of Britain: Geoffrey of Monmouth's Historia Regum Britanniae and Its Early Vernacular Versions* (Berkeley, 1950).

[7] Heinrich Pähler, *Strukturuntersuchungen zur Historia Regum Britanniae des Geoffrey of Monmouth* (Bonn, 1958), especially pp. 58–60 and 92–134, and Walter F. Schirmer, *Die frühen Darstellungen des Arthurstoffes* (Cologne, 1958).

[8] Hanning, *Vision*, pp. 121–172, especially pp. 126–130, 135–136, 142, 171.

of writing[9] and a "mirror of his own times" of considerable craftsmanship.[10] More recently still Geoffrey has himself been given fresh dignity as an historian, imaginative certainly, but in essence reliant upon, and faithful to, Welsh historiographical tradition.[11]

Then, in 1976, Professor Christopher Brooke pushed the question one stage further.[12] Geoffrey was a writer of parody, a poker of fun at contemporary society. He laughed at the laws, at the church, even, perhaps, at pressing national ambitions. His aim, and his success, in this exercise remained, however, literary: "This is a literary work of remarkable skill: a skill in story-telling above all, and in reconstructing the past out of fragmentary materials. It is in this sense that he takes his place both among the major literary figures and among the most ingenious historians of the age." "The motive most in evidence is the desire to display the literary gifts of the historian."[13] Fun, fiction, and fact are all means to this end. The conflict between "romance" and "history" disappears again but does so beneath this sharper purpose of mockery and satire.

I have only admiration for interpretations of Geoffrey's work that would expose him as an artist and a parodist of enormous skill; Geoffrey's desire to display his literary gifts is indeed the motive most in evidence in the *Historia*. But this was not, I hope to argue, his primary motive. Geoffrey was in appearance historian and littérateur because he was expert in both arts and could show himself to be so. Yet he did not use history purely in the service of parody or primarily to demonstrate higher standards of literary achievement. His purpose was more profound. If he displayed "the literary gifts of the historian," if, as well, he exaggerated certain trends in historical writing, it was to mock that literature and confound its authors. He meant to make telling points about the quality of the literature and to diminish the authority with which some of its exponents spoke. He meant, ultimately, to call into question the position held and hoped for in twelfth-century Anglo-Norman society by literate and celibate canons regular and monks.

* * *

The *Historia*, the story, reign by reign, of ninety-nine kings of Britain from Brutus to Cadwallader with that of Arthur as the centerpiece, was written at

[9] Reginald F. Treharne, *The Glastonbury Legends* (London, 1967), p. 66. Treharne also draws attention to the lack, in the *Historia*, of Christian spirit and feeling. Ibid., pp. 69–70.

[10] Antonia Gransden, *Historical Writing in England c. 550–c. 1307* (London, 1974), p. 206. Pp. 207–208 of the same work emphasize again Geoffrey's un-Christian, even sadistic, attitudes. The few pages devoted here to Geoffrey are full of insights.

[11] B. F. Roberts, "Geoffrey of Monmouth and Welsh Historical Tradition," *Nottingham Medieval Studies* 20 (1976), 29–40.

[12] Christopher Brooke, "Geoffrey of Monmouth as a Historian," in *Church and Government in the Middle Ages*, ed. Christopher Brooke, D. Luscombe, G. Martin, D. Owen (Cambridge, 1976), pp. 77–91. Professor Brooke supplies in his first footnote further directions on Arthurian bibliography.

[13] Ibid., pp. 88, 90.

II

or near Oxford in the 1130s, completed by 1138.[14] The early twelfth century produced in England a quite extraordinary amount of written material in Latin. We are confronted, first of all, with the physical stocking of abbey and cathedral libraries after the Conquest (those, for example, of Malmesbury, Canterbury, Abingdon, Lincoln, Salisbury, Rochester, Hereford, Worcester, Durham, Exeter, St. Albans, Bury) and the enthusiasm with which these collections were used and extended.[15] Secondly there was an increase in the records of government and, with it, in the demand for the services of those literate in Latin. The recent edition of the *Regesta Regum Anglo-Normannorum* bears witness to the great growth in quantity of writs and charters in the reigns of Henry I and Stephen, and in the *Constitutio Domus Regis* the Chancellor and the Master of the Writing Office are officials of considerable importance who are named first.[16] Thirdly there was literature newly translated in England from languages other than Latin or newly composed in Latin there. These three divisions comprehend an enormous variety of materials: patristics, lives of saints, legal compilations, instruments of bureaucracy and argument secular and ecclesiastical, histories.

A striking aspect of this enormous effort at copying, collecting, arguing, recording — all in Latin — is that it took on a special intensity in the third and fourth decades of the twelfth century, that is, in the years just before Geoffrey began to write. William of Malmesbury wrote his Latin life of St. Wulfstan, based in part upon the Anglo-Saxon life by Coleman, between 1124 and 1140,[17] and his life of St. Dunstan probably towards the end of that period.[18] Caradoc of Llancarfan perhaps began to write his lives of St. Gildas and St. Cadoc shortly after 1120, and the life of St. Dubricius, found in British Library MS Cotton Vespasian A.xiv and in the *Liber Landavensis*, seems to have been written then also.[19] So too, perhaps, was an edition of the life of St. Teilo.[20] The *Leis Willelme* is traceable in the French form and most

[14] Christopher Brooke, "The Archbishops of St. David's, Llandaff and Caerleon on Usk," in *Studies in the Early British Church*, ed. Nora K. Chadwick (Cambridge, 1958), p. 231 n.2. For a long and careful discussion of the bearing of the dedications upon the date see Griscom, *Historia*, pp. 53–85. The prophecies of Merlin were known to Orderic Vitalis in 1134/5 when the work as a whole was in the course of composition.

[15] For the collections added to Abbot Godfrey's library by William of Malmesbury see H. Farmer, "William of Malmesbury's Life and Works," *Journal of Ecclesiastical History* 13 (1962), 47–51, 54. At Abingdon between 1100 and 1117 Abbot Faricius had six *scriptores* copy manuscripts of the Fathers: *Chronicon Monasterii de Abingdon*, 2 (RS, London, 1858), 289. Many of the surviving manuscripts from this period are named and discussed by Neil R. Ker, *English Manuscripts in the Century after the Conquest* (Oxford, 1960), pp. 22–34.

[16] C. Johnson, ed., *Dialogus de Scaccario* (Nelson, London, 1950), p. 129.

[17] D. H. Farmer, "Two Biographies by William of Malmesbury," in *Latin Biography*, ed. T. A. Dorey (London, 1967), p. 166.

[18] This is suggested by the epilogue in which William speaks as though the better part of his own life is over. W. Stubbs, ed., *Memorials of St. Dunstan* (RS, London, 1874), p. 324.

[19] K. Hughes, "British Museum Ms. Cotton Vespasian A.xiv ('Vitae Sanctorum Wallensium'): Its Purpose and Provenance," in *Studies in the Early British Church* ed. Nora K. Chadwick, (Cambridge, 1958), p. 193.

[20] Gilbert H. Doble, *St. Teilo* (Lampeter, 1942), pp. 10 ff.

probably therefore in the Latin to the later part of the reign of Henry I, and the *Consiliatio Cnuti* may only have been completed in 1130. The *Leges Edwardi Confessoris*, a curiously titled collection of current and earlier law, in Latin, seems to have been put together between 1130 and 1135.[21]

Materials for the support of bureaucratic government and argument poured forth. The *Canterbury Forgeries* seem to spring from the years 1121–1123,[22] and a part of the *Liber Eliensis* was begun soon after 1131.[23] The core of the *Liber Landavensis* was almost certainly compiled in the years 1120–1129 and completed by 1140.[24] The *Constitutio Domus Regis* was itself written between 1135 and 1139, most probably in 1136.[25]

Of the nameable writers of histories John of Worcester attended to his part of the Worcester *Chronicon ex Chronicis* between 1124 and 1140,[26] and Hugh the Chanter's work was finished in 1127.[27] William of Malmesbury produced the *Gesta Pontificum* in 1125 and revised it thereafter, and the *Gesta Regum* by 1125, again with revisions between the years 1135 and 1140. Between 1129 and 1139 he wrote his *De Antiquitate Glastoniense Ecclesiae*, and between then and c. 1143 the *Historia Novella*.[28] Henry of Huntingdon began to write the *Historia Anglorum* between 1129 and 1133 and worked at it in the following years, perhaps adding a prologue, and certainly making changes, between then and 1135.[29] Of the unattributable histories and annals, the *Annales de Regnis et Ecclesiis* was written in the early 1130s and perhaps completed in 1137.[30] The third section of the Durham *Historia Regum* was written soon after 1129, and an abridgement of a part of this was made, again, in the last years of the reign of Henry I.[31] During the 1120s and 1130s copying too seems to have quickened.[32] The world of the literate, in

[21] Felix Liebermann, *Die Gesetze der Angelsachsen*, 3 (Halle, 1903–16), 340.

[22] R. W. Southern, "The Canterbury Forgeries," *English Historical Review* 73 (1958), 224. For different views on the date and purpose of these documents, however, see Margaret Gibson, *Lanfranc of Bec* (Oxford, 1978), pp. 231–237 (Appendix C).

[23] E. O. Blake, ed., *Liber Eliensis* (London, 1962), p. xlviii.

[24] W. Davies, "Liber Landavensis: Its Construction and Credibility," *English Historical Review* 88 (1973), 350.

[25] Johnson, *Dialogus*, p. 1.

[26] Reginald R. Darlington, *Anglo-Norman Historians* (London, 1947), p. 14.

[27] C. Johnson, ed., *Hugh the Chanter: the History of the Church of York 1066–1127* (Nelson, London, 1961), p. x.

[28] Gransden, *Historical Writing*, pp. 168, 181–183.

[29] Ibid., p. 194.

[30] Felix Liebermann, *Ungedruckte Anglo-Normanische Geschichtsquellen* (Strassbourg, 1879), pp. 15–24. We might ascribe a part of the *Annales Plymptonenses* to this period too: ibid., pp. 24–30.

[31] Hilary S. Offler, *Medieval Historians of Durham* (Durham, 1958), pp. 9–11; P. Hunter Blair, "Some Observations on the Historia Regum Attributed to Symeon of Durham," in *Celt and Saxon: Studies in the Early British Border*, ed. Nora K. Chadwick (Cambridge, 1963), pp. 63–118; S. T. O. d'Ardenne, "A Neglected Manuscript of British History," in *English and Medieval Studies presented to J. R. R. Tolkein*, ed. Norman Davis and C. L. Wrenn (London, 1966), p. 88. I am grateful to Professor Offler for this last reference and for generously sending me offprints of his own work.

[32] "Existing books suggest that in many of the great Benedictine abbeys the scriptorium was at its best in the second quarter of the twelfth century." Ker, *English Manuscripts*, p. 8.

short, was in these years very greatly expanded. Saints' lives and histories, especially histories of Anglo-Saxon England and its church, constitute a large part of this accumulation. Advocates of the regular religious life are heavily involved. Finally, the composition and copying of books, especially in Benedictine scriptoria, seems to have been undertaken with particular vigor in a region of England very close to that in which Geoffrey spent the major part of his career.[33]

* * *

Geoffrey refers to contemporary writers in the epilogue that is attached to what I take to be the earliest form of his work.[34] He names William of Malmesbury, Henry of Huntingdon, and Caradoc of Llancarfan. William and Henry are warned not to attempt to write about the kings of the Britons because of their own linguistic inadequacies — William and Henry do not possess a certain book in the "British" language which has been Geoffrey's strength and which he claims to have translated. Caradoc, on the other hand, is invited to continue where Geoffrey leaves off, and to write of the kings of Wales.[35] I shall return to him and to the book. For the moment there is a great wealth to be explored in Geoffrey's reference to the other two historians alone. This reference has long been regarded by some as a joke.[36] A closer look at Geoffrey's use of William and Henry, whose major works he certainly knew and drew upon, suggests that it was not just one joke but the end of a whole series of jokes. This has not generally been recognized.

The jokes begin, appropriately, at the beginning. In their prefaces both William and Henry lay stress upon the quantity and breadth of their reading. William, for example, in the preface to the *Gesta Pontificum*, speaks of his sources: "et hic et alibi traxi stilum per latebrosissimas historias, quanquam mihi non hic affluat eadem copia scientiae quae in Gestis Regum."[37] Henry explains that he used Bede: "nonnulla etiam ex aliis excerpens auctoribus, inde chronica in antiquis reservata librariis compilans."[38] Henry especially, and still in the preface, makes a great show of the profit he has derived from

---

[33] Ker speaks of "that region of the West of England centering on Gloucester which was, we can still dimly realize, one of the great regions of book production in the twelfth century." Ibid., p. 7.

[34] Griscom lists seven manuscripts which contain that double dedication to Robert of Gloucester and Waleran of Meulan which, for him, designates the earliest recension. Only one of these omits the epilogue. The remaining six, together with scores of others, both early and late, contain it. Griscom's preferences for this single manuscript (Cambridge University Library Ii. i. 14) is one of the least comprehensible of his editorial idiosyncracies. Griscom, *Historia*, pp. 31–33, 42–43.

[35] Griscom, *Historia*, p. 536.

[36] See Griscom's fierce and unconvincing defence of its seriousness, ibid., p. 52.

[37] William of Malmesbury, *Gesta Pontificum*, ed. N. E. S. A. Hamilton, *Willelmi Malmesbiriensis Monachi De Gestis Pontificum Anglorum* (RS, London, 1870), p. 4.

[38] Henry of Huntingdon, *Historia Anglorum*, ed. T. Arnold, *Henrici Archidiaconi Huntendunensis Historia Anglorum* (RS, London, 1879), pp. 1–3.

his readings in Horace, Homer, and the Old Testament, of his capacity to write prose and verse, and of his view of the high calling of the historian and of history in general, "quod ipsa maxime distinguat a brutis rationabiles." Geoffrey, in words not too far removed from those of William, sounds in his own preface a first clear note of discord: "infra alienos ortulos falerata verba non collegerim, agresti tamen stilo propriis calamis contentus." He is a simple man; he must content himself with little. For his history he has only one book (though one, he must remark, inaccessible to William and to Henry), to the translation of which he applies his rustic style.

We must return to the rustic style later. For the present: those offended by Geoffrey's "romantic" approach to history have long found vindication in, those who loyally support Geoffrey as an historian have long found their case hampered by, his use of his sources. To the second, save for "corrupt texts" or "oral tradition," unaccountably; to the first all too understandably — he makes mistakes. The works of William and Henry suffer directly and especially severely from these "mistakes." Take for instance the section in *Historia* 4.17 in which Geoffrey speaks of the British king Marius, grandfather of king Lucius, who beats the Picts and has an inscription commemorating his victory. The only known source for this is William's *Gesta Pontificum*, in which he describes a triclinium at Carlisle that bears the inscription "Marii Victoriae."[39] To William the work is Roman from Roman Carlisle and commemorates a Roman victory; to Geoffrey this is British work (as was, of course, 2.9, the foundation of Carlisle). Again in the *Gesta Pontificum* William earnestly attributes the construction of the hot baths in Bath to Julius Caesar.[40] Geoffrey (2.10) insists that they were the work of King Bladud, an extraordinary figure who met his death upon the temple of Apollo in London after an unsuccessful attempt to fly.[41] William in his works is fond of topography and monuments, and frequently allows them to support, even form, his historical narrative. Geoffrey too has frequent recourse to them; but he uses them to support "romance."[42]

Geoffrey's story of Estrildis seems to be taken from the *Gesta Pontificum*, but the name and country are changed and so is William's edifying ending.[43] Geoffrey does not use William as a source of edification for his readers; quite the reverse. A case in point is Geoffrey's now famous account (4.19) of the mission to Britain of Faganus and Duvianus. William's *De Antiquitate* contains plenteous reference to the missionaries Phaganus and Deruvianus, but in the revision of the *Gesta Regum* that he made between 1135–1140,

[39] William of Malmesbury, *Gesta Pontificum*, pp. 208–209.
[40] Ibid., p. 194.
[41] It is difficult not to see behind Bladud the shadow of another Malmesbury figure, aviator Eilmer, who made a similar attempt though happily without the same fatal result. L. White, "Eilmer of Malmesbury, An Eleventh Century Aviator," *Technology and Culture* 2 (1961), 97–111.
[42] Examples of Geoffrey's fanciful use of monuments, apart from those I have mentioned, may be found in 1.16, 6.17, 8.10–12, 10.3.
[43] Geoffrey, 2.2–5; William of Malmesbury, *Gesta Pontificum*, pp. 412–415.

which uses the *De Antiquitate,* William omits these names and declares, indeed, that the names of the missionaries have been forgotten.[44] The suggestion has been made that William expressed resentment against Geoffrey in this passage.[45] The problem of the Lucius legend is more complex than was then generally supposed,[46] as is the problem of the exact relationship between the *Gesta Regum,* in its revisions, and the *De Antiquitate.* However, an expression on William's part of resentment against Geoffrey between 1135 and 1140 would not have been wholly without justification. Early in the *Gesta Regum* William declared a generous belief that Arthur was worthy of a good history: ". . . Artur de quo Britonum nugae hodieque delirant; dignus plane quem non fallaces somniarent fabulae, sed veraces praedicarent historiae. . . ."[47] He followed this passage with an account of Arthur's victory at Mons Badonicus. In *Historia* 4.20, following his own account of the mission of Faganus and Duvianus Geoffrey cites a supposed book by the monk Gildas, Bede's famous precursor, as his source — the *De Victoria Aurelii Ambrosii.* According to William the victory was Arthur's; Geoffrey's source was spurious and so, it seems William later thought, were Faganus and Duvianus. If it was deliberate, then Geoffrey's mischief becomes outrage in the context of William's expressed hope for a "true" history of Arthur — especially if William's idea stood, as has been thought,[48] behind Geoffrey's work.

There is much more. William's treasured Glastonbury, for example, is ignored by Geoffrey, though the Giants' Dance built at Geoffrey's imaginary abbey of Amesbury by Merlin may be an echo of William's solemn description of its pyramid tombs.[49] William associates St. Patrick with Glastonbury in a passage very close to that in which he speaks of St. David's praise of the abbey. Geoffrey mentions Patrick only to rob St. David of the credit for founding the abbey of Menevia.[50] Behind Geoffrey's famous reference (12.14) to Bede's Chedwalda (according to Bede, of course, an Anglo-Saxon king) as the source for his own very different British Cadwaladrus stands the shadow of William's Cadwalla, who is very clearly Bede's.[51] Behind Geoffrey's wizard-consulting Edwin stands again the very different Christian convert of William and Bede. In short, William of Malmesbury's work was used by Geoffrey in a manner that closely resembles deliberate teasing abuse, and teasing abuse directed at least in part at William's monastic sources and treasured monastic foundations.

[44] William of Malmesbury, *Gesta Regum,* ed. W. Stubbs, *Willelmi Malmesbiriensis Monachi de Gestis Regum Anglorum Libri Quinque,* 1 (RS, London, 1887–9), 23.

[45] Tatlock, *Legendary History,* p. 233.

[46] See the remarks on it, and the appendix of texts given, in Christopher Brooke, "The Archbishops," pp. 207, 240–242. The Abingdon Chronicler, writing early the reign of Henry II, still accepted the story of Faganus and Duvianus.

[47] William of Malmesbury, *Gesta Regum,* p. 11.

[48] Christopher Brooke, "The Archbishops," p. 232.

[49] Geoffrey, 8.9–12; William of Malmesbury, *Gesta Regum,* pp. 25–26. .

[50] Geoffrey, 11.3; William of Malmesbury, *Gesta Regum,* p. 26.

[51] William of Malmesbury, *Gesta Regum,* p. 33; Bede, *Historia Ecclesiastica Gentis Anglorum* 4.15–16, 5.7, ed. B. Colgrave and R. A. B. Mynors (Oxford, 1969), pp. 381–385, 469–473.

Geoffrey's opening chapters of his first book are startlingly like those of Henry of Huntingdon. The two are alike in their praise of Britain, even to the measurement of the island with its twenty-eight cities, in their accounts of the Trojan origins of the Britons and the circumstances of the birth, exile, and early journeys of Brutus, in the mentions of kings Belinus and Cassivellaunus. Some of the resemblances, indeed all those I have mentioned, could have sprung from an independent use of versions of Gildas and "Nennius."[52] Other, closer resemblances, however, cannot be explained in this way. Henry and Geoffrey draw especially near to one another in three places: in their accounts of the death of Constantius and of the derivation of Helen, in the mention of Maxentius, and in their words on the roads of England. The problems of exactly when and in what ways Henry extended and revised the *Historia Anglorum* are far from being resolved, but it does seem clear that the first edition had appeared before Geoffrey began to write, and that the close similarities between the two works are to be found in this edition.[53] If we are right to assume that there was borrowing, then Geoffrey was the borrower.

In a way that is becoming familiar, the borrowing seems to be muddled and distorted. According to Henry, Coel of Colchester was a king, the father of Helen and grandfather of Constantine the Great. Helen was a saint; her husband, Constantius, a ruler of great stature. Geoffrey's Coel was a duke who seized the kingdom and made a pact with Constantius, a senator. Constantius married Helen to make sure of the kingdom. Henry's Maxentius is the son of the emperor Maximianus, against whom Constantine is directed by God. Geoffrey's is a tyrant against whom Constantine is directed by the suffering Britons. Henry's Constantine goes on to build churches and suppress heresy; Geoffrey's (4.8) to promote Helen's British relations, one of whom loses the kingdom to another duke. When he speaks of the roads, Henry involves no particular king and is accurate in his general description of the four major ones. Geoffrey attributes the building of the roads to the British king Belinus and is inventive in his description of one of them. This road, quite unknown to history, begins at St. David's and ends at Southampton. All Geoffrey's roads, moreover, are protected by the equally unknown Molmutine Laws. The Molmutine Laws first make their appearance in *Historia* 2.17. The work, according to Geoffrey, of the British king Dunwallo Molmutius, they guarantee the sanctuary of temples, cities, ploughs, and roads. Geoffrey concludes his chapter on the roads with another reference to Gildas: "Si quis autem scire voluerit omnia quae de ipsis statuerit, legat molmutinas leges quas gildas hystoricus de britannico in latinum, rex vero aluredus de latino in anglicum sermonem transtulit."

In each of these cases the distortion has consequences.[54] In the first,

[52] Ferdinand Lot, *Nennius et l'Historia Brittonum* (Paris, 1934), pp. 151, 153–155, 228.

[53] T. Arnold, ed., *Henrici Archidiaconi Huntendunensis Historia Anglorum* (RS, London, 1879), p. liii. A chapter is devoted to Henry's attitude to history in Partner, *Serious Entertainments*, pp. 11–48.

[54] Tatlock, *Legendary History*, p. 31 n.1, doubts whether Geoffrey borrowed King Lud from

II

Geoffrey provides a Helen who is musical, beautiful, and learned but not a saint, and a Coel, Constantius, and Constantine who are not of royal blood. The aura of sanctity, royalty, and divine direction conjured up by Henry has disappeared and been replaced by individual and family ambition. We have here a subtle but quite relentless substitution of images. A similar substitution, but one directed towards a different object, occurs in the case of Belinus and the roads. In the case of the Molmutine Laws and the roads, Geoffrey may have had a second source also in mind, the *Leges Edwardi Confessoris*.[55] This compilation purported to translate and, through translation, to record and defend the efforts of Anglo-Saxon lawgivers, especially those of the well-known and saintly founder of Westminster Abbey. This compilation, and behind it those of King Alfred the Great, are here reduced by Geoffrey to the role of mere translations into Latin of laws essentially British. In another part of his history (3.13) he attributes the laws of Mercia to a British queen, Marcia, and has Alfred, again, the mere translator into Saxon of her efforts. The insults would not have been lost upon a learned contemporary,[56] still less upon those who cared for the Anglo-Saxon monastic past with its reverence for its kings and for their protection of sanctuary law. And once again the insult is driven home by a reference to Gildas. Geoffrey makes six open and supposedly serious references in the *Historia* to Gildas as his source.[57] In the case of the first three references (1.17, Lud and Kaerlud; 2.17, the Molmutine Laws; 3.5, Belinus and the roads) at least one of his sources seems to have been Henry. The fourth, I suggested, may have been meant to express something of Geoffrey's attitude to William of Malmesbury. None of these four references can be traced in fact to Gildas.[58] The names of both Gildas and of Bede were dear to William and to Henry. When used by Geoffrey they seem to be meant on occasion to express not respect for the writing of the past but a profound lack of respect for the writing of the present. The two are used not primarily as sources but as scapegoats in a highly complex exercise in contemporary criticism.

Before turning to the larger scene, we may perhaps note one more sting that awaits contemporary historians in general and perhaps Henry in particular. At points in his narrative Henry inserts cross references to world history, a habit based perhaps on Jerome-Eusebius and pursued at length in the Worcester *Chronicon ex Chronicis*. Geoffrey does this too, for example in 1.18, 2.6 (twice), 9, 10, 15, 4.11, 15. The cross references inserted by Henry

---

Henry. This doubt cannot be resolved until we know more about the text of the *Historia Anglorum*, but if Geoffrey did borrow, then there is distortion here too, for Geoffrey fathers the "Kairlundene" of Henry and Nennius onto Lud, and declares, indeed, as they do not, that Kaerlunden is a corruption of Kaerlud.

[55] Liebermann, *Gesetze*, 1:637–638. A similar passage is found, too, in the *Leis Willelme*.

[56] The author of the *Leges Henrici Primi* and *Quadripartitus* also was greatly interested in West Saxon law: L. J. Downer, ed., *Leges Henrici Primi* (Oxford, 1972), p. 45.

[57] The references are in 1.17, 2.17, 3.5, 4.20, 6.13, 12.6.

[58] And on the free play Geoffrey makes with Gildas when he does use him see Schirmer, *Darstellungen*, pp. 25–27 and 38–39.

and the Worcester Chronicler are always, of course, seriously meant as a means of placing verified events within a wider context. Each of the cross references I have noted in Geoffrey's *Historia* follows a totally, in some cases glaringly, fictional passage. The first, for example, follows the section on Lud, Kaerlud, and the first source citation of Gildas. The second two follow the imaginary account of the rule of a woman, Gwendolen, and that of an equally imaginary tyrant supposedly modelled on William Rufus. The third follows the passage in which Geoffrey associates the founding of William of Malmesbury's Roman Carlisle with the British king Leil, and the fourth the attribution of the hot baths in Bath to Bladud and not to Caesar. It is hard to imagine that any of this was accidental.

The third person Geoffrey mentions in his epilogue is Caradoc of Llancarfan. After barring William of Malmesbury and Henry of Huntingdon, Geoffrey actively invites him to continue his history for him. This invitation has often been taken seriously. Now, we know little about Caradoc of Llancarfan, but the little we do know is an encouragement to suspect, not to trust, Geoffrey's invitation.[59] There is nothing in the accepted writings of Caradoc that have come down to us, the lives of Sts. Gildas, Cyngar, and Cadoc, to suggest that he was interested in the history of kings. The evidence points wholly to the contrary. Caradoc was one of a company of professionals who dealt in the lives not of seculars but of saints. Put at their simplest, the interests of Caradoc and his circle were not in the triumph but in the humiliation of kings. These humiliations were to be brought about preferably by ascetics exceptionally learned, endowed with powers far above the natural, and associated with distinguished monastic communities. Caradoc's Life of St. Cadoc is a good example of these preoccupations. It describes the saint admiringly in this way: "quamvis regis proles, regii cultus despiciebat pompam, sub vili habitu singulis horis frequentando ecclesiam."[60] In the face of his parents' desire for him to conduct himself properly as their firstborn and heir and become a soldier, Cadoc takes to learning, then to miracles (often at the expense of royal pride) and to the leadership of a large religious community. He is then instructed by an angel to end his life in exile from his homeland, and does so.

Some of the lives written by Caradoc's companions are to be found in the famous collection in British Library MS Cotton Vespasian A.xiv, apparently based on a collection made at St. Peter's abbey, Gloucester, in the 1130s.[61] Three of the lives in this collection have a special bearing upon Geoffrey's

[59] On Caradoc see J. S. P. Tatlock, "Caradoc of Llancarfan, SPECULUM 13 (1938), 139–152, expanded and corrected by P. Grosjean, "Vie de S. Cadoc par Caradoc de Llancarfan," *Analecta Bollandiana* 60 (1942), 35–45, and Brooke, "The Archbishops," pp. 228–236. Le Père Grosjean edits the Life of St. Cadoc, "Vie," pp. 45–67. Caradoc's Life of St. Gildas is edited by Th. Mommsen, MGH AA 13 (Berlin, 1898), 107–110.

[60] Grosjean, "Vie," p. 48.

[61] The Vespasian manuscript itself, interestingly enough, was possibly compiled at Monmouth Priory. K. Hughes, "British Museum Ms. Cotton Vespasian A.xiv," p. 197.

history because all deal in a particular way with Geoffrey's hero, Arthur.[62]
They are, the *Vita Cadoci,* the *Vita Carantoci,* and the *Vita Paterni.* All of them
diminish the stature of, even to the point of vilifying, Arthur. In the *Vita
Cadoci* Arthur is represented as a young man whose libidinous desires are
much in need of correction: "Arthurus . . . libidine in amorem adolescen-
tulae nimium succensus, ac iniqua cogitatione plenus. . . ." These are
restrained only by Kay and Bedevere. Later in the narrative Arthur's venge-
ful search for the slayer of three of his knights is stilled only by the intervention of the saint, who, with the help of others, among them St. David,
protects Arthur's victim. Arthur's demands are shown to be unreasonable
and a resort to "divine spells" is justified by the intensity of Arthur's rage
and greed. This story is repeated in Caradoc's life of the saint. In the *Vita
Carantoci* Arthur needs the saint's assistance in the domestication of a dragon. In the *Vita Paterni,* Arthur's greed reappears. "Confossus zelo avaritiae"
he tries to steal the saint's tunic, only to be threatened with a display of the
saint's power over nature. He is humbled and repents. Caradoc, though
more gently, had portrayed a repentant Arthur in his life of St. Gildas.

Neither Caradoc nor his companions emerge from this as writers about
Welsh kings of the stamp of Geoffrey. The likelihood is, I think, that
Geoffrey knew this well, and that he set himself quite deliberately to mock
their known propensities, not merely in the epilogue but in the text also. In
Historia 9.1, for example, when Arthur is crowned king, the virtues Geoffrey
gives him are the antithesis of the vices mentioned in the lives. Arthur is
"iuvenis inaudite virtutis et largitatis in quo tantum gratiam innata bonitas
prestiterat ut a cunctis fere populis amaretur." Such aggression as he showed
was never prompted by greed, still less by lust, but was the result of a
courageous disposition and a laudable desire to distribute largesse. Arthur is
never humbled before bishops and clergy. They are humbled before him
(9.6), though not by magic but by his prowess in battle. When Arthur
appears in Geoffrey's *Historia* as an avenger (10.3), he is avenging the cruel
death of a woman, and Kay and Bedevere appear not as his keepers but as
his helpers in this just cause. Arthur has no cause to domesticate the dragon
which appears to him in 10.2; he is, on the contrary, to treasure the symbol
in his just conflict with Lucius Hiberius. The invitation to Caradoc seems to
have sprung, in short, from the same spirit as the banning of William and
Henry. The latter were not to write because they lacked a source; the former
was to write, but upon a subject utterly opposed to his known interests. The
animating spirit was once again the desire to ridicule contemporary literary
pundits in the most devastating way possible; to ridicule them individually
and severally through a reversal some of the claims and features of the
sources that had been their supports.

With Caradoc, I had said we should return to that "liber vetustissimus"
which Geoffrey claimed to have translated in rustic style and for lack of
which William and Henry were excluded from British history. The mention

[62] The extracts are conveniently set out in Chambers, *Arthur,* pp. 243–249.

of the *liber* evokes as great a variety of responses as did the appearance of the *Historia*. This is Geoffrey's story. While musing about the singular lack of a history of the kings of Britain he was offered an ancient book in the "British" language — "quendam britannici sermonis librum vetustissimum." The book was offered to him by Walter, archdeacon of Oxford, "vir in oratoria arte atque in exoticis hystoriis eruditus." The work which follows, says Geoffrey, is a translation of this book. He refers to the book again in 11.1, as the authority for his account of the battles between Arthur and Modred. In the epilogue he refers to it once more. He adds that Archdeacon Walter brought it "ex britannia." To the first two references to the book he adds self-deprecatory remarks upon his own rustic style. The problem of whether this ancient Welsh or Breton book existed cannot be adequately explored by one not versed in those languages. Alfred of Beverley and Gaimar believed in the ancient book, but then they believed in Geoffrey. Archdeacon Walter certainly existed. As well as being an archdeacon, he was provost of the college of secular canons of St. Georges at Oxford of which it is almost certain that Geoffrey too was a member. He was canon of Warwick, and he was witness with Geoffrey at Oxford to charters dated between 1125 and 1139. Henry of Huntingdon describes Walter as "superlative rhetoricus," a description which is like Geoffrey's.[63] But was he sober helper or mischievous collaborator in Geoffrey's venture? That we cannot say for certain, though the balance of probabilities lies in favor of the latter.

We can say something about Geoffrey's "rusticity," though. This was pretence. For all its apparent simplicity, the *Historia* is a work of considerable learning and elaboration.[64] For example, Geoffrey refers openly to Juvenal, Lucan, and Apuleius. He writes eloquent speeches which on at least one occasion (9.17) he takes care to have described as Ciceronian. Names and places are borrowed from Ovid, Juvenal, Virgil, and possibly Livy.[65] The journeys of Brutus before his arrival in Albion owe much to the *Aeneid* and *Thebaid*,[66] and Geoffrey borrows the closing words in the preface containing the double dedication from Virgil's first *Eclogue*.[67] The last section of *Historia*

[63] H. E. Salter, "Geoffrey of Monmouth and Oxford," *English Historical Review* 34 (1919), 382–385, and "The Medieval University of Oxford," *History* 14 (1929), 57–58. Henry of Huntingdon, *Epistola de Contemptu Mundi*, p. 302. There is testimony to Walter's involvement in the process of translation in the late-fourteenth-century Red Book of Hergest and the late-fifteenth-century manuscript of Welsh materials, Jesus College, Oxford, MS LXI. Griscom, *Historia*, pp. 149–150, would have it that the latter reference was taken from an earlier version, but there is no earlier record and a muddled memory of Geoffrey's words could also be its source.

[64] Hammer's index of authors cited demonstrates this beyond doubt for the variant version: *Variant Version*, pp. 267–269.

[65] Other examples of Geoffrey's learned associations are to be found in Tatlock, *Legendary History*, pp. 379–380.

[66] Edmond Faral, *La Légende Arthurienne*, 2 (Paris, 1929), 79–81. M. Faral's commentary on the *Historia* is particularly rich in information about Geoffrey's classical sources.

[67] "Tityre, tu patulae recubans," *Eclogue*, I, 1; ". . . recipias ut sub tegmine tam patulae arboris recubans," Griscom, *Historia*, p. 220. In that same preface, of course, Geoffrey, in pointed contrast to Henry, had declared he would not gather flowers from other men's gardens.

7.4 is certainly an adaptation, perhaps a parody, of Lucan's *Pharsalia* 1, 643–665. Geoffrey's "rusticity" was a joke. Was the idea of a translation of a "liber vetustissimus" a joke too? If we attribute even some degree of truth to his statement, several very recent books are inherently more probable than one very old one as sources. But a joke is far more probable. As Latin literature was accumulating round him when Geoffrey was writing, so too was anxiety about translation.[68] As he made fun of the literature, so too it is extremely likely that he chose to make fun of this as well. There is an element of pure delight in the thought that the single source which Geoffrey claimed his learned contemporaries lacked, and for lack of which, in apparent deference to their professional standards, he barred them from exercising their craft in the history of Britain, was, all the time, make-believe.[69]

* * *

In this attempt to suggest that Geoffrey meant not to make one history book but to mock many, attention has been focussed upon the three contemporary authors he named. The quest becomes even more rewarding when we widen its scope. Though history was his means, historians qua historians were not his only prey. We may see this by turning to some of the most arresting parts of Geoffrey's work — those parts in which he deals with the church in Britain.

In 4.19, 20 and 9.12, 13, 15, Geoffrey devotes attention to the organisation of this church. He divides it into three secular metropolitan sees: London, York, and Caerleon. London commands England and Cornwall,

[68] The old Cornish glossary in British Library MS Cotton Vespasian A.xiv, the manuscript already mentioned as the source of many of the saints' lives of the circle of Caradoc, seems to have been made in the early twelfth century from a Latin–Anglo-Saxon glossary drawn up at Cerne. Kenneth H. Jackson, *Language and History in Early Britain* (Edinburgh, 1953), pp. 60–61. Another surviving list, this time of Anglo-Saxon law terms, was perhaps made for Alexander of Lincoln, dedicatee of Geoffrey's work on the prophecies of Merlin. H. Hall, ed., *Red Book of the Exchequer*, 3 (RS, London, 1896). cclvi–lxv, 1032–9. The translator Adelard of Bath was active in England in the 1130s, was connected with the Anglo-Norman court, and may have dedicated one work to a son of Robert of Gloucester. Charles H. Haskins, *Studies in the History of Medieval Science* (Boston, 1924), pp. 26–27, 34. I have mentioned the translation into Latin of the Anglo-Saxon Laws, and also William of Malmesbury's translation and adaptation of Coleman's Life of Wulfstan. We have in the Canterbury version (F) (London, British Library MS Cotton Domitian A viii) a bilingual Anglo-Saxon Chronicle made again at this time.

[69] It now seems certain that Geoffrey called upon authentic Welsh and even Breton sources, and that he did so with the contemporary concerns of these nations in mind. Roberts, "Geoffrey of Monmouth," pp. 34, 37–40. To suggest, as I do, that Geoffrey used the idea of the single "liber vetustissimus" as a multiple means of poking fun is not to deny that he also used genuine material nor to deny him knowledge of contemporary Welsh or Breton hopes. But did he use this material and this knowledge as others used it? This I doubt. If he was capable of using Latin sources and their topoi as a means of making mischief in one context, it is not impossible that he used his knowledge of sources in other languages to make similar mischief in another. In the single case of the "liber vetustissimus," if Welsh or Cornish or Breton historical materials were, in the early twelfth century, in as complex and fragmentary a state as one is led to believe, then the thought that they could be contained within a single book was perhaps as ludicrous to those who did have access to them as it was infuriating to those who did not.

York everything north of the Humber, Caerleon Wales. He ignores in this, of course, the monastic see of Canterbury at a time of peculiar sensitivity.[70] He gives prominence to York and to its control over Scotland when York's duty of subservience to Canterbury had only recently and with pain been relaxed.[71] He supports the dreams of London and he invents in Glamorgan a Welsh metropolitan see in the face once again of metropolitan ambitions very recently disappointed — those of St. David's and Llandaff.[72] Some named archbishops are assigned to Geoffrey's sees: Dubricius, then David, to Caerleon, Samson to York, Guithelinus to London (6.2). We know that this is mischief.[73] Less stressed, however, is the fact that once again behind this mischief is a *recent* accumulation of Latin literature of propaganda, especially of propaganda in the cause of religious communities of regular life. Dubricius of Caerleon who crowns Geoffrey's Arthur (a choice reflecting harshly upon the claims of Canterbury) is the namesake of the saintly founder of the hopeful see of Llandaff. His life forms a part of the *Liber Landavensis*. He is also the namesake of the predecessor claimed at St. David's for St. David himself. Geoffrey gives Dubricius the titles of primate and legate (9.12), titles which William of Corbeil had claimed for Canterbury. Three archbishops of England in the time of King Lucius and twenty-seven of Geoffrey's twenty-eight flamens are also to be found in a recent letter from St. David's to Pope Honorius, though of course not the see of Caerleon, the appearance of which distorts the whole.[74]

In reaching back to St. Patrick as the founder of the abbey of Menevia yet excluding St. David's from his sees (11.3), Geoffrey makes play both with the traditional association of Dyfed with the Dessi of Leinster (as represented, for example, in the Welsh genealogies in MSS B.L. Harley 3859 and Jesus College Oxford XX) and with inner conflicts present in recent supports for St. David's pretensions, the letter to Honorius and the life of St. David. The late-eleventh-century life of St. David by Rhigyfarch meant to leave no doubt in the minds of its readers that St. David's was a metropolitan see, that the abbey was its strong support, and that David and not Patrick was its founder. The letter to Honorius, on the other hand, shows sympathy with Patrick as David's subordinate and as subordinate too to direction from Rome. We are

---

[70] Canterbury finds mention in Geoffrey as a place the wicked Vortigern liked to visit (6.10), and as Merlin's prophesied successor to London (7.3).

[71] Donald Nicholl, *Thurstan, Archbishop of York (1114–1140)* (York, 1964), pp. 99–103.

[72] The canons of St. David's claimed metropolitan status for the see in the pontificate of Honorius II (1124–1130): J. Conway Davies, ed., *Episcopal Acts and Cognate Documents relating to Welsh Dioceses*, 1 (Historical Society of the Church in Wales, 1946), no. 80. For further information on the metropolitan claims of the see of St. David's and their fate later in the century see M. Richter, "The Life of St. David by Giraldus Cambrensis," *Welsh History Review* 4 (1968–69), 381–386, and "Professions of Obedience and the Metropolitan Claim of St. David's," *National Library of Wales Journal* 15 (1967–68), 197–214. Urban of Glamorgan's ambitions for Llandaff had only died with him in 1134: Martin Brett, *The English Church under Henry I* (Oxford, 1975), pp. 52–53.

[73] Christopher Brooke, "Geoffrey of Monmouth," pp. 80–82.

[74] Christopher Brooke, "The Archbishops," pp. 203–210.

here in the deep difficulties of contemporary divisions within the Irish Church;[75] Geoffrey's iconoclasm seems easily to comprehend these too. His own David, archbishop of the secular see of Caerleon, drawn in affection to the abbey of Menevia that St. Patrick had founded and in which David was buried by order of the king, and all while Rome was Britain's enemy, makes nonsense of it all. William, Henry, and Caradoc are, it might be noted, included in this nonsense; Henry allows St. David's at least a brief period of metropolitan status in succession to Caerleon and William has St. David uncompromisingly at St. David's itself and Patrick associated with him only in his praise of Glastonbury.[76] Caradoc may have lent his skill to the forging of the *Liber Landavensis*.[77] The nonsenses accumulate. The letter from the chapter of St. David's to Honorius, for instance, names a certain Samson, later archbishop of Dol, as St. David's successor as archbishop of St. David's. Geoffrey has an Archbishop Samson — but of the secular see of York. He mentions Samson of Dol (9.15) only to point out that he was succeeded at Dol by a certain Teilo, priest of Llandaff. The *Liber Landavensis* is familiar with Teilo and connects him, indeed, with Dol; but Teilo there is one of the founders of the metropolitan see of Llandaff and not just a priest.[78] To top it all, in 4.20 Geoffrey cites the familiar *De Victoria Aurelii Ambrosii* of Gildas as his authority for his metropolitan dispositions. He adds, as an excuse for shortening his own account: "Quod autem ipse tam lucido tractatu paraverat, nullatenus opus fuit ut inferiori stilo renovaretur." Neither the inferior penmanship nor the lucid exposition existed. Again we have the paradox of invented literary authority given the appearance of antiquity, combined with real inventive mockery of current literature. Mockery of the written supports of current metropolitan claims, through a spurious source, furthermore, had special point in the context of the many spurious compilations involved. Finally if Caradoc of Llancarfan, writer of a recent life of Gildas, did indeed help to forge the *Liber Landavensis*, Geoffrey's invocation of the authority of Gildas within this context for his own arrangements, turns again into outrage.

* * *

So far, we have been concentrating upon the immediate causes and objects of Geoffrey's mischief-making. I have attempted to show that the enormous accumulation of Latin literature and especially the literature with which he found himself surrounded formed his chief provocation, and that he constructed and directed his history to make fun of it. He made fun by parodying its sources and its method, by distorting its message, by directing known and named experts to tasks they hated or banning them on the most

[75] For a careful discussion of the literary aspects of these conflicts see N. K. Chadwick, "Intellectual Life in West Wales in the Last Days of the Celtic Church," in *Studies in the Early British Church*, ed. Nora K. Chadwick (Cambridge, 1958), especially pp. 136–142, 145–146.
[76] William of Malmesbury, *Gesta Regum*, pp. 26–27.
[77] Brooke, "The Archbishops," pp. 229–231.
[78] Ibid., pp. 204–206.

specious of grounds from tasks they loved, and by pretending throughout to a simplicity which, it must have been all too clear even to the semi-learned, he did not possess. On occasion, it seems, in addition, that he ridiculed, through literature, many of the principal motives behind its composition. Works that supported certain known ecclesiastical policies fell in ruins before Geoffrey's dispositions, and Geoffrey's apparently slipshod use of legal and historical compilations brought about subtle but quite devastating changes of emphasis and national sympathy. The supports and pretensions of some of the greater monastic sees and houses suffered especially severely from Geoffrey's teasing.

I have no doubt at all that there are many more hidden literary parodies in the *Historia* waiting to be discovered. Contemporary authors other than those he named may have suffered from the same treatment. Rather than pursue this line of investigation, however, I should prefer to end with a suggestion. The suggestion is tentative and cannot be resolved into a conclusion, but it calls upon evidence which has not, to my knowledge, previously been applied to an understanding of Geoffrey's work. For that reason alone it may claim attention. The evidence is of two kinds: that derived from an examination of the contents of the *Historia* as a whole, and that derived from an examination of the immediate social context within which Geoffrey lived. I wish to suggest that Geoffrey, through both his ridicule and his serious literary creation, held to one overriding purpose. By both mocking and writing Latin literature, he meant to exalt certain virtues he felt currently to be diminished both by the literature and by those supporters and exponents of the celibate and cenobitic life which were in the forefront of its production. He meant also to exalt certain of the ways of life that monasticism threatened. The virtues he meant to exalt were the physical bravery of men, the judicious influence of women, and the power for good in society of family care and pride. The way of life he meant to exalt was that of responsible rulership and marriage.

In the *Historia Regum Britanniae* Geoffrey seems to diverge from that Latin literature to which he was close in his treatment of three major (and interrelated) subjects: lay rulers, women, and churchmen. I have said something of his divergence from the views of contemporary hagiographers in the matter of Arthur. He diverges, too, from the kings of William and Henry. Geoffrey's hero has a greater moral stature than any of theirs, stature that comes from a revision of opinion about the relative status of specific virtues and vices. Put simply, qualities dismissed by certain of Geoffrey's contemporaries as vices become, for Geoffrey, virtues. Pride becomes prowess, covetousness the necessary forerunner to largesse, anger the righting of cruel wrong, lust the laudable will to beget and provide for heirs. Arthur's right to rule is hereditary and his virtue "innata" (9.1), not of grace, but of birth. His conquests are justified by his need to provide for those close to him: "Arturus ergo quia in illo probitas largitionem comitàbatur, statuit saxones inquietare, ut eorum opibus que ei famulabatur ditaret familiam. Commonebat etiam id rectitudo, cum tocius insule monarchiam debuerat hereditario iure obtinere." He provides accordingly, but especially for his own family (9.9), and these efforts clearly govern the dignity of a known terrestrial realm and the happiness of its inhabitants. Similar though less exalted instances of just such a collection of virtues may be found in Arthur's royal predecessors: Cassivellaunus, for example. Conversely family discord and the consequent breakdown of such efforts are the most frequent heralds of vice and failure (2.6, 15).

In Geoffrey's accounts of royal celebrations wives play an important part.[79] Though the crown passes through the male line, women are frequently given by him a vital role in the government of the kingdom.[80] The conflict of the brothers Brennius and Belinus is ended by their mother, and that between Arviragus and Vespasian by Queen Genuissa.[81] In these cases too we have the same concern for family prosperity. We have also the pattern of virtues and failings definable as such not according to an abstract terminology but according to the measure of happiness they give or refuse to groups of blood relations and the measure of prosperity they secure or fail to secure for the countries to which these are tied by birth and by affection. I have mentioned Geoffrey's changes to the story of Helen. A much more striking example of such changes is to be found in his version of the legend of St. Ursula. The previous versions have these points in common. Ursula is a British virgin desired in marriage by the son of a continental tyrant. Urged by a divine vision and accompanied by eleven thousand other virgins, she goes. She refuses a barbarian marriage, however, and all are slaughtered by the Huns as virgin martyrs; rousing stuff, with a very clear message. Geoffrey distorts it. According to him (5.15–16) Ursula goes not to a tyrant but to a man built much on the Arthurian model, Conan of Britanny, who "commissam patriam viriliter defendebat," and, after his victory, "voluit commilitonibus suis coniuges dare ut eis nasceretur heredes, qui terram illam perpetuo possiderent." The accompanying eleven thousand, therefore, are to be wives for a meritorious army, and Geoffrey never describes either them or Ursula as virgins, but as "filias" or "mulieres." The majority of those who hesitate do so because they love their kinsmen and country. A few prefer chastity or even death, but not, it seems, to the loss of virginity as such, but to marrying for money. The company resists not marriage but the barbarians' wish "lascivire cum eis."

The modifications look slight. They are in fact fundamental. All the inessentials of the story are retained in the guise of essentials. The true essential of the original, the "virtuous" opposition between virginity and

[79] For example 2.2–6, 4.8, 5.15, 16, 6.5, 12, 14, 15, 7.19–20, 9.13, 10.13. 2.8 is perhaps an excessive demonstration of the point.

[80] 2.6, Gwendolen reigns for fifteen years and concedes the throne to her son Maddan only when she considers him of age. 2.15, Cordelia reigns for at least five years. 3.13, Marcia writes the laws which King Alfred merely translates, then rules for her son until he comes of age. 5.6, Helen is instructed to succeed her father. In placing such an emphasis upon the role of women it may be that he used his knowledge of Welsh tradition here to serious effect.

[81] 4.16.

marriage is quite destroyed and replaced by a far more complex story about desirable and undesirable human motives and affections. Meritorious warfare and the desire to begét heirs are reconcilable and praiseworthy. It is not marriage itself but its abuse which leads to disaster. Virginity as a virtue seems to have no part.[82]

Finally we return to Geoffrey's ecclesiastical dispositions. I have mentioned that all his metropolitan sees are secular sees. There is no monk-bishop to be found in the whole work. Gloucester is lauded as a bishopric, which, when Geoffrey wrote, it was not, and not as an abbey, and a peculiarly important one, which it was.[83] Moreover, Eldod, the bishop of Gloucester, is a warrior who like Guithelinus of London and Dubricius of Caerleon stirs soldiers to meritorious warfare. Geoffrey never invokes that supernatural power which, according to Caradoc and his circle, comes of physical and mental asceticism, never directly exalts the regular religious life as such, and does much indirectly to diminish its place. King Elidur, for example (3.17), does not retire to a monastery in the Anglo-Saxon manner when he gives up his crown to his brother. The reign of the monk-king Constans is an unrelieved disaster to which the monastic life contributes materially: ". . . debilitas sensus ipsius id faciebat, nam infra claustra aliud quam regnum tractare didicerat" (6.6). Geoffrey pays tribute (9.15) to the pious wish of Archbishop Dubricius to become a hermit, but makes it clear that Dubricius's successor to the archbishopric, David, the king's uncle and appointed by the king, is a model of goodness. And the life of the hermit, of course, is by no means synonymous with the regular cenobitic life. There is a pleasantly perverse touch in a previous chapter (9.13). Habits of a single color are the badges of knights of prowess and of ladies who are appropriately demanding in their love. The abbey of which Geoffrey speaks most often, Amesbury, is praised primarily as a mausoleum for kings and faithful warriors. Geoffrey's abbeys are always, indeed, subject to kings, and his monks, when he does allow them a place, are devoted to a life of withdrawn and penitential prayer. I have said how marked, in context, is Geoffrey's omission of Glastonbury. The omission was in part pure fun at William's expense, but it had, I think, a deeper side too. To omit Glastonbury which claimed his bones

---

[82] The modifications become all the more important in view of the especially wide currency the legend had in early-twelfth-century England. Wilhelm Levison, *Das Werden der Ursula-Legende* (Cologne, 1928), pp. 91–96.

[83] K. Hughes, "British Museum MS Cotton Vespasian A.xiv," pp. 190–192, 197. On the aggressive part played by the abbey of Gloucester in monastic politics in both England and Wales in the period in question see also Christopher Brooke, "St. Peter of Gloucester and St. Cadoc of Llancarfan," in *Celt and Saxon, Studies in the Early British Border*, ed. Nora K. Chadwick (Cambridge, 1963), pp. 258–283. The comparatively recent acquisition of Welsh properties, especially the church of St. Cadoc at Llancarfan, by St. Peters, the likelihood that the collection of Welsh saints' lives, later copied into the Vespasian manuscript, was originally made at the abbey partly from Llandaff materials, and the possibility, mentioned by Ker, that the scriptorium at Gloucester was an important one, all of course give an extra edge to Geoffrey's mockery of the Welsh hagiographers and propagandists and to his omission of St. Peters. So does the fact that Robert, earl of Gloucester, was Geoffrey's main dedicatee.

while making so much of Arthur, and to invent a purely imaginary monastic mausoleum when real ones stood at Westminster and Reading, struck hard at monastic claims upon kings. Glastonbury may well have laid claim too to relics of St. Ursula and her ten chief companions.[84]

It is a singular fact that the later years of the reign of Henry I were occupied by a particularly intensive debate about clerical continence. Ecclesiastical councils legislated for clerical celibacy,[85] but strong legislation is often a measure of the strength of the opposition to it. In this case Henry I, in both condemning clerical marriage and ensuring that it was in practice possible, played a masterly dual role[86] and made certain that, in precisely those years in which Geoffrey began to write his *Historia*, the debate was far from being resolved. The claims of monks and canons regular to the priesthood and through that to episcopal office are of course reconcilable with and supported by a successful drive for celibacy; other claims not perhaps so easily so.

It is a still more singular fact that the Oxford in which Geoffrey lived and wrote yields, from a time still closer to his time of writing, independent evidence of an entry into this particular fray. In about 1132 Archbishop Thurstan of York asked one Master Theobald, then teaching at Oxford, whether monks should have pastoral care. His reply was unambiguous. They should have neither pastoral care nor tithes, for they had no rights to the public priesthood and to public clerical status and its rewards.[87] Monks were to withdraw from public power and revenues and to live of their own a life of penitence. This reply had perhaps been predicted, for Theobald had expressed himself equally unambiguously upon related matters earlier in his career.[88] He had earlier declared his belief that priests' sons were eligible for the priesthood and had made some very direct remarks about the pride which often lay in open chastity. There is some suggestion that Theobald was himself the son of a priest and that he held and expressed, though indirectly, to his friend Philip, views favorable to the marriages of priests.[89]

Theobald was probably a secular canon of St. Georges in Oxford. Geoffrey almost certainly was. Geoffrey's friend, Archdeacon Walter, to whose generosity Geoffrey attributed the provision of the "liber vetustissimus" was

[84] *De Antiquitate*, PL 179:1964. Gransden, *Historical Writing*, pp. 207–208, notes Geoffrey's use of the legend of St. Ursula and his attitude to monasticism, but suggests that his object was principally to amuse.

[85] We have some record of two of the last three councils of William of Corbeil, the councils of Westminster and London, 1127 and 1129. In both, clerical continence was the principal object of concern. In the first, of which we have versions of the canons themselves, clerical marriage and concubinage were very strongly condemned. Brett, *English Church*, pp. 81–82.

[86] Ibid., p. 220. See also the interesting remarks on Gratian's own ambivalence towards this question in J. Gaudemet, "Gratian et le célibat écclésiastique," *Studia Gratiana* 13 (1967), 341–369.

[87] R. Foreville and J. Leclercq, "Un débat sur le sacerdoce des moines au XII siècle," *Studia Anselmiana* 41 (1957), 52–53.

[88] Nicholl, *Thurstan*, p. 188.

[89] Pl 163:767–70; Foreville and Leclercq, "Un débat," pp. 10–11, 21.

provost of St. Georges. Walter, moreover, was almost certainly married.[90] St. Georges began to succumb to the claims of celibate, regular clergy in 1129, when the regular house of Osney was founded in part on its revenues.[91] It was closed in 1149. Theobald's virulence is understandable in the light of, and is very likely to have been prompted by, this threat to his origins and livelihood. If my description of at least some of Geoffrey's preoccupations is a correct one, then the two are most firmly allied. Both sought to defend the rights in public life of the virtues of the family from its enemy — aggressive monasticism equally anxious for public rights. The difference is that Geoffrey tried in addition to defend the delights of Latin literature, and largely from that same enemy, and did so with the most consummate skill.[92]

*   *   *

There are many levels to Geoffrey's achievement. I have tried to single out four. I have agreed that Geoffrey was primarily a parodist, and that he parodied the postures of sections of contemporary society. I have suggested in addition that he parodied in particular the literature which supported these sections of society in their laughable state, and 'that he tried to do so by using the same literature but in a very different way. Most important, however, are the third and fourth levels, those which rest upon Geoffrey's immediate surroundings and which provide help towards an understanding of his ultimate purpose. The last years of the reign of Henry I ,and the first years of the reign of Stephen were years in which the position in England of the secular and married clergy came under serious threat at the hands of a still powerful and celibate monastic church. The threat from canons regular and monks was felt with great intensity at Oxford. Perhaps from this fact, surely from the expressed position of his colleague Theobald, Geoffrey took the opportunity to devise a defence. The desire to defend the virtues of secular society and to rebut the claims of the celibate played a vital part in the composition of the *Historia* and perhaps in its success. Geoffrey constructed in it a powerful alternative to monastic literature and to monastic society. His work is literate, polished, learned, but, above all, amusing. And in the world he creates it is not celibates and monks but kings and queens with heirs to

---

[90] F. M. Powicke and A. B. Emden, eds., Hastings Rashdall, *The Universities of Europe in the Middle Ages*, 3 (Oxford, 1936), 17, notes 1 and 2. Archdeacon Walter passed on one of his prebends to his son. H. E. Salter, ed., *Cartulary of Osney Abbey* (Oxford, 1934), no. 20, p. 31.

[91] Geoffrey witnessed the foundation charter of 1129, in company with Archdeacon Walter. H. E. Salter, "Geoffrey of Monmouth," p. 385.

[92] An able demonstration of the effect of the 1127–1129 pressure for clerical celibacy upon the historical work of no less a person than Henry of Huntingdon is to be found in N. Partner, "Clerical Celibacy and the Writing of History," *Church History* 42 (1973), 467–475. I owe this reference to Ms. Jan Foote. Henry too regarded the pressure with distaste, a distaste made the more explicable by the possibility that he was married (Partner, *Serious Entertainments*, pp. 14–15). He expressed his displeasure, however, in a far less skillful way than, if I am right, did Geoffrey. He was wholly without Geoffrey's lightness of touch. This similarity of opinion, yet deep difference in style, may in part explain Geoffrey's open teasing and private neglect of Henry.

care for, a country to love, and the courage and imagination to provide for
them who rule the land and church of Britain. The recommendation of
these essentially human values in the face of increasingly vigorous and
articulate threats to them guided, perhaps prompted, Geoffrey's deeply
artistic creation. I do not wish to deny the existence of other interests and
other ends. The work is far too complex for that. But most of these other
interests need this perspective for their proper understanding. The friendship expressed in Geoffrey's dedications for Robert of Gloucester and, apparently, for the cause of Mathilda[93] is compatible, for example, with the
purpose I have ascribed to him, and is perhaps explained by it. The exaltation of the virtues of the family cuts two ways of course; the too free suffer
with the too severe (though not perhaps as much).[94] It may also cut across
the bounds of recent national allegiances.[95] This fact may explain the ir-
resolution with which attempts to define Geoffrey's larger political sympathies end.

Parody is not in general the stuff of which histories are made; and, if it is
good, the target or targets of parody are concealed. In both cases, if I am
right, Geoffrey's inventiveness and skill were very great. So too, though, was
his restraint. The *Historia Regum Britanniae* was a work of the gentlest
counterpropaganda; it was perhaps all the more telling for that reason. It
deserves to be given a far more important place than it has hitherto received
in the literature of the twelfth-century monastic reform.

[93] On Geoffrey's probable support of Mathilda see Tatlock, *Legendary History*, pp. 286–288,
426–427.

[94] Hanning, *Vision*, pp. 150–152.

[95] Though we know little about the conduct of Anglo-Norman crown wearings it is hard to
see Geoffrey's account of the company at Arthur's coronation feast (9.13), with its careful
separation of the sexes and its devotion to musical appreciation, as anything but a parody of
them. As Brooke points out, the previous chapter has stings too for the Welsh at the Norman
court. Brooke, "The Archbishops," p. 80.

III

THOUGHTS ABOUT THE CONTEXT
OF SOME EARLY MEDIEVAL TREATISES
DE NATURA RERUM

This is a rather dry title for a rather dampening subject. It is hard to emerge from a scrutiny of early medieval treatises On the Nature of Things without a sense of having been thundered and lightened and rained on several times, and misted over and covered in hail and frost, of having been dripped on by the stars and scarcely dried by the sun. In some such texts, in addition, one is expected to follow the Nile to its source, to watch the ways of the moon with the tides, to consider the nature of the waters above the firmament. And as though this were not enough there is the intellectually dampening effect of the present state of the material. We have two truly excellent modern editions of two of these treatises – the De Natura Rerum of Isidore of Seville, by Jacques Fontaine published in 1960, and the De Natura Rerum of Bede, by C.W. Jones, published in 1975.[1] For the third important one, that of Rabanus, we have the choice of Migne, with all its deficiencies, or that bewildering array of manuscripts and excerpts which both defeats editors and demonstrates the importance of the text. Anonymous extracts De Natura Rerum are to be found in equally anonymous and generally unedited computistical manuscripts especially. None of this inspires warm feelings or confidence. It may well then be asked with pertinence why I am attempting to say anything at all. It is certainly rash to do so, but I press on, nonetheless, for three particular reasons.

III

I hope these may justify to some extent the rashness. Firstly,
given the enormous numbers of surviving manuscripts of them and
the clear borrowings from them we can so consistently trace in
so very many later works, early medieval treatises De Natura
Rerum were clearly held to be of the highest importance and
were in fact copied with hope and enthusiasm. It is worth
trying, at least, to find out why. Secondly, the three treatises
I have mentioned have not been, so far as I know, closely
compared for contents and context. Thirdly I have had a few
thoughts about a common immediate purpose for which parts at
least of such treatises and collections of extracts may have
been compiled and so, as the title of this paper suggests, about
a common context which may have inspired in general their
composition. These thoughts, I think, are new. If they are
correct this may give us a new perspective also from which to
approach the treatises and extracts, and even a means of reviving
our own hope and enthusiasm for them.

The treatise De Natura Rerum first in time, is that by
Isidore of Seville (d. 636). Fontaine's edition makes the task
of handling this treatise a remarkably pleasant one. It is,
indeed, a model of how to present such a text to the modern
reader. His description of the manuscripts he uses is exhaustive,
his choice of exemplars to collate for the edition of the text
as Isidore wanted it to be read is unexceptionable, his sourcework and apparatus are impeccable. If I have a complaint it is
concerned with my own interests, not the realisation of Fontaine's
purposes. He collates only pre-Carolingian manuscripts, seventeen
of them - a remarkable number to survive. The Carolingians made
enormous use of Isidore and they adapted the text in ways which
cannot help but throw light upon the contexts within which they
expected it to be used. A great deal of work remains to be done
upon the Carolingian exemplars and their glosses and their
relationship to the Carolingian treatment of Bede and Rabanus.[2]
Fontaine's edition is, however, a marvellous start, and can take
us from the early seventh well into the eighth century in pursuit
of the many ways in which the text was employed.

Isidore, as he says in his preface, wrote it for King
Sisebut, ruler of visigothic Spain from 612 until 621. Sisebut
was a scholar, and was particularly interested in astronomy and
in celestial and meteorological phenomena. As a scholar-ruler his
concerns extended to his subjects, and he was deeply anxious for
the remedy of wrong belief and ignorance. Isidore tells us that
Sisebut asked specifically for a treatise on natural phenomena
and their causes, a task Isidore hastened (too literally, says
Fontaine, for the accuracy of his quotations)[3] to fulfill.
Isidore prepared two recensions of the treatise; one of 46
chapters and a second of 47 (after his discovery of Book II of
Pliny's Natural History). He set out a clear plan for the king.
First came time (8 chapters) and the changes of the seasons.
Then came the elements and the make-up of the cosmos, the world

and its parts, the sun, moon and stars, eclipses and planets,
thunder and lightening, rainbows and clouds, rain, snow and hail,
wind and weather signs, pestilence, tides, rivers and earthquakes,
Etna and the geographical divisions of the earth. A typical
chapter, and one which may help to explain the spirit of his
work and of works of this kind in general, is chapter xxix on
thunder:

> 'Thunder is produced by the collision of clouds. Winds
> dwell within the bosom of the clouds in which they are
> conceived, but when these clouds receive a shock, the
> natural mobility of the winds causes them to burst out
> in all directions, and they make a great noise, rather
> like the rumbling of wagons as they roll out of stable
> yards.

> Looked at differently, thunder is the voice of God,
> rebuking human kind from on high, or the ear piercing
> preaching of holy men, who shout aloud to reach the
> faithful throughout the world and admonish them for
> their sins.'

Concise, clear and unexceptionable, parts of this chapter were
borrowed both by Bede and by Rabanus. Isidore presented the first
recension of his De Natura Rerum triumphantly to the king in 613.
It was quickly copied and reached Fleury (probably via
Septimania) and Cambrai by the end of the seventh century at the
latest, and South Germany at least by the early eighth century.
A third, slightly longer recension, possibly put together in
Northumbria at the court of King Aldfrith (d. 705),[4] was widely
diffused in the eighth century in Germany and Austria. This was
transmitted, perhaps by the Carolingians, to North Italy.
Isidore's De Natura Rerum maintained from then on a consistent
popularity until the end of the twelfth century.

The De Natura Rerum of Bede cannot be dated precisely, but
it was certainly written before the De Temporum Ratione of 725,
which mentions it, and perhaps with, or shortly before the De
Temporibus (703), which seems to complement it. Both the De
Temporibus and the De Natura Rerum seem, on the surface at least,
to be relatively direct and simple works, produced by a scholar
less mature than the author of the De Temporum Ratione and suited
to the needs of a teacher in a monastic school. Fontaine argues
(not wholly convincingly, but credibly) that Bede did not know
the longer version of Isidore. Bede's treatise is certainly in
part a remaking of much of Isidore's. Isidore's first eight
chapters on time apart, Bede took material from at least thirty-
six of Isidore's remaining thirty-eight or thirty-nine. We can no
longer entertain any doubt about Bede's admiration for Isidore,
and he seems even to have spent his final hours translating
sections of Isidore's De Natura Rerum into Anglo-Saxon for his
less educated brethren.[5] For all this, the borrowings are never
slavish and Bede's text shews some interesting, and, illuminating,
departures from Isidore to which we shall return.

Jones's edition of Bede's text is, like Fontaine's edition of Isidore's, quite admirable, and equipped, like his, with splendid apparatus, sourcework and collations. It prints in addition, a set of late Carolingian glosses. It is deficient, however for us, as is Fontaine's edition, in one important, though different, respect. Jones does not provide an exhaustive description of any of the manuscripts of Bede's De Natura Rerum, not even of those he uses. We are thus deprived of a vital part of the evidence we need to help us to place the work within its context, for we have no immediate way of identifying the texts with which it was originally bound. This is an infuriating deficiency in editions of medieval texts, and always diminishes their usefulness to historians of ideas; but of course it does give them some interesting work still to do.

Bede's compilation may have excited even more enthusiasm than that of Isidore. Laistner published an impressive list of surviving texts and fragments of it as early as 1943,[6] a list reproduced with corrections by Jones in his edition. This shews that in the ninth century Bede's De Natura Rerum was turned into a veritable best seller - largely, it seems, by the enthusiasms of the Carolingians. Over forty ninth-century copies of the whole or parts of it survive, five from St. Gall alone. We can assign fifteen surviving copies to the tenth century, sixteen to the eleventh and, interestingly, an upsurge in the twelfth to thirty-three. Even allowing for the replacement of elderly copies and the vagaries of individual collectors it does seem possible that at least some of the reasons for which, and at least an element of the context within which, Bede originally wrote the treatise, persisted into the ninth century and enjoyed some sort of revival in the twelfth.

Like Isidore, Bede equips us with a plan. He begins not with Sisebut but with God, and the creation of things in time to run their natural course. He has fifty-one chapters to Isidore's forty-seven, and misses out time, to which, of course, he devoted the De Temporibus. He then takes us across some seemingly familiar ground; the world and its parts and elements and zones, the heavens and their stars and planets, eclipses, winds, thunder and lightening, clouds, rain and hail, weather prognostics and pestilences, tides, seas and rivers, earthquakes and Etna and the parts of the earth again.

Rabanus wrote 'de rerum naturis' within his enormous compilation modestly entitled De Universo - of everything.[7] This, the first preface tells us, was given to Louis the German in response to a request seemingly made personally to Rabanus by the king. The king, says Rabanus, had heard that Rabanus had written a little work - 'opusculum' - about the properties of words and the mystical meanings of things, and so had asked to have it. Rabanus met the king, we know, at Rasdorf, most probably in the autumn of 843.[8] He had been compiling the De Universo in retirement from Fulda during the previous year, and there is

every reason to believe that the royal request was speedily
fulfilled. We may, then, date the first recension of the De
Universo tentatively to 844. The king must have been a little
shattered. The De Universo is a collection of twenty-two books
which lives up to its title. Together with the properties of
words and the mystical meanings of things for which the king had
asked, Rabanus has also, he says, 'plura exposita de rerum
naturis.' Thus, he continues, one might find both fact and
allegory, 'historicam et mysticam singularum rerum explanationem'
(hard to translate; perhaps 'the meaning of things in the world
and in the spirit'). We go from God, to heavenly and earthly
creatures, to holy men, to man himself, to the world, to time, to
human constructs and social groups, to minerals and metals, to
weights and measures, to agriculture and war, to the practical
arts and food and drink and implements. The scale of the whole is
immensely more vast than that of the treatises of Isidore and Bede
and has, as I said, for that reason, and by reason of its
popularity, daunted modern editors. It is dangerous to try and
deal with it. But it has large sections in Books IX and XI and
a little in Book XII which are to our purpose, because they may,
I think, throw a little more light upon the context, and
especially the new context I am going to propose, of concern for
knowledge about the nature of things. In Book IX Rabanus deals
with the same familiar subjects; the world, the elements, the
heavenly bodies, clouds and thunder and storms and winds. In
Book XI he treats of the waters of earth and heaven, in Book XII,
briefly with the earth itself; the same concerns as those of
Bede and Isidore - and perhaps, to some extent, the same context
and purposes.

There are some very evident differences between the three
treatises. First comes the obvious one of time and place - early
seventh-century Seville, early eighth-century Jarrow, mid-ninth-
century Petersberg, near Fulda. Isidore and Rabanus wrote for
kings, but for kings of a very different stamp. Bede wrote
initially perhaps for the monastic schoolroom, perhaps for active
monastic priests. I shall incline towards the latter for reasons
which I hope will become clear. Isidore was a bishop when he
wrote; Bede and Rabanus were both distinguished Benedictines,
though Rabanus was three years later to become Archbishop of
Mainz. Isidore and Rabanus were at more advanced stages of their
career than it appears was Bede, and arguably more mature in their
approaches. Isidore has a slight, Rabanus an extended, tendency
to construct allegories of a doctrinal and moral kind upon the
simple facts of nature. To Isidore, for example, hail is a
representation of the cold harshness of unbelief, snow the
unbelievers themselves, cold as ice, or one-time believers, now
grown cold in love and frozen in the pure whiteness of their
baptismal purity.[9] To Rabanus hail foreshadows the anger of God
and snow represents the purity of justice.[10] He mentions
Isidore's interpretation in this particular chapter, but he does
not take his allegories from Isidore often. Rabanus is full of

spiritual interpretations piled one upon the other and of biblical
reference of a far more extensive kind than is Isidore. Bede
mentions the bible very little and allegory not at all. This
distinction between Bede's treatise and those of the other two is
a very striking one. Certainly Bede drew upon Isidore's De Natura
Rerum as I have already said. The attached table, based upon
Jones's sourcework with a few observations of my own, is an
attempt to shew how much. But he did not draw on him exclusively
nor even particularly literally. And Rabanus did not draw upon
either.[11] One might plausibly suggest as an explanation for
Rabanus's neglect the facts that he must have had available to him
copies of both Bede and Isidore and that he must have known how
widely copied both were. Medieval plagiarism was neither so blind
nor so insensitive to economy of effort as to indulge in copying
simply for the sake of copying. Yet there is a little more, I
think, to be said than this. A complex operation is in process.
Both Rabanus and Bede are selecting and extending, and Rabanus,
above all, is hammering christian teaching home in a way which
makes even Isidore seem faint-hearted.

The differences between the treatises, then, are many, and
some of them are deep. Why then try to treat them as an entity?
I do so for three reasons. The similarities between them, to
which we shall now turn, are in fact, I hope to prove, more
important than their differences. Furthermore, these similarities,
and one of them, the new one, in particular, may help to throw
these differences into relief and to explain them. This last may
even help towards a deeper understanding of these treatises'
underlying unity.

* * *

One must never underestimate the pressure of a simple desire
to know. Sometimes, this desire to know can be, and was,
stimulated by readings in the seven liberal arts. Rabanus says
this explicitly, in a second preface to the De Universo in which
he dedicates the work this time to a Bishop Haimo, apparently a
former pupil.[12] Bede's and Isidore's treatises were also clearly
affected by the enthusiastic enquiries of school pupils. Grammar
left a firm impress upon certain chapters of that of Isidore, in
some of which he drew especially heavily from scolia upon
Lucretius, Virgil and Lucan.[13] Astronomy stood behind much of the
information upon the stars and planets in each of the three
treatises, and especially behind some of Bede's expansions of
Isidore.[14] Geometry in its geographical extension may account for
the introduction (in Isidore's case, the late introduction) of
material on the parts of the earth, or chapters on the names of
rivers and seas, zones and climates, the ways of the oceans.
Thus, the purest curiosity, aided by a measure of education, would
have welcomed much in our treatises De Natura Rerum. Isidore's
description of how the stars move as the universe moves, the
seemingly large ones nearer the earth at a pace different from
that of the seemingly small ones further away, would have satisfied

many an observer. So would Bede's additions from Pliny, Book II, which allowed him to expand upon the nature of stars; how some give off moisture, some are hardened into frost, some packed into snow or frozen into hail. Others, he adds, give off a blast of air, sometimes hot, sometimes dewy, sometimes cold.[15] As well as being stimulated by the liberal arts, curiosity of this last kind was invited by the practical needs of the monastic horarium. The times at which the night offices were sung were determined by the positions of the stars in the night sky. Gregory of Tours wrote his De Cursu Stellarum specifically for the assistance of the watcher in charge of awakening the brethren at the appropriate hour. Precision and the avoidance of mistakes were essential to so delicate an operation; so was wakefulness and, if possible, interest on the part of the watcher. It comes as no surprise, then, to find that some codices bind the De Cursu Stellarum together with a De Natura Rerum.[16]

Should anyone seek to challenge the curious, moreover, he could always have recourse to Solomon. In his preface, Isidore quotes Wisdom 7, 17:

> 'Sure knowledge he has imparted to me of all that is; how the world is ordered, what influence have the elements, how the months have their beginnings, their middle and their ending, how the sun's course alters and the seasons revolve, how the years have their cycles, the stars their places.'

Rabanus quotes from the same book in his letter to Bishop Haimo. Scriptural and patristic[17] authority to support an interest in the facts of nature could readily be found should anyone need to look for it. The pressure of a justified desire to know seems, in short, to have operated upon all three compilers and upon those who copied their works, and this, together with captive royal ears, perhaps allowed Isidore and Rabanus more latitude in the matter of allegory and sheer preachiness than they might otherwise have had.

The beginnings of a 'scientific' interest, in our sense of scientific, then, there was. It is unlikely, however, that it predominated. Its practical benefits were by no means obvious to all, and recourse to Solomon may, indeed, indicate that pure curiosity had its opponents from the very beginning. Each of our three writers and their dedicatees, moreover, had functions to fulfil which took them, (though of course to varying degrees), beyond the confines of the study, the library and the monastery. If they fed the private world of the mentally alert, and saved from a more public disgrace those liable to fall asleep, the three treatises had to look, I would argue, mainly to a world far larger than either of these. This larger world is the one I am concerned now principally to explore. In one part, it certainly contained the mentally irritating: the simple and dogmatic opponents of the

factual. Such a one was Bishop Philaster of Brescia, who, despite
dying in 397, continued to make his presence felt, for his vigorous
railings against heretics were copied and available well into our
period.[18] Philaster held it to be heretical to advance a natural
explanation for an earthquake, or to doubt that God nightly placed
the stars in the sky, or to give names to the stars which were not
in the bible.[19] Fontaine was the first to draw attention to the
challenge such figures posed,[20] and, though their assertions were
not always preserved on vellum, we may very credibly suppose that
they formed a permanent feature of the landscape. They are
important, indeed crucial, to the proper understanding of the
development of medieval science - but we cannot pursue them here.
Rather, I wish to turn to portions of this larger world different
again. The portion at which I wish in particular to look is that
made up of the flock of christians, largely anonymous, for whom
Isidore and Rabanus, as bishops, and Bede, as priest and educator
of priests, felt themselves responsible; the wide world of the
pastorate. I would argue that pastoral needs acted strongly upon
all three of these compilers and so upon their treatises De
Natura Rerum. I would suggest that they may have been the
strongest of the pressures the compilers felt. And I would
attempt to prove that, among these pastoral needs, two,
especially, stand out. To one, attention has been drawn, although
fleetingly, in the secondary literature. The second has been
almost entirely passed over; although I have come to believe that
it may have been the most important of all. We may consider these
two in succession.

* * *

King Sisebut asked Isidore for his treatise, but Fontaine
gave us an additional reason for his writing it. This reason
had, as far as I know, not been advanced before and Fontaine
offered it tentatively and did not pursue it. It deserves
pursuit, however, for it is a most convincing one. It need not
be confined in its application, moreover, to the De Natura Rerum
of Isidore alone. It is, that the treatise was written in large
part the better to explain the Apocalypse.

The Apocalypse was, in the early middle ages, firmly
believed to record a revelation made to the apostle John, and to
furnish a set of signs by which the faithful might recognise the
second coming and the end of the world. It is full of clouds and
thunder and lightning, of earthquakes and of falling stars. Thus
Christ will come again in clouds, (1, 7) the prophetic angel of
chapter ten is wrapped in a cloud, the grim reaper comes in a
cloud (10, 1; 14, 14-16). Thunder and lightning issue from the
throne on which God sits (4, 5) and there are 'peals of thunder,
loud noises, flashes of lightning and an earthquake 'after the
opening of the seventh seal and the angel's throwing of the
censer to earth (8, 5). Again, when the prophetic angel calls
out we hear 'seven thunders' (10, 3-4), and when the temple of God

is opened after the blowing of the last trumpet there are 'flashes of lightning, loud noises, peals of thunder, an earthquake and heavy hail' (11, 19). Peals of thunder accompany the coming of the lamb (14, 2). The opening of the sixth seal is followed by a great earthquake (6, 12) as is to be the seventh. An earthquake follows the rising into heaven of God's two witnesses as well as the opening of the temple (11, 13). There is an earthquake at the pouring out by the seventh angel of the seventh bowl of wrath (16, 17).

These preoccupations begin to look familiar. They become even more so as we press on. Eclipses, falling stars, winds and pestilences, hail, waters of blood and bitterness and rainbows march across the pages. The darkening of the sun and moon follow the earthquake of the sixth seal, and so do falling stars (6, 12-14). The sun, moon and stars are eclipsed again after the sound of the fourth trumpet (8, 12) and stars fall again at the sounds of the third and the fifth (8, 10; 9, 1). John sees four angels holding back the four winds (7, 1). The fourth rider of the Apocalypse is to unleash pestilence (6, 8). We have noted the hail at the last trumpet. It follows the blowing of the first, also (8, 7) and 'great hailstones, heavy as an hundredweight' drop upon the people after the seventh angel has poured out his bowl of wrath (16, 20). The second and third bowls of wrath turn rivers, fountains and the sea into blood (16, 3-7) and God's two witnesses have 'power over the waters to turn them into blood' (11, 16). The star which falls at the sound of the third trumpet 'fell on a third of the rivers and on the fountains of water'. It turns these waters bitter (8, 10-11). The angel of chapter ten, wrapped in a cloud, has a rainbow over his head (10, 1). All very stirring stuff. There is also a sea of glass which might easily be confused with ice (4, 6; 15, 2).

The _Apocalypse_ needed simple elucidation as did other books of the bible, and in simple ways; such elucidation as providing the names of the four winds, for example, which Isidore, and Bede, and Rabanus all did. A knowledge of the everyday nature of the phenomena it described could also be of assistance to the teacher concerned to illustrate a simple moral point. In a treatise on the _Apocalypse_ almost certainly of Carolingian origin we find the following comment on the 'sea of glass, like crystal' of 4, 6:

> 'Just as the ice produced by the cold of winter
> becomes hardened like rock crystal after many
> years of such cold, so is the faith of saints
> made solid as rock by the impact of striving
> through time.'[21]

The _Apocalypse_ needed elucidation in more complex ways, however, as well. On the one hand it was a very difficult text indeed. On the other, because it was so stirring, it was an extremely useful tool in the hands of pastors, moral directors, missionaries, preachers of every kind, for it was peculiarly

capable of inspiring fear. Gregory the Great used it and
expansions of it in 601 to instruct King Ethelbert of Kent –
perhaps with a view to humbling him a little:

> 'When the end of the world is nigh, many
> frightening things will happen which have
> not happened before. For instance, there
> will be changes of climate, fearsome things
> in the sky, unseasonal storms, wars, famines,
> diseases, earthquakes.'[22]

Two hazards confronted the apocalyptic preacher and the would-be
humbler of kings, however. One was that no one would take any
notice. The second was that they would take too much notice and
conclude that, for example, the first cloudburst which followed
the sermon was a herald of the second coming. There was a danger,
in other words, that they would be consumed by a fear which was
excessive and not conducive to a true understanding of the
processes of salvation. It was vital, therefore, if both contempt
and hysteria were to be avoided, to distinguish between which
signs were supernatural signs, and which were not. Phenomena
for which natural causes were knowable must be described and set
apart. Hence then the concern to explain in treatises De Natura
Rerum, the ordinary causes of clouds and thunder and lightning,
rain and earthquakes and falling stars, loud noises and eclipses,
hail and winds, pestilences and rainbows and ice. One of the
chapters Bede adds to Isidore's discussion of these subjects deals
with the purely natural origins of sweet and bitter waters
(chapter xxxviii). Another, (xlii), explains that the redness
of the Red Sea, though blood coloured, has purely earthly causes.
Bede draws attention too to places which normally do not have
storms or lightnings or eclipses, (xxiii), and so, by implication,
to places where such occurrences just might be apocalytic.

Bede, of course, wrote a treatise upon the Apocalypse; his
Explanatio Apocalypsis.[23] He completed it certainly before 716,
for in that year Eusebius, to whom he had dedicated the treatise
and whom he had addressed as 'brother', became Abbot of Jarrow.
How far before we do not know, but it is tempting to place it, in
its similar preoccupations, close to his De Natura Rerum. Bede's
explanations of the biblical text, which he takes section by
section, are largely allegorical and moral. Some of the
allegories he uses are to be found in sections of Isidore's De
Natura Rerum. He seems to have rejected these allegories when
composing his own De Natura Rerum, but to have been ready to
include them in his work on the Apocalypse. Thus, when commenting
upon Apocalypse 8, 5:

> 'and there were peals of thunder, loud noises,
> flashes of lightning and an earthquake,'

Bede declares, as Isidore had before him, that the thunder
represents God's wrath and is the voice, too, of exhortation.
He adds likewise, that lightning represents the miracles of

saints, which make the earth move and its people believe.[24] The later earthquake of Apocalypse 11, 3 represents Judgement Day, when every city built upon sand will fall. Isidore too had allowed in his treatise De Natura Rerum that an earthquake might represent the Day of Judgement, and he had added a comment that it is unusual for there to be earthquakes where the soil is sandy.[25] Rabanus, though treating of each matter at far greater length, also used some of these allegories. Thus, to him too thunder is the voice of God, lightning the luminous miracles of the saints.[26] There are many more examples of such use. Many are allegorical commonplaces and are certainly not confined to work upon the Apocalypse; but their presence especially in Bede's work on this text and in the two related treatises De Natura Rerum helps to illustrate the ways in which the two could, and sometimes did, come together. Isidore and Rabanus, who did not themselves write commentaries upon the Apocalypse but who both lived in a world where the second coming was thought to be both vital and imminent, seem to have been content to leave material appropriate to its understanding within their treatises; Bede, who did write such a commentary, left it out of his. This may, indeed, be one of the reasons for some of the differences between Bede's De Natura Rerum and theirs to which I earlier drew attention. It does, at the very least, seem possible to extend Fontaine's idea and to argue that, as Isidore's De Natura Rerum was written partly with an understanding of the Apocalypse in mind, so too were those of Bede and of Rabanus, although Bede preferred to separate his 'scientific' from his allegorical discussion of the phenomena there described.

Bede also wrote a latin poem on the Day of Judgement,[27] in a part of which he set out vividly the signs which would precede this day. There would be earthquakes, mountains crashing down, hills turning to liquid. The sky would grow black, the sea terrible, stars would fall, the light of the moon would be hidden.[28] The poem was translated into Anglo-Saxon and became, it seems, highly popular.[29] Again, and perhaps not too surprisingly, Bede's poem, in early manuscripts, is sometimes found bound together with a De Natura Rerum.[30] This same poem is, in places, reminiscent of far older verses on Judgement Day, verses drawn from the tradition of the Sibylline Oracles. These verses are to be found in many places; in the Contra Iudeos of Quodvultdeus, for example, in a version of the Sibylline Oracles once erroneously ascribed to Bede himself and, most importantly, in Book XVIII, chapter xxiii of Augustine's City of God.[31] They were, then, very widely known. These verses also speak of unnatural earthly and heavenly portents. The earth will be drenched with sweat and will crack, there will be fire on land and sea and raining down from the sky, the light of the sun and of the moon will be extinguished, the planets will cease to move, fountains will be quenched by fire. We may perhaps find in such verses some additional reasons for the careful descriptions of volcanoes and of rainbows we are given in our treatises, as well

III

as for the more familiar explanations of eclipses and of earthquakes. Book XVIII of the <u>City of God</u> is also the book in which
Augustine expressed his reservations about a too careful search
for the signs of the end of the world.[32] Had God wished us to
know, says Augustine, Christ would have told his disciples.
Natural explanations were a way of quelling curiosity of this
sort: advanced relentlessly they might easily defeat them
altogether. I have not yet been able adequately to enquire into
the make-up of codices containing the verses and/or Book XVIII,
and so to discover whether they appear often together with any
of our three treatises; but such coincidences would not surprise
me.

Interest in the <u>Apocalypse</u>, then, and in the Day of
Judgement stood behind much of the 'scientific' material chosen
for our treatises. They had before them the twin task of
explaining the <u>Apocalypse</u> more fully, as Fontaine had hinted
of Isidore's, and of confining fear of the Day of Judgement to
its rightful and most salutary place. The separation of a
proper fear from both an improper anxiety and an impertinent
searching for signs was a difficult separation to sustain. The
difficulty was perhaps meant in part to be met by that
combination of the rational with the allegorical which we see
in Isidore and in Rabanus. Thunder and lightning, for instance,
might be explained away or given a meaning purely symbolic and
moral, and so with many another of the apparent terrors. The
needs of active apocalyptic preachers added urgency to the
production of texts such as these. We might remember that all
three of our writers were to some extent involved in the sending
of preachers to as yet unconverted peoples. The combined
purposes of exposition and appropriate exhortation seem to
explain admirably the emphasis placed by these treatises upon
those extraordinary meterological and earthly phenomena for
which convincing natural and symbolic explanations could be
found. It is also conceivable, though without an adequate
analysis of surviving manuscript codices impossible to prove,
that the upsurge of interest in Bede's work in the twelfth
century, for example, was associated with that parallel upsurge
of interest in apocalyptic material which the crusading movement
helped to bring about.

Other sections of the bible were served by our treatises
as well, especially, of course, by Rabanus's huge work. This
should be noted. It was useful to know the ways of the Nile
and the position of the Red Sea, and storms, plagues, celestial
portents, earthquakes, clouds and rainbows were by no means
confined to the <u>Apocalypse</u>. It does seem likely, however, that
the <u>Apocalypse</u> as a text and the fear it might be used to inspire,
exercised an influence upon our treatises which was very powerful
indeed. In their attention to fear, furthermore, the authors of
our treatises came close to Lucretius, the author of the first
century poetic treatise <u>De Natura Rerum</u> from whose title our first

two compilers may have borrowed their own. Lucretius wrote also
to counteract fear, although the fear he sought to calm was the
individual fear of death, of everlasting punishment and of the
'terrific utterances of priests':

> 'This terror of mind therefore and this gloom
> must be dispelled, not by the sun's rays or the
> bright shafts of day, but by the aspect and law
> of nature.'34

The universe, Lucretius sought to prove, was purely material, and
contemplation of this fact in its many aspects would calm
unreasoning anxiety. Not surprisingly, this immediate motive
and this solution did not recommend themselves to Isidore, Bede,
Rabanus or their followers, and Lucretius's work, though available,
was not widely used or copied. It seems, however, that the
general impulse which motivated him, the desire to put at rest
that unreasoning fear of the unknown which possessed so many
humans may have been common to them all. Although the objectives
of the christian writers were in detail very different from those
of Lucretius, in this impulse to write, and in the provision of
much of the material the satisfaction of this impulse demanded,
all may have been remarkably alike.

The desire to know more about the facts of nature, annoyance
at an excessively simplified understanding of the christian faith,
the need for an enhanced appreciation of the message of the
Apocalypse, cynical disregard on the part of some of its fearsome
possibilities, excessive curiosity about or terror at them on the
part of others, all of these explanations may severally and
together, and with due allowance for degree, account for the form
and composition of all of our treatises De Natura Rerum in a wholly
satisfying way. They may explain the efforts of their authors,
the times and places of their composition, the schemes they
followed, the vigour with which they were copied. They may do so;
but I do not think they do.

* * *

In the foregoing section I have tried to build on the clues
I have found in Fontaine in two ways. I have suggested that Bede
and Rabanus were every bit as concerned as was Isidore to explain
the Apocalypse; and I tried to point out how crucial to all of
their efforts was the problem of fear. Fear was to be neither
excessive, nor wrongly directed - nor wholly lacking. The
problem of the rightful ordering of fear is a factor new to
discussions of medieval scientific texts. It deserves, however,
to be given far greater attention than it ever has been, even
when we set the Apocalypse aside. Fear is, after all, one of the
strongest of human emotions, and christianity came to cast the
wrong sort out. One of the answers to fear is, indeed, 'natural'
knowledge, as Lucretius saw. I propose now, therefore, to press
the problem of fear a little further; and, in doing so, to attempt

to uncover the presence of other, still more hidden, forces at work
upon the compilers of our treatises.

One means of whipping up a proper kind of fear then, as so
often, was especially popular with preachers - appeal to demons.
The idea that wicked demons were everywhere on the prowl for the
souls of men, an idea vividly expressed, for example, by Augustine
in his De Divinatione Daemonum, could be an exceedingly effective
weapon in the armoury of discipline. It was an idea not
unconnected with the Day of Judgement, of course, but it was
capable both of more extensive and more immediate application.
Demons and their assaults might be associated with every kind of
evil; but in the early middle ages they tended to be associated
with one in particular; the continuance of pagan superstition.
An especially vivid example of such an association is provided,
interestingly, by one of Isidore's episcopal predecessors, Martin,
Archbishop of Braga. Some forty years before Isidore presented
his De Natura Rerum to Sisebut, Archbishop Martin had written a
homily 'For the correction of country people', much on the model
of Augustine's De Catechizandis Rudibus, to combat rustic 'superstition'.35 In his preface Martin states that it is his aim to:

'Chastise the rustics who are still bound by the
old pagan superstition and offer more veneration
to demons than to God.'

The homily which follows is a quarry full of Vizigothic pre-
christian beliefs, recalled so as to be firmly ascribed to the
Devil and his followers, and to be combatted by a summary of the
christian faith, and its reassertion according to Augustine's
plan. Demonically inspired superstition is, according to Martin,
a major obstacle in the way of the progress of christianity, and
he sets himself the task of removing it in the best way he knows;
the convincing restatement of christian doctrine.

We need not enter at this point, perhaps, into the sleight
of hand with which wicked demons were made to turn 'superstitio'
into a term of abuse allied to 'maleficium'; nor into the probably
insoluble question of how much notice was taken of Martin's homily.
I suspect not much. I would suggest that, at this juncture, there
are two important points for us to mark. Firstly, as with our
notional misunderstandings of the Apocalypse and the signs of the
Day of Judgement, we are dealing here too with obstacles in the
way of christianity and, especially, with obstacles which feed
deeply upon human fear and so stand in the way of a proper
religious awe. Secondly, and most importantly for our present
purposes, certain of the superstitions which Martin describes
here bear a remarkable resemblance, in their subject matter, to
certain of the chapters in our treatises De Natura Rerum.

Like Bede, and like Rabanus, Martin appeals first of all to
Genesis for an account of the creation and constitution of the
universe to be revered by christians. He goes on then to condemn
certain specific demonically inspired beliefs. Among the beliefs

he condemns are wrongful homage paid to the powers of the sun and
moon and the stars and to those of fire, deep waters and springs;
and he inveighs against wrongful practices for the protection of
crops from plague or vermin.[36] He is also furiously opposed, as
was the second Council of Braga over which he presided, to pagan
forms of divination.[37] He reinforces his objections with good,
solid reference to the events expected at the Day of Judgement.[38]

When Isidore presented his De Natura Rerum to King Sisebut,
Sisebut thanked him with a poem explaining in natural terms the
lunar eclipse. This poem is attached to many of the early copies
of the treatise. The king, most interestingly, gave in it a
reason for writing his poem. He wanted to combat by his own
scientific explanation a wrongful superstition about the moon
of the kind to which Martin, it seems, referred. He describes
this superstition. When the moon is in fact in eclipse, says
Sisebut, 'the populace' believes that it is being drawn down into
an underground cavern by the enchantments of a sorceress, who
wields a magic mirror to attract it, or that it is being plunged
into the Styx or ensnared with the help of magical herbs. He
refers to the great shouts and clamours with which the people made
manifest this belief.[39] The belief was evidently widely held, for
we have good independent evidence of it. Maximus of Turin refers
with irritation to the shouts and clamours - thought necessary,
apparently, to comfort the moon in its distress and to distract the
sorcerer - and so does Eligius of Noyon, in a sermon reported in
his Vita.[40] Crashes and bangs in aid of the moon clearly troubled
the consciences and the sleep of many a pastor. Reference is
made once again to the belief in the tantalising mid-eighth
century Indiculus Superstitionum, and in the Scarapsus of Pirmin
of Reichenau (d. 754), and it surfaces once more in a sermon of
Rabanus and in the Decretum of Burchard of Worms in the early
eleventh century.[41] Sisebut's rational explanation had clearly
not succeeded in suppressing it, nor, seemingly, had those
similarly rational explanations of an eclipse we find in each of
our three treatises. But it seems possible to argue that the
explanations in the treatises, like that in Sisebut's poem, were
written, perhaps even were mainly written, with such a superstition in mind.

Again interestingly, in his own preface, Isidore himself
used the word 'superstitious':

> 'Neque enim earum rerum naturam noscere
> superstitiosae scientiae est, si tantum
> sana sobriaque doctrina considerentur.'[42]

This is hard to translate into English. Perhaps we may render it
loosely as:

> 'There is nothing wrong with getting to know
> the nature of things, provided that one under-
> takes such an enquiry with care and with an
> eye to orthodox teaching.'

Isidore was here clearly looking towards such as Bishop Philaster;
but his contrast between the sort of enquiry he was himself
attempting, and that which was 'superstitious' or harmful, is at
least in harmony with those of King Sisebut and of Archbishop
Martin.

Enquiries De Natura Rerum must be defended, then, against
charges of superstition; but they may also, if we are to believe
Sisebut at least, be used to defy, and if possible to undo, popular
pagan superstitions. The purpose, and indeed perhaps the
conclusion, of this last section of my enquiry may perhaps at this
point be Divined. Is it possible, on the basis of these small
clues so far presented, to argue that sections far greater than
those devoted to the eclipse of the moon were also directed to
popular superstitions of this kind? Have we, even, evidence of
'science' in direct conflict with superstition allied to the
magical in at least some of its popular manifestations? I think,
perhaps, we have.

Thanks to the efforts of Martin of Braga, in his homily and
his own collections of canons, to the enthusiastic copying of the
canons of the second Council of Braga and of the fourth Council
of Toledo (over which Isidore himself presided), to the Vizigothic
law codes and to much recent research,[43] we can build up quite a
good picture of that which was seen as 'superstitious' or 'magical'
in Vizigothic Spain. Our picture is a little less good for
Northumbria in the time of Bede, partly because we appear to have
less immediately accessible contemporary evidence and have to
argue backwards from such texts as Lacnunga, or sideways from such
difficult problems as the knowledge and use of Pliny, and the date,
character and use of discovered magical remains. It is, however,
there.[44] The situation improves considerably when we come to the
time of Rabanus. To the evidence of the Salic Law, the Indiculus
Superstitionum and the Carolingian capitularies, we may add that
of ninth century penitential literature (not least that ascribed
to Rabanus) and the fulminations of at least one episcopal spokesman for the period. And we have in addition, of course, the
treatise Rabanus himself devoted to the condemnation of magic, the
De Magicis Artibus.[45] Even at this point we can say one thing with
certainty. This is, that the pre-christian magical beliefs of
those to whom they came as teachers and as pastors troubled our
three compilers greatly. Let us look now, once again, then, but
this time a little more closely, at some of the chapter headings
and contents of their three treatises. We might note once more
that we have a great deal in all three on the weather, especially
on storms and thunder and lightning, on winds and prognostics and
the natural causes of rain and hail. We have something on the
natural causes of pestilence. We have much on the heavenly
bodies, sun, moon, stars and planets. We have rather more on the
zodiac in some treatises than in others (to this, briefly, we shall
come). We have a little, in Rabanus, on springs and rivers - all
very heavily biblical. All of these preoccupations have echoes of
the kind we are now to explore.

Efforts to manipulate winds and weather, to call down rain
and fend away (or bring down upon enemies) damaging storms are
common to many agricultural societies. We have evidence that the
largely Germanic societies which form the immediate object of our
scrutiny were no exception. 'Weather magic', the attempt to
control the elements in ways considered unchristian, was very often
condemned by councils and christian authorities. Among Martin of
Braga's collection of canons, for example, is one, canon 72, which
forbids christians to 'worship the elements'.[46] Isidore names
'agitating the elements' among the nefarious activities of the
magicians he is later to describe in his Etymologies, and whom he
abhors.[47] More striking still is a canon (canon 8) among those of
the first Council of Braga[48] and a passage in the Forum Iudicum
(codified by King Chindaswinth of the Vizigoths, 642-653, but
reaching back to the Lex Romana Vizigothorum).[49] The Forum Iudicum
condemns 'invokers of tempests' in general and prescribes fierce
penalties. The Council of Braga anathematizes those who think
that the devil has control over thunder and lightning and storms
and droughts. This last is a clear reference to Priscillianist
beliefs, but it is worth noticing that it reappears word for word
in Spanish penitentials of a far later date, and when the immediate
danger of the Priscillianists had long disappeared.[50] Penitential
material which has both Anglo-Saxon and Old Saxon associations
similarly condemns 'those who conjure up storms' and Bede, it
seems, may have had amulets against the weather in mind in parts
even of his Explanatio Apocalypsis. Thunderstones, certainly, are
often to be found in Anglo-Saxon England.[51] Most interesting of
all, however, are two short treatises on storms, both of the ninth
century, and both of which give explanations of the origins and
power of storms which are, to say the least, very different from
those put forward in our treatises.

The first of these is a strange little book 'On Thunder'.[52]
In Migne, this is printed among the works of Bede, but it is now
thought instead to be a ninth-century translation of a work by
the Greek John Lydus. It survives only in a single manuscript
of the late tenth or early eleventh century, and it is, in fact, a
simple divinatory treatise, containing a series of predictions
based upon the times when, and the directions from which, thunder
is heard. Thus, thunder coming from the east portends the
shedding of human blood, thunder coming in December means
prosperity for everyone, thunder heard on a Thursday means lots of
crops and fish, and so on. Given the abundance of patristic and
conciliar evidence we have prohibiting, often on pain of anathema,
divination and augury of all kinds, it is hardly surprising that
the author of this little work felt impelled to defend himself in
his preface against possible charges of magic. Nor is it startling
that it was so little copied. The De Tonitruis is important
evidence, however, of an attitude to prognostication, and to
thunder, which was both ancient and at least to this extent
persistent.

The second treatise is even more informative. This is a
tirade, possibly delivered shortly after 816, at the beginning of
his episcopate, by Agobard, Archbishop of Lyons. Migne heads it
'Against the ridiculous views of the masses concerning hail and
thunder storms' and this title gives a fair indication of its
contents.[53] The particular ridiculous belief which Agobard reports
is a belief in 'tempestarii' or storm-bringers. These, Agobard
tells us, are thought to be able, through incantations, to raise a
special wind which can draw down storms and hail to cut down
harvests. They then sell the fallen harvests to persons coming
from a region they call Magonia, in airborne ships. Middlemen are
involved in these arrangements, persons who can buy off the
'tempestarii' for a price. To pay these middlemen (and here we see
why the Archbishop writes with such detail and such fury) tithes
and alms remain unrendered. We are here clearly dealing with a
very well managed protection racket but, equally, one which derives
its profit from a deeply seated superstition. Agobard speaks only
of his region and we have no sure means of knowing quite how
commonly such beliefs and rackets were to be found in other
districts. It is a story, however, not dissimilar to that found
in the Forum Iudicum, the Penitentials and in Burchard. Pirmin of
Reichenau, moreover, in his Scarapsus condemns belief in, or gifts
to, 'tempestarias'.[54] All of this goes to shew, I think, that
superstitious practices concerning storms were reasonably widely
held during the period, and close to the places, within which our
three treatises were compiled.

When we read passages, then, such as the one from Isidore on
thunder I quoted at the very beginning of this paper, when we
contemplate the seemingly naive prognostics about the weather
contained in, and often bound with, our treatises, or when we read
in them that fire, such as lightning, comes from the simple
collisions of hard things like stones or that storms can be the
result of air stirred into winds by God [55] we may with good reason
look at them afresh. Here we have signs which portend storms,
indeed; but not storms which portend anything unless it be the
Day of Judgement.[56] And storms arise from purely natural causes
and from God. One interesting small point I have noticed. In
Isidore's chapter xxx, 'On lightning', he illustrates his point
about the collisions which produce it by referring both to the
fire-producing collisions of hard stones and to the fire produced
by striking wood upon wood. He uses both illustrations again
(with the addition of fire struck by wheels) in his Etymologies
XIII, ix. The first illustration comes from Pliny; the second
does not. Bede (xxviii) omits the second illustration and so does
Rabanus (IX, xix) although both use the illustration of the stones
and Rabanus, drawing on the Etymologies, the illustration of the
wheels as well. Economy perhaps; and yet it is worth remembering
that item 15 of the Indiculus Superstitionum, the mid-eighth
century list of outlawed, possibly Saxon, superstitious practices,
names among these 'fire struck from wood', or 'nodfyr'. We do not
know exactly what this was, but reference to it is to be found

again in a capitulary of Carlomann, dated 742, and recording
seemingly a ruling made by Boniface at a synod of that year.
Carlomann forbids 'sacrilegos ignes, quod nied fyr vocant'.[57]
It is possible that both Bede and Rabanus were aware of the
inappropriateness of this second illustration to a treatise written
at least in part as a counter to such superstitions, and
accordingly shied away from it.

Often associated with fear of storms is fear of pestilence;
thunderstones, indeed, were thought to afford protection against
both. We may also, therefore, look afresh at the information we
find in some of our treatises about the origins of pestilence.
Pestilences, we are told, arise from excessive heat or drought or
rain, all of which trouble the order of nature. They may be
carried to distant parts by winds or clouds, and be breathed in by
humans. They may be brought to this point by man's sins;[58] but
they may not, by implication, be conjured into or out of being on
the orders of human beings or by supernatural agencies other than
the Christian God. Like weather conjurors, pestilence magicians
were well known to both the secular and the ecclesiastical laws of
our period. There were magicians who claimed to be able to bring
down pestilences, and magicians who claimed to be able to free
persons and crops from these pestilences, often with the help of
amulets and incantations. We find these magicians condemned, once
again, in the Forum Iudicum, by Isidore, by Bede, by Rabanus and
again in the Decretum of Burchard.[59] Belief in 'fairy' agencies
in the spreading of pestilence, too, was very widespread. The
notion, for instance, that elves brought down pestilence by
shooting it into persons or beasts was especially popular. 'Elf-
shot' might be assisted by thunder. Our Anglo-Saxon sources are
especially rich in charms to counteract the effects of this
malevolent elf-born magic.[60] Evidence of the spent weapons of
elves lay, after all, all around in the form of neolithic arrow
heads or fossil belemnites.[61] Christian counter-charms, the
incantation of a prayer, the bearing of a cross or relic, were one
way of dealing with the problem, and such charms are often to be
found in early manuscripts. To use such charms widely, however,
was to tread a path perilously close to the one which was
condemned. It must to many have seemed far safer, if in some ways
more demanding, to resort to reasoned explanation. Thus wind or
clouds, not elves, nor, come to that, the moon,[62] delivered
pestilence to man according to our treatises; and if there was any
supernatural agency involved, then it was the agency of God,
bringing man proper and salutary chastisement.

As with the weather, so with pestilence we are confronted
once more by the presence of fear. It confronts us this time,
however, even more directly. Whilst in the matter of the
Apocalypse and Day of Judgement it is a matter of exciting fear
to an appropriate degree, here it is a matter of calming it by
appropriate means. When I discussed the bearing of our texts
upon the proper understanding of the Apocalypse, I suggested that

they were used to interpose reason between two main obstacles to
this; superstitious fear and cynicism. Here the texts interpose
reason again, but between different obstacles and with, I would
maintain, an increased urgency and subtlety. They must place it
this time between superstitious fear and excessive unreason within
the church itself; an excess sometimes manifest in counter-charm
or ritual dangerously like the ones to be defied.[63] As in the case
of the Apocalypse, so here we meet the need to convert fear from
an unreasoning (and in Agobard's case unprofitable) terror to an
appropriate and informed sense of awe; but the fear is of something
more ever-pressing and immediate than the Day of Judgement, and
the need commensurately greater, the more so in that counters were
being developed within the church which must have seemed to many
alarmingly close to the outlawed superstitions.

We may perhaps see in this last purpose too one additional
reason for Rabanus's tremendous excursions into biblical reference.
Excursions on this scale were novel in such a treatise, and so too
was Rabanus's large use of both secular and sacred works.
Certainly Rabanus wrote his work as a further aid for exegetes[64]
but the matter did not, I suggest, end there. Exegesis itself has
larger incentives and it may be that we can uncover one of these.
Whilst by no means ignoring the efforts of Isidore and Bede, and
under headings much the same as some of theirs, Rabanus saw a
different way of approaching the self-same problem. Natural
explanations were helpful in the battle against pagan superstition
and its over simple counters, but they could hardly compete with
the bible. Biblical science could be added to natural science,
and so produce an accumulation of right reason infinitely greater
than that of natural science alone. Rabanus seems to have made
the bringing of this accumulation to bear upon this particular
scene his own especial task. Rabanus's exegetical excursions
within a treatise De Natura Rerum should not be placed primarily
against a background of the needs of exegetes but within the
context of these treatises. Identical purposes stood, on occasion,
behind both work upon the nature of things and work upon the
meaning of the scriptures. 'Science' and the exegesis of the
bible work together here for the same, in part hidden, ends.

All I have said so far seems, to me at least, to contribute
powerfully to one conclusion. This is that this last aspect of
our texts, and this last purpose, the correct countering of non-
christian superstitions, was the most important of them all.
There is, moreover, a further dimension in the struggle. When
they are placed against a background in which superstition and
magic were rife and reason hard to find our texts may be seen to
have had before them social problems additional to and different
again from those which moved our apocalyptic preachers; and
social problems arguably even more urgently in need of a solution.
Non-christian 'tempestarii' or 'magi' attending to fear in their
own ways, posed a threat to christian belief, authority and even
livelihood. This we have seen, but there is even more to be
deduced. We might pursue some of these deductions with the help

of those welcome studies on the social origins and impact of magic
produced so energetically by anthropologists above all. The ways
of 'magi' might invite immediate unfortunate results; unfortunate
both for the magician and for others. Readers of anthropological
work on witchcraft will be familiar with two particular and
arresting ideas; the idea that witchcraft developed as an answer
to misfortune, and the idea that accusations of witchcraft spring
from misfortunes unresolved. It is now, I think, established that
accusations of the malevolent manipulation of the supernatural –
the bringing down, as it might be, of storms or pestilences or
earthquakes, or the darkening of the moon – may arise from many
social needs and strains, but that the need to explain away
persistent misfortune is especially prominent among them. [65] The
manipulators, 'magi', 'tempestarii' and even, should they take
upon themselves too much, christian priests, may, in such
situations, themselves become the scapegoats for such fears. So
may the wholly innocent. If there was a need in our period to
reduce the power of those who safely profited of magical beliefs,
we may suppose also that there was a need to save from unjust
punishment those whom the community might wish to blame.

This dimension to the problem is an enormous one, and full
of possibilities. In this context one extra piece of information
Agobard gives us in his tirade against the 'tempestarii' is
especially interesting. Agobard tells us that he had had brought
before him four people, three men and a woman, whom the populace
believed had fallen from the ships from Magonia. They had bound
them in chains and they wanted to stone them.[66] The archbishop's
scorn had clearly helped to rescue these unfortunates. In this
particular social context the provision of a rational explanation
produced social results of a most important kind. We may add this
last aim, then, too to the accumulating pressures on our treatises.

Popular and immediately pressing 'magical' superstitions,
then, together with certain features of these superstitions which
had socially and pastorally alarming effects, exercised a powerful
influence upon the compilers of our treatises. I would suggest
that this influence, least mentioned of all, was in fact the most
powerful. I should like to turn now, as a postscript, to one
last, still highly controversial but I hope illuminating aspect
of this influence; one which I hope, perhaps needless to say, will
add support to the suggestions I have made so far.

* * *

When one compares the treatises of Isidore and Bede in
detail one feature in particular emerges rather strikingly; a
feature which, so far as I know, has not been given prominence
before. Bede has both less and more to say about certain specific
subjects. He abandons, for example, Isidore's chapter xxvii, (on
whether the stars have a soul) and he inserts a small block of
chapters of his own between his borrowings from Isidore xx and

xxii. Chapter xxvii of Isidore, which Bede abandons, and this new
block which he inserts (chapters xiii-xviii) all shew a single
interest. They all deal with the planets, stars and zodiac. This
single interest, moreover, characterises many of Bede's additions
to Isidore within individual chapters. He adds material on the
zodiac, for example in his own chapters ix and xxx, (taken in part
from Isidore x and xviii) to his chapter xiii (in part from
Isidore xxiii), and to his chapter xxi, which shews no connection
with Isidore's treatise at all.

Now, there are simple ways of explaining these additions.
The naturally curious may have needed more food; the wakeful
monastic hour-keeper may have needed more amusement. The sections
Bede adds depend extremely heavily upon the Natural History of
Pliny, especially upon Book II. Perhaps, then, Bede had access to
a section of Pliny Isidore did not then know. None of these
explanations is wholly satisfying, and Isidore did know Book II
of Pliny, even if he did not quote from these specific sections.
I should like to advance another one; one related to the one I have
tried to attach to the treatises as a whole. This is, that the
additions concerned a sub-section of non-christian belief and
practice; the sub-section of divination and astrology.

Isidore was curious about the stars, the planets and the
zodiac. They interested him, indeed, exceedingly; but he was
forced to be guarded in his interest. He was forced to be guarded
above all because of the trust the Priscillianist heretics and
their successors had given to astrology. He had thus to steer the
most careful of courses between a proper interest in the stars and
an heretical reliance upon them.[67] To help to steer this course,
he formulated his famous distinction between 'natural' and
'superstitious' astrology, a distinction which was to have an
important future and to help many besides himself to express their
sympathy for a scientific knowledge of the powers of stars and
planets.[68] This, however, was in his Etymologies, Isidore's last
work. In his far earlier De Natura Rerum he seems to have felt
himself bound to be more discreet,[69] though not so discreet, of
course, as to refuse to ponder upon the problem of whether the
stars have a soul.

These last ponderings, in Isidore's chapter xxvii, seem to
have been too much for Bede, but the additional material in Bede's
De Natura Rerum to which I have drawn attention here, is, when we
look at it, all material which bears upon 'natural' astrology. The
question of Bede's attitude to 'natural' astrology is a huge one,
full of difficulties, set positions,[70] incipient controversy. It
cannot possibly be pursued far here. Equally, however, I cannot
resist the making of a suggestion about a possible pursuit. In
that the problem bears so closely upon my argument I can resist it
even less.

'Natural' astrology had, I would suggest, become a pressing
concern; and it had become pressing because non-christian 'superstitious' astrologers, like non-christian 'magi' and 'tempestarii',

and the skills to which they pretended, had become forces to be
reckoned with. They had,moreover, become forces at least as great
as, and perhaps even greater than, those which had confronted
Isidore. Diviners and augurers, so often mentioned in our
penitentials and conciliar rulings, and, above all, 'haruspices',[71]
practised, after all, many arts of prediction. It is more than
possible that a primitive, or even not so primitive, form of
astrology was one of these. A few years after he had written his
De Natura Rerum Bede was to write as though the activities of the
'mathematici' were then a contemporary problem. Aldhelm had
mentioned them too in terms which should not, I think entirely be
dismissed as mere derivatives.[72] In such a situation the provision
of a little further 'scientific' information upon the planets,
stars and zodiac, could be seen to be helpful and this for several
reasons. It was a means by which educated christian pastors might
effect a reckoning with non-christian astrologers and soothsayers;
just as 'natural' explanations for the weather and for disease
might put other 'superstitious' practitioners at bay. It was a
way, too, in which christian priests might set themselves
informedly apart. Bede in c. 703 felt both braver about, and
more in need of information on, 'natural' astrology than did
Isidore in 613. We might note furthermore that many of the
additional extracts from Pliny found in Bede's De Natura Rerum
were thought worthy of a separate circulation. We have a number
of especially interesting surviving ninth-century manuscripts of
these, some of which copy with them 'natural' weather prognostics
as well.[73] Such collections were designed in part to help the
priest with the computus, and doubtless they did this. Rabanus,
it is worth remarking, built many of the extra sections Bede took
from Pliny Book II into his own De Computo, in 820.[74] The
correspondence between Rabanus's borrowings here from Bede's De
Natura Rerum and Bede's additions to Isidore is, indeed, very
striking. Such information might help him with these other
problems too. 'Natural' astrological material of this sort was
clearly important to the Carolingians; it is possible that the
problems posed by this survival of superstitious astrology, and
which I have suggested acted upon Bede acted upon them also, and
among them, of course, Rabanus.

The question of the rehabilitation of 'natural' astrology,
and its restoration to the christian curriculum as a respectable
object of scrutiny is a remarkably complex one. In an earlier
article I tried once more to go a small way towards exploring it.[75]
My emphasis was then, however, on the twelfth century, upon the
very evident revival of astrology then, and upon the equally
evident (I thought) reactions to it. The composition of world
histories was one of these reactions; an activity in which Isidore,
Bede, and above all in his De Universo, Rabanus, readily engaged.
This is to go far; but the revival of 'natural' astrology in the
twelfth century is clearly, I think, related, on the one hand to
the revival of an interest 'de natura rerum' and on the other to
the need to combat non-christian 'superstition'. As in the

twelfth century, so here. Though by no means as evident in its
impact as it was in the twelfth century, when it does rear its
head 'natural' astrology is still a part of the response to
superstitious practices; to 'magic', in short. Signs of the
astrological sub-section of this battle are more easily to be
found in some of our treatises than in others, but they are
present in all of them and they are a part of an important whole.
The crucial factor behind the composition of our three treatises
De Natura Rerum was the pressing need to overpower non-christian
authority and practice, and, above all, to prevent the exploit-
ation of a non-christian emotion of fear.

* * *

   Early medieval treatises upon the nature of things seem, at
first glance, to have been designed to meet two needs. They were
to satisfy those curious of scientific knowledge and they were to
provide the biblical exegete with such 'natural' information as
might be demanded by his pupils. Calming intellectual nourishment
is therefore offered to each in such treatises and it was for this
that they were compiled.

   My purpose in this paper has been to look at this picture
again, and, as a result of this second look, I have tried to expose
it as a counterfeit. Though natural curiosity is appeased in our
treatises, and though exegetes are certainly supplied, neither
commanded the main attention of our writers. Nor did these chiefly
aim at intellectual calm. Their priorities were wholly different.
By distinguishing the natural from the supernatural they meant to
concentrate attention on the latter, not the former; and they
proposed to raise and redirect, and not to lower, the emotional
temperature of their audience. 'Science', here, was not employed
to diminish the realm of the supernatural but to extend it; and
exegesis, in being concentrated in this context upon the
Apocalypse, emerges from the schoolroom and enters the mission
field. It is primarily concerned, furthermore, not with the
provision of simple instruction, but with the re-ordering of the
complex emotion of fear. Above all, our texts confront paganism,
'superstition' and 'magic', and this is the area of their chief
concern. Finally, they do not confront it by attempting to
overwhelm it, but by trying instead to transform it. In this way
early medieval treatises De Natura Rerum kept alive two hopes.
The emotions which were generated by paganism might yet be re-
aligned towards christian salvation; and man might still be freed
from his destructive terrors. This was a large ambition for
writers of scientific works to cherish, and one perhaps not wholly
familiar to us; but it does deserve, I think, our careful
attention.

1. J. Fontaine, Isidore de Séville. Traité de la Nature (Bordeaux 1960); C.W. Jones, Bedae Venerabilis Opera, Pars 1, Opera Didascalica (Corpus Christianorum 123A, Turnholt 1975), pp. 174-234. Fontaine provides a translation into French, parallel with the text.

2. Later manuscripts are listed by M.C. Diaz Y Diaz, Index Scriptorum Latinorum Medii Aevi Hispanorum, pars prior (Acta Salmanticensia 13, Salamanca 1958), 31-32.

3. Op. cit., pp. 13-14.

4. Ibid., pp. 79-80.

5. The monk Cuthbert reported this; edit. C. Plummer, De Obitu Bedae, in Venerabilis Baedae Opera Historica i (Oxford 1896) clxii. Cuthbert's phrasing had led to the belief that Bede despised Isidore's works; thus C.W. Jones, Bedae Opera de Temporibus (Cambridge, Mass. 1943), p. 131. A larger knowledge of his use of them and a more credible translation of Cuthbert have, however, combined to revise this view. Fontaine, op. cit., p. 79, n 1.

6. M.L.W. Laistner, A Hand-List of Bede Manuscripts (Cornell U.P. 1943), pp. 139-144.

7. PL 111, 9-614. This title is not found in the surviving early manuscripts, however, and so may not go back to Rabanus.

8. Edit. J. McCulloh, Rabani Mauri Martyrologium (Corpus Christianorum, Continuatio Medievalis 44, Turnholt 1979), p. xix. The introduction to this edition provides an excellent summary of Rabanus's career, and much relevant bibliography.

9. xxxv; Fontaine, op. cit., pp. 290-291.

10. XI, xvi, xviii; PL 111, 326, 328.

11. I have compared the three texts with the help of the magnificent sourcework in E. Heyse, Hrabanus Maurus Enzyklopädie 'De rerum naturis' (Munich 1969).

12. Most probably Haimo of Halberstadt, d. 853. PL 111, 11.

13. Especially upon chapters xxvi and xliv; Fontaine, op. cit., pp. 10, 264-265, 312-317.

14. Chapters xiii-xviii, for example; Jones, op. cit., pp. 204-210.

15. Isidore xxii, Fontaine, op. cit., pp. 254-255; Bede xi, Jones, op. cit., p. 202.

16. For example Ms. Bambergensis patr. 61 of the Staatliche Bibliothek, Bamberg, an eighth century codex from Monte Cassino, binds the De Cursu Stellarum with Isidore's De Natura Rerum.

17. For instance that of Augustine in his De Trinitate III, ix-x; edit. W.J. Mountain and F. Glorie, Sancti Aurelii Augustini De Trinitate Libri xv (Turnholt 1968), pp. 143-146.

18. At least three ninth century manuscripts are known now of Philaster's work on heresies, and one fragment from the eighth century.

19. Diversarum Hereseon Liber, CII; 'Alia est heresis quae terrae motum non dei iussione et indignatione fieri, sed de natura ipsa elementorum opinatur ... Non adtendentes dei potentiam, elementorum naturae audent adscribere potentiae motionem, ut quidam filosofi vaniloqui, qui rerum naturae hoc adscribentes dei potentiam non cognoverunt.' Also CIII and CXXXIII. Edit. F. Heylen, Filastrii Episcopi Brixiensis Diversarum Hereseon Liber (Turnholt 1957) pp. 266-267, 297-298.

20. Op. cit., p. 12.

21. Commentariorum in Apocalypsin Libri Quinque, III, iv; PL 100, 1118.

22. Edit. L.M. Hartmann, Gregorii I Registrum, XI, 37; MGH Ep. Sel. i (2) (Vienna 1899), 309. Bede found the letter important enough to include in his Ecclesiastical History. Edit., B. Colgrave and R.A.B. Mynors, Bede's Ecclesiastical History of the English People, I, 32 (Oxford 1969), pp. 112-113.

23. PL 93, 129-206.

24. Bede, 1, PL 93, 155; Isidore, xxix-xxx, xlvi, Fontaine op. cit., pp. 278-9, 282-283, 320-321.

25. PL 93, 164; Isidore xlvi, ibid., pp. 320-321.

26. De Universo IX, xix; PL 111, 277. The author of the Carolingian commentary mentioned above agrees; PL 100, 1136. Rabanus prefers to see the day of judgement as portrayed by the tempest of Nahum 1, 3. Isidore made this equasion in his chapter xxxviii, ibid., pp. 298-299.

27. PL 94, 633-638.

28. 'Praecurrunt illum vel qualia signa, repente Terra tremet, montesque ruent, collesque liquescent Et mare terribili confundet murmure mentes. Tristius et coelum tenebris obducitur atris,

III

-27-

Astra cadunt rutilo et Titan tenebrescit in ortu,
Pallida nocturnam nec praestat luna lucernam
De coelo venient et signa minantia mortem.'
Ibid., 635.

29. It is printed in E. van K. Dobbie, The Anglo-Saxon Minor
Poets (The Anglo-Saxon Poetic Records vi, New York 1942),
58-70.

30. Ms. London, B.L. Cotton Domitian A I, for example, a manuscript
of the late tenth or early eleventh centuries from St.
Augustine's, Canterbury binds it with Isidore's De Natura
Rerum. N.R. Ker, Catalogue of Manuscripts containing Anglo-
Saxon (Oxford 1957), pp. 185-186.

31. Edit. R. Braun, Opera Quodvultdeo Carthaginiensi Episcopo
Tributa (Turnholt 1976), pp. 248-249; PL 90, 1186; edit.
E.M. Sanford and W.M. Green, Saint Augustine, The City of God
against the Pagans, V (Loeb, London and Harvard 1965), 442-445.

32. In chapter liii especially; ibid., vi (edit. W.C. Greene),
78-81.

33. Among many other treatises, admittedly, a ninth century West
German codex nonetheless binds the Contra Iudeos of
Quodvultdeus with the De Natura Rerum of Bede; Ms. Leiden Voss
Q 75.

34. Edit. W.H.D. Rouse, Lucretius, De Rerum Natura (Loeb, London
and Harvard 1966), p. 13.

35. Edit. C.W. Barlow, Martini Episcopi Bracarensis Opera Omnia
(Yale U.P. 1950), pp. 183-203. The editor has translated the
text in Iberian Fathers (The Fathers of the Church 62,
Washington 1969).

36. Ed. cit., chapters 6 and 11, pp. 186, 190-191.

37. Ibid., ch. 12, pp. 191-192.

38. Ibid., ch. 14, pp. 194-196.

39. Fontaine, op. cit., pp. 330-331.

40. Maximus of Turin, Homilia Cl 'De Defectione Lunae', PL 57, 485;
edit., B. Krusch, Vita Eligii'Episcopi Noviomagensis II, 16,
MGH Scriptores Rerum Merovingicarum iv (Hanover and Leipsig
1902), 707.

41. Indiculus, ch. 21 'De Lunae defectione quod dicunt "vince
luna"', edit., G.H. Pertz, MGH Leges i (Hanover 1835), 20;
Scarapsus, PL 89, 1041; Rabanus Homilia xlii, PL 110, 78-80;
Decretum X, 33, PL 140, 837.

III

42. Fontaine, op. cit., pp. 166-167.

43. In particular that of S. MacKenna, Paganism and Pagan Survivals in Spain up to the Fall of the Vizigothic Kingdom (Washington 1938).

44. Indispensable is the work of A.L. Meaney, in particular her Anglo-Saxon Amulets and Curing Stones (B.A.R. 96, Oxford 1981). I am indebted to Professor Meaney for the generous provision of proofs and offprints.

45. PL 110, 1095-1110.

46. Barlow, ed. cit., p. 141.

47. Edit. W.M. Lindsay, Isidori Hispalensis Episcopi Etymologiarum sive Originum, VIII, ix, 9 (Oxford 1911).

48. Barlow, ed. cit., p. 108.

49. This is discussed by MacKenna, op. cit., pp. 122-123.

50. J.T. McNeill and H.M. Gamer, Medieval Handbooks of Penance (New York 1938), p. 289.

51. Ibid., p. 227 and note; Meaney, op. cit. pp. 77, 92, 118-119 and notes.

52. De Tonitruis, PL 90, 609-614. The authorship of the tract is discussed in C.W. Jones, Bedae Pseudepigrapha (New York 1938), pp. 45-47.

53. PL 104, 147-158. An improved edition is to be found in L. Van Acker, Agobardi Lugdunensis Opera Omnia (Turnholt 1981), pp. 3-15.

54. PL 89, 1041.

55. Bede, xxv, xxvi; ed. cit., pp. 216-218.

56. Isidore, xxxviii; ed. cit., pp. 298-299.

57. Edit. A. Boretius, MGH Capitularia Regum Francorum, i (Hanover 1883), 25.

58. Ibid., xxxix, pp. 302-305.

59. MacKenna, loc. cit.; Isidore, Etymologiae, VIII, ix, 30-31, ed. cit.; edit. B. Colgrave, Two Lives of Saint Cuthbert, IX, 17 (Cambridge 1940), p. 184; Rabanus, De Magicis Artibus, PL 110, 1099 (copying Isidore); Decretum XIX, PL 140, 961B.

60. For example, an early charm recounted in J.H.G. Grattan and
    C. Singer, Anglo-Saxon Magic and Medicine (Oxford 1952),
    p. 50. They take the charm from the eighth century manuscript
    B.L. Royal 2 A xx, f. 45v. This, interestingly, conjures the
    elf by God, 'and by the awful day of Judgement'. Christian
    fear here outdoes non-christian.

61. Meaney, op. cit., p. 111.

62. In a revealing passage in his History of the Lombards VI, 5
    the eighth century historian Paul the Deacon associated a
    severe pestilence with an eclipse of the moon; edit. L.
    Bethmann and G. Waitz, Pauli Historia Langobardorum, MGH
    Scriptores Rerum Langobardicarum et Italicarum Saec. VI-IX
    (Berlin 1878), p. 166.

63. Sometimes we have a codex containing different kinds of
    interposed reason. Such a codex is B.L. Cotton Domitian A I,
    of the late tenth or early eleventh century and from St.
    Augustine's Canterbury, described in Ker, op. cit., pp. 185-
    186, and mentioned above (n. 30). Together with Bede's De
    Die Iudicii and Isidore's De Natura Rerum it has a
    'scientific' recipe (as opposed, that is, to a charm) for
    the curing of wens.

64. All this is made clear by E. Heyse, op. cit., especially pp.
    36-39.

65. See for example the discussions in edit. M. Douglas, Witch-
    craft Confessions and Accusations (London 1970), passim but
    especially pp. xvii-xxii, 113-114, 208-231.

66. Ed. cit., p. 4.

67. Indispensable to an understanding of Isidore's approach to
    astrology is J. Fontaine, 'Isidore de Séville et l'astrol-
    ogie,' Revue des Etudes Latines, 31 (1953), 271-300.

68. Etymologiae, III, xxvii; ed. cit..

69. See J. Fontaine, Isidore de Séville et la Culture Classique
    dans l'Espagne Wisigothique, ii (Paris 1959), especially pp.
    503-540.

70. Laistner, long ago, argued that astrology, starved of texts,
    was never a serious threat in the early medieval west, and
    certainly not one as serious as such heathen practices as
    sorcery. M.L.W. Laistner, 'The western church and astrology
    during the early middle ages,' Harvard Theological Review 34
    (1941), 251-275. He was taken to task a little by Fontaine,
    art. cit. p. 272. I hope eventually to argue at greater
    length that the threat to the early medieval church from

astrologers whose lore was largely orally transmitted, but
no less effective for that, was far greater than has
previously been supposed.

71. Fontaine, art. cit., pp. 280-282.

72. De Temporum Ratione, chapter iii; ed. C.W. Jones, Bedae Opera
    De Temporibus (Cambridge, Mass. 1943), pp. 183-184. Aldhelm,
    De Metris et Enigmatibus; edit. R. Ehwald, MGH Auctorum
    Antiquissimorum xv (Berlin 1919), 72-73.

73. These are listed and discussed by C.E. Finch, 'Excerpts from
    Pliny's Natural History in Codices Reg. Lat. 309 and Vat. Lat.
    645,' Transactions and Proceedings of the American Philolog-
    ical Association 96 (1965), 107-117.

74. I have set out his borrowings in the appendix of tables, and
    have taken them from the admirable edition of W.M. Stevens,
    Rabani Mogontiacensis Episcopi De Computo (Turnholt 1979).

75. Reprinted as no. XIII below.

Appendix

These tables give chapter headings for the De Natura Rerum (DNR) of Isidore and of Bede and those of the relevant sections of the De Computo of Rabanus. The columns which follow indicate inter-relationships, when these are close. In the De Computo Rabanus occasionally turns to Bede's De Temporum Ratione (DTR) instead of his DNR.

The sources for the relevant books of Rabanus's De Universo are set out clearly in tabular form in E. Heyse, Hrabanus Maurus' Enzyklopädie 'De rerum naturis' (Munich 1969), pp. 102-107 and 110-114. She shews convincingly that for his exegetical materials he casts his net very widely indeed, and for his scientific information he chooses to pass by the treatises De Natura Rerum of both Bede and Isidore and to draw instead upon Isidore's fuller Etymologies. Whilst Isidore's treatise, De Natura Rerum had, with a few expansions, clearly sufficed for Bede, and Bede's for much of Rabanus's De Computo, with the De Universo both the scale of the work and the pool from which information is drawn change.

Rabanus De Computo contents		Bede DNR	DTR	Isidore DNR
xxxvii.	De planetis et origine nominum earum.	–		
xxxviii.	De planetarum cursu per signiferum et natura signiferi.	xvi		
xxxviiii.	De Duodecim signis.	xvii		
xl.	Demonstratio signorum per solis cursum.	xxi		
xli.	De lunae cursu per signa.		xvii	
xlii.	Argumentum ad investigandum lunae cursum.		xviii	
xliii.	Argumentum de eo quot horis luna luceat.		xxiv	
xliiii.	De magnitudine solis et lunae.	xix		
xlv.	De natura et situ lunae.	xx		
xlvi.	De eclipsin solis sive lunae.	xxii	xxvii	
xlvii.	Ubi eclipsin non sit et quare.	xxiii		
xlviii.	De indicio qualitate planetorum.	xv		
xlviiii.	De natura caeli.	v		x
l.	De quinque circulis mundi.	ix		
li.	De his signis stellarum quae extra zodiacum sunt.	xviii		
lii.	De cometis.	xxiiii		

Isidore DNR contents		Bede DNR
I.	De diebus.	No
II.	De nocte.	equivalent.
III.	De hebdomada.	
IV.	De mensibus.	
V.	De concordia mensuum.	
VI.	De annis.	
VII.	De temporibus.	
VIII.	De solistitio et aequinoctio.	
IX.	De mundo.	iii/x
X.	De V circulis mundi.	ix
XI.	De partibus mundi.	iv/?xliv/xv
XII.	De caelo et eius nomine.	v/vii/?xlv
XIII.	De planetis caeli.	vii
XIV.	De aquis caelestibus.	?viii
XV.	De natura solis.	xix
XVI.	De quantitate solis et lunae.	xix
XVII.	De solis cursu.	xix
XVIII.	De lumine lunae.	xx
XIX.	De lunae cursu.	-
XX.	De eclipsin solis.	xxii
XXI.	De eclipsin lunae.	xxii
XXII.	De cursu stellarum.	xi/xii (close)
XXIII.	De positione VII stellarum errantium.	xii/xiii
XXIV.	De lumine astrorum.	xi
XXV.	De lapsu stellarum.	xi
XXVI.	De nominibus astrorum.	?xxiv
XXVII.	Vtrum sidera animam habeant.	-
XXVIII.	De nocte.	-
XXIX.	De tonitruo.	xxviii (close)
XXX.	De fulminibus.	xxv/xxix (close)
XXXI.	De arcu.	xxxi
XXXII.	De nubibus.	xxxii
XXXIII.	De pluuiis.	xxxii/xxxiii
XXXIV.	De niue.	xxxv
XXXV.	De grandine.	xxxiv
XXXVI.	De natura uentorum.	xxvi (close)
XXXVII.	De nominibus uentorum.	xxvii (close)
XXXVIII.	De signis tempestatum.	xxxvi (close)
XXXIX.	De pestilentia.	xxxvii
XL.	De oceani aestu.	xxxix
XLI.	Cur mare non crescat.	xl
XLII.	Cur mare amaras habeat aquas.	xli
XLIII.	De Nilo flumine.	xliii (close)
XLIV.	De nominibus maris et fluminum.	-
XLV.	De positione terrae.	xlv
XLVI.	De terrae motu.	xlix
XLVII.	De monte Aetna.	l (close)
XLVIII.	De partibus terrae.	xlv/li

Bede DNR contents		Isidore DNR
I.	De quadrifario Dei opere.	–
II.	De mundi formatione.	–
III.	Quid sit mundus.	ix
IIII.	De elementis.	xi
V.	De firmamento.	xii
VI.	De uaria altitudine caeli.	–
VII.	De caelo superiore.	xii/xiii
VIII.	De aquis caelestibus.	–/xiii/xiv
VIIII.	De circulis mundi.	x
X.	De plagis mundi.	ix/xi/xii
XI.	De stellis.	xxii/xxiv/xxv
XII.	De cursu planetarum.	xxii
XIII.	De ordine earum.	?xxiii
XIIII.	De apsidibus earum.	–
XV.	Quare mutent colores.	–
XVI.	De zodiaco circulo.	–
XVII.	De XII signis.	–
XVIII.	De lacteo circulo.	–
XVIIII.	De cursu et magnitudine solis.	vii/xvi/xvii
XX.	De natura et situ lunae.	?xviii
XXI.	Argumentum de cursu lunae per signa.	–
XXII.	De eclipsi solis et lunae.	xx/xxi
XXIII.	Vbi non sit et quare.	xxi
XXIIII.	De cometis.	xxvi
XXV.	De aere.	xxx
XXVI.	De uentis.	xxxvi
XXVII.	Ordo uentorum.	xxxvii
XXVIII.	De tonitruo.	xxix
XXVIIII.	De fulminibus.	xxx
XXX.	Vbi non sit et quare.	–
XXXI.	De arcu.	xxxi
XXXII.	De nubibus.	xxxii/xxxiii
XXXIII.	De imbribus.	xxxiii
XXXIIII.	De grandine.	xxxv
XXXV.	De niue.	xxxiv
XXXVI.	Signa tempestatum uel serenitatis.	xxxviii
XXXVII.	De pestilentia.	xxxix
XXXVIII.	De natura aquarum duplici.	–
XXXVIIII.	De aestu oceani.	xl
XL.	Cur mare non crescat.	xli
XLI.	Cur sit amarum.	xlii
XLII.	De Rubro Mari.	–
XLIII.	De Nilo.	xliii
XLIIII.	Aquis terram necti.	–/?xi/?xlv
XLV.	Terrae positio.	xlviii/?xii
XLVI.	Terram globo similem.	–
XLVII.	De circulis terrae.	–
XLVIII.	Gnominica de hisdem.	–
XLVIIII.	De terrae motu.	xlvi
L.	Incendium Ethnae.	xlvii
LI.	Diuisio terrae.	xlviii

IV

MONSTERS AND THE ANTIPODES IN THE EARLY MIDDLE AGES AND ENLIGHTENMENT

The question of the Antipodes, that is, the question of whether a place and a people on the opposite side of the known world could be said to exist, was a rich subject for debate until the very time of their discovery. Sometimes this debate became sufficiently public and acrimonious to leave clear record. It left such record on two particularly notable occasions, and these occasions form the pretext for this discussion. The first of them took place in the early eighth century, the second in the early seventeenth. It is upon the first that I wish to concentrate here, but not without some little reference to the second.

We have evidence of the first occasion from the year 748. In that year, Pope Zachary I (741–752) wrote a letter in response to a series of questions about ecclesiastical discipline which had been put to him by Archbishop Boniface of Mainz. One of Boniface's questions concerned the Antipodes, both the place and its inhabitants. Boniface was critical of the opinions held upon the matter by one Virgil. Zachary's reply left no room for ambiguity:

> In the matter of that perverse and evil teaching, of which he delivers himself against God and his own soul—to be specific, his declaring that there is another world and other men underneath the earth, and another sun and moon—you are to hold a council and expel him from the church, stripping him of the honor of the priesthood.[1]

---

[1] "De perversa enim et iniqua doctrina, quae contra Deum et animam suam locutus est—si clarificatum fuerit, ita eum confiteri, quod alius mundus et alii homines sub terra sint seu sol et luna—hunc habito concilio ab ecclesia pelle, sacerdotii honore privatum"; MGH Epp. 3.360, no. 80. I have included the Latin text because the translation is my own; in the case of translations available in print I shall cite only references. The pursuit of these thoughts was made possible by the award of a membership at the Institute for Advanced Study, Princeton, for which I am most grateful. This paper was first delivered as a seminar at Dumbarton Oaks, Washington, D.C. I derived great profit from the discussion there.

The mere expression of the idea that there was another place and people on the other side of the earth merited deprivation of priestly office.

We do not know the exact outcome of the dispute, but Virgil / Fergal prospered. His friendship with the duke of Bavaria (of which the pope had complained earlier in the same letter), and his defiance of Archbishop Boniface evidently did him no worldly harm, for he was awarded the bishopric of Salzburg (consecrated 767) and presided over it, Irish fashion, from the abbey of Saint Peter's in Salzburg until his death in 784.[2] We do know, however, that Pope Zachary was wrong. There are other men and other habitable areas on the opposite side of the earth, and the sun and moon do shine on them both. The pope's pronouncement against Virgil was seen, at least tacitly, to have been in error in 1233, when Virgil was canonized by Pope Gregory IX; and it was publicly denounced as ridiculous in that burst of astronomical and cosmological rebellion and pope-baiting which characterized the early seventeenth century. Here we have the second of the notable occasions on which the question of the Antipodes rose to the surface. On this second occasion the materials of the first were reviewed, their conclusions then discredited. The letters to and from Archbishop Boniface were published in a complete edition in 1605, and Kepler, when defending the Copernican theory, cited the letter of Pope Zachary as evidence of clerical ignorance and obduracy in the face of scientific inquiry (wrongly adding that Zachary had recanted). In 1633 the matter was raised again at the condemnation of Galileo, and in 1634 Descartes questioned the papal position and papal attitudes in general to scientific hypotheses and experiment.[3]

We seem to have, in these two occasions, classic instances of the difference between the Middle Ages and the "Enlightenment." On the first occasion we appear to be witnessing the attempted aggressions of an apparently typical medieval combination: that of pope and archbishop set upon a course repressive of legitimate and (with hindsight) profitable intellectual inquiry. On the second occasion, there emerges at last the beginning of a victory of intelligent man over ecclesiastical obscurantism. "Science" seems to be on the verge of banishing the last lingering traces of medieval, and, by the same token, superstitious, ideas about the Antipodes.

I hope in this paper to argue for an interpretation of these two occasions which is very nearly the opposite of the one I have set out here. Without actually wishing to assert the scientific truth of that which has become known as the medieval view of

---

[2]This Virgil was earlier ingeniously identified by Löwe with the author of a well-known eighth-century cosmography; H. Löwe, "Ein literarischer Widersacher des Bonifatius: Virgil von Salzburg und die Kosmographie des Aethicus Istricus," *Abhandlungen der Akademie der Wissenschaften und der Literatur in Mainz* 11 (1951) 908–988. Recently, however, serious doubt has been cast upon this identification: K. Hillkowitz, *Zur Kosmographie des Aethicus* 2 (Frankfurt a. M. 1973) 1–19.

[3]An excellent summary of this aspect of the dispute is provided by H. van der Linden, "Virgile de Salzburg et les théories cosmographiques au VIIIe siècle," *Bulletin de la classe des lettres: Académie royale de Belgique* 4 (1914) 163–187. The best survey of literary references to the Antipodes from Plato to Columbus is still G. Boffito, "La leggenda degli Antipodi," *Miscellanea di studi critici edita in onore di Arturo Graf* (Bergamo 1903) 583–601.

the Antipodes—a difficult task, especially for one who lives there as I do—I wish to suggest that this view, the view which maintained with vigor that there was no such place and no such people, had, within its context, an enormous amount to be said for it, and that we should look first to this context when judging the rightness or the wrongness of this view, and its "superstitious" content. In the same way (though, as a medievalist, with rather more wariness) I would aver that the seventeenth-century attempt to have this view reversed had—and has—a lot to be said against it.

I

One thing may be said immediately in defense of Zachary's pronouncement, and that is that it was firmly consistent with current learned Christian opinion. As recently as 725 Bede, a countryman of Archbishop Boniface and one whom the archbishop held in very high esteem, had expressed the same view. He expressed it in his *De temporum ratione*, which was one of the most carefully compiled of his *opera didascalica* and one of the most widely read and respected. In a passage at the end of his chapter on the five zones of the earth, Bede discusses Pliny's account of the Antipodes:

> Those zones rendered temperate by their nearness both to sun and ice are called the summer and winter zones: and both are said to be habitable, that is, capable of being inhabited, because they are not rendered unfit for mortals by extremes of heat and cold. Only one of them, however, is known for certain to be inhabited. We must refuse credence to the legends about the Antipodes, and the idea that anyone has historical or aural or visual evidence that people can cross through the fiery heat of Ethiopia and, leaving the northern sun behind them, find there temperate lands fit for mortals. Pliny, that relentless inquirer into the facts of nature, though he does not deny that the earth, "resembling a pine cone is inhabited all round," does say this of the zones; "There are only two temperate zones between the torrid and the frozen ones, and these have no communication with each other because of the fiery heat of the heavenly body."[4]

Pliny leaned towards the possibility that a habitable zone on the other side of the world might indeed, once postulated, be inhabited.[5] Bede is prepared to report

---

[4]"Solstitialem et brumalem significat, quae vicina utrinque ferventis et gelidarum sunt vi temperatae: ideoque ambas dicunt habitabiles, id est habitationi habiles, et nec frigoris immanitate nec caloris mortalium a se repellentes accessum. Quamvis unam solummodo probare possunt habitatam, neque enim vel antipodarum ullatenus est fabulis accomodandus assensus, vel aliquis refert historicus vidisse vel audisse vel legisse, qui meridianas in partes solem transierunt hibernum ita ut eo post tergum relicto, transgressis Aethiopum fervoribus, temperatas ultra eos hinc calore illinc rigore atque habitabiles mortalium repererint sedes. Denique solertissimus naturalium inquisitor Plinius, qui non negat terram, 'etsi sit figura pinea nucis, nihilominus undique incoli,' vide quid de his scribens zonis dicat: 'circa', inquit, 'duae tantum inter exustam et rigentes temperantur, eaeque ipsae inter se non perviae propter incendium sideris' "; Bede, *De temporum ratione* 34; ed. C. W. Jones, *Bedae Venerabilis Opera* 6.2, Corpus christianorum 123B (Turnholt 1977) 390.

[5]Pliny, *Naturalis historia* 2.65; ed. H. Rackham (London 1938) 297.

68

Pliny's idea about the habitable land, but not to allow that there might be men on it. His denial is flat, as was Zachary's. And in departing from Pliny Bede agrees, in turn, with Isidore, who in the early seventh century set out his own conclusions in his very popular *Etymologies*:

> We cannot believe in the existence of a people who are called 'Antipodae' because they are thought to be opposite ourselves, and placed under the earth with their feet against ours, for neither the solidity nor the center of the earth will allow of them. The proposition does not spring from historical evidence but from the affectations of poetic reasoning.

> Besides these three parts of the world there is a fourth, across the ocean and in the south. This is unknown to us because of the heat of the sun. Legends place the inhabited Antipodes there.[6]

Isidore may, in his turn, retain some traces of Lactantius who, at the end of the third century, expressed himself with even greater vehemence:

> And what shall we say of those who think there are "Antipodae" with their feet opposite ours? Is there anyone silly enough really to believe that there are men whose feet are higher than their heads? Or that things which lie on the earth with us hang downwards with them, and trees and fruits grow the wrong way up, and rain and snow and hail fall upwards onto the ground? Who would number the hanging gardens among the seven wonders of the world when serious thinkers postulate hanging trees and cities and seas and mountains?

> . . . and so within the curvature of the earth there is contained another world, inhabited by men and all sorts of animals. But we cannot hear or speak of the Antipodes without a smile. It cannot seriously be suggested that we believe in the existence of men whose feet are opposite ours.[7]

And then, at the center point of all this, as of so much, stood Augustine. In his *De civitate Dei* 16.9, Augustine gave magisterial utterance on the matter:

[6]"Jam vero ii qui Antipodae dicuntur eo quod contrarii esse vestigiis nostris putantur, ut qui sub terris positi adversa pedibus nostris calcent vestigia nulla ratione credendum est, quia nec soliditas patitur nec centrum terrae; sed neque hoc illa historiae cognitione firmatur, sed hoc poetae quasi ratiocinando coniectant"; "Extra tres autem partes orbis quarta pars trans oceanum interior est in meridie, quae solis ardore nobis incognita est, et in cuius finibus antipodes fabulose inhabitare produntur"; Isidore, *Etym.* 9.2.13, 14.5.17; ed. W. M. Lindsay, *Isidori Hispalensis episcopi Etymologiarum sive originum libri XX* (Oxford 1911).

[7]"Quid? illi qui esse contrarios vestigiis nostris antipodas putant num aliquid locuntur? aut est quisquam tam ineptus qui credat esse homines quorum vestigia sint superiora capita? aut ibi quae aput nos iacent, inversa pendere, fruges et arbores deorsum versus crescere, pluvias et nives et grandines sursum versus cadere in terram? Et miratur aliquis hortus pensiles inter septem mira narrari, cum philosophi et agros et urbes et maria et montes pensiles faciant?"; ". . . itaque intra sinum eius (terrae) aliam terram contineri, quae ab hominibus et omnis generis animalibus incolatur. De antipodis quoque sine risu nec audiri nec dici potest, adseritur tamen quasi aliquid serium, ut credamus esse homines qui vestigiis nostris habeant adversa vestigia"; Lactantius, *Divinae institutiones* 3.24; *Institutionum epitome* 34; ed. S. Brandt, *L. Caeli Firmiani Lactanti Opera omnia* 1 (Prague 1890) 254–255, 709–710.

IV

But in regard to the story of the *antipodes*, that is, that there are men on the other side of the earth, where the sun rises when it sets for us, who plant their footprints opposite ours, there is no logical ground for believing this. Its authors do not claim that they have learned it from any historical evidence, but offer it as a sort of logical hypothesis. Their theory is that the earth hangs suspended within the heavenly sphere, so that the lowest and middle points of the world are one and the same. From this they conjecture that the other half of the earth, which lies beneath our portion, cannot lack human occupants. They fail to observe that even if the world is held to be global or rounded in shape, or if some process of reasoning should prove this to be the case, it would still not necessarily follow that the land on the opposite side is not covered by masses of water. Furthermore, even if the land there be exposed, we must not jump to the conclusion that it has human inhabitants.[8]

The cumulative effect of all these pronouncements is indeed the same as that of Zachary.

Zachary was faithful, then, to current and past tradition;[9] but since loyalty to tradition is not the strongest of defenses against accusations of obscurantism, more must be advanced in his support. With this purpose in mind we may look a little more closely at the authorities who stood behind him.

While Pliny had left open the general question about whether the hypothetical land was inhabited, he closed one specific aspect of it. Bede quoted with approval a part of this section of Pliny, and Isidore, in the passage cited above, clearly agreed with it, too. Pliny says:

But the middle portion of the lands, where the sun's orbit is, is scorched by its flames and burnt up by the proximity of its heat: this is the torrid zone. There are only two temperate zones between the torrid one and the frozen ones, and these have no communication with each other because of the fiery heat of the heavenly body.[10]

Now while this still allowed Pliny to postulate inhabitants, for Bede and Isidore it ruled such a possibility out completely. They argued from the assertion to the denial as though the logic of the argument were obvious, and there was nothing more to be said about it. Fortunately, Augustine sets out the reasons Bede and Isidore (and Zachary) took for granted. In the concluding passage of that section of his *De civitate Dei* I have already quoted, he says,

For there is absolutely no falsehood in the Scripture, which gains credence for its account of past events by the fact that its prophecies are fulfilled. And the idea is too absurd to mention that some men might have sailed from our part of the earth to

[8]Augustine, *De civitate Dei* 16.9; ed. E. M. Sanford and W. M. Green, *Saint Augustine: The City of God against the Pagans* 5 (London 1965) 49–51.
[9]Non-Christian literature too could be hostile to the idea of the Antipodes; Lucretius, *De rerum natura* 1.1052–1082, for instance: ed. A. Brieger, *T. Lucreti Cari De rerum natura libri VI* (Leipzig 1905) 30–31; and Plutarch: L. Thorndike, *A History of Magic and Experimental Science* 1 (New York 1923) 219–220.
[10]Pliny 2.68 (n. 5 above) 307.

70

the other and have arrived there by crossing the boundless tracts of ocean, so that the human race might be established there also by descent from the one first man.[11]

Even if there is a habitable zone on the other side of the world, by the very fact that it is inaccessible there cannot be men on it; for all men were and are descended from the first man. Here Augustine has in mind above all Genesis 9.19, and the declaration that all men were descended from Adam through the three sons of Noah. The story of Genesis declares that the human race is one. Since this race is manifestly placed in the known world, and since the unknown world is inaccessible, it follows that there can be no human beings there.

We may add, then, to the support of tradition in general, Christian and some non-Christian, the support of Genesis, and the giving through this of some substance at least to an argument which looked slender. Of course, this is still not enough; but from this position we may now see far further. This particular section of patristic teaching and biblical exegesis had a wider context, and was liable to have much further reaching consequences than has so far appeared. The principal concern of the inquiry is not now learned tradition and the Bible, but the human race itself, and its means of communication above all. Here we confront its whole moral outlook and that which conditions it for good or ill.

II

Even for those most passionate in the defense of their existence, the people of the Antipodes were odd. The best that could be said of them was that they were upside down, and experienced, for example, the heat and cold of the seasons at different times of the year, and saw different stars.[12] From this, however, more elaborate fantasies could be invented and much stranger features adduced.[13] Isidore, for instance, for all his resolute dismissal of the idea of an inhabited Antipodes, could still believe in, and even relish, a curious race of that name: "The Antipodes in Libya have their feet facing backwards from their legs, and eight toes on each foot."[14] The upside down people have turned into a kind of monster, with feet turned backwards and an excessive number of toes.[15]

---

[11] Augustine (n. 8 above) 51. It should be noted that the question at issue throughout this discussion was not whether the world was round or flat, but whether the other side of it, round *or* flat, was accessible or inaccessible. The first problem has no necessary connection with the second.

[12] As, for instance, by Martianus Capella; ed. A. Dick, *Martianus Capella, De nuptiis Philologiae et Mercurii* (Leipzig 1935) 298–299, §605.

[13] Some of the maps of the world springing from illustrations to the *Commentary on the Dream of Scipio* of Macrobius (2.5), for example, place one-footed Sciapods in the Antipodes; M. Destombes, *Mappemondes A.D. 1200–1500* 1 (Amsterdam 1964) 40–42, 79–80.

[14] "Antipodes in Libya plantas versas habent post crura, et octenos digitos in plantis"; Isidore 11.3.24 (n. 6 above).

[15] Isidore's description became popular and was familiar to illustrators of bestiaries. One such illustration is reproduced by J. B. Friedman, *The Monstrous Races in Medieval Art and Thought* (Cambridge, Mass. 1981) 12.

These people so described readily took their place among a formidable series of strange races, "monsters," indeed, whose ancestry stems from a tradition far longer than that to which Pope Zachary paid immediate tribute, a tradition which had, furthermore, a very wide currency. Stories of strange peoples and monsters were extraordinarily popular in antiquity and the Middle Ages. They owed their popularity and extensive literary record partly to mythical projection, partly to observation, partly to the attractions they had for artists, always to the appeal they made to the human imagination. The tradition seems to begin with Herodotus, in the fifth century B.C. It was handed on from him through Ktesias of Knidos and Megasthenes in the fourth century B.C. and, to the Latin West in particular, through Pliny in the first century A.D. and Solinus in the third, and through the stories of Alexander the Great's travels to India.[16] From all of these accounts spring those lists of extraordinary creatures, in appearance part human part animal, so well known to medieval cosmographies and bestiary collections.[17] In the early Middle Ages, indeed, the tradition seems to run riot. Isidore's "Antipodes," for example, appear to be a mixture of the Indian people described by Megasthenes, whose feet faced backwards, and the eight-toed people of Ktesias and Pliny. They are part of a full chapter, largely drawn from Pliny and Solinus, in which Isidore reports upon the more remarkable aspects of the earlier monster tradition, and which was to assist greatly in its transmission.

Ideas varied, of course, about how these monstrous races came to be, about the meaning of their existence and about how, above all, they should be treated. A strong current of thought, originating perhaps with the Babylonians, saw monstrous births as presages, in Latin "monstra," usually of disaster.[18] Cicero maintained a form of this view, doing so seemingly in the face of a very different opinion, stemming from Aristotle. According to Aristotle, monsters are not divinatory signs, but stem from Nature's straying from the generic type.[19] On all these views monsters, arresting as they are, are very hard to incorporate acceptably within the bounds of common humanity. Elements of the unnatural and of the deformed, and the fear which springs from this, cling to them. It is tempting to keep them, at the very least, at a distance and to sever them from the responsibility of creatures more evidently "human." This fact may in part account for their being so often placed, in cosmographies and maps, at the outermost fringes of the known world.

Now Pope Zachary had nothing directly to say about monsters nor, it now seems,

---

[16]For these remarks and for his superb discussion of the history of the monstrous races see R.Wittkower, "Marvels of the East: A Study in the History of Monsters," *Journal of the Warburg and Courtauld Institutes* 5 (1942) 159–197, esp. 182. For the Alexander literature see W. J. Aerts et al., eds., *Alexander the Great in the Middle Ages* (Nijmegen 1978).

[17]A good summary description of many of these monsters may be found in Friedman (n. 15 above) 9–21.

[18]F. Lenormant, *La Divination et la science des présages chez les Chaldéens* (Paris 1875) 103–126, and Wittkower (n. 16 above) 168, n. 5.

[19]Cicero, *De divinatione* 1.42.93, ed. W. A. Falconer (London 1923) 325; *Generation of Animals* 4.3.767, ed. A. L. Peck (London 1953) 400–404.

IV

had Virgil; but some of those who subscribed to the medieval view of the Antipodes had. And with these we encounter an apparently quite extraordinary paradox. They were as open to a belief in the existence in the known world of these remarkable creatures as they were closed to the idea that man could subsist in the Antipodes. We have seen that Isidore was prepared to subscribe to the monsters; indeed he declared in the same chapter that they were products of the Divine Will. So too believed Augustine. Augustine has, in his *De civitate Dei*, a long section on the monstrous races (in which he too mentions the people whose feet face backwards, though without actually giving them their name). In this he shows, like Isidore, a knowledge of Pliny and Solinus. He says, however, a little more than Isidore; and through this we may begin to explain the paradox. Augustine enters another dimension. In doing so he at last brings us to that larger understanding of the events of 748 for which we have sought.

Augustine speaks of the monstrous races in the context of a discussion about the ways of God and of human kind, and with the purpose of inculcating a complex but very firm moral lesson. The lesson is this. As long as we lack the certainty that these monsters are animals, the presumption must be that they are human, and so descended, as Genesis tells us, from the race of Adam. The fact that they appear strange must on no account allow them to be set apart from, let alone beneath, humanity, accusing God, as it were, of bad workmanship. It is unthinkable, of course, to set aside monstrous human births, says Augustine. These are, we know, an act of God's will. This same attitude must govern man's relations with the monstrous races:

> Furthermore, the same explanation that is used to account for monstrous human births among our race can be applied to certain monstrous races also. For God is the creator of all things, and he himself knows at what place and time a given creature should be created, or have been created, selecting in his wisdom the various elements from whose likeness and diversities he contrives the beautiful fabric of the universe. But one who cannot see the whole clearly is offended by the apparent deformity of a single part, since he does not know with what it conforms or how to classify it. We know instances of men born with more than five digits on their hands and feet. This, to be sure, is too slight to be considered a serious aberration from the norm, yet far be it from anyone to suppose in his folly that the Creator made a mistake in the number of human fingers, even though he may not know why God acted as he did. So even if a greater variation were to arise, he whose works no one has the right to censure knows what he has done.[20]

Augustine goes on, then, to give examples of monstrous births, and he does so, it seems, with a dual purpose. He insists in the first place that monstrous births of human parents are quite clearly descended from the race of Adam, and, in the second, that there is therefore a very strong presumption that the monstrous races are similarly descended:

[20] Augustine 16.8 (n. 8 above) 45.

At Hippo Zaritus there is a man with feet that are roughly crescent-shaped, with only two toes on each, and his hands are like his feet. If there were any race like this it would be added to the curious marvels of natural history. Surely, then, we shall not on this account deny, shall we, that this man is descended from that one man who was first created? . . . Moreover, who could enumerate all the human infants that are very unlike the parents of whom they were indubitably born? Therefore, since we cannot deny that these are descended from that one man, such is the case also with any races whatsoever that are reported to have deserted, as it were, by their divergent physical types, the normal path of nature that the majority and, in fact, nearly all men follow. If these peoples are classified among rational and mortal animals, then we must admit that their stock is descended from that single first father of all mankind, always providing that the tales told about the diverse characteristics of these races and their great differences from one another and from us are authentic.[21]

It is even possible, concluded Augustine, that God created the monstrous races precisely to reassure human beings that monstrous human births are all a part of the divine plan:

What if God willed to create some races of this sort expressly to prevent us from thinking that the wisdom by which he moulds the forms of men was at fault in the case of such monsters as are duly born among us of human parents, as if it had been the craft of an unskilled artisan? It should not then seem to us unnatural that, even as there are certain monsters among individual races of man, so also within the human race as a whole there may be certain monstrous tribes.[22]

I have quoted Augustine's discussion of the problem of monsters at some length because it is of an extraordinary importance to the question in hand. In this section of his *De civitate Dei* Augustine sets himself, with the help of Genesis, explicitly to counter views he regards as narrow and inhumane. His insistence that it is unthinkable to treat monstrous births as subhuman is, of course, rhetorical; in the late Roman Empire this was far from unthinkable.[23] He counters this inhumanity by making an ingenious connection. He binds together the race of Adam with creatures whom "normal" human beings could be tempted to treat as at best subhuman, and at worst as not human at all, but by whom they were also fascinated, as they were by more materially rewarding wonders.[24] In so binding the two together he urges upon human beings an extension of their tolerance and sympathy. While doing this, Augustine emphasizes repeatedly that the human race is descended from Adam, and

[21] Ibid. 47–49.
[22] Ibid. 49.
[23] Seneca, *De ira* 1.15 (3); ed. G. Viansino, *Dialogorum libri III, IV, V* (De ira) (Turin 1963) 22. Cf. also M. Delcourt, *Stérilités mystérieuses et naissances maléfiques dans l'antiquité classique* (Liège 1938) 59–66.
[24] Augustine makes equally ingenious use of this fascination with "mirabilia" at 21.5 (n. 8 above) 7.25–33.

IV

that it is this common descent which must compel it to accept that even the most curious aberrations are a part of the divine purpose. Descent from Adam is the crux of the whole argument for behavior properly humane.

It is the crux, finally, of the argument about the Antipodes. This fact explains the passion with which early medieval thinkers asserted that no human being could possibly be found there. The section of the *De civitate Dei* in which Augustine deals with the monstrous races directly precedes his discussion of the Antipodes. It precedes it for a very good reason. His position on the Antipodes is the logical conclusion of his argument about monsters and monstrous births. To this argument the announcement in Genesis that the whole human race is one in its descent from the first man is vital. The idea that the Antipodes could be inhabited and yet be, at the same time, inaccessible to the human race as we know it was wholly destructive of this notion of single descent. To accept such habitation would be to sever the human race into noncommunicating parts and to bring Augustine's construction, with all its inner ingenuity and moral urgency, tumbling about his ears. The argument had, furthermore, another dimension to it. Augustine clearly expected it to broaden human sympathy. But if common descent was to compel mankind to accept as a part of humanity the very strangest of peoples, and to extend thereby its tolerance by the acceptance of God's apparently aberrant behavior, then separate descent, once postulated, might allow of the opposite. The existence of beings demonstrably not descended from Adam and probably monstrous would at best confuse the argument and rob it of its force; and it might, at worst, prompt second thoughts about those previously accepted as a part of the human race.

That was why the expression even of the idea of an inhabited Antipodes was declared to be close to heresy. Common descent is not, of course, the only support available to an argument designed to inculcate improved principles of human behavior, but it was the support chosen in this instance; and, given that a belief in Genesis was not confined to Christian peoples, nor was belief in the importance of descent without wide appeal, it was a very useful one. It was not that Augustine or those of his successors to whom I have referred objected to geographical or anthropological inquiry as such, nor that they wished to subscribe blindly to biblical authority. They were bent upon the pursuit of an ambitious moral end, one humane in its widest sense, and to the achievement of this end the question of the existence of the Antipodes was at best irrelevant and at worst destructive.[25]

The early medieval position on the Antipodes must, then, to be properly under-

[25] We might add that, conversely, the more riotous were the features of the medieval monster tradition, the more helpful they might be to the achievement of Augustine's purpose. This tradition should be seen not as the result of an impoverished learned legacy, supplemented by a self-indulgent preference for fantasy, but as a careful and purposeful means of extending the human imagination; the more improbable were the monsters the more this aim was fulfilled. In this I take issue with small sections of an otherwise most interesting book; M. T. Hodgen, *Early Anthropology in the Sixteenth and Seventeenth Centuries*, ed. 2 (Philadelphia 1971) 33–35, 51–54. I owe this reference to Professor John Elliott.

MONSTERS AND THE ANTIPODES

stood, be placed within its whole context. It was an appendix to a long and passionate discussion about the attitudes human beings should hold toward their own kind. Augustine's pleas for a more extensive humanity demanded the acceptance within the human race of creatures whom it was often man's first instinct to shut out. He chose the idea of single descent, of possible communication, and the biblical authority behind it, as his main support in this plea. These pressures towards acceptance would, it was hoped, work against those first instincts of rejection. The notion that men existed not so descended was a separate question, to be dealt with separately and at the proper time. Posed within this particular request for human breadth of mind it could only make mischief. Two possible courses were available for the avoiding of the problem for the time being. One could do as Augustine did and dismiss the Antipodes; "nulla ratione credendum est"; or one could do as Isidore did, that is, admit the existence of monsters of that name but place them securely within accessible Libya.

This brings us at last back to the context within which Pope Zachary uttered so apparently crude and laughable a condemnation of the idea of an inhabited Antipodes. His purpose was the same as that of Augustine. This purpose was to try to keep alive, untrammelled by distractions, an argument for human tolerance; an argument which, while not freed of imperfections and not final, showed every promise of being serviceable at a time when human tolerance and breadth of mind badly needed such service. Zachary, furthermore, was writing to the leader of a missionary effort confronted by strange and savage peoples, consisting indeed not merely of heathen Germans but perhaps of members of the monstrous races themselves.[26] We hear much about the resistance of non-Christians to missionary endeavors, less about the tolerance required of existing Christians to their incorporation within the fold.[27] Yet the demands upon such tolerance must have been great, and the idea that these potential Christians were of common human stock must have been a very necessary aid to meeting them. The importance of Genesis in Anglo-Saxon and Old Saxon hardly needs further demonstration here, although we may from the present discussion perhaps understand its popularity a little better. Certainly Boniface appeals to it.[28] To have one of Boniface's supposed helpers, therefore, publicly claiming that human creatures existed who were demonstrably not of the race of Adam was, at the very least, of no help to those struggling for the incorporation of possibly very strange converts within the existing German church. The acceptance of the existence of inaccessible

---

[26]Aethicus Ister, for example, placed dog-headed Cynocephali near to the Germans (2.28); H. Wuttke, *Die Kosmographie des Istrier Aethikos* (Leipzig 1853) 15–16.

[27]Boniface and his missionaries did encounter internal opposition, however, because they were foreigners; W. Levison, *England and the Continent in the Eighth Century* (Oxford 1946) 168–169. We know, too, from the manuscript tradition of the *Liber monstrorum*, that there was an interest in monsters in southern France, modern Switzerland, and southwest Germany certainly by the mid-ninth century, and, from the text, that this interest contained a large element of hostility; A. Knock, "The 'Liber Monstrorum': An Unpublished Manuscript and some Reconsiderations," *Scriptorium* 32 (1978) 28; Friedman (n. 15 above) 149–150. See also the letter of Ratramnus to Rimbert, *Epistola de Cynocephalis*, PL 121.1153–1156.

[28]Boniface, *Sermones* 2 and 3; PL 89.845, 848.

Antipodean monsters could, indeed, at one stroke destroy the basis upon which the whole argument for the acceptance of closer strangers had been built. And there was an even greater hazard. The impetus for these often very difficult and dangerous missions was, during this period, drawn very largely from the conviction that the Apostles were commanded to go out and preach to *all* nations (Matthew 28. 19; Acts 2. 4–5). The thought that there might exist inaccessible nations could only detract from this conviction, too. Zachary could not afford such indulgences. It was not that either he or his predecessors wished to exalt biblical authority and inhibit scientific hypotheses as such. The inhibition of this particular hypothesis and the emphasis laid upon this particular section of the Bible were simply necessary by-products of this far larger purpose.

III

I have tried to suggest in the foregoing pages that the early medieval view of the Antipodes had, within the context within which it was propounded, a lot to be said in its favor. I have attempted to prove that attitudes towards monstrous births and unfamiliar forms of humanity, and attitudes towards the existence of Antipodean inhabitants, are very closely linked, and I have concluded that the rejection of the idea of an inhabited Antipodes was, at the time at which it was rejected, necessary to the sustenance of a credible plea for tolerance and "humanity." Is it possible, as a postscript, to press this conclusion further? With this in mind, may we look rather differently upon the so-called enlightenment of the second occasion upon which Zachary's views on the Antipodes were discussed?

In that same article upon the history of the monstrous races, Wittkower has this to say about attitudes to them in the sixteenth century. He refers especially to the *Prodigiorum ac ostentorum chronicon*, published in 1557 by Conrad Wolffhart, known as Lycosthenes:

> While the Augustinian conception had made the monsters acceptable to the Middle Ages and monuments like the tympanum at Vézelay had given them their due share in the creation, while the later Middle Ages had seen in them similes of human qualities, now in the century of humanism the pagan fear of the monster as a foreboding of evil returns. We are faced with the curious paradox that the "superstitious" Middle Ages pleaded in a broad-minded spirit for the monsters as belonging to God's inexplicable plan of the world, whilst the "enlightened" period of humanism returned to Varro's "contra naturam" and . . . regarded them as creations of God's wrath and to foreshadow extraordinary events. Lycosthenes is an exponent of ideas which having long been in abeyance were revived in the circle of the German emperor Maximilian. Their effect was immediate and widespread, and they brought to the surface popular beliefs which had no place in the official medieval conception of the world.[29]

[29]Wittkower (n. 16 above) 185–186.

Evidence of this fascination for, and fearfulness of, monsters abounds in the sixteenth century.[30] The works of Ambrose Paré and Martin Weinrich stand out among a number of serious and careful treatises about the related problems of monstrous races and monstrous human births. The famous French surgeon, for example, for all that he allowed, in his *Des monstres et prodiges*,[31] for the possibility that the production of certain monsters may help to reflect the glory of God, gave most space to explanations in which sexual wrong-doing, demonic intervention, and God's wrath took pride of place.[32] Monsters "sont le plus souvent signes de quelque malheur à advenir."[33] Paré drew heavily, although probably through a French intermediary, upon the work of Lycosthenes. Further, Martin Weinrich, in his *De ortu monstrorum commentarius* (first published 1595), opposed explicitly the views of Augustine and Isidore. According to Weinrich, the idea that monsters are an ornament to creation is absurd. They are part of God's curse after the Fall, a manifestation of divine displeasure, lessons to us to mend our ways. We must distance ourselves from them and all that they represent. Some of the passion evoked by this discussion was born of painful medical investigations and experiences, some of a dislike of contemporary popular fascination with the macabre, some of a distaste for divination and especially for the notion that monsters are necessarily portents. Nonetheless, for all its varied origins, the spirit of much of the argument was, in the fearfulness of monsters it inspired, and the gloom it expected to surround their conception, remarkably similar. The thought that strange peoples and births could be meant to gladden the heart of man and that he should be encouraged to welcome these creatures into common humanity began to seem ridiculous. While it would be wrong to suppose that early medieval attitudes to monsters were free from this terror and despair,[34] it seems true to say that these last emotions were not allowed then quite the triumph they enjoyed in the sixteenth century.

In the seventeenth century, the gloom was compounded; and it was compounded, most interestingly, especially in those areas and among those scholars that are associated with revived discussions about Zachary, Virgil, and the Antipodes. As in the sixteenth century, so in the seventeenth pessimistic views of monsters and monstrous births abounded among medical practitioners and astronomers. In the same year in which the letters to and from Boniface were published, 1605, a medical practitioner,

[30] Ibid. 186–188 and notes, especially on the rediscovery and popularity of the fourth-century writer *Julius Obsequens*. A masterly study of sixteenth-century French attitudes to the monstrous is J. Céard, *La Nature et les prodiges: L'insolite au XVIe siècle en France* (Geneva 1977).

[31] J. Céard, *Ambroise Paré Des monstres et prodiges* (Geneva 1971), presents a critical edition and discussion of this important text. The treatise, first published in 1573, enjoyed great popularity and was republished in French in 1575, 1579, 1585 (with a long addition on astronomy), 1598, 1607, and in Latin in 1582; ibid. xi–xix.

[32] A summary of Paré's views may be found in G. Lascault, *Le monstre dans l'art occidental* (Paris 1973) 250–251.

[33] Céard (n. 31 above) 3.

[34] Friedman contributes some eloquent pages on the supposedly monstrous and degenerate progeny of Cain and Ham (n. 15 above) 92–107.

IV

Jean Riolan, published his *De monstro nato lutetiae*. In this he pressed the prevalent fear of monsters to a logical conclusion. He argued that monsters, that is, humans of an "unnatural" form, born of human parents, should be put to death because their being was contrary to the laws of nature. He argued, furthermore, that such beings were the products of an intercourse which was itself illicit. This extreme application of the views of Aristotle was not allowed to go unchallenged,[35] but it seems that the voices of such as Riolan were loud and insistent, and were raised during those very years in which Pope Zachary's views upon the Antipodes were being most ridiculed. Fortunio Liceti, for instance, another medical practitioner, in his *De monstrorum causis, natura et differentiis*, published in 1616, subscribed strongly to Riolan's propositions. In this treatise he took the opportunity to eliminate the Plinian races themselves as figments, and fiercely to oppose the idea that such figments could in any way be reconciled, as Augustine tried so hard to reconcile them, to the beauty of the world.[36] Such voices were not those of an unimportant minority on the fringes of society, but of respected public figures at the center of professional life. Their works were, furthermore, widely read. The second edition of Liceti's treatise appeared, interestingly, in 1634, the very year in which Descartes turned his own attention to Zachary and Virgil. If we turn to Descartes it becomes clear that although Cartesianism could find a place for monsters, it was well down the hierarchy of creation. Certainly there was no trace of the dignity, still less of the moral value, attributed to them by Augustine. There was no question of their being fully incorporated within mankind.[37]

Thus, on that second occasion on which the views of Zachary and Virgil upon the question of an inhabited Antipodes were publicly aired, we find, in tandem, as it were, with this discussion, a lively debate about the monstrous races and about monstrous births. Here, however, the outcome of the twin discussion is very different from the outcome of those of the early Middle Ages. In the seventeenth century, as it was thought acceptable, even desirable, to remove monstrous births and monstrous races so far from the responsibility of mankind that mankind might even be allowed to kill them, so it was thought possible to admit of the idea of an inhabited Antipodes. In this matter there was undoubtedly a lifting, or rather rejection, of restrictions and a freeing of the "scientific" imagination. But as in the case of the original restrictions, so in the case of the freeing, the wider context is instructive. Such postulated inhabitants could now impose no great demands. Pressure to receive strange or monstrous races upon equal terms by man had all but vanished, and ample measures for subjection and even elimination had taken their place. It is difficult to argue

[35] J. Roger, *Les sciences de la vie dans la pensée française du XVIIIe siècle: La génération des animaux de Descartes à l'Encyclopédie* (Paris 1963) 397–418. See also, on the anxieties of La Mothe Le Vayer, and his efforts after 1633 to incorporate the monstrous within the human race, R. Pintard, *Le libertinage érudit dans la premier moitié du XVIIe siècle* (Paris 1943) 528.

[36] A summary of the views of Weinrich, Riolan and Liceti may be found in Céard (n. 30 above) 442–456.

[37] Lascault (n. 32 above) 178–179.

at this point that this development was conducive to any great increase of "enlightenment"; and one might well at least begin to ask whether their admission on these terms into the realm of the scientifically possible boded very well for the postulated inhabitants of the supposed Antipodes themselves.

This is not the place for an examination of the atrocities which followed the discovery of inhabited land in the Antipodes; nor must it be imagined for one moment that either all the discoverers, or all those scholars who gave their attention to revisions of the scale of being, would knowingly have contributed to the violence of its outcome. Many manifestly did not. Two points may, however, be made. The first is that the reduction of the savage to a level on the scale of being lower than that of man does indeed seem to have accompanied the discovery of lands previously thought to be inaccessible.[38] The second point is that, on Augustine's view, and on Zachary's, these atrocities could not have happened.[39] For Augustine, preparedness to accept common human descent was the only basis upon which man could approach man or monsters. The maintenance of this principle of unity had, for Augustine, priority over all else. Once it was established, adventure and discovery might follow; but they may not precede its establishment and, above all, they may not imperil it. That was why he, and those who agreed with him, could not admit of an inhabited Antipodes; and it is hard from the subsequent history of exploration and discovery to prove them wholly wrong.

The question of the Antipodes, then, in the early Middle Ages, was a test; and it was a test in pursuit of an end far from superstitious. Linked as it was with the question of the fabled monstrous races, it was a test of the attitude of man to man. Wide tolerance and extended human sympathy demanded that the answer to the question about the monsters be the opposite of the answer to the question about the Antipo-

[38]Early settlers in the American colonies, for example, and early travellers to Africa were, when it came to the point, unprepared to accept Indians and Negroes as truly man. A way was then made open for the justification of such a position, and such justifications began, accordingly, to appear; Hodgen (n. 25 above) 416–424. (Albertus Magnus cannot, however, be credited with the first expression of the idea of an intermediate class of creatures between animals and man. Tertullian, for instance, clearly held a similar view; "Tertium genus dicimur cynopennae aliqui vel sciapodes vel aliqui de subterranea antipodes"; *Ad nationes* 1.7; PL 1.640). It was a short step now to the decision that inferior man-beasts ought to be subjected by right to the will of superior humans, even to a position similar to that of Riolan on monsters. This step was taken too; L. Hanke, *Aristotle and the American Indians: A Study in Race Prejudice in the Modern World* (London 1959) 40–48, 68–73, 76–78; and idem, *All Mankind Is One* (De Kalb, Ill. 1974), 34–56. For the ill-sustained efforts of Pope Paul III to defend the rights of the American Indians to humane treatment, in the bull "Sublimis Deus" of 1537, see Hanke, "Pope Paul III and the American Indians," *Harvard Theological Review* 30 (1937) 65–102. My attention was drawn to this bull at the Dumbarton Oaks seminar (see n. 1 above).
[39]"As long as all men were considered brethren in the family of God, *as long as no efforts were made to classify some men among the beasts* [italics hers], as long as no political or economic interest called for a theoretical imputation of debasement with respect to any group of dependent people, neither skin color nor the natural anxiety caused by conflict with enemies such as the Muslims or Tartars led to anything like what we now know as racial 'tension' "; Hodgen (n. 25 above) 213–214.

IV

des; belief in the possible humanity of accessible monsters involved disbelief in the existence of the inaccessible and possibly monstrous inhabitants of the Antipodes. The moral growth of mankind seemed, on this argument, to require an absolute denial of the idea of an inhabited Antipodes. This denial in the eighth century Zachary gave; this denial the "enlightenment" refused. We cannot prove that Zachary's stand did in fact help towards the extension of human sympathy;[40] but we can, I think, now argue that it was meant to do so. We can also note that the expansion in the period of the enlightenment, of a "scientific" attitude to the Antipodes, and its condemnation of Zachary, was accompanied by a singular contraction in the matter of humane behavior. On these grounds alone the approach of the early Middle Ages to monsters and the Antipodes deserves some reconsideration, and perhaps some defense.

Department of History
University of Auckland
Auckland, New Zealand

[40]Ratramnus of Corbie in the ninth century is still involved in the apparently unresolved question of whether Cynocephali should be considered a part of the human race, and his line of reasoning is not as liberal as that of Augustine. His tests for admission are more severe, requiring civilized rational behavior and sexual compunction, and he refuses to accept all monstrous births as human: *Epistola de Cynocephalis*, PL 121.1153–1156.

V

THE CAREER
OF HONORIUS AUGUSTODUNENSIS

SOME FRESH EVIDENCE

The problem of the career of Honorius Augustodunensis is an extremely testing one. This article cannot pretend to solve it. It seeks instead to extend the discussion of it to include some new material. This new material has come to light in the course of an attempt to locate and examine the surviving twelfth century manuscripts of Honorius's works ; and it is hoped that it will at least suggest that Honorius may have been associated with two places quite new to the scene. The places are the abbey of Lambach, in Austria, and the cathedral priory of Worcester, in England. The attempt which follows to explore this evidence falls into three sections : (I) the évidence for an association between Honorius and Lambach, (II) the evidence for an association between Honorius and Worcester, (III) the possible impact of the new material upon previous hypotheses.

I. THE EVIDENCE FOR AN ASSOCIATION
BETWEEN HONORIUS AND LAMBACH

Two surprising facts have emerged from an attempt to compile a hand list of surviving twelfth century Austrian manuscripts of Honorius. The first of these is that the abbey of Lambach can claim the largest share of the surviving manuscripts. Eight Lambach books can be identified now, containing between them fifteen of Honorius's known works, and some small fragments which are rare, and which are also probably by him. VIENNA N.B. 382, a manuscript of the *Summa Totius* formerly owned by Lambach, is the only twelfth century manuscript of this work which survives. Two manuscripts of works, by Honorius, and at the abbey of Lambach now, deserve special notice.¹ One, LAMBACH CXXXIX, is a manuscript of a collection of sermons and observations drawn primarily from Honorius's *Speculum Ecclesiae* and *Gemma Animae*. This work could be the lost *Refectio Mentium*. Another is a manuscript of the *Gemma Animae* which has an unique addition. They will be described in detail below.

The second surprising fact is that a list of Honorius's works, contained in a twelfth century manuscript at the abbey of Göttweig, (GÖTTWEIG 14, fol. 148ᵛ), is apparently unique. This list, written in a twelfth century hand, has been known about for some time, ² but has somehow escaped a detailed examination. The percentage of the works in the list which are works by Honorius himself is a very high one. All save three of the first twenty three works listed are certainly by Honorius, and one of the three may be by him. Of the fifty works listed twenty two are his. The descriptions used in the list, moreover, are in places markedly similar to the descriptions used by Honorius in his account of his own works in the *De Luminaribus Ecclesiae*. ³ The Göttweig list contains every work named in the *De Luminaribus*, with the possible exception of the "evangelia quod beatus Gregorius non exposuit". The connexion, therefore, between this list and Honorius is a close one.

The list is in fact a list of a gift of books made by a certain "Heinricus". It has about it one other particularly interesting aspect ; that is, that it may not have been made to Göttweig at all. Few of the works mentioned in it can be found in abbey catalogues or in the library of Göttweig now, and the manuscript

---

1. The librarian of Lambach, Hofrat Dr. Hans Zedinek, and his assistant, Frau Edeltraut Korompay, gave me generous help. I am deeply indebted to them, and to the administrator and community of the abbey for their hospitality.

2. The list of books was printed by MIGNE, *PL* 172, 34-5, and then in T. GOTTLIEB, *Mittelalterliche Bibliothekscataloge Österreichs*, I, Vienna, 1915, 11-12. Gottlieb refers to the manuscript as Göttweig 33, but it has since been re-catalogued.

3. *PL* 172, 232-234. Doubts have been expressed about the authenticity of this passage, but not, it seems to me, with good cause. The objection that Honorius would not boast about his own work is not easy to sustain when one reads his own prefaces. For the rest, the passage appears without any sign of interpolation in the two earliest extant manuscripts, KLOSTERNEUBURG 949 and ZWETTL 225, and its last sentence is picked up in some manuscripts of the *Imago Mundi* ; « Quis post hunc regnum adepturus sit posteritas videbit ». Mss. MUNICH *Clm.* 22225, CAMBRIDGE *Corpus Christi College* 66, LONDON *British Museum* Harley 4348, Royal 13 A xxi.

of the gift does not mention Göttweig by name; "huic contulit ecclesiae" is all we have. H. Menhardt, in a masterly effort to draw together all that was known of the legacy of Honorius, made the extremely tentative alternative suggestion of Lambach. [1] The emergence of more information about the Lambach manuscripts of Honorius's works encouraged a further exploration of this suggestion. I have therefore made an attempt to trace other twelfth century Lambach manuscripts which would fit the descriptions given in the gift. Of the works not by Honorius a possible seven existing manuscripts can be traced, and a further thirteen can be found mentioned in Lambach catalogues. The medieval catalogues are, unfortunately, incomplete, but even so this is a large number. It is certainly larger than the number which can be associated with Göttweig. The presence at Göttweig of a manuscript recording a gift to Lambach can easily be explained. Relations between Göttweig and Lambach were, and indeed are, close. Göttweig gave shelter to a group of Lambach monks very early in the history of the foundation. [2]

It may be convenient at this point to set out the evidence for the proposed association between the gift of Frater Heinricus and the abbey of Lambach in tabular form. In the first column, the books in the gift are set out in the order in which they appear, and with the names given to them. In the second, those Lambach manuscripts which survive and which fit the descriptions are listed against them. The third column marks books which appear by name in certain catalogues of the abbey library, but which seem since to have disappeared from the abbey. Three surviving book lists have been consulted ; two are twelfth / thirteenth century ones, and are numbered [1] and [2] ; the third is the most recent complete one, made in the eighteenth century by P.F. Resch (d. 1789), and in manuscript at the abbey now [3]. Many of the books which appear in the first two catalogues have been traced by K. Holter. [3] The list of the

1. H. MENHARDT, Der Nachlass des Honorius Augustodunensis, in Zeitschrift für Deutsches Altertum und Deutsche Literatur 89 (1958), 30, 51-4. Gottlieb, ubi supra p. 9, had been worried about it : « Der Einband weicht von sämtlichen anderen Hss. der Bibliothek ab... Und schon Bernh. Pez, Thesaur. anecd. II (1721) p.xi hatte bemerkt, dass fast alle Bücher dieser « Schenkung » überhaupt und besonders in Göttweig vermisst werden ».
2. Vita Adalberonis Episcopi Wirziburgensis, MGH SS XII, 136-7.
3. K. HOLTER, Zwei Lambacher Bibliotheksverzeichnisse des 13. Jahrhunderts, in Mitteilungen des Instituts für Österreichisches Geschichtsforschung 64 (1956),

66

gift of Frater Heinricus is written in prose form across the folio. It is set out in columns here merely for convenience. The list ends "nota quinquaginta libri". The titles cannot describe fifty codices for some of the works mentioned are very slight indeed. Nor, if the following identifications are correct, can the works be listed in the order in which they appear in the codices. The word "item" seems, in the list, to mark not the beginning of a codex but a work by the same author of, or of a type similar to, the one named before. The list gives, then, no information about the size and constitution of separate volumes, but is a rough description of contents only. I have underlined those of the works named which are certainly by Honorius. The descriptions given in the list for the *Offendiculum*, the *Eucharistion*, the *Neocosmus* and the *Summa Gloria* are precisely the same as those given by Honorius in the *De Luminaribus*, and the *Expositio Psalterii* and *In Cantica Canticorum* are praised in both in similar words.

Isti sunt libri, quos frater Heinricus huic contulit ecclesie.

Psalterium insigniter expositum.

Cantica Canticorum mirabiliter exposita.	BALTIMORE, *Walters Art Gallery* 387	[2] [3] XLIV
Matheus glosatus.	VIENNA *N.B.* s.n. 3604	[2] [3] XCVI
Apocalipsis exposita.	LAMBACH VI, Bede and Haimo	[2]
Item Cantica Canticorum cum glosis.		? [3] LXXIX, Bede and Gregory in Cant.
Clavis phisice, scilicet de perifision excerptus.	VIENNA *N.B.* s.n. 3605	
Speculum Ecclesie, in quo sermones dulcissimi ad populum.	*Bodley* Lyell 56	[2]
Refectio Mentium, in quo sermones ad fratres in capitulo.	? LAMBACH CXXXIX	
Pabulum Vite, in quo sermones in festis diebus.		
Elucidarium bene correctum.	VIENNA *N.B.* 807	[2]
Offendiculum de incontinentia sacerdotum.		

271-6. I have not been able to see the first list. The second, on fol. 227ᵛ of LAMBACH XIX, appears to me, however, to be in a twelfth-century hand. Unhappily a part of the list is missing.

Eucharistion de corpore domini.		
Neocosmus de VI primis diebus.	BALTIMORE, *Walters Art Gallery* 387	[3] XLIV
Scala celi de tribus celis.	*Bodley* Lyell 56	
Gemma Animae de divinis sacramentis.	LAMBACH XXXV	[2]
Sacramentarium de mysteriis.	*Bodley* Lyell 56	
Summa Totius, in quo cronica ab initio mundi usque ad nostra tempora.	VIENNA *N.B.* 382	
Imago Mundi, in quo totus mundus describitur.		
Summa Gloria de apostolico et Augusto.	*Bodley* Lyell 56	
Suum quid virtutis, De virtutibus et vitiis.	*Bodley* Lyell 56	
Sigillum Sancte Marie, in quo cantica ad personam sancte Marie exponuntur.	BALTIMORE, *Walters Art Gallery* 387	[3] XLIV
Cognitio vite.	*Bodley* Lyell 56	
Inevitabile, in quo de libero arbitrio et predestinatione et gratia dei disputatur.	*Bodley* Lyell 56	
Anshelmus de libero arbitrio.		
Eucherius de hebreis nominibus.	? VIENNA *N.B.* s.n. 3612	
Ysidorus breviter super totam bibliothecam.		
Item sententie Ysidori de utroque testamenti.	VIENNA *N.B.* s.n. 4837	
Thimeus Platonis.		
Bucolica Virgilii.		
Theodolus.		[1]
Musica Odonis.		[1] Musica Guidonis
Serenus de medicina arte, in quo excerpta Bede de Gallieno et Ypocrate.		? [3] CXI Liber Physicorum
Abacus Gerlandi.		
Priscianus adbreviatus.		[3] CXXII
Abbo de regulis.		[1] Libellus regularum
Focus de arte grammatica.		
Item libellus de penultimis.		
Libellus versuum, in quo Vita Marie Egiptiace et novus Cato.		? [3] C Codex metricus ; Petrus Abaelardus

V

68

Rethorica Alcuini.		? [1] Disputatio Albini cum Karolo de dialectica
Excerpta de Martiano.		
Priscianus constructionum, in quo et exemplar metrorum.		[3] CXLVII
Liber orationum.		[3] CLVI
Liber *de Luminaribus ecclesie*, id est de scriptoribus ecclesiasticis.		
Liber in quo sancte cantilene.		
Excerpta de libris sancti Augustini *de deo et anima*.	*Bodley* Lyell 56	
Questiones diverse.	*Bodley* Lyell 56	[3] LXXIX Orosius
	? Vienna *N.B.* 807	[3] CI Augustine
Glose diverse.	Vienna *N.B.* s.n. 3600 3602 3603 3604	
Computus Dyonisii grece, in quo abacus et mappa mundi.		
Martyrologium in quo diverse pagine computi.	? Lambach XLII	[2] [3] CXXXI
Rodale in quo VII liberales artes depicte.		
Item rodale, in quo Troianum bellum depictum.		
Item rodale, in quo varia pictura.		
Item quaternio depictus.		
Nota quinguaginta libri.		

Some of the manuscripts which I have set beside the descriptions in the gift deserve special attention. One is Vienna *N.B.* 807. This was at some point the property of the Schottenkloster of St. Mary in Vienna, for it carries an ascription on fol. 1. The ascription is written however in a hand later than the hand of the scribe. This manuscript contains a particularly well corrected *Elucidarius*, and the sets of *Quaestiones, In Proverbia,* and *In Ecclesiasten, In Johannem* and *In Mattheum* of which I have previously argued Honorius was the author. [1] The copy

---

1. V.I.J. Flint, *The true author of the Salonii Commentarii in Parabolas Salomonis et in Ecclesiasten,* in *Recherches de Théologie ancienne et médiévale* 37 (1970), 174-186.

of the *Elucidarius* contains the later variant for II 7, and a series of marginal additions which are, without exception, drawn from the last recension. [1] It fits, therefore, better than any manuscript I have examined, the description "Elucidarium bene correctum" of the gift. The four sets of *Quaestiones*, moreover, are closely associated with the *Glossa Ordinaria* on *Proverbs*, *Ecclesiastes* and *John*, and with glosses on Matthew. Three twelfth-century Lambach manuscripts of the *Glossa Ordinaria* of the first three books survive now, VIENNA N.B. *Series Nova* 3603, 3600, and a further most important exemplar of an anonymous gloss on Matthew, again from Lambach, is very closely related to these particular *Quaestiones in Mattheum*. This gloss is now VIENNA N.B. *Series Nova* 3604, another Lambach manuscript. Because of the closeness of the relationship, this manuscript has been set against the "Matheus glosatus" of the gift. It is just possible that this gloss is by Honorius himself. Honorius says in the *De Luminaribus* that he wrote an "evangelia quae beatus Gregorius non exposuit". The only considerable work by Honorius which does not appear in the gift is this "evangelia", and it has not indeed been identified. Menhardt points out, however, that St. Matthew would be a good candidate for such an exposition, for Gregory only devoted eleven of his *Homeliae in Evangelia* to him. [2] It is not possible yet to decide upon this, and the "evangelia" may have been, as Endres suggested, an homiletic supplement to Gregory. [3] This particular manuscript seems, however, to deserve careful treatment. [4] As I have argued for the attribution to Honorius of these particular *Quaestiones*, so, because this examplar of them is in the same hand as the "Elucidarium bene correctum", I have included it tentatively among the "Questiones diverse" of the gift. Because, too, of the relationship between the *Quaestiones* and the *Glossa*

---

1. See V.I.J. FLINT, *The original text of the Elucidarium of Honorius Augustodunensis from the twelfth century English manuscripts*, in *Scriptorium* 17 (1964), 91-94.
2. H. MENHARDT, *Der Nachlass des Honorius Augustodunensis*, ubi supra, p. 56.
3. J-A. ENDRES, *Honorius Augustodunensis*, Kempten-Munich, 1906, p. 61.
4. The *Quaestiones in Mattheum* are throughout very closely related to VIENNA N.B. s.n. 3604, but the question of Honorius's authorship of the latter cannot be satisfactorily solved until we know more about the early tradition of glosses on St. Matthew.

Ordinaria, I have included the above Lambach manuscripts of these, but again tentatively, among the "Glose diverse". Also among the *Series Nova* manuscripts of the Nationalbibliothek, Vienna, is a fine examplar from Lambach of the Gloss on the Canonical Epistles.

A particularly interesting manuscript is LAMBACH CXXXIX. (Twelfth century, vellum 5" x 7", single cols., 23 lines, rubricated headings, much abbreviated, same hand until last three folios.) This manuscript contains a collection of heavily compressed sermons, beginning with the first sunday in Advent. There is no title and no author's name until fol. 32 when the note "Onorius. Gemma Animae" appears. The text is, for the most part, composed of selections from the *Speculum Ecclesiae* and the *Gemma Animae.* Selections from the *Speculum Ecclesiae* are to be found on folios 6ᵛ, 10ᵛ-11, 14, 32-52, 56ᵛ-88. They come from *PL* 172, 845, 853, 895, 965-1106, 815-958. Folios 90-118 contain selections from the *Gemma Animae,* differently arranged. The arrangement begins at Book IV of the *Gemma Animae,* and goes through it, and then proceeds through Books I, II and III, selecting and compressing, often by a curious system of alternative chapters. Folios 1-32 and 118-125 contain selections I have not yet been able to trace. The story of Thais, referred to twice in Honorius's *Speculum Ecclesiae,* appears on fol. 70, in the same form as in WORCESTER F.48 (see section two). The suspicion that this manuscript may be the lost *Refectio Mentium* springs from a note on fol. 125 (in a hand different from that of most of the text) : "Fidelis anima tamquam bono terre suo frumento refecta dicit". The description of the *Refectio Mentium* given in the gift of Frater Heinricus points out that it was addressed to the brothers in chapter ; certainly the understanding of this abbreviated collection, often of references only, demands a certain amount of prior knowledge.

A last important manuscript is LAMBACH XXXV, the *Gemma Animae.* (Twelfth century, vellum 8" x 10", double cols., 30 lines, same hand throughout.) This manuscript has an addition to the *Gemma Animae,* written in the same hand as the text, and attached, without differentiation, to the end of it, fol. 95ᵛ-96ᵛ. The additional passage describes the translation of Pagan Roman honours, of many kinds, into Christian terms. The emperor has his equivalent in the pope, the patricius in the patriarch, the rex in the archbishop, and so on. Particular attention is paid to the symbolism of the Roman triumph and

V

the Christian rendering of it, for example in the celebrations of Palm Sunday. Honorius used symbolism of this sort in his *Speculum Ecclesiae* (*PL* 172, 955 f.), and also in his *Gemma Animae* (I, LXXii-LXXviii). Small sections of this addition appear in an almost identical form in the text of the *Gemma Animae*, for example fol. 96ᵛ :

> Propter tres causas sunt picture vel imagines in ecclesia, prima propter ornatum, secunda quod est litteratura laicorum, tercia quia sunt admonitiones clericorum.

The *Gemma Animae* I, cxxxii :

> Laquerarium picturae sunt exempla justorum, quae Ecclesiae repraesentant ornamentum morum. Ob tres autem causas fit pictura : primo, quia est laicorum litteratura : secundo, ut domus tali decore ornetur ; tertio, ut priorum vita in memoriam revocetur.

The passage is, therefore, closely connected with Honorius's work. It may be a summary of his thoughts upon this theme put together by himself. The defence of pictures is interesting. A magnificent series of romanesque frescoes of the late eleventh century have recently been discovered at Lambach.

One notable omission in the range of Honorius manuscripts from Lambach is the *Imago Mundi*. No exemplar of this can yet be certainly associated with Lambach. [1] One Windberg manuscript, however, now at Munich, *Clm.* 22225, as a collection bears a striking resemblance to the Lambach collection of Honorius in Ms. *Bodley* Lyell 56, and contains an unique version of this text. It is, then possible that this version is related to a lost Lambach exemplar. If this were so, this would be exciting, for the Windberg version of the *Imago Mundi* appears to represent an early stage in the composition of the work.

It appears from this investigation that it is at least conceivable that the gift of Frater Heinricus was made to Lambach, and that, if this is so, the fact that the gift contains so high a proportion of the works of Honorius explains the large number of twelfth century

---

1. ZWETTL 172 was not always at Zwettl, for it bears the monogram of Otto Gnembhertl, "plebanus S. Marie Virginis in littore in Wienna", fol. 1. It is a most interesting manuscript of the early twelfth century, and contains, before the *Imago Mundi*, a collection of complex computistical texts and diagrams of precisely the kind Honorius seems, in this work, to be trying to explain.

Lambach manuscripts of his works which survive. It may, however, be possible to advance a little further than this, and this with the help of one further early manuscript, again now at Lambach, LAMBACH XXVII.

LAMBACH XXVII (late eleventh/early twelfth century, vellum 7¼" x 9½", fol. 80, single cols., 30 lines, rubricated headings, same hand throughout) contains a compilation, in three books, of extracts from works on the liturgy. The extracts are not identified in the text, but are in fact drawn from the *Liber Officialis* and the *Eclogae* of Amalarius, the *De Divinis Officiis* of the Pseudo-Alcuin, the *De Divinis Officiis* of Isidore, and from sources I have not yet been able to identify. The extracts are arranged without division and in a haphazard manner within the three books. The books deal, respectively, with the major feasts (to fol. 23), the mass and the canonical hours (to fol. 61) and with the externals of the liturgy, buildings, vestments, special prayers and rites. The special interest of this manuscript lies in the fact that it appears to be related in an unique way to two of Honorius's works, the *Gemma Animae* and the *Sacramentarium*. In these two works Honorius uses all the sources named above. The *Gemma Animae* and the *Sacramentarium* are, however, closely related to LAMBACH XXVII itself by the fact that Honorius, on a number of occasions, uses his extracts in the order in which they appear in this manuscript. This order is not always an obvious one. In order to make the closeness of the relationship apparent, it is again set out in tabular form. The left-hand column contains references to the sources of the Lambach compilation in the order in which they appear. The right-hand columns contain references to those chapters in Honorius's works which use these sources in this order.

Lambach XXVII		*Gemma Animae*	*Sacramentarium*
		Honorius	
fol. 1	Amalarius III xl	III i	
fol. 3	Amalarius I xli	III xiv	
fol. 4	Pseudo-Alcuin V	} III xviii-xx	lxviii
fol. 4ᵛ	?	} III xxx	lxviii
fol. 5	Amalarius IV xxxiv	III xxi	
fol. 5-5ᵛ	Pseudo-Alcuin VII	III xxiv	
fol. 5ᵛ-7	Amalarius I i-iii	III xxxvii-viii ; xl	i-iii
fol. 7	Amalarius I iv-vi	III xliv-xlv	V
fol. 7ᵛ	Amalarius I vii	III xli-xlii	IV
		III xliii	

fol. 9v-10	Amalarius I ix / Pseudo-Alcuin XIV	} III lxxx-xxxii / lxxxviii	} VIII (both chpts in order)
fol. 10v-11	Amalarius I xii / Pseudo-Alcuin XVII		} X (both chpts in order)
fol. 13	Pseudo-Alcuin XVIII	III xciv, xcvii	
fol. 14-14v	Amalarius I xviii, xvii, xxi, xix	III ci-cii / III ciii, cvi-cvii	XII / XII
fol. 15v	Amalarius I xxviii	III cx	XII
fol. 16	Amalarius I xxv-xxvi	III cxi	
fol. 16v	Isidore II xxv / Pseudo-Alcuin XIX / Amalarius I xxvi	} III cxi-cxii	
fol. 17v-18	?	III cxv	
fol. 18	Amalarius I xxxi	III cxviii	XII
fol. 18v	Amalarius I xxxiv / I xxix	III cxxxiii	XV
fol. 19	Amalarius I xxxii / Pseudo-Alcuin XXI	}	XIII / XIII
fol. 20	Amalarius I xxxiii		XIV
fol. 20v	?	III cxxxviii	XIX
fol. 21	Amalarius I xxxvii-xxxviii / xxix	III cxlvi / III cxlix	XX
fol. 23	Amalarius II i	III cliv	XXI
fol. 24-25	Amalarius II ii / Amalarius II xiv		XXII / XXII-XXIII
fol. 25	Amalarius II iii	III clii	XXIII
fol. 26v	Isidore II iv		XXIII
fol. 27-28	Pseudo-Alcuin XXXVI / Pseudo-Alcuin XXXIV / » XXVI / » XXIV / » XXVI		XXIII / XXIV / XXIV / XXIV
fol. 65	Pseudo-Alcuin XXIX / Amalarius II xxi	} I ccxi-ccxii	XXIV
fol. 66v-67	Amalarius II xxiii / Pseudo-Alcuin XXIX	} I ccxxii / »	

Some of the sections for which no source has as yet been found are reflected in the *Gemma Animae* and the *Sacramentarium*. For example, on fol. 17v the text leaves Isidore at II, xxv, and continues :

> Patrini vero illorum previdere debent ut cum ad intellegibilem etatem pervenerint, fide et bonis operibus instruant seu orationem dominicam vel simbolum eos instanter erudiant. Quod si neglexerint norint se rationem pro eis reddituros ante deum, quorum fide iussores existerunt.

74

A corresponding passage is to be found in the *Gemma Animae* III,
cxv :

> Sacerdos omnes infantes de baptismo levat, et iedo omnium pater et
> debitor fideique jussor manet. Sed quia debitum jus singulis persolvere
> minime praevalet, ideo eos patrinis commendat, ut ipsi eos fidem
> catholicam et orationem Dominicam instruant... Nullus nisi unus vel
> una ad levandum infantem accedat, iisque se fidejussorem illius sciat,
> ut ita eum, sicut suscepit, restituat. Quod si eum Christianitatem
> docere neglexerit, pro eo supplicium subibit.

Fol. 4 also :

> Canitur tamen *venite* pro sexto psalmo ea videlicet ratione quoniam
> vocatio gentium facta est in sexta mundi etate. Secunda antiphona
> *fluminis impetus* letificat civitatem dei quae est ordine secunda.
> Canitur alleliua quia nimirum post vocationem gentium sequitur
> baptisma, quod proprie sonat prenominata antiphona. Tertia noc-
> turna tangit novum testamentum quod inicium habet a baptismo.
> Qua propter habet in capite antiphonam fluminis impetus letificat
> cum alleliua. Que antiphona cum psalmo suo adliquidum sonat de
> novo testamento sequentes similiter. *Cantate domino canticum novum.*
> Psalmus aperte narrat de novo testamento. Similiter *dominus regnavit
> exultet terra.* Qui tres psalmi monstrant precipue perturbationem et
> commotionem gentilium contre predicationem apostolorum et subver-
> sionem ydolorum atque conversionem christianorum.

In LAMBACH XXVII, this passage follows an extract from the
Pseudo-Alcuin V. Passages exactly similar to this follow chapters
modelled upon *Pseudo-Alcuin* V in the *Gemma Animae* III, xx,
and the *Sacramentarium* LXVIII.

So far these fragments of evidence about the number and
distribution of Honorius's in Austria are, in separation, significant.
In separation, if we do not believe that the gift of Frater Heinricus
was made to Lambach, it still remains true that Lambach was
interested in Honorius's works to a quite singular degree, and
that, in LAMBACH XXVII, it may have furnished Honorius
with a source for two of them. Not far away, at Göttweig,
there was a similar centre of interest in the form of a devoted
collector of Honorius's works. In combination, however, the
fragments may be part of an exciting larger construction. If the
gift was made to Lambach, then it might, as I have said, account
for the presence there of so many Honorius manuscripts. It
does not, however, account for LAMBACH XXVII, which is not
mentioned in it ; and it does not account for the concern of the
donor with Honorius. It is hardly satisfactory to explain away
the uniqueness of this collection in terms of the possible disap-

pearance of others. We have here something singular, not easily dismissed. There is one solution which would resolve all these conflicts. It cannot be proved to be the right one, but it has much to recommend it. This is, that Frater Heinricus was in fact Honorius himself, attached at some point to the community of Lambach, and, understandably, an enthusiastic collector of his own works.

There is one quite independent support for this thesis. The author of Honorius's *Imago Mundi* is, in an important twelfth century manuscript of this work, Ms. *Corpus Christi College, CAMBRIDGE, 66*, described as a canon *Henricus*, and this name has persisted in the English tradition of the *Imago Mundi*, so much so that it is often ascribed in early catalogues to Henry of Huntingdon. One other important English manuscript, the earliest exemplar we have of Honorius's *Sigillum*, Ms. *Jesus College*, OXFORD, 54, has, on the first folio and written in an early twelfth century hand, "Nobilis henrici cuius pereunt inimici". Honorius appears to have wished to conceal his identity, [1] and he certainly adopted, in Augustodunensis, a surname which has confused large numbers of historians. Dom Bauerreiss suggested that he adopted the name Honorius whilst he was in England. [2] It is not, therefore, impossible that his name, before he took Honorius, was Henricus ; and that Honorius himself, in token of his associations with Lambach, made this gift, consisting so largely of his own works, to the abbey.

II. HONORIUS AND WORCESTER

It has long been accepted that Honorius spent at least a part of his career in England. So far, all attempted reconstructions of Honorius's life have agreed that his English associations were with Canterbury. The evidence which has led to this conclusion is good ; the dependence of Honorius's works upon the works of St. Anselm, and the greetings to the Canterbury brethren in some manuscripts of the *Speculum Ecclesiae* and the *Gemma Animae*. It is not, however, completely compelling.

---

1. *Elucidarius*, preface : « Nomen autem meum ideo volui silentio contegi, ne invidia tabescens suis juberet utile opus contemnendo negligi. » Y. LEFÈVRE, *L'Elucidarium et les Lucidaires*, Paris, 1954, p. 360.
2. R. BAUERREISS, *Zur Herkunft des Honorius Augustodunensis*, in *Studien und Mitteilungen zur Geschichte des Benediktiner Ordens* 53 (1935), 32.

The preface to the *Speculum Ecclesiae* makes it clear that Honorius spent some time at Canterbury ; "cum proxime in nostro conventu resideres", say the brothers in their request for the work ; but it does not make it equally clear that he spent all his time in England there. It is in fact possible that the accepted picture of Honorius's career in England can be adjusted, again with the help of the manuscript evidence. This is not great in quantity, but the little there is suggests an association not with Canterbury but with the diocese of Worcester.

Again, as with Lambach, the first hint of this comes from the examination of the surviving manuscripts. The largest number of surviving twelfth century manuscripts of Honorius's works which can be assigned to a certain place in England must be assigned to the diocese of Worcester. Four come from Worcester itself, and one from Evesham (the early copy of the *Sigillum* mentioned above, Ms. *Jesus College*, OXFORD, 54). No important early manuscript can be assigned with certainty to Canterbury. This reconstruction of the distribution of English manuscripts is not of itself, of course, significant ; it is erected over too many gaps in the evidence. Taken together with other, rather sounder, facts however, it is indicative. These are set out below in what seems to be the order of their importance.

1. Large sections of Honorius's *Speculum Ecclesiae* appear to have been drawn from collections of the lives of saints. Two early English copies of the earliest large collection of saints' lives in use in England survive now, Mss. *Bodley* Fell 1 and 4, of the early twelfth century, from Salisbury, and Mss. *Corpus Christi College*, CAMBRIDGE, 9, and *British Museum* Cotton Nero E i (the same collection, but deposited in two places), of the eleventh century, from Worcester. [1] The second collection is known as the *Worcester Passionale*. There are marked similarities between the *Speculum Ecclesiae* and the *Worcester Passionale*. I have not found a similar combination of materials in any south German or Austrian manuscript which Honorius could have used. [2] The Fell books do not contain the sermons

---

1. N.R. KER, *Salisbury Cathedral Manuscripts and Patrick Young's Catalogue*, in *The Wiltshire Archaeological and Natural History Magazine* 191 (1949), 178-79.

2. A summary of this material, including that of the English manuscripts, is to be found in W. LEVISON, *Conspectus Codicum Hagiographicorum, MGH Scriptores Rerum Merovingiarum* VII, 2 (1920).

from which Honorius seems to quote, and they are in any case perhaps a little too late for the *Speculum Ecclesiae*. [1] Similarities are to be found in the following sections.

a) The sermon on the Purification.

> Augustine : " Exultent virgines, virgo peperit christum, nihil in ea quod vovet putent exterminatum, mansit virgo post partum. Exultent vidue infantem christum vidua anna cognovit. Exultent coniugate nasciturum christum elizabeth nupta prophetavit. Nullus gradus praetermissus est, de quo non haberet testimonium " (*CCCC* 9, fol. 140).

> Honorius : " Virgines exultent et Christo devotis laudibus persultent, quia virgo Maria mundo Salvatorem edidit qui castis virginibus coelestia munero tribuit. Viduae gaudeant et Christo votive plaudant, quem vidua Anna hodie cum Symeone templo intulit, qui continentes coeli templo inducit. Conjugatae jocundentur et Christo laudes consono ore modulentur, ad cujus matris ingressum Elizabeth maritata, Spiritu sancto repleta, prophetavit, qui in legitimo conjugio viventes in coelesti thalamo sibi copulabit " (*PL* 172, 851).

> Augustine : " Agnovit symeon infantem tacentem ... Cum ergo cognovisset accepit eum in ulnas suas hoc est in brachia sua amplexatus est eum " (fol. 140ᵛ).

> Honorius : " hunc hodie senex Symeon tremulis ulnis portat " (*PL* 172, 851).

In the next section of his sermon Honorius expands on the fact that all ages welcome the coming of Christ and his miracles. An anonymous sermon in the *Passionale* makes this statement : "omnis aetas et uterque sexus eventorum miracula, fidem credenti generationem eius affirmant" (fol. 141ᵛ). This sermon also enters into a discussion of the symbolism of the offering made by Mary in the temple. So does Honorius, and although their interpretations are very slightly different, they are by no means incompatible (*PL* 172, 850-1).

b) The sermon on the Nativity of the Blessed Virgin Mary.
The story of Joachim and Anna in this sermon is a clear and good paraphrase of the story told in the sermon on the same subject in the *Passionale* (*PL* 172, 1000 ; Cotton Nero E i, fol. 322ᵛ-324).

c) The sermon on the Exaltation of the Cross.
The story of Cosdras of Persia in this sermon is a paraphrase

---

1. LEVISON, *ibid.*, p. 545, points out that the Fell manuscript and the *Worcester Passionale* depend for the saints' lives upon a common source, now lost. Honorius can, of course, be supposed then perhaps to have drawn upon this lost source for the lives ; but this still does not account for the sermons.

of the same story in the *Passionale* (*PL* 172, 1004-5 ; *Passionale*, fols 373-4).

d) The lives of the saints.

Honorius speaks of saints Sebastian, Agnes, Vincent in this order (*PL* 172, 857-60). Their lives occur in this order in the *Passionale* and give him the information he uses and many of the words. Other lives of saints apparently drawn directly from the *Passionale* are these ; St. Agatha (*PL* 172, 861-2, fols 148-149ᵛ) ; St. Laurence and St. Hippolytus (*PL* 172, 989-92, fols 275-279) ; St. Maurice (*PL* 172, 1005-08, fols 343ᵛ-345ᵛ) ; St. Dionysius (*PL* 172, 1011-14, fols 88ᵛ-100ᵛ) ; St. Martin and St. Briccius (*PL* 172, 1021-6, fols 139ᵛ-151) ; St. Cecilia (*PL* 172, 1027-31, fols 162-168ᵛ) ; and St. Nicholas (*PL* 172, 1033-8, fols 13ᵛ-26ᵛ).

2. The *Sigillum* and Worcester.

Four of the five surviving twelfth century English manuscripts of the *Sigillum* are associated with the diocese of Worcester, and three with Worcester itself. The *Worcester Passionale* (fol. 285) contains the "Cogitis me" of Paschasius, upon which large sections of the *Sigillum* are modelled. The *Passionale* also contains two of the miracle stories mentioned in the *Sigillum*, Theophilus and Mary of Egypt (fols 155, 177).

3. Ms. CAMBRIDGE *University Library* Kk iv 6.

This manuscript, written in the hand of John of Worcester, contains a heavily corrected copy of the *Elucidarius* (group 1). The text of the *Elucidarius* is followed by another series of questions and answers (fols 60-62ᵛ) in a hand similar to that which performed most of the corrections. A section of the additional series has been printed, in a somewhat confusing manner, by J.B. Pitra. [1] Pitra prints it, apparently, as the third section of the *Testimonia Fidei* of Augustine. The manuscript from which he takes the preceding passages, and the one following this, (NAMUR 64) does not however contain this particular section. I have only found it in this Cambridge manuscript. The questions and answers are about isolated points arising, it seems, from the discussion of the Old Testament. There is no reference in them to their author, and no distinction is made

---

1. *Analecta Sacra Spicilegio Solesmensi Parata* 5 (1888), 160. I am most grateful to the Librarian and Assistant Librarian of the Cathedral Library of Worcester for allowing me to explore the resources of the collection now at the Cathedral.

V

in the manuscript between them and the *Elucidarius*. They are certainly in the style of Honorius ; it is not impossible that they are by him. If this is so, then the association between Honorius and Worcester is upheld, for they may be a record, otherwise lost, of his teaching there. The least that can be said of this manuscript is that it shews there was a lively interest early in the twelfth century in Honorius's work at Worcester. The same manuscript (fol. 216) contains the *Sigillum*.

4. The *Speculum Ecclesiae* and the *Liber Comitis* of Smaragdus, WORCESTER F.91.

For other sections of the *Speculum Ecclesiae*, Honorius draws upon the *Liber Comitis* of Smaragdus (*PL* 102, 13-552). The correspondence between the two early works begins at Septuagesima Sunday. Worcester cathedral has an early eleventh-century copy of the *Liber Comitis* (WORCESTER F.91) which itself begins at Septuagesima Sunday (*PL* 102, 99). This is not a common work.

5. Work upon the liturgy was of interest at Worcester in the eleventh and twelfth centuries. One of the most important Worcester manuscripts which gives evidence of this interest is *Corpus Christi College*, CAMBRIDGE, 265. This manuscript contains many of the extracts from Amalarius used in the *Gemma Animae* and the *Sacramentarium*. It contains also one passage which is reflected in a chapter in the *Gemma Animae* for which I have been able to find no other source :

> Misse autem officium totum in quatuor dividitur species, id est in precationes, orationes, postulationes, gratiarum actiones. Quicquid enim agitur in officio misse, antequam oblate ponantur super altare, precationes nominantur, quia precantur bona populo. Et quicquid ab hora fit qua secreta canitur usque ad agnus dei oratio vocatur. Et oratio post agnus dei postulatio appellatur. Quod autem in fine misse a populo respondetur, deo gratias, gratiarum actio nuncupatur (*CCCC* 265, fol. 308ᵛ).

Gemma Animae I, cxii :

> Missa dividitur in quatuor species, secundum obsecrationes, orationes, postulationes, gratiarum actiones : ab initio missae usque ad offertorium sunt obsecrationes ; a secreta usque ad Pater Noster sunt orationes ; deinde usque ad communionem postulationes ; exinde usque in finem gratiarum actiones.

6. The Worcester manuscript *Bodley* Hatton 42 (ninth century) has in it a text of the *Collectio Hibernensis*. Fol. 11ᵛ contains the particular version of the chapter in this text used by Honorius in his *Sacramentarium* XXIV (R.E. Reynolds,

V

"Further Evidence for the Irish Origins of Honorius Augustodunensis", in *Vivarium* 7 [1969], 1-8).

7. WORCESTER F.48, eleventh century. This manuscript
contains, on fol. 166ᵛ, the story of Thais. The story of Thais
is referred to twice by Honorius in his *Speculum Ecclesiae* (*PL* 172,
881, 892-3). The second reference is a paraphrase of the story
in the form in which it is told in this manuscript. The story
appears in this same form in LAMBACH CXXXIX, fol. 70.

8. Honorius may have used the sermons of Wulfstan, according
to W. Matz, *Die altdeutsche Glaubensbekenntnisse seit Honorius
Augustodunensis* (Diss. Halle 1932), p. 8-10, 45, 49-51.

To establish that Honorius used Worcester manuscripts, and
that the diocese of Worcester maintained an interest in Honorius's
work, is not quite the same as establishing that he lived and
worked there for any great length of time. He could have
travelled there from Canterbury. This accumulation of evidence,
however, does, it seems, establish that he may have been more
closely associated with Worcester than has been suspected
hitherto.

III. THE POSSIBLE IMPACT OF THE NEW MATERIAL
UPON PREVIOUS HYPOTHESES

Ever since the publication of J-A. Endres's fundamental
work on Honorius, [1] historians have agreed to free him from all
links with Autun, and to link him instead with southern Germany,
perhaps with Austria, and with England. If the above evidence
is accepted his associations with England must be widened to
include Worcester, and his connexions with southern Germany
must give place to those with Lambach, in Austria. So far the
change of ground is not a great one. It does, however, involve
a withdrawal from certain positions which have been held until
now with some firmness.

The first positions from which to stage a withdrawal are
those erected upon the proposed identifications of certain persons
to whom Honorius's works were dedicated. Five names or
capital letters make their appearance in prefaces and dedications : Henry, C., Christian, Gotteschalk and Thomas. [2] These

1. J-A. ENDRES, *Honorius Augustodunensis*, Kempten-Munich, 1906.
2. Henry, *Imago Mundi*, Mss. CAMBRIDGE *Corpus Christi College* 66,

V

are all, unfortunately, names which are common in Germany
and Austria. Numbers of efforts have been made to identify
the bearers of these particular ones, some more confident than
others. Among the confident ones can be counted that for
C. and for Cuno, and that for C. and for Christian. For C. and
for Cuno, Dom Bauerreiss has suggested Cuno of Raitenbuch,
abbot of St. Michael's at Siegburg 1105-1126, and bishop of
Regensburg 1126-1132. [1] Appointed abbot by Frederick of
Schwarzenburg, archbishop of Cologne, Cuno was an ardent and
active reformer. He may have been a literary figure of some
distinction ; certainly he was inclined to support promising
young authors, among them Rupert of St. Laurence of Liège,
whom he received at Siegburg, and appointed abbot of Deutz
in about 1120. Rupert is full of praise for Cuno, both as a patron
and as a protector. [2] Christian, in turn, is described in the
Annales Palidenses (which, apart from the *De Luminaribus*,
contains the only nearly contemporary notice about Honorius)
as Honorius's friend, and the annalist describes Christian's
request for the *Imago Mundi* : " ... familiaris suus quidam nomine
Christianus, quae praescripta sunt petiit et impetravit. " [3]
He has been identified by Endres with Christian, abbot of the
Schottenkloster of St. James of Regensburg (1133-53). [4] Christian of Regensburg is another distinguished figure. He was
apparently a member of the royal family of Macarthy, and the
Life of Marianus of Regensburg tells of two journeys he made
to Ireland to seek help for his monastery. On his last journey
he was chosen as archbishop of Cashel, and was buried there
at the seat of the Macarthy family. [5]

The identification proposed for Cuno led to the possibility
that Honorius may have been connected with the abbey of

LONDON *British Museum* Cotton Cleopatra B iv, Royal 13 A xxi, *Lambeth
Palace* 371. — C., Cuno, *Expositio Totius Psalterii, In Cantica Canticorum,*
PL 172, 347, Mss. MUNICH *Clm.* 5118, 4550. — Christian, *Imago Mundi,*
Expositio Selectorum Psalmorum, PL 172, 119, 269, Mss. *Clm.* 536, 14731. —
Gotteschalk, *De Libero Arbitrio,* PL 172, 1225, Ms. ZWETTL 298. — Thomas,
De Animae Exsilio et Patria, PL 172, 1241.
   1. R. BAUERREISS, *Honorius von Canterbury (Augustodunensis) und Kuno I,
der Raitenbucher, Bischof von Regensburg 1126-1136,* in *Studien und Mitteilungen
zur Geschichte des Benediktiner Ordens* 67 (1956), 306-13.
   2. *De Vita Cunonis, MGH SS* XII, 637, *Epistola ad Cunonem abbatem
Siegebergensem,* PL 167, 195-6.
   3. *MGH SS* XVI, 52.
   4. ENDRES, *ubi supra,* p. 4.
   5. A. GWYNN, *The continuity of the Irish tradition at Wurzburg,* in *Herbipolis
Jubilans,* Wurzburg, 1952, p. 66-8.

Siegburg. The quite independent discovery of a piece of evidence connecting Siegburg with Canterbury lent this possibility support. This evidence is contained in a document preserved in the archives of Christ Church Canterbury ; a death roll of the monks of Siegburg for whom the prayers of the Canterbury monks are asked. The death of Cuno's successor, Markward, is included in the list, and so it seems that the list was drawn up during Cuno's term of office. [1] Honorius could, then, have been connected through Canterbury with Siegburg. From this it was a short step to the supposition that he depended upon the works of Rupert of Deutz. [2] The identification of Christian opened the way to even more speculations. Several of these attempt, through Christian of Regensburg, to explain Honorius's mysterious surname "Augustodunensis". Endres proposed that "Zigetburg" would be an appropriate German rendering, "hill of imperial victory", and declared that Honorius Augustodunensis described Honorius correctly as a monk of the Schottenkloster of Weih St. Peter, later St. James, of Regensburg, closely connected, therefore, with abbot Christian. The convent was founded on a hill which was associated in legend with a Çarolingian victory The equation of "Zigetburg" with Siegburg is an obvious further step, but one which seems not yet to have been taken. Dr. Sanford, instead, attempted to link the surname with Regensburg itself, by way of an identification of Augustodunum with terms for Rome and terms for Rome with Regensburg. [3] Augustodunum, she argued, means "mount of emperors". Endres, fired by his enthusiasm for Honorius's associations with the Schottenkloster, [4] proposed that the name of a further dedicatee, Thomas, was one commonly used by Irishmen, and that a dedication to a man of this name strengthened the possibility that Honorius was at St. James. Most recently, Professor R.W. Southern has argued with conviction that Honorius may himself have been an Irishman, and that "Augustodunensis" may mark his association with an Irish "hill of kings", Cashel. [5]

---

1. *Historical Manuscripts Commission. Various Collections*, I, 1901, 217. Pointed out by W. WILBRAND, *Unbekannte Urkunden zur Geschichte der Abtei Siegburg*, in *Annalen des Historischenvereins für den Niederrhein* 137 (1940), 76.

2. M. MAGRASSI, *Teologia e Storia nel Pensiero di Ruperto di Deutz*, Rome, 1959, p. 248, 272-6.

3. E.M. SANFORD, *Honorius, Presbyter et Scholasticus*, in *Speculum* 23 (1948), 402-3.

4. *Ubi supra*, p. 84f., and *Das St. Jacobsportal in Regensburg und Honorius Augustodunensis*, Kempten-Munich, 1903.

5. R.W. SOUTHERN, *St. Anselm and his Biographer*, Cambridge, 1963,

The appearance of Worcester and Lambach upon the scene makes some of these positions less attractive than they were. The first connexion to begin to dissolve is the connexion between Honorius and Siegburg. The suggestion that Honorius spent at least part of his time in England at Worcester diminishes the importance of the Canterbury-Siegburg confraternity document. When one adds, furthermore, considerations of time to those of space, the connexion between Honorius and Siegburg becomes even less convincing. The question of the exact timing of the associations proposed for Honorius with Worcester and Lambach has so far been studiously avoided ; this because the introduction of this dimension into any reconstruction of Honorius's career waits upon the establishment of a firm chronology for his writings. I hope shortly to be able to set this out. This much can, however, be said in anticipation. It appears that the list of Honorius's works given in the *De Luminaribus* is a chronological one, and that the earliest works named were written in England at a time earlier than has previously been supposed. For Book III of the *Elucidarius*, especially, Honorius used a particularly early version of the *De Beatitudine* of St. Anselm. [1] The works dedicated to Cuno, that is, the *Expositio Psalterii* and the *In Cantica Canticorum*, are, on the other hand, late ones. The works dedicated to Cuno do not seem, either on the basis of the present distribution of the manuscripts of them or on that of their content, to be products of the time Honorius spent in England. Nor can they be linked directly with Cuno's tenure of office as abbot of Siegburg. The connexion between Canterbury and Siegburg, and Honorius and Cuno, cannot, then, be allowed to hold Honorius firmly to Canterbury.

The other patterns of associations to which some modifications may have to be made are those between Honorius and Christian and between Honorius and Ireland. If Honorius was for any length of time a member of the community of Lambach, the period of his life spent at Regensburg is by so much diminished, and the extent of his relationship with abbot Christian of St. James perhaps by so much limited. Regensburg must not be removed from the scene. A special reference to the city appears

---

p. 216.   He has been supported by R.E. REYNOLDS, *Further Evidence for the Irish Origins of Honorius Augustodunensis*, in *Vivarium* 7 (1969), 1-8.
1. Honorius used a version of the *De Beatitudine* close to that of Eadmer but without Eadmer's additions.   Eadmer's was possibly first put together in 1100.   R.W. SOUTHERN and F.S. SCHMITT, *Memorials of St. Anselm*, Oxford, 1969, p. 273-91.   This first version ends at "societatem daemoniorum", p. 287.

V

84

in Book I, xxiv, of Honorius's *Imago Mundi*, and the dedications to Cuno could have been made when Cuno was bishop of Regensburg. The solution of Regensburg for "Augustodunensis" is still the best we have. It seems, however, that the part played by Regensburg may be a small and a late one. The *Expositio Selectorum Psalmorum*, which is one of the two works by Honorius which carries the dedication to Christian, is a late work, and, more important, the dedication in the second work, the *Imago Mundi*, only appears in its later recensions. [1] It seems, then, that, if the identification is correct, abbot Christian of St. James of Regensburg can be relegated to a later part of Honorius's career. If this is so, then to decide upon this fragile relationship that Honorius was an Irishman appears to be quite unjustified. Demonstrations of Irish sympathy are notably lacking in his works. The passage on Ireland in the text of the *Imago Mundi* is cursory in the extreme. [2] Two of Honorius's works, the *Imago Mundi* and the *Gemma Animae* are often to be found with works of an Irish flavour, but that may mean only that their owners were eclectic in their tastes, and that they, and not Honorius, were interested in Ireland. No good independent evidence of an association between Honorius and Ireland has yet been found.

The identifications proposed for Cuno and for Christian cannot now be asked to yield any helpful information about the early part of Honorius's career. Worcester and Lambach can be fitted without violence into the space left by their withdrawal. Lambach, moreover, can perhaps provide explanations for some problems which have puzzled scholars for a long time, and upon which the identifications have thrown no light. A great deal of interest has been aroused in the past by the fact that Honorius seems to speak at one point as a canon and at another as a monk, [3]

---

1. The only two surviving twelfth century manuscripts which represent early recensions of this text, *Corpus Christi College*, CAMBRIDGE, 66, and *British Museum*, Cotton Cleopatra B iv, dedicate it to Henry.
2. Ms. *Corpus Christi College*, CAMBRIDGE, 66, contains an additional passage on Ireland, but this passage appears in no other twelfth century manuscript of the work, and there is no reason to suppose that it is by Honorius. The support for Honorius's Irish origins adduced by REYNOLDS, *op. cit.*, which is drawn from Honorius's use of an especially Irish redaction of the *Collectio Hibernensis*, is unconvincing. This text was, as he himself admits, readily available. It was, of course, available at Worcester.
3. Honorius speaks as a canon in his *Liber Duodecim Quaestionum*, cfr I. DIETERICH, *MGH Libellus de Lite* III, 31. Chapter vi of this work tackles the question of the relative merits of the monastic and canonial orders, and

V

and also by the apparent incompatibility between the monastic state, and the adjectives "inclusus" and "solitarius" so often attached to Honorius's name in early manuscripts of his works. Lambach can provide solutions to both of these problems, although it must be admitted that the solutions are tentative. For the first, it seems possible to say with some firmness that Honorius was at one time a canon and at another a monk, that the logical progression in such matters is from the first state to the second, and that the evidence suggests that this was the course Honorius took. This progression accords extraordinarily well with the history of the community of Lambach. Count Arnold of Lambach, when he gave his castle to the new foundation, certainly meant it to be a house of secular canons ;

> Aggregavit preterea, sicut seniorum percepimus relatibus duodecim clericos, non cenobiali lege in cenobio degentes, sed in vicinia claustri circumquaque in singulis tuguriis conmorantes, deputatis eis, prout cuique opus esset, necessariis. [1]

The house was, however, turned into a "cenobium" by Adalbero, bishop of Wurzburg and son of the founder. The transformation was not an easy one, and Adalbero had to make at least two attempts. The exemplar of Adalbero's charter which we now have, confirming the conversion, gives as the date of the first 1056, and of the second 1089. [2] There is some doubt about the first of these dates, for in that part of the charter which refers to Adalbero's first attempt specific reference is made to the approval of Pope Gregory VII. Wattenbach dismisses this reference as a mistake ; yet the early date could as easily be mistaken. [3] Moreover, the acceptance of such a transformation as early as 1056 does not accord well with what we know of the policy of Altmann of Passau, in whose diocese Lambach lay. If the date of the first attempt is altered, and placed at some point within Gregory's pontificate, these difficulties are lessened ;

---

answers it firmly in favour of the canon. Yet Honorius includes St. Benedict's feast day and the feast of his translation in his *Speculum Ecclesiae*, and in his *Quod Monachis Liceat Predicare* he argues forcefully that the profession of the monk is superior to that of the canon regular. This last work is printed by ENDRES, *op. cit.*, p. 147-150.
1. *Vita Adalberonis Episcopi Wirziburgensis, MGH SS* XII, 132.
2. *Ibid.* 133.
3. If we accept the early date we have only two abbots for the period 1056-1106, a long period for two men, especially in view of the fact that the first did not stay in office until the end of his life. *Ibid.* 136.

V

86

and Honorius could, as a young man, be involved in the difficulties involved in the transformation. The difference of views marked in the works mentioned could be a measure of his reaction to it. He may even have left for a time because of it.

The second problem, that of the incompatibility between the monastic state and that of the "solitarius" has caused more difficulty than it need have. It was quite possible for a member of a monastic community to lead a solitary life for a time, and in Honorius's lifetime it may even have been quite common, [1] Students and scholars particularly were encouraged to do so, and were apparently allowed the title of hermit as a courtesy. Such courtesies were possibly widespread ; but we have excellent contemporary evidence that they were practised at Lambach. An unpublished and extremely interesting letter on the verse of the last folio of the Lambach collection of liturgical sources mentioned above, LAMBACH XXVII, speaks of "fratrum Lambacensium et solitariorum".

Many unsolved problems remain. The chronological ones are crucial. There is clearly a place for an association of some sort between Honorius and Canterbury and Honorius and Regensburg, for Honorius's known use of the works of St. Anselm, and for the dedication of some of his works to Cuno and to Christian. Neither Worcester nor Lambach provides a solution to "Augustodunensis" nor to these particular debts and ascriptions. It has not been possible, on the basis of the evidence available, to transform the probability that Honorius was connected with these two places into a certainty. The identification of the Frater Heinricus of the gift with Honorius must remain a hypothetical one only. Nonetheless, it remains true that Lambach and Worcester were interested to a striking degree in the works of Honorius, and that their claims must be considered closely before any serious attempt can be made to reconstruct his career.

University of Auckland, New Zealand.

---

1. Dom Jean LECLERCQ demonstrates this most convincingly in an article *Pierre le Vénérable et l'érémitisme clunisien*, in *Studia Anselmiana* 40 (1956), 99-120.

VI

HEINRICUS OF AUGSBURG
AND HONORIUS AUGUSTODUNENSIS :
ARE THEY THE SAME PERSON ?

In short order: yes, I think they are. At least, one person may be made of *one* of the Henrys of Augsburg and of Honorius. In making this one person, confusion becomes to some degree more confounded, for one has, in a way familiar to medievalists, now to divide the one previously known Henry into two, one slightly earlier than the other. The gain, I hope, outweighs the loss; for in fusing Honorius with one, the later, Henry, a problem which has been puzzling students of Honorius literally for generations will at one stroke be solved. The problem is that of Honorius's mysterious surname, 'Augustodunensis'. This must mean Augsburg. At last. This solution is the main contribution this paper sets out to make. It will try also, however, to say a little more about Honorius. It may be possible to add short works on music to Honorius's known output, and so both to reinforce and to expand the picture we have of him as a passionate teacher of Benedictine monks to be articulate in the pastorate.[1] Whilst the written achievement of the former single Henry of Augsburg will be by this diminished, that of Honorius will be extended into one of the very few areas of twelfth century learning about which he has seemed so far to have had little to say. These short works on music may even have been among Honorius's first productions.

I

The identification of the previously one Henry of Ausburg has seemed, since 1891 quite clear.[2] The story, via Manitius and Langosch,[3] was summed up more recently by Marvin Colker.

> Almost all that can be learned about him is to be derived from two passages in the *Annales Augustani*. From the chronicle it is clear that Henry, formerly of Aquileia, was made a canon of Augsburg in 1077, when Wigold became bishop of the German city, and that in 1083, Master Henry, expelled with Wigold, died in the monastery of St. Magnus (at Füssen) and was buried there: "(1077) Heinricus Aquileia pridem Augustensis canonicus, Wigoldus ex familia ecclesiae episcopus constituitur. (1083) Magister Heinricus, Augustensis canonicus, cum Wigoldo episcopo expulsus, in coenobio sancti Magni obiit et sepultus est."[4]

The identification of this Henry's works seemed also a comparatively simple affair. A long poem called the *Planctus Evae*, which Colker edits in the same article, is described in one of the two surviving twelfth century manuscripts of it, Ms. Österreichische Nationalbibliothek, Vienna, 1063, (f. 124), possibly from St. Florian, as 'versus Heinrici Augustensi (sic) Magistri.' A further twelfth century manuscript, Ms. Bamberg Lit. 10 (f. 98 v) ascribes a quatrain on the melodies of the Introit to 'Heinricus auguste urbis scolasticus'. The quatrain, then, seemed to belong to the same Henry. The second surviving manuscript of the *Planctus Evae*, also of the twelfth century, Ms. Österreichische Nationalbibliothek, Vienna, 388, (f. 75 v), again associates its author, Heinricus scolasticus, with Augsburg. Two more twelfth century copies of works coming from South German libraries and attached to a certain Heinricus were noticed by Colker and so added tentatively to the collection. One, Ms. Bayerische Staatsbibliothek, Munich, clm. 18580 (from Tergernsee)

---

1. I attempted to set out the state of our knowledge to date upon Honorius in V.I.J. FLINT, *The place and purpose of the works of Honorius Augustodunensis*, in *Revue Bénédictine* 87 (1977) 97-127. Earlier bibliography is scrupulously cited in M.-O. GARRIGUES, *Quelques recherches sur l'œuvre d'Honorius Augustodunensis*, in *Revue d'Histoire Ecclésiastique* 70 (1975), 388-425, *especially* 388-398.

2. J. HUEMER, *Zur Geschichte der mittellateinischen Dichtung. Heinrici Augustensis Planctus Evae*, in *Jahresbericht über das K.K. Staatsgymnasium im II Besirke im Wien* 24 (1890-91), 5-8.

3. M. MANITIUS, *Geschichte der lateinischen Literatur des Mittelalters*, II (Munich 1923), 615-618. K. LANGOSCH *in* W. STAMMLER and K. LANGOSCH, *Die deutsche Literatur des Mittelalters : Verfasserlexicon* II (Berlin-Leipsig 1936), 248-251.

4. M.L. COLKER, *Heinrici Augustensis Planctus Evae*, in *Traditio* 12 (1956), 150-151. The passages quoted from the *Annales Augustani* are edited by G.H. PERTZ in *MGH.SS*, III, 129 and 130.

150

contains (f. 83) a poem on grammar by one 'Heinricus', and a second, Ms. Bayerische Staatsbibliothek, Munich, clm. 14506 (from St. Emmeramm's, Regensburg), has (f. 73) some 'proverbia Heinrici'. A last and clearly headed twelfth century manuscript, Ms. Österreichische Nationalbibliothek, Vienna, 51, contains a small Dialogue between a Magister and a Discipulus upon the theory and mathematics of music. [1] This has as its title (f. 89 v) 'Incipit musica domini heinrici augustensis magistri', presumably the same Henry again. The corpus of works certainly and plausibly ascribed in manuscripts to the Heinricus of Augsburg of the *Annales Augustani* appears to be complete.

The last work mentioned, the Dialogue on music, has been recently edited. [2] It is the appearance of this edition, with its firm attribution to the Henry of the *Plantus Evae* which has prompted me to this reconsideration of the whole, and to this introduction, almost injection, into the picture of Honorius. In the first, rather negative, instance, the *Planctus* and the Dialogue are very unlike one another. The *Planctus Evae* is a long and sophisticated poem, taking up some sixty five pages of *Traditio* in its printed version. It is a finely constructed piece of verse and, according to Manitius, was likely to have been used as a school exercise and as a means of guiding pupils into the difficulties of the composition of latin poetry. [3] The ascription of it to a scolasticus teaching at the distinguished cathedral school of Augsburg in the third decade of the eleventh century is wholly consonant with its content (nothing less than the divine plan of creation and the completion of Adam's mission by Christ) and composition. The Dialogue is wholly different. Unfortunately the sole manuscript in which it has come down to us is incomplete, [4] but enough of it survives to give a clear indication of its nature. It is a short, simply constructed, prose conversation between a master and his pupil. It begins by setting out the three stock divisions of music — mundana, humana, artificiosa — and proceeds *seriatim* to elucidate the theory and purpose of the last. It is unsophisticated and unrefined, and is devised not in order to help the already practised to become more proficient in a difficult art, but to reduce such an art to dimensions assimilable even by those barely exercised in it. Distinct contents, style and purpose do not automatically presuppose, of course, distinct authors; [5] but the second style and purpose do have a remarkably familiar ring to students of Honorius. And indeed, in the second and positive instance, the Dialogue is remarkably like certain of Honorius's works.

II

The will to reduce the most complex to the most simple, to substitute the answers of learning for its process, and so supposedly render that process

1. A short note on this appeared in 1967 ; M HUGLO, *Un théoricien du XI*ᵉ *siècle : Henri d'Augsbourg*, in *Revue de Musicologie* 53 (1967), 53-59.
2. J. SMITS VAN WAESBERGHE, *Musica Domni Heinrici Augustensis Magistri*, in *Divitiae Musicae Artis, Schola Paleographica Amstelodamensis Conspirante Collectae* (1977).
3. MANITIUS, *loc. cit.*
4. It ends, in fact, half way down f. 91, which is cut, at a most trying point, where its author had just begun to speak of the music of the planets.
5. SMITS VAN WAESBERGHE, *ed. cit.*, pp. 25-27, made a spirited effort to maintain that the *De Musica* and the *Planctus Evae* were products of the same pen, but his evidence, based as it is upon lack of actual opposition, shared thoughts and Greek-rooted words, is capable of other explanations, see below.

unnecessary by the deft finding of short-cuts, is now so grimly familiar a feature of Honorius's writings that it perhaps needs no further stress. The Dialogue is very like these writings in this. It is like them also in certain other features. It is like them in its passion for scene setting, in its concern for charm and movement, in its choice of words and perhaps even in its choice of sources. I will set out here the more striking of these resemblances.

I have drawn attention elsewhere to Honorius's love of views and of vantage points. [1] The author of the Dialogue enjoys spectacle too. Here is a parallel with Honorius's *Imago Mundi*:

> D. Et ubi est, quod illa postreme inaequalitatis genera dixisti secerni a musica ?
> M. Memor esto me ita ut hoc excipere locutum fuisse. Si enim inter tortuosos montium et vallium anfractus aliquando planities invenitur, non mirum est inter horum generum tortuosas qualitates aliquid plani et hoc in uno tantum et semel reperiri (Dialogue, p. 44.)
> Si enim quis in aere positus eam desuper inspiceret, tota enormitas montium et concavitas vallium minus in ea apparet, quam digitus alicuius si pilam praegrandem in manu teneret (*Imago Mundi* I, v, *PL* 172, 122).

Charm, again as I have said, is very evident in Honorius's works, and especially so in his dialogues. There are many examples of a technique very similar to that employed by the charming discipulus of Honorius's *Elucidarius*, for example, at work here too in the Dialogue on music. Here, anxious questions, half-seriously answered, urge the discussion along;

> D. Qui sunt minus pleni musici?
> M. Qui mei sunt similes; hoc est, qui aliquam tam artis quam instrumentorum rationem sed non pleniter exequuntur.
> D. Quid igitur ego faciam, qui de arte te interrogare disposui?
> M. Quod esurientes faciunt, qui hoc, quod minus sufficit, avidius sumunt (Dialogue, p. 36). [2]

This manner of progression is very familiar to readers of Honorius. So is a certain sharpening in the rhythm of question and answer; a sharpening very often brought about by the use of one word; 'minime'. 'Minime' in the *Elucidarius* is used frequently in reply to a peculiarly obvious question, introduced merely as an excuse for further exposition on the part of the Master;

> M. Si igitur tu stares coram Deo et aliquis diceret: "Respire retro aut totus mundus interibit," Deus autem diceret: "Nolo ut respicias, sed me inspicias," deberes tu Deum contemnere, qui est creator omnium rerum et gaudium angelorum, ut liberares transitorium mundum?
> D. Minime.
> M. Hoc Adam fecit... (*Elucidarius*, I, 98-99, p. 378).

Exactly the same happens in the Dialogue;

> D. Satisne de inequalitatis generibus interrogavi?
> M. Minime. Audisti ea tantum esse, sed nondum scis quid sint, unde dicantur, cui quantitati deputentur, que ex quo consonantie prodeant. (Dialogue, p. 40). [3]

---

1. *The place and purpose...*, *art. cit.*, pp. 110-111. The references to the Dialogue which follow are to the pages of the printed edition cited above. Those to the works of Honorius are to the page numbers of the relevant volume of the *Patrologia Latina* (vol. 172), with the exception of Honorius's *Elucidarius* for which reference is made instead to Y. LEFÈVRE, *L'Elucidarium et les Lucidaires* (Paris 1954).

2. I have made small emendations here to the edition from the manuscript, f. 89.

3. See also Dialogue pp. 38, 45, 46, 51.

A clear verbal parallel between the Dialogue and yet another of Honorius's works, the short treatise on the seven liberal arts called the *De Animae Exsilio et Patria*, is to be found;

> D. Quae est artificiosa?
> M. Quae arte hominum composita, aut tactu, ut in fidibus, aut flatu, ut in organis, aut percussione, ut in cymbalis et tibiis perficitur. (Dialogue p. 35).

This is very like the central part of the short chapter Honorius devotes to music in the *De Animae*;

> Quinta civitas est musica, per quam transitus est ad patriae cantica. In hac urbe per Boetii doctrinam hinc chorus viris gravibus, inde puerilis acutis vocibus Deo jubilat: organa fistulis, citharae fidibus concrepant, cymbala pulsu tinniunt: septem dissonae voces consonam harmoniae efficiunt. Triplex modulatio, quae fit flatu, tactu, pulsu, septem consonantiis senarii dignitatem, universitatem continentem, concinit; dum intervallis et proportionibus tono tum dulce melos reddit... (*De Animae* VI, *PL* 172, 1244).

It appears, furthermore, from this passage, that Honorius lays special stress on the authority of Boethius. Boethius's *De Musica* is the main source of the Dialogue. The author of the Dialogue follows Boethius closely, sometimes re-arranging Boethius's order, a trick with which explorers of Honorius's use of sources again become very familiar. After Boethius, the author of the Dialogue draws most heavily upon the writings on music of Hermannus Contractus. [1]

Finally, there is a little to be learnt from the trying ending of the Dialogue. The dialogue ends, incomplete, just after this passage;

> D. Quae voces sunt in vice planetarum?
> M. E Lune, F Mercurii, G Venere, A id est mense Solis, B Martis, C Iovis, D Saturni.

The argument goes no further but, as Huglo pointed out, the Master had earlier in the work drawn attention to a very recent development, that is, the beginning of musical notation with Gamma. The discipulus asks;

> Quare quidam in primis Γ gamma gregi (greci) et post a b molle, guod synemen(on) vacant ponuntur?

and the Master replies;

> Moderni gamma grecum licentiae tantum non naturae vel institutionis causa ponunt, et quia ex libitu musicorum saepe infra finales diapente inveniunt. [2]

Huglo went so far as to propose that Heinricus of Augsburg may have originated this new form of notation. [3] It is, then, to say the least interesting to discover that the idea of beginning with Gamma is advanced by Honorius in his *Imago Mundi*. Here I must part from the Migne text of the *Imago*, which is inaccurate, and quote the passage from one of the best manuscripts of the work, Ms. Bayerische Staatsbibliothek, Munich, clm. 536, from Prül. [4] In this

---

1. This dependence on Honorius is especially evident in *Imago Mundi*. I hope to make this clear in my forthcoming edition.
2. HUGLO, *art. cit.*, p. 56.
3. He repeats this proposition in a further article on Heinrich von Augsburg in *Die Musik in Geschichte und Gegenwart*, 16 (Kassel-Basel-Toul-London 1979), 633; ''Es ist jedoch bemerkenswert, dass die Position des Gamma am Anfang der alphabetischen Notenskala auf Heinrich von Augsburg zurückgeht''.
4. Book I, LXXXI, *PL* 172, 140; clm. 536 f. 19r.

chapter Honorius draws together the notation of the musical scale and the
music of the planets, and the entry runs;

In terra namque si gamma, in luna A, in Mercurio B, in Venere C, in sole D,
in Marte E, in Iove F, in Saturno G ponitur, perfecto mensura musice invenitur.

III

There are, I suggest, only two ways in which these parallels may adequately
be explained. One of the possible explanations is that Henry of Augsburg
and Honorius were in close contact. We could then maintain Henry as the
Dialogue's author but suppose that Honorius learnt many of his techniques.
We could, furthermore, keep Henry intact. The other explanation is, of
course, that Honorius was at some point called Heinricus of Augsburg and
wrote the Dialogue. Each of these explanations brings Honorius into
contact with Augsburg. We may perhaps examine at this point the independent evidence for such a connexion.

As early as 1903 J.-A. Endres, the first scholar seriously to work upon Honorius, drew attention to a clear association between a work certainly by Honorius
and a *Rituale* almost certainly the property of the cathedral church
of Augsburg. [1] This *Rituale* (ms. Bayerische Staatsbibliothek, Munich, clm.
226 and, in my view, of the twelfth century) describes itself as a possession
'augustense ecclesiae' and shews a concern for the archiepiscopal see of Mainz
by the mention of masses in memory of Archbishops Bruno and Embrico.
Augsburg was, of course, in the province of the metropolitan of Mainz. The
Rituale also manifests that independence of spirit appropriate to a great
church within a province by an acrimonious rejection (f. 46) of certain customs
followed at Mainz in the rite for the octaves of Easter and Pentecost. A third
feature of the *Rituale* bears directly upon the supposed contact between
Honorius and Augsburg, for a series of marginal passages contained in the
manuscript are almost exclusively drawn from Honorius's *Gemma Animae*.
My own examination of these passages has established that they are not direct
representations of the printed version of this work, and may indeed represent
an early recension.

One other manuscript, also, proposes a connexion between Honorius and
Mainz. Ms. Corpus Christi College, Cambridge, 66, a relatively late copy of
a very early (probably the first) recension of Honorius's *Imago Mundi*, gives
(f. 4) a description of the author of work;

Iste Henricus, qui hunc librum edidit, fuit canonicus S. Mariae civitatis Maguntie, in qua ecclesia sunt canonici bis quater quaterdeni.

We may note the description of Honorius as Henricus and return to it. For
the moment we have in this description another association with the archdiocese of Mainz, and we have the statement that Honorius was a canon.

We have long known that Honorius moved from the canonial to the monastic life, and we have long suspected that he made this change early in his
career. We have been virtually certain that he spent a period of time, at
the beginning of his active life, in England, perhaps deciding with the help
of St. Anselm, whose work he so clearly reveres, upon his monastic vocation.
His chosen profession as a monk was followed largely in the city of Regensburg,

1. J.-A. ENDRES, *Ein Augsburger Rituale des 13 Jahrhundert*, in *Passauer Monatschrift* 13 (1903), 636.

at the abbey of St. Emmeramm or that of Weih St. Peter, later St. James. He was a vehement supporter of reforming ideals. [1] We have not known, however, what impelled Honorius to make these journeys and take these decisions. The events at Augsburg in the last years of the eleventh century and the first years of the twelfth provide a peculiarly appropriate *mise en scene* for all these different events; certainly one more appropriate than any advanced so far.

The cathedral school of Augsburg, built up especially by Bishop Ulrich (923-973), was an excellent one, and boasted active and outstanding school-masters. [2] But, towards the end of the eleventh century, the support of Augsburg for the reform, was, especially under Bishops Siegfried (1077-1096) and Hermann (1096-1133), less than enthusiastic. Both Siegfried and Hermann held the see in the imperial interest, and Siegfried in particular held it in competition with that Bishop Wigold whose name is linked in the *Annales Augustani* with that of the scolasticus Henry. Henry arrived, indeed, in the middle of the schism over the appointment to the bishopric in 1077, [3] and presumably had a full share in the disorders which followed this schism and which resulted in the expulsion of himself and Wigold in 1083 and the near destruction of the city. Hermann's appointment as bishop seems to have been, if possible, a change for the worse for such religious idealists as had survived there so far. Considerable, if somewhat partisan, light is thrown upon monastic reactions to Hermann's episcopal style by the author of a treatise on the abbacy of Egino, abbot of the Benedictine house of Sts. Ulrich and Afra in Augsburg [4]. Hermann's election, ordination and consecration were seen as direct affronts to the movement for ecclesiastical reform, and he was a scourge of the regular religious life. Not only did he render Abbot Egino's office insupportable but he persecuted the regular clergy from the very beginning of his episcopate. The *Annales Augustani* provide additional testimony to the state of affairs. The entry for 1098 runs;

> Nullus religionis splendor. Provintiae quaedam non solum pontificali sed etiam sacerdotali sunt regimine privatae; sua quique quaerentes. non quae Dei sunt assectantes. [5]

Hermann was certainly later responsible for the expulsion of that most redoubtable of later spokesmen for the reform, Gerhoh of Reichersberg, [6] and he also forced a change upon Augsburg which brought the disaffected directly into contact with the city of Regensburg. The entries in the *Annales* for 1101 and 1104 respectively describe the crisis into which the canons of Augsburg were plunged;

---

1. V.I.J. FLINT, *The chronology of the works of Honorius Augustodunensis*, in *Revue Bénédictine* 82 (1972), 238-242. I have summed up the evidence for Honorius's time in England and at Regensburg, and for the dates of his movements in *The career of Honorius Augustodunensis*. *Some fresh evidence*, in *Revue Bénédictine* 82 (1972), 80-85; (I have strategically to withdraw from my suggestions that Honorius was associated early in his career with the abbey of Lambach and that "Augustodunensis" may refer to Regensburg).

2. HUEMER, art. cit., pp. 5-6.

3. *Ed. cit.*, pp. 130-131.

4. *Uodascalcus de Eginone et Herimanno*, ed. G. PERTZ, *MGH.SS*, XII, 429-448.

5. *Ed. cit.*, p. 135.

6. P. CLASSEN, *Gerhoch von Reichersberg* (Wiesbaden 1960), 15-19.

In Augusta dissensio inter episcopum et canonicos, canonicae conversionis exterminium, restitutio praediorum canonicorum Gisenhusae et Strubingae et aliorum.

In epiphania canonici Augustenses, possessionibus ad se pertinentibus diu despoliati, Gisenhusa, Strubinga, Chreina, Reginboldeshusa, cum aliis tam ad oblationem quam ad stipendium eorum pertinentibus, ab imperatore et ab episcopis et regni principibus Ratisponae benigne suscipiuntur, quorum communi suffragio cuncta illis subtracta ab episcopo Herimanno denuo restituuntur. [1]

The dates of these crises and difficulties coincide remarkably well with those dates proposed so far for major changes in Honorius's life. A short while ago I suggested that Honorius's conversion to the monastic life may have taken place in the very early twelfth century, and that he spent these very years in England among canons of Lotharingian sympathies pursuing reform, perhaps leaving at Anselm's last exile in 1103. [2] Robert Losinga, bishop of Hereford 1079-1095, had recently, it might be remembered, re-established close relations with the archdiocese of Mainz through his interest in the chronicle of Marianus Scotus. A departure, perhaps to the West of England, in 1098, and a return to Regensburg perhaps early in 1104 is then, very much what we might expect of a young and enthusiastic canon of Augsburg. The fragments previously collected about Honorius's life and writings, and especially about his fierce reforming sympathies, fit into this new picture with an amazing ease.

IV

The idea that Honorius began his active life as a canon of Augsburg provides, then explanations for his choices and his movements of an order which had previously been lacking. The surname 'Augustodunensis' may indeed apply to Augsburg. Two questions remain. Was he taught there by the scolasticus Henry who wrote the Dialogue on music; or was he himself the author of the Dialogue 'dominici Heinrici augustensis magistri'?

For Honorius to have been taught by Henry before Henry's withdrawal and death in 1083 does strain the chronology we have so far for Honorius's life. All the signs so far indicate that Honorius began his public career in the very last years of the eleventh century and that he continued to be active until about 1140. Thus to be taught by Heinricus scolasticus between 1077 and 1083, Honorius would have had to have been born at the latest in perhaps 1065, and to have been about thirty three when he started on his travels. None of this is impossible and the biblical authority for a career in the priesthood beginning at such an age will escape no one. There are, however, two more shreds of evidence to support the view that Honorius/Heinricus wrote the Dialogue himself. They lie in the likelihood that Honorius was indeed at one point called Henry, and deep in the elusive so-called gift of Frater Heinricus.

It does seem to be highly probable that Honorius was himself called Henry, and that he was called this early in his life. Some time ago I drew attention

1. *Ed. cit.*, p. 135.
2. V.I.J. FLINT. *The Elucidarius of Honorius Augustodunensis and the reform in late eleventh century England*, in *Revue Bénédictine* 85 (1975), 186-188, 197-198. I tried to suggest that Regensburg was a particularly attractive centre in the early twelfth century for those interested in the Lotharingian style of articulate reform in *The place and purpose...*, *art. cit.*, pp. 103-107.

to two facts. Some early manuscripts of early works known to be by Honorius attribute them to one 'Henricus'; and the so called gift of Frater Heinricus to Gottweig contains an extra-ordinary number of Honorius's writings. [1] Three manuscripts of that recension of the *Imago Mundi* which I am now sure is the earliest, attribute this work to 'Henricus'. [2] One more manuscript, once again of an early work, the *Sigillum*, and the earliest copy we have of it, Ms. Jesus College, Oxford, 54, has on its first folio, and written in an early twelfth century hand, the legend 'Nobilis henrici cuius pereunt inimici'. All these manuscripts are English ones, which lends strength to the notion that Honorius continued to use his own name, Henry, when he left Augsburg for England, changing it to Honorius firmly only later in his career.

The gift of Frater Heinricus contains, among the fifty works it lists, twenty two which are known to be by Honorius. It contains, too, every work named as his own by Honorius in his *De Luminaribus Ecclesiae*, with the possible exception of the 'evangelia quod beatus Gregorius non exposuit'. In view of this remarkable proportion, I argued that Frater Heinricus must be Honorius himself and that the gift must contain his own collection both of his own works and of works he had collected carefully during his life. We may now be in a position, with the help of the present codex which includes the Dialogue on music, Ms. Österreichische Nationalbibliothek, Vienna, 51, to take one further step. It may be possible to identify this codex with one of the items listed in the gift of Frater Heinricus, and so to draw Honorius and the Dialogue at last firmly together.

The thirty first item in the Gift is a 'Musica Odonis'. I associated this tentatively with the work of Guido of Arezzo. Ms. Vienna 51, however, begins its very large collection of treatises on music with a 'Musica Odonis', that is, the *De Musica* of Odo of Cluny. This codex may, in short, be the missing 'Musica Odonis' of the Gift. It has to be said that this identification cannot be made with certainty. We know no more of this codex than that it is of the right date, that it comes from South Germany or Austria, and that the hand in which the Dialogue is written is not unlike the hands to be found in other manuscripts I have suggested were originally a part of the Gift. [3] Within the large collection the codex contains, however, are all the sources the author of the Dialogue actually used (Boethius, Hermannus Contractus), as well, of course, as the Dialogue itself. It is excellently well fitted to be the original collection of the author, containing a copy of the author's rendering down to workable dimensions of sections of this collection. The author of the Dialogue certainly regarded himself as semi-expert in the field;

> D. Qui sunt minus pleni musici?
> M. Qui mei sunt similes, hoc est qui aliquam tam artis quam instrumentorum rationem sed non pleniter exequuntur.

---

1. I have set out these facts in detail in *The career...*, *art. cit.*, pp. 63-86, especially 64-68 and 75.

2. Mss. Corpus Christi College, Cambridge, 66, British Library, London, Cotton Cleopatra B IV, and Royal 13 A. XXI.

3. The codex as a whole is described by Dr. Eva IRBLICH in *Wissenschaft in Mittelalter, Ausstellung von Handschriften und Inkunabeln der Österreichischen Nationalbibliothek* (Vienna 1975), 231-232. I am grateful to her for much kind assistance. I have compared this hand with those to be found in Mss. Österreichische Nationalbibliothek, Vienna, s.n. 3604 and 3605, both books possibly part of the Gift. Dr. Irblich and I agree upon the similarities.

The Vienna codex would be more than adequate to provide such expertise. [1] Taken together with the evidence of similarities between Honorius's possible writings and the style and purpose of the Dialogue, and for Honorius/Heinricus's early presence at Augsburg, it is hard to refrain from the conclusion that the Vienna codex is the missing *Musica Odonis* of the Gift, and that the Dialogue it contains is Honorius's own copy of his own work.

As a postscript, we may add that if Honorius wrote this small piece, he may well have written the quatrain (composed as an aid to the different psalm tones for the Introit) previously ascribed to the one earlier Henry of Augsburg too. Huglo [2] was able to point to the survival of ten early copies of this. It is, of course, attributed in Ms. Bamberg Stiftsbibliothek Lit. 10 (the only copy found so far with an attribution) to 'Heinricus auguste urbis scolasticus', and this should mean the first Henry. Most of the surviving copies come from South Germany or Austria, which is what we would expect of a work either by the original Henry or by Honorius. One of the earliest manuscripts, however, Ms. Rouen 1386, is from Jumièges. [3] The associations of Jumièges and England in the early twelfth century are far closer than the associations between Jumièges and Germany, and Jumièges and the West of England, especially Malmesbury, enjoyed an especially close relationship. It is tempting to connect the possession by Jumièges of an early copy of the quatrain with Honorius's time in the west of England. [4]

CONCLUSION

It seems at least possible that we may have two Henrys of Augsburg, and that the second became more widely known under a different name; Honorius Augustodunensis. 'Augustodunensis' will then refer to Augsburg. Honorius, I suggest, began his career there, perhaps as a canon of the cathedral, and therefore under the primatial jurisdiction of the see of Mainz, and he incorporated this beginning to his active life in the pseudonym he chose.

The first Henry, the scolasticus of Augsburg, died a little too early for us to be sure that he taught Honorius. Honorius may still, however, have been influenced by him, perhaps by being taught by men who were his pupils, perhaps by having ready access to Henry's works. If the first Henry of Augsburg wrote in truth the Dialogue on music which has, until now, been attributed to him, then this influence would explain the clear similarities to be found between the Dialogue and some of the works of Honorius. I have tried to put forward, however, another explanation for these similarities. We

---

1. « Sie enthält alle bedeutenden Musiktractate des Früh- und Hochmittelalters, und zwar, des Boethius († 524), Odos von Cluny († 942), Hucbalds von Elnon († 930), Bernos von Reichenau († 1048), Guidos von Arezzo († um 1050), des Hermannus Contractus († 1054), Wilhelms von Hirsau († 1091), sowie zahlreiche anonym gebliebene Abhandlungen über Instrumente, » E. IRBLICH, *op. cit.*, p. 232.

2. *Art. cit.*, p. 57.

3. Huglo gives as the date for this manuscript the late eleventh century, but the section containing the quatrain is in fact of the twelfth century ; H. OMONT, *Catalogue Général des Manuscrits des Bibliothèques Publiques de France. I. Rouen* (Paris 1886), 362.

4. I tried to associate Honorius's stay in England with the West country in particular in *The career...*, art. cit., pp. 75-80.

cannot yet be precisely sure which were the works of the first Henry. More analysis is needed of the *Planctus Evae*, the *Proverbia* and the poem upon grammar. It may be noted that none of these survives in copies earlier than the twelfth century. I have attempted to suggest with as much firmness as the evidence allows that the Dialogue and the quatrain on music belong in fact to the corpus of the writings of Honorius. They may be placed among those others of Honorius's works he felt it unnecessary to mention in the *De Luminaribus Ecclesiae*, and so tentatively assigned to his very early years as a writer. This Dialogue may constitute the twenty third item known to be by Honorius in the Gift of Frater Heinricus. The codex in which the Dialogue is to be found now may, indeed, have been a part of that original gift. The association between Honorius and the gift would, if that is so, be by so much strengthened.

Should this attribution be upheld, then one more dimension to Honorius's interests is revealed. He instructed his pupils in the theory, and perhaps the practice, of music. That a canon of Augsburg should be well versed in music should not surprise us; [1] but that Honorius should add this interest too to his already enormous range is, perhaps, somewhat remarkable. He becomes even more of a polymath than we had thought; and we have yet another reason to suspect that his real talent lay in the dramatic. The movement for ecclesiastical reform may well, by the early twelfth century, have needed to assume a dramatic and popular shape if memories of the discomforts it had brought in its train were to be assuaged, and Honorius's capacity to provide for this need was perhaps one of the main factors governing his success.

If the foregoing argument is accepted, then the Gift of Frater Heinricus will assume considerable importance as a source. It becomes a source not merely for our better appreciation of the wider interests of Honorius (though it certainly is a source for these, and should be given far more careful treatment than I have been able to give it so far), but for our understanding of a whole section of the activities of the reformed church. We have very probably in the Gift the teaching library of an active agent of that reformed church. We may learn from it both the limits and the extent of the learned ambitions of the early twelfth century monastic schools; certainly those of South Germany, perhaps those of other regions of Europe. The extent, not the limits, of those ambitions appears at first sight to be the more striking aspect of them.

University of Auckland,
New Zealand.

---

1. On the importance of Augsburg as a musical centre in this period see A. LAYER, *Augsburger Musikpflege im Mittelalter*, in ed. L. WEGELE, *Musik in der Reichsstadt Augsburg* (Augsburg 1967), pp. 11-26.

THE CHRONOLOGY OF THE WORKS OF HONORIUS AUGUSTODUNENSIS

In an earlier paper I set out a little new evidence ; evidence drawn primarily from the surviving manuscripts of Honorius's works, and bearing upon Honorius's career. This evidence led to the suggestion that the scope of Honorius's activities in England and Southern Germany was more extended in space than had been thought before ; that, in short, they encompassed not only Canterbury and Regensburg, but the cathedral priory of Worcester, in England, and the Benedictine abbey of Lambach, in Austria. All consideration of time was however, carefully avoided, and the possibility that Honorius's early works were written in England and his later ones in Germany was mentioned as a possibility only. This paper is an attempt to fill this gap. We have no direct chronological evidence about Honorius. The problem can only be approached through his writings. These, then, their contents and the more important manuscripts of them, will now be examined in some detail. The discussion falls naturally into four parts. The first deals necessarily with the corpus of Honorius's works and with some of the suggestions already made about their dates ; necessarily with the corpus because the editions have by no means removed all the confusions, and necessarily with the suggestions because they must now be modified. Some works can be associated quite clearly with England : these will be treated in the second part. The third part will concern itself with the rest of the works acknowledged as his own by Honorius in the *De Luminaribus*, and the last will treat of the *De Luminaribus* and the unacknowledged works.

I. THE "CORPUS HONORII"

The *De Luminaribus* lists Honorius' works in this order : *Elucidarius, Sigillum, Inevitabile, Speculum Ecclesiae, Offendiculum, Summa Totius, Gemma Animae, Sacramentarium, Neocosmum, Eucharistion, Cognitio Vitae, Imago Mundi, Summa Gloria, Scala Coeli de gradibus visionum, De Anima et de Deo,*

Expositio Totius Psalterii, Cantica Canticorum, Evangelia (' quae beatus Gregorius non exposuit '), *Clavis Physicae, Refectio Mentium, Pabulum Vitae, De Luminaribus.* The *Annales Palidenses* contain the only other nearly contemporary list. This credits Honorius with an *Expositio Super Cantica Canticorum*, another on the Psalter and one on the Gospels, again ' quae beatus Gregorius non exposuit ', also with a *Speculum Ecclesiae*, a *Gemma Animae*, ' et insuper alia quam plurima '. All of these except the ' Evangelia ' can be traced again in the gift of Frater Heinricus. [1]

Some of these works are lost. The *Evangelia* and the *Pabulum Vitae* have not reached us. One Lambach manuscript, M.S. LAMBACH CXXXIX, may contain the *Refectio Mentium*, but the attribution is not certain. Some works can, on the other hand, be added to the list. Migne contains a number of these. [2] Thus in a section ' didascalica et historica ' appears a catalogue of Roman pontiffs. A work *De Haeresibus* makes up the same section. Into an exegetical section comes the *De Decem Plagis*, and into that labelled ' Dogmatica et Ascetica ' the *De Libero Arbitrio* and the *Libri XII* and *VIII Quaestionum*, the *Scala Coeli Minor*, the *De Animae Exilio et Patria* and the *De Claustrali Vita.* [3] Endres has a few more short pieces to contribute ; the *Quod Monachis Liceat Predicare*, [4] three questions from a Melk manuscript which has the only text we know of the *De Anima et de Deo*, [5] and additions to the *Cognitio Vitae* and the *Clavis Physicae.* [6] A small text from important Windberg and Lambach

---

1. I have discussed the importance of the gift of Frater Heinricus in the earlier paper : V.I.J. FLINT, *The Career of Honorius Augustodunensis. Some Fresh Evidence*, in *Rev. bénéd.* 82 (1972), p. 63-86. The *Annales Palidenses* is a world chronicle produced at Pöhlde, near Brunswick. It ends at the year 1182 and uses Honorius's *Imago Mundi*. Its author, for this reason, refers to Honorius's other works. *MGH SS*, XVI, 52.

2. Two of the works attributed to Honorius in MIGNE, the *De Solis Affectibus* and the *De Philosophia Mundi*, are undoubtedly spurious. Endres first expressed doubts about the former, mainly because it is in a style so unlike that of anything else Honorius wrote. It is a dry piece of work, with none of the helps to the slow reader one finds in the *Imago Mundi*. The *De Philosophia Mundi* has, of course, long been proved to be the work of William of Conches.

3. *PL* 172, c. 239-244, 233-240, 265-270, 1223-1226, 1226-1230 (Sententiae Patrum), 1177-1186, 1187-1192, 1239-1242, 1241-1246, 1247-1248.

4. *Honorius Augustodunensis*, Kempten-Munich, 1906, p. 147-150.

5. MELK 850, now *Bodley Lyell 58*. ENDRES, *op. cit.*, p. 150-154. The *De Anima et de Deo* has not been published.

6. *Ibid.*, p. 138-141. The *De Vitiis et Virtutibus* is, in some manuscripts, inserted between chapters 37 and 38 of the *Cognitio Vitae* : MSS. *Bodley Lyell* 56 and 58, and Clm 22225. It stands on its own in the gift of Frater Heinricus.

manuscripts, which contributed the first of these last two additions should also perhaps be attributed to him, and also some small fragments, as yet unpublished, in the same manuscripts. [1] The *Quaestiones et ad easdem responsiones in duos Salomonis libros Proverbia et Ecclesiasten*, printed by Migne but denied to Honorius by Endres, should now be reassigned to him, and with them the *Quaestiones in Joannem and in Mattheum*. [2]

Some of the works, especially those which I shall argue are the earlier ones, appear in different recensions. Some bear references to authorities which may be meant as guides for further work, and some are glossed. Few, in fact only those which were among Honorius's last works, appear to have been meant to be definitive. Honorius seems, for the most part, to have kept his writings before him, and worked over them with care. His output is remarkably varied ; it includes biblical exegesis, primitive theology, cosmology, history, polemic. He moves easily between the dialogue and narrative forms. There is about the whole, however, a singular unity. His style and technique become, after a little reading, unmistakable. One has, when reading his works, the sense of a vigorous and in some ways original writer. A little of this sense can be gathered even from this bland list of titles. Few of them are obvious ones. Many of them appear to have been created by the author, and some of them convey no impression at all of what the work is about. [3] Honorius is rich in small, sometimes irritating, tricks of invention. He has, above all, the instinct of a performer for timing. This instinct is, fortunately, a help in establishing a chronology for his writings.

It has always been clear that Honorius produced a great deal of work. It has never been clear exactly when he produced it. The *De Luminaribus* gives no help with chronology beyond the

---

1. *Quid sit vasa honoris et quid sit vasa contumeliae ; Bodley* Lyell 56 and Clm 22225. This is also in MSS. HEILIGENKREUZ 77 and KLOSTERNEUBURG 931. *Bodley* Lyell 56 contains extra sets of short *quaestiones*, ff. 191-192, 205ᵛ-206. There are nine in all. Three in the first group are printed by I. Dieterich in *MGH Libelli de Lite*, III (1897), p. 34-35, from Clm 22225 and ST. FLORIAN XI. The first question from the second group is also in KLOSTERNEUBURG 931. The manuscript also contains short pieces. Those on ff. 272ᵛ-273 are contained also in Clm 22225 and ST. FLORIAN XI. Others are : f. 195, *De legione ;* ff. 236-237, *De quatuor modis scripturarum, De Hierusalem, De VI etatibus, De numero.*
2. *PL* 172, c. 311-348 ; ENDRES, *op. cit.*, p. 73-75. See V.I.J. FLINT, *The True Author of the ' Salonii Commentarii in Parabolas Salomonis et in Ecclesiasten '*, in *Rech. de Théol. Anc. et Méd.* 37 (1970), p. 174-186.
3. The titles of some may be drawn from astrological terms : the seal, the mirror, the image, fate. If so, they are consciously christianised.

VII

218

general assertion that Honorius flourished in the reign of the
Emperor Henry V. The *Annales Palidenses* give none, save the
fact that Honorius was associated with a certain ' Christianus '.
I have said that some of Honorius's works bear dedications.
The attempted identification of these has led to some remarkable
assertions. Endres pursued this path, and his particular identifications gave him a period for Honorius's active life which
stretched from the England of St. Anselm to the end of the life
of Abbot Christian of Regensburg (1153), perhaps even to that
of Abbot Gregory (1156-85). [1] The later possibility was strengthened by the supposed dedication of the *De Libero Arbitrio* to
Provost Gotteschalk of Bamberg (d. after 1170). Endres was
free therefore to station Honorius's writings at arbitrary intervals
within this liberal time span. These preferences led him to set
aside the ' sub quinto Henrico floruit ' of the *De Luminaribus*.
Manitius and after him Miss Sanford, neither of whose primary
task was to establish the chronology of Honorius's works, accepted
Endres's liberal assessment and, it seems, his method of reaching
it. Manitius placed the *Elucidarius* in or after the year 1120 and
let the rest follow where they would, with the exception of one
or two attempts at precise dating. [2] Rooth, interested in the
possible German origins of the *Speculum Ecclesiae*, the *Summa
Totius*, the *Gemma Animae* and the *Sacramentarium*, tried in the
meanwhile to relate these, the *Expositio Totius Psalterii* and the
In Cantica Canticorum with what was known of Honorius's
German career. [3] In an important few pages he cast doubt upon
Endres's reckoning. Some of his observations are no more than
suspicions and some of his detailed criticisms hang upon dates he
had taken to be established ones but which are now open to some
doubt. His suspicions, however, can be shown to be well founded.
The last person to make a serious effort at setting out in outline
the chronology of Honorius's career and that of his works was
H. Menhardt. [4] His contribution is helpful because it is clear,

1. The *Exposition in Cantica* is addressed to the successor of ' C '. Taking
' C ' to be Christian, Endres supposed this to be Gregory of St. James of
Regensburg. *Op. cit.*, p. 60.
2. M. MANITIUS, *Geschichte der Lateinischen Literatur des Mittelalters*,
Munich, 1931, III, p. 366.
3. E. ROOTH, *Kleine Beiträge zur Kenntnis des sogennanten Honorius
Augustodunensis*, in *Studia Neophilologica* 12 (1939), p. 128-133.
4. H. MENHARDT, *Der Nachlass des Honorius Augustodunensis*, in *Zeitschrift für Deutsches Altertum und Deutsche Literatur* 89 (1958), p. 67-69.

but in content it summarises the opinions of those authors I have already mentioned, and differs from them very little. This method of inquiry was, in fact, a dangerous one. It led to too summary a dismissal of the earliest evidence. Its conclusions have not so far been supported by an examination of the contents and sources of the individual treatises. The following discussion seeks to remedy this lack. The result will, it is hoped, lead to a radical revision of all the dates offered so far, and to a return to the general outline suggested by the *De Luminaribus*.

II. THE WORKS ASSOCIATED WITH ENGLAND

Six works bear some signs of being associated with England. The first two on Honorius's list bear the clearest of these signs ; that is, the *Elucidarius* and the *Sigillum*. The *Speculum Ecclesiae*, the *Offendiculum*, the *Gemma Animae* and the *Imago Mundi* have associations slightly less uncompromisingly marked. The first version of the first of these works can be dated with some precision. It seems well, then, to begin the process of dating the Corpus with these.

Large sections of the *Elucidarius* rely directly upon works of St. Anselm and upon his spoken word. The reliance was acknowledged in the early manuscripts, and was confined to opinions written or expressed before 1100. Honorius uses, for example, a version of the *De Beatitudine* which is far more closely related to Eadmer's first version of this than to any of the later ones ; it may even be an earlier transcription than Eadmer's. Conversely one can point to later works which do not seem to have been available to Honorius when he wrote. In Book I (3-5) he shows no sensitivity to the difficulty this comparison had caused Anselm in his *De Processione Sancti Spiritus*. [1] This suggests that this part of the *Elucidarius* at least may have been written before the appearance of this work, dated by Father Schmitt to the years 1099-1102. [2] Similarly the controversial definition of free will contained in Book II chapter 7 of the first version of the *Elucidarius* seems to have been decided upon before St. Anselm had formulated fully the definition set out in the *De Concordia Praescientiae*

---

1. Chapter VIII. *S. Anselmi Opera Omnia* (ed. F. S. Schmitt), Edinburgh, 1946-1961 (New Edition : Stuttgart, 1968), II, p. 199-201.
2. F. S. SCHMITT, *Zur Chronologie der Werke des hl. Anselm von Canterbury*, in *Rev. bénéd.* 44 (1932), p. 347-348.

et Praedestinationis (1107-1108). [1] At least three recensions were made of the *Elucidarius* ; the first was written in England at the very beginning of Honorius's career, and the other two appear to have been put together after the completion of this last work.

The preface to the second work on the list, the *Sigillum,* suggests that it followed the *Elucidarius* directly.

> Omnium fratrum conventus tuae diligentiae grates solvit, quod eis spiritus sapientiae tot involucra per tuum laborem in *elucidario* involvit.

The first part of the *Sigillum* is a summary of the work printed in Migne as St. Anselm's ninth homily. [2] The summary, with some changes, is to be found again in the *Speculum Ecclesiae* as part of a sermon on the feast of the Assumption. [3] The homily was not in fact St. Anselm's but, as Dom Wilmart has shown, was written by Ralph D'Escures, monk and abbot of St. Martin's of Séez, who took refuge in England in about the year 1100 and later became Bishop of Rochester (1108) and Archbishop of Canterbury (1114). [4] He wrote it, the preface tells us, in Normandy, probably while he was abbot of Séez. Prior Eastry's catalogue shows that Canterbury had two copies of it in his day. [5] It may have reached Canterbury quite early, but, if not, the flight to England of Ralph himself is good surety for its arrival. It is safe to say that Honorius could have had access to it in England in 1100 or thereabouts. This is the latest of the material used in the *Sigillum.* The work could, therefore, have been written very early in the twelfth century.

The preface to the *Speculum Ecclesiae* suggests that Honorius had been on a journey before he was asked to write it :

> Cum proxime in nostro convento resideres, et verbum fratribus secundum datum tibi a Domino sapientiam faceres, omnibus qui aderant visum est non te sed angelum Dei fuisse locutum.

---

1. See V.I.J. FLINT, *The Original Text of the ' Elucidarius ' of Honorius Augustodunensis from the twelfth century English manuscripts,* in *Scriptorium* 18 (1964), p. 91-94, for corrections to Lefèvre's edition.

2. *PL* 158, c. 644-649.

3. *PL* 172, c. 991-992.

4. A. WILMART, *Les Homélies attribuées à S. Anselme,* in *Arch. d'hist. doctr. et litt.* 2 (1927), p. 16-23. Ralph had to leave Normandy because of his support of the papal prohibition of lay investiture and led for a time a peripatetic life in England. WILLIAM OF MALMESBURY, *Gesta Pontificum* (ed. N.E.S.A. Hamilton), London, 1870, p. 127.

5. M. R. JAMES, *The Ancient Libraries of Canterbury and Dover,* Cambridge, 1903, p. 32-33, n⁰ˢ 146 and 161.

The heading given to the work in some manuscripts, ' fratres Cantuariensis ecclesiae ' suggests that it was Canterbury he had left. [1] This tempted Endres to decide that he had left England. It should be noted however that both the *Sigillum* and the *Inevitabile* imply that Honorius was some way away from his petitioners. In the preface to the *Sigillum* he talks of the community's grateful acceptance of the book he had sent them (' quem misi libellum ') and in the *Inevitabile* the discipulus describes himself as an embassy, ' Illorum ergo nunc fungor legatione '. It could be that Honorius was not as far away from Canterbury when he wrote the *Speculum* as Endres supposed. It is true that the *Speculum* is now to be found in manuscripts from South Germany and Austria. Also Baesecke has drawn attention to the fact that Honorius had relied for parts of it upon a latin collection of prayers which came from Germany. [2] Honorius may, however, have used for it Worcester material, [3] and, if this is so, then he may merely have left Canterbury for Worcester. Honorius's relations with the West Country of England will be more fully treated later, and I hope to show that they are marked in the *Sigillum* as well as in the *Speculum Ecclesiae*. For the moment it is perhaps enough to say that all the material apparently used by Honorius here too could have been available in the very early years of the century ; and that the two could be connected in time as well as in space and in some of their sources.

In the *Offendiculum* and the *De Apostatis*, which seems to be attached to it, Honorius expresses strong views about unworthy priests and apostate monks. The title, the sentiments expressed and some of the ways in which they are expressed suggest England, where monumental efforts were made under St. Anselm to prohibit clerical marriage, and decrees against it promulgated in 1102 and 1108. [4] The archbishop was uncompromising on the matter, and, although the decrees of the councils of Westminster are nowhere explicitly mentioned in Honorius's texts, it is clear that St. Anselm's opinions played an important part in their formation.

---

1. For example, Clm 7700 and St. FLORIAN XI. ENDRES, *op. cit.*, p. 30.
2. G. BAESECKE, *Die Altdeutschen Beichten*, in *Beiträge zur Geschichte der Deutschen Sprache und Literatur* 49 (1925), p. 268 ff.
3. *Rev. bénéd.*, *art. cit.*
4. J. KELLE, *Untersuchungen über das ' Speculum Ecclesiae ' des Honorius und die ' Libri deflorationum ' des Abtes Werner*, in *Sitzungsberichte der Kaiserlichen Akademie der Wissenschaften* 145 (1903), fasc. VIII. MANSI, XX, 1151 and 1230. Decrees were also passed at these councils against apostate monks.

The title Honorius uses is very like that given to a work of St. Anselm's ; the *De Presbyteris Concubinariis seu Offendiculum Sacerdotum*. [1] This forms the central part of a letter on the subject to a certain Abbot William [2] and this and Honorius's treatise are closely related. [3] Anselm, for example, recommends, as Honorius does, that priests of unwholesome life are to be avoided totally, but is prepared to admit that the sacraments they administer might be valid :

> Non quo quis ea quae tractant contemnenda, sed tractantes exsecrandos existimet.

Honorius had held this opinion in the *Elucidarius* (I, 190) :

> Quamvis damnatissimi sunt, tamen per verba quae recitant fit corpus Domini.

He would offer it again in the *Eucharistion* (ch. VI). He maintains it now in the *Offendiculum* (ch. 41). [4] Again Anselm decides in his letter that the orders of such priests remain valid and that if they repent they may come back to the full practice of their priesthood. Honorius is of this opinion too in the case of Simoniac priests :

> Inde canonica auctoritate, si quis a symoniacis ordinatur, ab omni officio aecclesiae sequestratur ; sed si ad aecclesiam convertitur, et eius vita utilis in clero iudicatur, non reordinatur, sed per manus impositionem catholici episcopi reconciliatur. (Ch. 51.)

St. Anselm, who deals so much more briefly with the matter, does not make this last condition, but the general agreement is clear enough. [5]

---

1. *PL* 158, c. 555-556.
2. SCHMITT *op. cit.*, III, ep. 65, p. 182-185.
3. The only surviving English manuscript of Anselm's *Offendiculum*, CAMBRIDGE *Corpus Christi Coll.* 34, has the letter of St. Anselm bound with it (f. 427).
4. It is true that at the beginning of the chapter he seems to take a fiercer line than Anselm ; so ENDRES, p. 35. He thinks Honorius departs here from his original idea. Honorius modifies his apparent statement that such priests have no sacramental power, however, later in the chapter : ' Substantia quoque panis et vini non fit melior in manibus boni oblata nec peior per manus impii sacrificata '.
5. Honorius seems to be somewhat preoccupied with the idea that there is no need to re-ordain erring priests. In the *De Luminaribus* he stresses this one point in the writings of Peter Damian : ' Petrus, cognomento Damiani, ex monacho et eremita episcopus, scripsit librum contra illos qui Simoniacos reordinare censuerunt, et multa alia ' (IV, XI).

In the *De Apostatis* too Honorius shows great deference for the opinions of St. Anselm. As well as in the decrees passed in his councils, St. Anselm gives his opinions on apostate monks in three letters. [1] He leaves the recipients in no doubt about his conviction that such monks are damned unless they repent. To Adrian, monk of Canterbury, he says :

> Nullus enim homo in praesenti vita vivens potest te absolvere ab his vinculis excommunicationis et anathematis, nisi quod vera dilectione precor et consulo feceris.

Adrian's departure, says Anselm, can only have been at the prompting of the devil and neither he nor his companion can merit Anselm's prayers unless they return. Honorius is quite unrelenting on this matter too. Such monks are wolves in sheeps clothing and are to be shunned utterly (ch. 4). In chapter 10 he makes it clear that he too thinks they will be damned :

> Si illi non debet in cibo communicari, qui in aecclesia probatur formicari, ab omni communione aecclesiae sunt reprobandi, qui Deum et aecclesiam per apostasiam reliquerunt et extra aecclesiam publice in fornicatione sordescunt. Quis ergo eos sciens « ave » eis dixerit, eorum malis operibus communicat et ideo dampnationis etiam illorum particeps erit.

Honorius uses the standard quotation from Luke (IX, 62) too, in chapter 8. All of these views could have been gathered from Anselm and in England. There is one other very important piece of evidence which suggests that they were in fact gathered there. This is to be found in the wording of the text of two sections of the *Offendiculum*. The two sections in question, chapters 17 and 18, bear a close resemblance to a letter sent by Paschal II to Henry I of England. Both take for their texts John X, 1-18. Honorius says in chapter 17 :

> Audi : Qui per ostium Christum non intrant aecclesiam, sed aliunde ascendunt per pecuniam, non sacerdotes, sed fures et latrones.

He expands this and in chapter 18 goes on :

> Qui a pastore non intromissus per ostium non intraverit, sed scandendo per murum in ovile irruerit, aut fur aut latro aut lupus est.

---

1. Schmitt, *op. cit.*, IV, ep. 162 (written 1093), p. 34-35 ; V, ep. 333, p. 269-270 ; ep. 431 (undated), p. 377-378.

224

The similar passage in the letter from Paschal II is this one :

> Cum autem ecclesiae ostium reges esse arrogant, fit profecto ut, qui per eos ecclesiam ingrediuntur, non pastores, sed fures et latrones habeantur, eodem domino dicente : « Qui non intrat per ostium in ovile ovium, sed ascendit aliunde, fur est et latro » [1].

This letter arrived in England after Pentecost 1101. It is given by Eadmer. [2] Honorius could then have had access to it at Canterbury or in the West Country. There is, indeed, still extant an important early twelfth century copy of it which belonged to the Cathedral of Christchurch Canterbury. [3] This evidence, together with the fact that Honorius cites nowhere the decrees of the council of Westminster, tempt one to conclude that he at least gathered the material for this part of the *Offendiculum* between Pentecost 1101 and the council of 1102. This is to put forward the date usually accepted for the composition of the *Offendiculum* by some twenty years [4] which is a startling revision but one which seems to be not unjustified.

Honorius set himself up as a purveyor of fierce views on reform in his first recension of the *Elucidarius*. The *Offendiculum* may have been drawn up specially to give greater substance to the passages on reform in this early work, and its appearance may have been one of the reasons for their disappearance in later renderings. Verbal similarities between the two are on occasion striking, [5] and some of these similarities are to be found in passages of the *Elucidarius* which belong only to its earliest recension. [6] The epilogue to the *Offendiculum* shows, moreover, that here too Honorius was writing surrounded by enemies ; it may have followed the *Elucidarius* very quickly. Did the *Speculum Ecclesiae*, then, follow the *Offendiculum* ? It could have done so but there seems no reason to destroy at this point the order of Honorius's list. It seems more likely that they were written concurrently and that both took shape in England before their publication in Germany. The only surviving early manuscripts of the

1. SCHMITT, *op. cit.*, IV, ep. 216, p. 115.
2. *Historia Novorum* (ed. M. Rule), London, 1884, p. 128-131.
3. CAMBRIDGE *University Library*, I.1.3.33, f. 195. This manuscript is as a whole attributed to Christchurch Canterbury by N. R. KER, *Medieval Libraries of Great Britain*, London, 1964, p. 30.
4. Thus Miss E. M. SANFORD, *Honorius, Presbyter et Scholasticus*, in *Speculum* 23 (1948), p. 413, gives as an approximate date 1122.
5. *Elucidarius* I, 185-189. *Offendiculum* 42-43. *Elucidarius* I, 193-194, 198.
6. *Elucidarius* I, 200a. *Offendiculum* 47. Many of these opinions are ascribed in early manuscripts of the *Elucidarius* to St. Anselm.

VII

Offendiculum and of its companion, the *De Apostatis*, are German ones. They are rare works and were perhaps not intended for wide distribution.

So far, with the exception of the *Inevitabile* which will be discussed below, the works which appear to have some connection with England are those mentioned first in the list in the *De Luminaribus* ; they seem to have been put together during the late eleventh century and the very early twelfth.

There was certainly an interest in the eleventh century in England in works upon the liturgy. Two magnificent manuscripts which give evidence of this interest come from Worcester. One comes from Exeter. [1] One of the Worcester ones contains extracts from the two works of Amalarius Honorius used. He may have copied these and an additional passage from it. [2] If Honorius's use of Amalarius is suggestive, his use of one other source in the *Gemma Animae* is compelling. The work of Maurilius of Rouen, *De Officiis Ecclesiasticis*, survives in one twelfth century manuscript. [3] Maurilius undertook this work in his last years as archbishop of Rouen (d. 1067). It appears to be a revision and expansion of a treatise on the same subject written at his command by John, bishop of Avranches. [4] In two places, Honorius and Maurilius have passages in common which cannot be traced to any third source. It is likely that Honorius took a miracle he uses to prove the authenticity of the feast of the Nativity from Maurilius, [5] and it is more than likely that he

---

1. MS. CAMBRIDGE *Corpus Christi College* 265 (Worcester), 190 (Exeter), *B.M.* Cotton Nero A 1 (Worcester).
2. CCCC 265. M. BATESON, *A Worcester Cathedral Book of Ecclesiastical Collections, made c. 1000 A.D.*, in *English Historical Review* 10 (1895), p. 712-731. Dom Wilmart, who declares that Amalarius was little known in England before the twelfth century, does not mention this manuscript ; A. WILMART, *Pour une nouvelle édition du traité d'Amalaire sur les Offices*, in *Rev. bénéd.* 37 (1925), p. 99, n. 1. There is still in existence also a tenth century English manuscript of the *De Ecclesiasticis Officiis* of Amalarius : CCCC 192. William of Malmesbury, of course, confirmed the interest, in the Worcester diocese, by his abridgment of Amalarius. This is preserved in three early manuscripts : *All Souls* 28 (twelfth century), *Lambeth* 380 (twelfth century) and *Lambeth* 363 (twelfth-thirteenth century).
3. MS. *Bodley* 843.
4. R. DELAMARE, *Le ' De Officiis Ecclesiasticis ' de Jean d'Avranches*, Paris, 1923, p. XLVIII-LI.
5. ' De primordiali cultu divino ' : *Gemma Animae* I, CXXII ; *Bodley* 843, f. 127. ' Quod Christus sit fundamentum Ecclesiae ' : *Gemma Animae* I, CXXIX ; *Bodley* 843, f. 127ᵛ. DELAMARE, *op. cit.*, p. LVIII, points this out, but his references are inaccurate. The possibility has been advanced by ENDRES, *op. cit.*, p. 39, and ROOTH, *op. cit.*, p. 129, that the *Gemma Animae* was in some way involved with the *De Divinis Officiis* of Rupert of Deutz, which was in the

took these two passages from him. The passages, widely separated in Honorius, are close together in Maurilius, and the dependence is very close indeed. If Honorius did borrow from Maurilius, then he is virtually certain to have read him in England. To judge from the manuscript evidence, the *De Officiis Ecclesiasticis* was not popular and it is most improbable that it circulated widely outside England and Normandy. The *Gemma Animae* too, then, bears a trace of Honorius's early English interests, and none of the material in it suggests a date later than that of the other works associated with England, or with it, in Honorius's list.

Finally, the *Imago Mundi*. I hope later to suggest that in Books I and II of this work Honorius may again have drawn upon sources available in England. More important for the present purpose, however, is the fact that the *Imago Mundi* is the one work to which we can assign firm dates. The *Imago Mundi* is an earlier work than was previously supposed. Wilmanns, following Föringer, distinguished five recensions of it. The first, he decided, ended in 1123. [1] This dating was accepted by Endres and Manitius and more recently by Rooth. [2] On the reckoning, then, that Honorius produced roughly a book a year (for which reckoning, incidentally, there is no evidence other than the quality of his work, and some of that could lead one to assign a far shorter time to it), and relying on the accuracy of the list in the *De Luminaribus*, Wilmanns decided that the years 1122/23 would be appropriate for the production of the *Imago Mundi*. Unhappily the other delicate points upon which this theory is poised have for themselves no support. The fact that there have now come to light two manuscripts, one of the twelfth century and one of the thirteenth, which end the *Imago Mundi* in the year 1110 must do it serious damage. [3] Both of these manus-

course of composition in 1111 ; *PL* 170, c. 215. I have so far found no evidence of a connection beyond the general one of purpose and the common use of sources, and certainly no reason to suppose that Honorius depended upon, and therefore wrote after, Rupert.

1. *MGH SS*, X, p. 127. The first recension was contained in a single manuscript : LONDON *B.M.* Cotton Cleopatra B. IV. The other recensions ended at 1132/33, 1139, 1152, after 1152. Besides these variants at its end, in some early manuscripts the book begins at ' non arbitror infructuosum '. This led Duhem to suggest that it was not by Honorius at all ; P. DUHEM, *Le système du monde. Histoire des doctrines cosmologiques de Platon à Copernic*, Paris, 1913-1917, III, p. 27. The suggestion has, however, no further support.

2. *Op. cit.*, p. 129. Endres in a footnote mentioned the evidence of CCCC 66 ; *op. cit.*, p. 45, n. 1.

3. CCCC 66. The thirteenth century MS. is *B.M.* Cotton Vespasian E.X (f. 119) ; this has not previously been cited.

VII

cripts are English ones. The first is a particularly important
one. I have mentioned MS. CAMBRIDGE *Corpus Christi College*
66 before. It will be mentioned again. The evidence it provides
deserves to be taken seriously.

The works in which English material appears to have been
used fall within a period which stretches from approximately
1098 to 1110. The works associated with England are also
among those works which are mentioned first in the *De Luminaribus* and appear to have been written in the order given in it.
So far, the list in the *De Luminaribus* seems to be a roughly
chronological one. The order given in the *De Luminaribus* for
the other works appears also to correspond to their order in time.

III. THE OTHER WORKS LISTED IN THE "DE LUMINARIBUS"

The *Inevitabile*, and the rest of the works grouped round the
Gemma Animae and the *Imago Mundi*, that is, the *Summa
Totius*, the *Sacramentarium*, the *Neocosmum*, the *Eucharistion*, the
Cognitio Vitae, are difficult to date exactly. There seems,
however, to be no reason why any of them should be far removed
from the *Gemma Animae* or the *Imago Mundi* in time. The
prologues of all of them make it clear that Honorius is still
involved in his twofold task of resolving difficulties for the simple
minded and remedying the sad lack of books. Honorius seems
to draw, too, for some of them, upon a stock of material which
has not undergone any radical change or increase.

In the prologue to the *Inevitabile*, Honorius associates this
work with the *Elucidarius* and with the *Sigillum* as cleverly as he
associated the last two. Clearly there were ways round his
anonymity for persons he chose :

Discipulus. Fratres in domo Dei ambulantes cum consensu, sunt pro
tua salute orationi instantes : diligentiae quidem tuae, orationes :
Clavi autem David Christo, gratiarum solvunt actiones : qui ob Gene-
tricis suae merita, tot eis in Canticis, de ea *per te reservavit* mysteria.
Ob hanc causam, et ob alia quae multis incognita, *elucidans* in laudem
ejus, debitores fecisti.

There are open references here to the two preceding works and
Honorius puts into the mouths of his petitioners many of the
words he had himself used in his reply to the request for the
Sigillum. In this he had said :

Igitur quia vestrum collegium gratanter suscepit, quem misi libellum, dabo operam per *clavem David vobis reserare*, de quibus videmini dubitare.

It looks, therefore, as though the *Inevitabile* may have followed these two immediately in fact, as it does in the *De Luminaribus*. There are two recensions of the *Inevitabile*. [1] The two are distinguished by a variant, similar to that which distinguishes the recensions of the *Elucidarius*, on the definition of free will. [2] The first recension adopts the Augustinian definition which had appeared first in the *Elucidarius*. [3] The second has the Anselmian which had appeared in Anselm's treatises *De Libertate Arbitrii* and *De Concordia Praescientiae et Praedestinationis*. [4] This definition may only have been properly formulated in the last years of St. Anselm's life, for although the *De Libertate Arbitrii* had been drawn up most probably in the years 1080-1085 [5] its full exposition in the *De Concordia* was to wait until 1107-1108. [6] The first recension known so far could, then, be placed in time shortly after the first recension of the *Elucidarius*, and after the *Sigillum* ; that is, in about 1100-1101. [7] The second might conveniently take its place after the public appearance of the views of St. Anselm on free will. This would mean that it too was produced after 1108. In date, in its references to the two first works, in its interest in St. Anselm's preoccupations, and in its place in the *De Luminaribus*, the first version of the *Inevitabile* falls among the works associated with England.

---

1. Kelle first drew attention to a recension differing from that printed from J. Conen's edition in Migne ; J. KELLE, *Untersuchungen über des Honorius ' Inevitabile sive de praedestinatione et libero arbitrio dialogus '*, in *Sitzungsberichte der Kaiserlichen Akademie der Wissenschaften*, phil.-hist. Klasse, 150 (1904), fasc. III, p. 1-24. He printed the different recension from Clm 13105, cod. 142 (Liège, thirteenth century) and Cassander's edition of 1552. LEYDEN Vulc. 100 appears to be the MS. Cassander used but Kelle could not find.

2. F. BÄUMKER established that the recension printed in Migne was the second of the two : *Das ' Inevitabile ' des Honorius Augustodunensis und dessen Lehre über das Zusammenwirken von Wille und Gnade*, in *Beiträge zur Geschichte der Philosophie des Mittelalters* 13 (1914), fasc. 6, p. 1-93.

3. ' M. Dic ergo mihi imprimis, quid liberum arbitrium vocitari dicis. — D. Ut tu diffinisti, libertatem bonum vel malum eligendi ' (KELLE, p. 12).

4. ' Libertas arbitrii est potestas servandi rectitudinem voluntatis, propter ipsam rectitudinem ' (*PL* 172, c. 1200).

5. SCHMITT, *art. cit.*, p. 350.

6. *The Life of St. Anselm of Canterbury by Eadmer* (ed. R. W. SOUTHERN). Nelson Medieval Texts, 1962, II, LXIV, p. 140.

7. The twelfth century manuscripts of this recension are MS. LEYDEN Vulc. 100 (St. Pantaleon), Clm 13105 (Prüfening ?), 14348 (St. Emmeram's, Regensburg), KREMSMÜNSTER CXXXIII, *Bodley* Laud. Misc. 237.

I have been unable to trace in it, however, any source which is certainly English.

The *Summa Totius* clearly preceded the *Gemma Animae*, for Honorius in the latter work returned to his old tactics of open reference in the preface :

> Postquam, Christo favente, pelagus Scripturae prospero cursu in summa totius transcurri, atque naufragosam cymbam, per syrtes et piratas multo sudore evectam, vix ad optatum litus appuli, rursus habitatores Sion me in fluctus cogitationum intruditis, et nec vires recolligere, nec navis armamenta reficere sinitis. [1]

The *Summa Totius* was perhaps a preliminary to the *Imago Mundi*. [2] There are difficulties in the way of dating it more precisely. The only complete manuscript of it is a fifteenth century one and ends in the twelfth year of the reign of Lothar of Supplinburg (1135-36) ; it may, as Wilmanns pointed out, be a second or even a third recension. [3] One marginal noted placed next to the passage reporting the accession of Henry V of Germany may give a slight clue :

> Anshelmus episcopus in Anglia claret.

The tense of the verb contrasts with an earlier note :

> Heriger episcopus claruit.

The *Summa* may, then, have been written while Anselm was alive. Very little of it has been published, and the only twelfth-century manuscript of it to have been discovered so far shows that it was an extremely thorough and painstaking piece of work ; [4] one which perhaps because of its very thoroughness did not become popular.   In it special attention is paid to classical history, and the bulk of this manuscript (f. 28^r - f. 72^r) is devoted to the fifth age.   After Justinian, marginalia suddenly decrease.   There are few early mentions of it ; I have found it only in the medieval catalogue of the abbey of Prüfening and in the gift of Frater Heinricus.   It is quite likely, then, that the *Summa Totius* was

---

1. *PL* 172, c. 541.
2. So R. Wilmanns : ' Hanc summam denuo in epitomen redegit Honorius cum in libro tertio Imaginis Mundi de dispositione orbis adumbratam historiam rerum ab Adam ad sua usque tempora gestarum dare sibi proposuisset ' (*MGH SS*, X, p. 127).
3. *Ibid.*, p. 126.
4. VIENNA *Nationalbibliothek* 382.   It is very carefully and fully annotated in the same hand.

a comparatively early effort, which shewed that Honorius, when he wrote it, had himself ready widely and was capable of producing a substantial historical exposition. Like many works of this nature, however, it proved a little too substantial and was easily superseded by the superficial, but comprehensible, *Imago Mundi*. The *Sacramentarium* is very closely associated with the *Gemma Animae*. It seems to be in fact an expansion of select parts of it, and founded upon similar sources. Unlike the *Gemma Animae* it is a rare work and again, unlike the *Gemma Animae*, all the surviving manuscripts of it are German ones. There is no independent means by which this work can be dated. The *Neocosmum* (or *Hexaemeron*), according to its prologue, sought to enter again debates about the days of creation and to try to resolve them. The *Eucharistion* Endres sees as one of the last waves of the storm started by the Berengarian controversy. [1] He points out that although the treatise shows no particular dependence on St. Anselm's letter on the matter, Honorius takes up much the same position as it does. The letter he means is in fact part of a commentary of Anselm of Laon on the First Epistle of St. Paul to the Corinthians, long falsely attributed to Anselm of Canterbury. [2] Honorius's defence here of the orthodox position on the Eucharist has echoes in the *Elucidarius* and in the *Speculum Ecclesiae*. [3] The *Cognitio Vitae* is particularly interesting. Many questions are the same as those asked in the *Elucidarius*, and the same illustrations are used for their solution. [4] The *Cognitio* is, however, a work of far greater substance. Answers are given at greater length and with far more conside-

---

1. ENDRES, *op. cit.*, p. 41 f.
2. O. LOTTIN, *Anselme de Laon, auteur de la ' lettre ' de S. Anselme sur la Cène*, in *Rech. de Théol. Anc. et Méd.* 13 (1946), p. 222-225.
3. It draws upon Paschasius, like the *Elucidarius* ; for example, *Eucharistion* XII (PL 172, c. 1256) ; *Elucidarius* I, 180 ; Paschasius, *Liber de Corpore et Sanguine Christi* (PL 120, c. 1303-1310). Honorius's literal understanding of the doctrine of transsubstantiation is demonstrated in his elaboration of the miracle of the Jewish boy in the *Speculum Ecclesiae*, sermon on the Purification (PL 172, c. 852) and in the sermon ' In Coena Domini ' (*ibid.*, c. 928). It is demonstrated also in the *Gemma Animae* I, CXI (*ibid.*, c. 673).
4. *Cognitio Vitae* II   *Elucidarius* I, 2

»	VIII	»	I, 2
»	X	»	I, 3
»	XI	»	I, 7-9
»	XXI	»	I, 112
»	XXIII-XXIV	»	I, 12, 16
»	XXIX	»	I, 10
»	XXXII	»	I, 6, 59
»	XLIII	»	I, 11.

ration, even at times calling simple logic to their service. It is the sort of work which could well have been prompted by a more mature reading of the *Elucidarius*. The *Cognitio* marks a return too to the dialogue form. Honorius depends in it upon St. Anselm's *Monologion*, but fragments of Anselm's long expositions are inserted by Honorius as conclusions. In some places the condensation is so extreme that he may be depending only on his memory of his master's words.

The sum of this evidence suggests that all the works which precede the *Imago Mundi* in the list in the *De Luminaribus* could have preceded it in time. They have some links with the works associated in part with England, but the links are tenuous. There are no surviving twelfth century English manuscripts of any of them ; those which do survive are associated with South Germany and Austria. The *Summa Totius*, above all, is primarily concerned with German history, as is the last section of the third book of the *Imago Mundi*. We have reached the years approximately 1109-1110, and we have surely reached the continent. This change of place and date will become more interesting when we return to consider Honorius's career. For the time being, the order given by the *De Luminaribus* appears to be a chronological one.

With the *Summa Gloria*, the next work on the list, Honorius puts into writing principles his association with St. Anselm had perhaps fortified in him, and thereby launches himself, with characteristic forthrightness, at one of the most sensitive concerns of contemporary politics ; the relationship of the regnal to the sacerdotal power. The preface to the *Summa Gloria* makes it clear that it was written where the problem of regnal versus sacerdotal power was a highly topical one :

> Quia igitur plerique nomen scientiae sibi usurpant, nescientes, de quibus locuntur vel affirmant, atque imperita scientia apud indoctas vulgi aures inflantur seque fautores secularium potestatum iactanter gloriantur, quatenus horum inpudentia reprimatur, hic libellus ad honorem veri regis et sacerdotis, Iesu Christi, edatur.

Honorius occupies himself furthermore (chapters 30-31) with the problem of imperial power. Again the only surviving manuscripts are Austrian. This work is closely associated with imperial concerns.

Dieterich, in his edition, makes the suggestion that the controversial chapter 22, in which Honorius asserts that the king should be elected with the consent of his bishops, refers to the election of Lothar of Supplinburg in 1125, which certainly depended upon episcopal help. [1] This, on the chronology at present suggested, would leave a great time gap between the *Imago Mundi* and the *Summa Gloria*. Honorius's assertion could, however, refer to that state of affairs which made the election of Lothar of Supplinburg possible. Endres was quite sure that the work was dedicated to a bishop and, because of his conviction that the *Imago Mundi* was written in Regensburg, supposed that the bishop was Cuno of Regensburg (1126-1132). [2] It does seem that the work was asked for by an important person :

> Injungis mihi, sermone et scientia imperito, pervigil ovilis Christi ductor, stylo depromere, utrum eaedem personae pares sint in collato principatus apice, an altera alteri in dignitate sit preferenda, vel altera ab altera sit iure constituenda ?... videtur scelus idolatriae tibi in vice Christi imperanti nolle obedire.

but it is not possible on this evidence to go further than that. It is unfortunately impossible to be quite sure about the dedication or to date the work exactly, but if the *Imago Mundi* was as seems certain, first written in 1110, and if the *Summa Gloria* followed it in time as it does on Honorius's list, then 1111 is at least a likely date for the beginning of the undertaking. This, moreover, is the year of the capture and humiliation of Paschal II. In that year those who opposed imperial policy would have been especially appreciative of an assertion of the rights of sacerdotal power.

The *Scala Coeli*, which follows the *Summa Gloria* in the list, seems to complement the *De Animae Exsilio et Patria*, which is not mentioned in the *De Luminaribus*. The latter provides the way to intellectual improvement, the former, to spiritual. The *De Animae Exsilio et Patria* was, it seems, written just before the *Scala Coeli*, for the preface of the *Scala Coeli* refers back to it :

> Sunt namque plures qui ad spiritualia scandere nituntur, sed ordinem graduum ignorantes, per abrupta se praecipitant... Quorum animi inopia pie permotus, navem eis *de exsilio ad patriam* opimis opibus instruxi... [3]

Again it expresses Honorius's desire to supply the needs of those struggling for improvement. No firm date can be given to these

---

1. *MGH Libelli de Lite*, III, p. 73.
2. *Op. cit.*, p. 49-50.
3. *PL* 172, c. 1229.

two works but it is possible that they were not far removed in
time from the *Cognitio Vitae*. The prefaces of the *Cognitio* and
the *De Animae* are remarkably alike, both in the by now familiar
fear of envy they express and in the vision of the way to truth
they both try to present. The unlearned are represented as
wandering in the realms of error ; by learning is constructed the
pathway to truth. One sentence is repeated in both :

> Ego autem cum invidia tabescente iter non habeo.

In chapter IX, moreover, the *Cognitio Vitae* catches the title of
the *De Animae* as the *Scala Coeli* had done :

> Nolo ut inde mihi, sed Deo, cujus donum est, gratia referatur : qui
> saepe per abjectos servos ad haereditatem suae visionis filios suos
> convocat, et per hostes *de exsilio ad patriam* iter salutis amicis
> praenotat. [1]

The *De Animae* and the *Scala Coeli* are slight works, and the only
surviving manuscripts of them are Austrian ones. The years
after 1111, perhaps soon after because of their apparent nearness
to the *Cognitio Vitae*, would be appropriate for them too.

The *Expositio Totius Psalterii* and the *In Cantica Canticorum*
seem to be linked in fact, as they are in their position in the
De Luminaribus. Honorius regarded the production of these
two works as the high point in his career :

> Expositionem totius Psalterii cum Canticis miro modo ; Cantica canti-
> corum exposuit, ita ut prius exposita non videantur.

Endres, although anxious to ascribe them to the period of Christian of Regensburg (1133-1153) and of his successor Gregory
(1156-1185), points out that in the case of the *Expositio Totius
Psalterii* the dedication to Christian is not found in the earliest
manuscripts. [2]   C. and Cuno are more common. [3]   This brings
us back, if we are to think of Bishop Cuno of Regensburg, tentatively at least, to the years before 1132. The *Expositio Totius
Psalterii* is an enormous work, quite the longest Honorius wrote.
He comments in it upon the whole of the Psalter and makes use of
a large number of recent sources as well as of older ones. [4]   He

---

1. *PL* 40, c. 1013.
2. *Op. cit.*, p. 56.   Rooth draws attention to this fact too ; *art. cit.*, p. 132.
3. Pez, *Thes.*, v, p. 1622, and *PL* 172, c. 269, n. 111.
4. V.I.J. Flint, *Further Notes on the twelfth century ' Commentarii in*

234

divides his commentary on each psalm into two parts and discusses the application of each psalm to Christ and the Church respectively. It must have taken a very long time to assemble. Again, no exact date can be given to it, but if it was written for Cuno, and if it was written also after the *Summa Gloria* and *Scala Coeli*, it could have been begun in approximately 1112 and ended at any point before 1132.

The prefatory letter in the *In Cantica Canticorum* suggests that it followed the *Expositio Psalterii* directly :

> Quia praedecessori tuo beatae memoriae venerando abbati C. librum David utcunque explanavi, poscis a me, imo jubendo exigis successor ejus, librum Salomonis tibi explanari, justum asserens ut qui patri patris opus magno sudore elaboratum obtuli, tibi quasi filio filii opus stylo elucidatum debeam offerre. [1]

It also suggests that Abbot C. had left or indeed had died. Cuno of Regensburg had, because of his tenure of office at Siegburg, some claim to be called abbot, and he was of course succeeded in 1132. This is unsatisfactory as evidence in itself, but there is, on the other hand, a lot of internal evidence to show that the *In Cantica Canticorum* was a late production. Honorius had developed his approach to a difficult subject. He says himself that the subject is one which requires a certain maturity. In his preface to his Quaestiones he readily supports the opinion that Proverbs is fit reading for beginners, Ecclesiastes for the rather more advanced, the Canticle for the 'perfecti'. [2] A commentary such as this is a heavy task and needs a lot of material ; this may have led Honorius to postpone his efforts at it.

The ' Evangelia quae beatus Gregorius non exposuit ', the

Psalmos ', in *Rech. de Théol. Anc. et Méd.* 37 (1971), p. 80-88. As well as the sources cited in this article, Honorius used Cassiodorus and Jerome and, it seems from the marginal references in MS. VIENNA *NB* 910, parts of the lost commentary of Rabanus. Certainly I have found no other source for the passages for which Rabanus is cited in this manuscript.

1. *PL* 172, c. 347.

2. *PL* 172, c. 311. ' Quid ait Salomon in Proverbiis ? Aut quid docet in Ecclesiaste, vel in Cantico Canticorum ? In Proverbiis docet parvulum, et per varias sententias instruit, quasi filium. In Ecclesiaste vero jam perfectae aetatis virum imbuit, ut intelligat quia in hujus mundi rebus nihil sit perpetuum, nihil gloriosum aut magnum, sed omnia brevia et caduca, et vana sint quae cernimus. In Cantico Canticorum, jam virum consummatum, atque in omnibus et variis exornatum virtutibus sponsi Domini nostri Jesu jungit amplexibus '.

Refectio Mentium and the *Pabulum Vitae* were thought not to have survived. The last two appear in the gift of Frater Heinricus, and from this one learns that they were sermon collections :

> *Refectio mentium,* in quo sermones ad fratres in capitulo. *Pabulum vite,* in quo sermones in festis diebus.

Their position just before the *De Luminaribus* in the order which Honorius gives to his writings suggests that they were late compositions, although the phrase ' pabula vitae ' is used in the preface to the *Summa Gloria* and this could mean that Honorius was using his old trick of referring back to an earlier work. The two may have been reissues of the *Gemma Animae* and the *Speculum Ecclesiae,* and it is just possible that one manuscript, of the twelfth century and now at Lambach, is the *Refectio Mentium.* This manuscript is certainly a reissue of the *Speculum Ecclesiae* and the *Gemma Animae.* [1] It could well have been a late reissue. The *Evangelia* was, in the opinion of Endres, an attempt to complete the series of forty *Homiliae in Evangelia* of Gregory the Great. [2] It will, he thinks, have been an homilectic one and perhaps, like the *Refectio Mentium* and the *Pabulum Vitae,* designed for the liturgical year. It is possible, however, that the ' Matheus glosatus ', which appears in the middle of Honorius's works in the gift of frater Heinricus, was in fact written by him and that it is the ' Evangelia '. His other directly biblical works were exegetical and not homiletic. This in itself, of course, brings one no nearer to a date for it. It seems, however, on the evidence of the *Expositio Totius Psalterii* and the *In Cantica Canticorum,* that Honorius may have postponed his efforts at exegesis until late in life. There is good reason to suppose, then, that if the *Evangelia* was in fact an exegetical work, its position in the *De Luminaribus* list is chronologically the correct one. The *Clavis Physicae* is as yet unpublished although Pez went so far as to transcribe the Zwettl manuscript of it. [3] It is in fact a simplified rendering of the *De Divisione Naturae* of John Scotus Erigena. Miss Sanford suggests that it is a late work. [4] The magnificent schemata in the Paris manuscript

---

1. LAMBACH CXXXIX ; *Rev. bénéd.* 82 (1972), p. 63 ff.
2. *Op. cit.,* p. 61.
3. The transcription is now *Codex Mellicensis* 1655. At the date of writing Dr. Paolo Lucentini is preparing an edition.
4. *Art. cit.,* p. 417.

of it may be by Honorius. [1] If so, they shew his abilities as a teacher. Again it seems possible to leave this work where it stands in the list.

We have now reached the end of the list in the *De Luminaribus*. It appears to be without doubt a chronological one, and it appears, furthermore that a large part of Honorius's work can be placed approximately within the years proposed by the *De Luminaribus*, that is, the years 1106 to 1125. This revises the dates usually accepted for them by about twenty years. It remains to be seen whether Honorius's other works can also be placed within these limits, and to place the *De Luminaribus* itself.

IV. THE "DE LUMINARIBUS" AND THE UNACKNOWLEDGED WORKS

The *De Luminaribus Ecclesiae* was clearly written with Imperial interests very much in mind. The floruits of the writers named in Book IV (even that of Lanfranc) are placed by relating them to the reigns of German emperors. It was the last of the works Honorius chose to list as his own at the time of writing. The last author Honorius mentions before himself is Rupert of Deutz, although there is no indication, as there is in the *De Scriptoribus Ecclesiasticis* of the so-called Anonymous of Melk, [2] that Rupert was dead when Honorius wrote. The *De Luminaribus* could, then, have been completed before 1130. If it was, then, given the date suggested for the composition of the *In Cantica Canticorum*, it was written shortly before the latter work. This date, c. 1132/3 is, however, tentative. It seems possible to say that the *De Luminaribus* was among the last works Honorius wrote and to place it within the years 1130/33.

Finally those writings which are not mentioned in the list but which are known to be by Honorius can be fitted into the period which the sum of these conclusions suggests for Honorius's active life ; that is, c. 1098 - c. 1133. First of all, the shorter ones.

Many of these seem to be preparations for, or extensions of, the

---

1. PARIS *B.N.* lat. 6734. This is perhaps from St. Michael's Bamberg and is illustrated and discussed by Mlle M.-Th. D'ALVERNY, *Le Cosmos symbolique du XIIᵉ siècle*, in *Arch. d'hist. doctr. et litt.* 20 (1953), p. 31, 36-37 ; plates, p. 46-47.

2. E. ETTLINGER, *Der sogenannte ' Anonymus Mellicensis de Scriptoribus Ecclesiasticis '*, Karlsruhe, 1896, chap. CXVIII, p. 97.

larger works Honorius mentions and this helps greatly to date them. Early manuscripts of the *Series Pontificum*, for instance, show that it was devised as an appendix to the *Imago Mundi*. The prologue to the *De Haeresibus* demonstrates that it was written immediately after the *De Luminaribus* and suggests that it too was an appendix :

> Cum eos summatim notavimus, qui claro lumine Catholicae doctrinae Ecclesiam illustraverunt, restat ut etiam illos strictum notemus, qui ean quasi tetro fumo haeretici dogmatis obfuscaverunt.

The *De Decem Plagis* and the *Scala Coeli Minor* are both incorporated practically wholesale into the *Speculum Ecclesiae*. [1] I have already tried tentatively to place the *De Animae Exsilio et Patria* by way of its connexion with the *Cognitio Vitae* and the *Scala Coeli*. The *De Libero Arbitrio* and the *De Claustrali Vita* can be given a date post hoc. The former rejects the definition of free will given in the first recension of the *Inevitabile*, in favour of that of St. Anselm. [2] It seems indeed to improve on the *Inevitabile* in concision and in clarity and so may have been written after the second recension too. [3] The *De Claustrali Vita* is a fervent defence of the monastic life and was surely therefore written after Honorius had begun to champion this — perhaps just after. I shall suggest that his interest in the monastic life first becomes noticeable in the *Sigillum*. By the time he came to write the *De Apostatis* he had, of course, become quite uncompromising. The *De Claustrali Vita* may fall within this period. The *Quod Monachis Liceat Predicare* is also, as its title suggests, greatly concerned with the rights of those professed as monks. This is a puzzling little work. Endres describes it as an expanded paraphrase of a work on the same subject by Rupert of Deutz, [4] written at some point before 1126. [5] He, and after him Miss Sanford, decided therefore that Honorius's treatise was written under Cuno when the latter was bishop of Regensburg, and facing

1. *PL* 172, c. 1048, 869-872.
2. ' Libertas arbitrii est potestas servandi justitiam propter ipsam justitiam (*PL* 172, c. 1224).
3. The discussion of the two *voluntates* (chap. VI) for instance seems to put more clearly an idea Honorius had merely outlined in the *Inevitabile* (*PL* 172, c. 1212-1213).
4. The treatises are printed by ENDRES, p. 145-147, and in *PL* 170, c. 537-542.
5. Rupert refers to the work in a letter to Everard of Brauweiler (d. 1126). *PL* 170, c. 544.

the legacy of struggles on the subject left by Hartwig's episcopate. Evidence that Cuno took up the struggle at Regensburg on behalf of the monks is given by Idung of St. Emmeramm in his *Liber IV Quaestionum*. [1] There is no ground at all, however, for the supposition that Honorius expanded Rupert's treatise. Honorius, it is true, has a lot more to say, especially about the place of regular canons in the complex ; but there is in fact very little connexion between the two works, and what connexion there is could be as well, or better, accounted for by supposing not that Honorius expanded Rupert's remarks but that Rupert borrowed from and compressed Honorius's for his own use at Liège or at Deutz. The *Quod Monachis* is knowledgeable about the position of canons regular [2] but is at the same time insistent that the monastic vocation is the higher one :

> Regularium itaque vita quanto a canonica est districtior, tanto a monachica remissior, et quanto ab illa altior, tanto ab ista inferior ac seculari vicinior, scilicet in splendore vestium et esu carnium, in laxa loquendi licentia, in minori psalmorum mensura. Unde sicut a canonica licet cuique ascendere ad regularium vitam, ita licet a regulari cuique ascendere ad monachicam, nulli autem licet a monachica ad regularem sicut nec de regulari ad canonicam.

This insistence would be the most readily understandable if Honorius had recently decided to support the monastic life as against the canonial. Endres points out that the *Speculum Ecclesiae* was clearly meant to be an aid to preaching ; 'hoc igitur speculum omnes sacerdotes ante oculos ecclesiae expendant'. Because of this he thinks that this too may have been devised as a weapon in the struggle for the preaching rights of monks. [3] The *Quod Monachis* could have been written at no great distance in time from the *Speculum Ecclesiae*, the *Sigillum*, the *De Apostatis* and, perhaps, the *De Claustrali Vita*.

---

1. *Idungi Argumentum super IV Quaestionibus*, in Pez, *Thes.*, II, 2, p. 529. Dedicated to a master Herbord, Pez thinks it will have been written for Herbord of Bamberg and so dates it to the mid-twelfth century.
2. ' Sicut ergo in ecclesia habet duo officia utriusque vite, sc. active et contemplative administrationis, sic habet duas professiones religionis, videlicet monachicam et regularem, hoc est communem vitam sub regula sancti Benedicti vel sancti Augustini ducentium. Que utraque professio assumit sibi viros de utroque officio tam laicos quam clericos. Ita quippe possunt laici esse monachi quam clerici, similiter ita possunt laici esse regulares quam clerici ' (Endres, *op. cit.*, p. 148).
3. *Op. cit.*, p. 30 f. R. Cruel, *Geschichte der Deutschen Predigt im Mittelalter*, Detmold, 1879, p. 129, puts the *Speculum Ecclesiae* in the forefront of the literature produced to support monks in their preaching.

The only considerable works certainly by Honorius and yet not mentioned in his list are the four sets of *Quaestiones* attributed it now seems erroneously, to Salonius of Geneva, the *Octo Quaestionum de Angelis et Homine*, and the *Liber Duodecim Quaestionum*. The first three of the sets of quaestiones later attributed to Salonius appear in a particularly early manuscript. [1] It seems, then, that they may have been compiled very early in Honorius's career. The *Quaestiones in Mattheum*, the fourth of the sets, may have been written with them. Because they are so closely related, however, to glosses on St. Matthew, they may have been written later, whilst Honorius worked upon the ' evangelia '. The sets of *Quaestiones* certainly appeared in at least two recensions. The earliest recension may be the one contained in MS. KARLSRUHE Codex Aug. CCV, which does not include the *In Mattheum*, the later, that of VIENNA NB 807, which does and which includes, in addition, an important revised version of the *Elucidarius*. [2] Both recensions fall easily within the dates set for the *De Luminaribus*.

The *Libellus Octo Quaestionum* is, as its title says, concerned with the problems of men and angels, their fall and the possibility of their redemption. The *Liber Duodecim Quaestionum* treats of many of the same questions again, although its preface declares that its real task is to report a battle in words for superiority between a canon and a monk ; a battle won by the canon. In both books, Honorius takes a firm position on the question of whether man was created to replace the fallen angels. This suggests a place in time for them. He considered this problem in the *Elucidarius* and the *Inevitabile*, and he decided both that man had an independent right to creation and that more men were in fact created to make up the number of the elect :

> D. Nonne casus malorum minuit numerum bonorum ?
> M. Sed, ut impleretur electorum numerus, homo decimus est creatus. [3]
> Quot autem sunt in hoc numero a Deo praescripti hi ante mundi consti-

---

1. KARLSRUHE Codex Aug. CCV. I am greatly indebted for the help of Dr. Kurt Hannemann of the Badische Landesbibliothek. He is not responsible, however, for my opinions !

2. I have made out the case for Honorius's authorship in my article in *Rech. de Théol. Anc. et Méd.* 37 (1970), cited above. The most recent printed editions of these *quaestiones*, based as they are upon the supposition that the *quaestiones* were originally by Salonius of Geneva, and that VIENNA NB 807 contains his work, give a somewhat confusing impression of the order of the recensions. The editions need badly to be re-done.

3. *Elucidarius* I, 57. Man's independent right to creation is given in I, 23-26.

240

tutionem sunt ad beatitudinem electi... Et quia hic numerus angelis cadentibus est imminutus, hominibus nascentibus est restitutus. [1]

In both these works Honorius is clearly following the *Cur Deus Homo*. [2] In the *Liber Duodecim Quaestionum*, chapters I, III, IV, and V, Honorius takes up the same position. In chapter V especially, he denies the validity of the parallel drawn by Gregory the Great between the ten orders of angels and the fall of one and the parable of the woman with ten drachmas. He denies in fact that the tenth order fell.

In the *Libellus Octo Quaestionum*, Honorius uses the very phrase he uses in the *Elucidarius* and expands upon its implications :

> D. ...cum enim auctoritas cujusdam magni dicat, ut impleretur electorum numerus, homo decimus creatur : videtur ad hoc solum facta multiplicatus hominum, ut impleretur imminuta numeros itas angelorum, et sic consequenter ruina angeli fuit causa conditionis hominis.
> M. Nihil est aliud auctoritas, quam per rationem probata veritas : et quod auctoritas docet credendum, hoc ratio probat tenendum. Evidens scripturae auctoritas clamat, et perspicax ratio probat : si omnes angeli in coelo permansissent, tamen homo cum omni posteritate sua creatus fuisset [3].

The great man whose opinion Honorius here tries to refute could be again Gregory the Great.

It seems reasonable to deduce from the evidence available so far that the *Libri Quaestionum* were written early in Honorius's life, when he was concerned about the relative merits of the canonial and monastic vocations, when he was thinking about the problems to which he gave more careful attention in the *Elucidarius* and the *Inevitabile*, and when he was enthusiastic about St. Anselm's opinions. The *Liber Duodecim Quaestionum* is certainly an ill-organized work. It is neither consistent nor well set out. It seems, despite its pretensions, to be merely a collection of somewhat hastily constructed questions and answers on quite random topics. The fact that Honorius wrote these books early and hastily may explain why he would not wish to include them in the list in the *De Luminaribus* and why there are so few manuscripts of them. [4]

---

1. *Inevitabile* ; PL 172, c. 1211.
2. *Cur Deus Homo* I, XVIII ; SCHMITT, II, p. 76-78.
3. *PL* 172, c. 1185.
4. If this early date is accepted, then the similar opinions expressed by Rupert of Deutz were perhaps owed by him to Honorius, and not by Honorius

Conclusion

The list of works given by Honorius in his *De Luminaribus Ecclesiae* is not exhaustive, gives no information about revision and amendment and does less than justice to Honorius's labours of composition. It is, however, broadly reliable, although, the dates given for Honorius's floruit should be liberally interpreted. Honorius's active life stretched, it seems, from the mid-1090s to approximately the mid-1130s, and the works in the list were written in this order within this time.

It is now possible to found a few further conclusions upon this evidence. When we set this account of the contents and chronology of Honorius's writings beside the distribution of the surviving manuscripts of them, there appears to be, in c. 1100/1102, a break. Some of the earlier of those works which seem to have contained English material, that is, the *Speculum Ecclesiae*, the *Offendiculum*, the *De Apostatis*, are now only to be found in German or Austrian copies. So are some of the other works mentioned early in Honorius's list, for example the *Inevitabile*. There may, of course, have been English copies of all of these which do not now survive. It is, however, at least equally possible that at this point in time, that is in the years 1100/1102 (the dates suggested for the composition of the *Inevitabile* and the *Offendiculum*) Honorius left England. He must have been in Germany or Austria when he wrote the *Summa Totius*. This work appears immediately after the *Offendiculum* in his list and he may, then, have left England for the continent in 1102. It is most tempting to suggest that he left, in fact, in 1103, the date of St. Anselm's last exile. If we accept this date we are left with some anomalies. If Honorius did indeed leave England in 1102/3 he must either have taken with him, or have had access to, material sufficient for the composition of the English sections of the *Gemma Animae* and the *Imago Mundi*. Such propositions are not, however hard to accept.

This revision of all the dates previously attached to Honorius's works has wide repercussions. First of all, of course, it throws a little more light upon Honorius's career. Secondly, and this is of greater importance, it rescues Honorius from the Limbo to

---

to Rupert as has been thought ; M. MAGRASSI, *Teologia e Storia nel Pensiero di Ruperto di Deutz*, Rome, 1959, p. 248, 272-276. As in the case of the *Quod Monachis Liceat Predicare*, so in this, the supposition that Rupert was the borrower is quite consistent with the state of the texts.

which Endres had consigned him. Honorius's life and works can now be placed firmly down in one of the most formative periods in the history of medieval learning. He is caught up in the midst of the movement for ecclesiastical reform, and clearly involved in that complex of exegetical activity which goes under the name of the ' school of Laon '. His writings stand now not on the edge but at the origins of the twelfth century renaissance. They may be expected to increase our understanding even of this.

The University of Auckland
(New Zealand).

VIII

THE ORIGINAL TEXT
OF THE *ELUCIDARIUM* OF HONORIUS AUGUSTODUNENSIS
FROM THE TWELFTH CENTURY ENGLISH MANUSCRIPTS

In 1954 M. Yves Lefèvre brought out a new edition of the *Elucidarium* of Honorius Augustodunensis (1). This improved on the edition in Migne in a number of ways. In the first and perhaps the most important place it did make clear how very complex a state the text is in, the foremost of the complications being the existence of two series of passages, independent of each other and variously distributed throughout the whole of its length. M. Lefèvre noticed that " seuls les manuscrits manifestement contaminés comportent les deux séries à la fois," (2) and distinguished them in his edition by printing the one in brackets alone and the other in brackets and italic letters. He then grouped the manuscripts into families according to whether they included one or the other or neither of the series, and having done that attempted on this basis to establish the original text of this Honorius's first work. M. Lefèvre committed himself firmly to the opinion that since it was impossible to decide which of the two series of passages came first, the only safe course was to assume that those manuscripts which contained neither represented the original text.

This assumption confronted him sharply with another textual problem; that of variants within this shortened version. One variant in particular invited treatment; the reply to the question : " *Quid est liberum arbitrium?*" in Book II Chapter 7. Two readings are to be found : " *In potestate hominis esse et velle et posse bonum vel malum*" and " *Libertas eligendi bonum vel malum.*" In manuscripts which contain the shortened version only the first reading prevails. M. Lefèvre concluded therefore that the first reading is grammatically the more satisfactory and that since " on peut sans doute admettre que, pour le sens, les deux formules sont à très peu près équivalentes," it is reasonable to suppose that this first reading was the original one (3). This despite the fact that Honorius's *Inevitabile*, his second work and one which often follows the *Elucidarium* in early manuscripts, gives a definition of free will identical with the second reading :

" *M. Igitur, dic mihi in primis quid liberum arbitrium vocitari dicis.*
" *D. Ut tu diffinisti, libertatem bonum vel malum eligendi.*" (4)

---

1) Y. LEFÈVRE, *L'Elucidarium et les Lucidaires* (Paris 1954).
2) *Ibid.*, p. 68.
3) *Ibid.*, p. 71.
4) J. KELLE, *Untersuchungen über des Honorius Inevitabile* (Vienna 1904), p. 12.

The decision to stand by the short version which contained this variant carried in its train a series of decisions about less important variants, and a major conclusion about the classification of the manuscripts containing one or other of the two series of passages and the development in time of the text. The major conclusion is that, because they have the " *in potestate* " variant for Book II Chapter 7, those manuscripts with a proportion of the series marked by brackets alone are next in line—" family A." This puts a subsidiary family, having this series, or a section of it, together with the " *libertas eligendi* " reading, third in line, and pushes the third family and by far the largest,—" family B "—which has sections of the other series and again the reading " *libertas eligendi*," to the end. On the ground of this conclusion, M. Lefèvre printed as his original the text of the shortest manuscripts, with the " *in potestate* " variant and, where other choices had to be made, those variants common to the short manuscripts and the manuscripts of family A. The readings common to family B are relegated to the footnotes.

Unfortunately, however, the edition does suffer from one serious limitation and one which M. Lefèvre himself did not hesitate to point out; namely that he had been compelled to concentrate almost entirely upon manuscripts available to him in France. He had to hand over manuscripts in other countries to research in those countries (5). Work on the English manuscripts casts some doubt on his conclusions.

There are eleven manuscripts of the *Elucidarium* in England and Scotland which date from the twelfth century; CAMBRIDGE, Corp. Christi Coll., 308, 439; —, Univ. Libr., KK IV 6; GLASGOW, Univ. Libr., 244; LONDON, Br. Mus., Royal 5 E VI, Royal 11 A VII, Royal 15 A XX;

—, Lambeth Palace, 358; OXFORD, Bodl. Libr., Fairfax 26, Lat Th. e 9, Laud Misc. 237.

All but the last mentioned, Laud Misc 237 (which, because it has bound up with it a German version of the Rule of St. Benedict may be a German manuscript), are most probably of English provenance. These manuscripts do provide a great deal of evidence to support M. Lefèvre's researches. Each of them falls into one or other of the broader groups he describes. Eight of them include at least some proportion of one of his series, the one marked by bracket and italic letters. The three remaining include a proportion of the other. Thus

" *Family B* "

CAMBRIDGE, Corp. Christi Coll., 308, 439 —, Univ. Libr., KK IV 6; LONDON, Br. Mus., Royal 5 E VI, Royal 11 A VII, Royal 15 A XX; —, Lambeth Palace, 358; OXFORD, Bodl. Libr., Lat. Th. e 9;

" *Family A* "

GLASGOW, Univ. Libr., 244; OXFORD, Bodl. Libr., Fairfax 26, Laud Misc. 237.

This is in itself an interesting balance to be found in early manuscripts, and for M. Lefèvre's general deductions sinister one. In view, moreover, of the extreme likelihood that the *Elucidarium* was written in England it assumes special importance (6). There is no early English exemplar of the shortened text. The shortest we have is C.C.C.308 containing as it does only the additions marked by brackets and italic letters to Book I Chapter 185 from the series. It displays, however, all the variants listed by M. Lefèvre as typical of the greater part of the manuscripts of family B (7). These variants are common in their turn to MSS. B. M. Royal

(5) LEFÈVRE, *op. cit.*, p. 11.
(6) R. W. SOUTHERN, *Saint Anselm and his Biographer* (Cambridge 1963), p. 211-212.
(7) LEFÈVRE, *op. cit.*, p. 79 n. 1.

5 E VI and Lambeth 358 and most of them to C.U.L. KK IV 6, B. M. Royal 11 A VII, B. M. Royal 15 A XX and Bodley Lat. Th. e 9.

Seven of the eight manuscripts of this group are, then, drawn together. They are associated again by their inclusion of a common variant reading for Book I Chapter 185; " *vel ecclesias vel ecclesiasticos honores vendunt vel emunt.*" This is again, according to M. Lefèvre, the predominant reading for family B. We thus have the bulk of the early English manuscripts in close correspondence with each other, but the correspondence is supposed to be that of a late rendering of the text. The difficulty in reconciling these two apparent truths is increased by the fact of an even greater internal similarity between two manuscripts of the group, B. M. Royal 5 E VI and Lambeth 358. The texts of these two are identical in almost every respect (8). They include, moreover, identical passages from the family B series (9).

To attempt an exhaustive summary of the individual variants here would be to go beyond the bounds of a note meant only to point to the material of the English manuscripts. This much can, however, be said. The indications there are, taken from bulk and internal agreement, are indications towards a text based not on the shortest manuscripts but on the manuscripts of one of the families; and that family not family A but family B. The text will include, therefore, many of the internal variants marked as common to family B and a selection from the passages relegated by M. Lefèvre as the second of the supplementary series.

The state in England of the variants to Book II Chapter 7 lends strength to this argument. Nine of the eleven manuscripts have the reading " *Libertas eligendi bonum vel malum.*" One, C.C.C. 439, has the two variants running successively, and one, Bodley Fairfax 26, has the " *in potestate* " variant. Of these two, C.C.C. 439 is a late and contaminated exemplar. It has the largest number of inclusions from the family B series of passages of any of the eight manuscripts containing them, with none of their common variants and several peculiar to itself. The only resemblance it bears to any of the manuscripts in its group is to the two identical ones, B. M. Royal 5 E VI and Lambeth 358 (10). It is most closely associated, therefore, with the group I should like to identify with the earlier tradition. The other exponent of the " *in potestate* " variant, Bodley Fairfax 26, is most likely the latest of the eleven. It contains all the passages of the series common to family A, and this fact together with the variant should place it, in M. Lefèvre's scheme, at only one remove from the original text. In the revised scheme this type of text should be placed at the end of the line of development.

The reading "*libertas eligendi*" should be accepted as the original. Even leaving aside that given in the *Inevitabile* mentioned above, this definition of Free Will makes much more sense in the broader historical context. Heated discussions on the exact nature of Free Will were, of course, maintained throughout the twelfth century in an attempt to refine the Augustinian definition " *potentia bene vel male operandi.*" One of its most notable critics, Robert of

---

8) The only dissimilarities of any note are a division of the questions in Book II 50 and Book III 106 in Lambeth 358, and a slight omission in Book II 6 in the same manuscript.
9) Book I 185 (2 & 3), Book II 10a, 44 (1), 76a-b. Of the seven manuscripts with which we are at present concerned, only C.C.C.308 has the addition to Book I 185 (3). It, C.U.L. Kk iv 6, B.M. Royal 11 A VII, and Bodley Lat. th. e 9 have Book I 185 (2). These last three diverge in their inclusion of 185 (1). B.M. Royal 11 A VII alone has the additions of B.M. Royal 5 E VI and Lambeth 358 to Book II and it has not 44 (1) but 44 (3).
10) It includes all the additional passages they have in common and also omits, like them, a passage in Book II 76a (quae sive... parem). This omission does not occur in any other English manuscript nor, apparently, in any of those examined by M. Lefèvre.

Melun, drew a distinction between the internal act of discerning and the external act whereby one realises one's internal choice, and relegated the use of the word " *electio* " to the performance of the external act. It could therefore no longer describe the full activity involved in the use of Free Will. Alain of Lille used " *potestas* " and " *voluntas* " to describe the grace given for the internal act. Into this later context fits most excellently " *in potestate hominis et velle et posse bonum vel malum* " (11).

It seems, therefore, that there is still room for a simplified and amended edition of this very important early English handbook to theological subjects. The manuscripts from which M. Lefèvre actually selected his shortened text are in fact only four in number and all late ones (12). The best of his early ones are in the same family as the two identical English manuscripts. It would be on this family that the new text would be based. There is, lastly, one piece of evidence that both helps towards this conclusion and adds to the importance of the text in general. This is that those passages from the controversial series which the new text would include all bear, in their concern for the making of money from churches by priests, upon the Investiture Contest and its preoccupations. Perhaps the repercussions of this Contest in England, especially on Saint Anselm, in some way provoked the compilation. In this case the *Elucidarium*, as well as being one of our earliest popular guides to church matters in general, would be one of our earliest witnesses too to the results in England of this particular crisis.

---

(11) O. LOTTIN, *Psychologie et Morale aux XIIe et XIIIe siècles* (2e éd., Louvain 1959), vol. 33-34, p. 44.
(12) Paris Bibl. Nat. 15688 (XIIIth cent.), Rheims 456 (XIVth cent.), Laon 146 (XVth cent.) Metz 149 (XVth cent.).

IX

THE «LIBER HERMETIS MERCURII TRIPLICIS DE VI RERUM PRINCIPIIS» AND THE «IMAGO MUNDI» OF HONORIUS AUGUSTODUNENSIS

The purpose of this short note is primarily to draw attention to a new fragment of this complex work. Only four complete texts were known to its editor ([1]). Of these four, only one manuscript is an early one ([2]). The present fragment comprises chapters 46-55 (inclusive) of the text, and is contained in ms. Corpus Christi College, Cambridge, 66, f. 3^v ([3]), and concealed as a part of the *Imago Mundi* of Honorius Augustodunensis. The concealment is thorough, in that the fragment is simply inserted, without heading, and without change of hand, as an expansion of chapter one of the present edition of the *Imago Mundi* ([4]). Corpus 66 is dated by James to the early thirteenth century ([5]), and so the present fragment is one of the earliest copies of the *Liber Hermetis* we have. It contains some variant readings, which I set out here against the readings of Silverstein's edition.

---

(1) Th. SILVERSTEIN, « Liber Hermetis Mercurii Triplicis de VI rerum principiis », *Archives d'histoire doctrinale et littéraire du Moyen Age*, 22 (1955), 217-302.

(2) Ms. Bodleian Library, Oxford, Digby 67. This manuscript is of the late twelfth, early thirteenth, century.

(3) I am grateful to the Librarian and Fellows of Corpus Christi College for their permission to examine this manuscript.

(4) PL 172, 121. The insertion is a continuation of the chapter, beginning after « gutta includitur ».

(5) M. R. JAMES, *A Descriptive Catalogue of the Manuscripts in the Library of Corpus Christi College* I (Cambridge 1912).

Chapters	Silverstein	Corpus 66
46	sinzugiis	siniugiis.
48	mundi machina oritur	machina mundi confirmatur
49	motus appellatur	dicitur motus
	secundum omnes motus	secundum generationem et cor-
	species universis	ruptionem et ceteras motus spe-
	convenire monstratur	cies universis convenire ma-
		nifestatur
50	discordi circularium	discordii circularium
	motuum concordia	octo mortuum concordia
	contemperantur	contemperantur
51	dicitur	nuncupatur
	et sustentativo	vel sustentativo
53	omnia sustinendo	omnia elementa continendo con-
	continentur	tinentur
54	proportionaliter	proportionaliter id est dissimi-
	consistit mundus	liter et concorditer consistit
		mundus
	ad centrum	a centro
	ad eternitatem consistit	ad eternitatem qua proportiona-
	mundus temporarius	liter consistit mundus tempo-
		rarius
55	Motus autem nature repugnantes	Motus etiam repugnantes
	sinzugiis constringens	siniugiis (id est conexsionibus
		above line) constringens
	passivas contrarias sinzugiis	passivas contrariis connexionibus
	et dulcibus convenienciis	dulcibus convenientiis
	sic eiusdem	sic et eisdem

Simple notification once made, this fragment does have a little more to tell us, I think about the history of the text. I would draw brief notice to this too. Firstly, the fragment adds some substance to all its editor has already said about the influence and the date of the *Liber Hermetis*. Secondly, and perhaps more importantly, the context within which this particular section is found may be allowed to add to our surmises about the context within which the *Liber Hermetis* was written, and that within which it was read.

Corpus 66, though now in a very complicated state ([6]), is certainly an English manuscript, and carries an ex-libris of the Cistercian abbey of Sawley in Lincolnshire (f. 2) and a rather less tangible association with Hereford ([7]). It falls securely, then, within the English ambience to which Silverstein assigned the *Liber Hermetis* ([8]). The recension of the *Imago Mundi* within which the fragment is found is, furthermore, a particularly early one. It may, indeed, be the first edition of the work ([9]). We do not know at what point in the circulation of the text the interpolation of a part of the *Liber Hermetis* was made (it is not, it must be said, to be found in any other of the copies of the early version of the *Imago Mundi* I have examined), but its insertion here is, at the very least, not incompatible with the early date so far assigned to the *Liber*.

---

(6) The original is now broken into two books. The first part of the original (items 1-8 inclusive) forms the first volume of Corpus 66 ; the second part comprises items 1-18 (inclusive) of Ms. Cambridge University Library Ff. i. 27.

(7) The *Mappa Mundi* on f. 1ᵛ of the Corpus manuscript has long been shewn to bear a particularly close relationship to the more famous Hereford Map. W. L. BEVAN and H. W. PHILLOTT, *Medieval Geography. An Essay in Illustration of the Hereford Mappa Mundi* (London, 1874), p. xxxvi-xxxix.

(8) *Art. cit.*, p. 235, 240-41.

(9) The work is dated in it to the year 1110 (f. 2), contains a dedication to « Henricus » and incorporates a series of variations which I take to be characteristic of an early stage in composition. I hope to make these points at greater length in my forthcoming edition.

Thus, the fragment supports the first remarks of the editor of the whole *Liber Hermetis*. The context within which it is found may now help to expand these. The *Liber Hermetis* is described as a « pseudepigraph apparently concocted during the twelfth century by an unknown Western writer with a bias in favour of astrology », and as a « cento » from sources such as Bede, Macrobius and others drawing on them, Adelard of Bath, William of Conches, perhaps Hugh of St. Victor and especially Firmicus Maternus, Zahel ben Bischr, Alcabitius, « and others of this stamp », « with several others as yet undetected » ([10]). This catholicity of source material, and sensitivity to new developments, is very like all we know of the context and sources of the *Imago Mundi* itself. Moreover, the *Imago Mundi* is in fact one of the undetected sources of the *Liber Hermetis*. At least six sections are borrowed word for word ([11]). I have already suggested that the *Imago Mundi* has early connexions with England ([12]) and, together with their shared eclecticism, the monastic compilations within which the *Imago Mundi* and the *Liber Hermetis* are to be found shew remarkable similarities. The two works are drawn together not merely as borrower and borrowed, but within a whole network of similar associations.

It is here, I suggest, that we may allow this fragment to add a little to our knowledge as it stands of the context of the *Liber Hermetis*. The *Imago Mundi*, into which the fragment is so neatly fitted, is not a work of Parisian, still less of « Chartrain » cosmological speculation. It springs instead from that demi-monde of cosmological interest which both preceded and reacted upon the world of the twelfth century schools. So too, perhaps, does the *Liber Hermetis*. We should look for its roots not to the French cathedral schools, but to the often deliberately contrasting efforts of monks to retain their hold upon popular cosmology. Both works are simply written, but there is no reason to suppose that the eclecticism manifested in them both was random. On the contrary, quite specific points were to be made by it. We see, in both texts, the desire of their compilers to demonstrate their knowledge of the latest cosmological materials ([13]), and thus maintain their scholarly respectability, whilst retaining close touch with, even leaning consciously towards, the anciently mythical and astrological ([14]). There is much in each text of both social and emotional appeal. We are allowed, I think, through both treatises, a glimpse into the world of early twelfth century monks and canons engaged in that pastoral care to which *Genesis*, and those cosmologies which sprang from a need to interpret this most difficult of moral texts, were vital. In the case of the *Liber Hermetis* we have a further way into the English corner of that world. This corner had recently come into the forefront of

---

(10) *Art. cit.* p. 217.

(11) Sections 265, 271, 272-273, 278-279 (SILVERSTEIN, *art. cit.* p. 271-272). These are taken, respectively, from the *Imago Mundi*, I, LV, LVI, LIX, LXII, PL 172, 136-137. Honorius drew for these sections on Bede, *De Natura Rerum*, XXVII, XXXII-XXXIII (PL 90, 247-249, 252-253) and on Augustine, *De Genesi ad Litteram*, I, (lxii) (PL 34, 285), but the *Liber Hermetis* is closer to Honorius than to these, and the early version of the *Liber* is especially close.

(12) V. I. J. FLINT, « The chronology of the works of Honorius Augustodunensis », *Revue Bénédictine*, 82 (1972), 226-227.

(13) This is especially true, of course, of the *Liber Hermetis*. The *Imago Mundi* as a text is more old fashioned, but it appears on occasion bound with the very latest.

(14) Again, the *Liber Hermetis* leads the field, and the author's use of Firmicus Maternus and his indulgence in prediction (e.g. sections 325-339) go further than anything attempted in the *Imago Mundi*. Honorius does, however, make extensive use of mythographers such as Hyginus— and in a curious passage on Saturn (I, (lxxvi), PL 172, 139) draws close to the Latin Asclepius ; ed. A. D. NOCK and A.-J. FESTUGIÈRE, *Corpus Hermeticum*, II (Paris, 1946), VIII, XIII, 326, 347-349.

astronomical and scientific enquiry ([15]), had rediscovered ancient astrology and its more modern interpretations ([16]), had become both fearful of, and mesmerised by, the possibilities these new interests revealed ([17]). The *Liber Hermetis* was one of the answers to the anxieties of this world. It may be treated as an English social document of some importance ([18]), and as a witness to the contortions demanded of those who would integrate popular beliefs and responses with ecclesiastical credibility and control.

The University
of Auckland
(New Zealand)

---

(15) M. C. WELBORN, « Lotharingia as a centre of Arabic and scientific influence in the eleventh century », *Isis*, 16 (1931), 188-199 and C. H. HASKINS, « The introduction of Arabic science into England », *Studies in the History of Medieval Science* (Harvard U.P. 1924), p. 113-118.

(16) William of Malmesbury provides evidence of both these interests. He draws attention to the use of Firmicus Maternus, and has astronomical collections drawn up for his own use. Ed. W. STUBBS, *Willelmi Malmesbiriensis Monachi de Gestis Pontificum Anglorum* (RS London, 1871), p. 259, n. 6 ; N. R. KER, « William of Malmesbury's handwriting », *English Historical Review*, 59 (1944), 374 ; L. WHITE, « Eilmer of Malmesbury, an eleventh century aviator », *Technology and Culture*, 2 (1961), 107, n. 7.

(17) STUBBS, *ed. cit.*, 193-203.

(18) The intrusion from the *Liber* in Corpus 66 is to be found only three folios away from the Mappa Mundi. For the continuing interest shewn in astronomy and cosmology in the diocese of Hereford see J. C. RUSSELL, « Hereford and Arabic science in England about 1175-1200 », *Isis*, 18 (1932-33), 14-25.

X

THE « ELUCIDARIUS » OF HONORIUS AUGUSTODUNENSIS AND REFORM IN LATE ELEVENTH CENTURY ENGLAND

The *Elucidarius* is a remarkable work. It is remarkable in three particular respects. In the first place it is a curious compound of crude theological statement and sophisticated construction. The crudity of the theology contained in it has already been exposed, [3] but the very real ingenuity which went into its making has not yet been fully explored. The first part of this paper will be directed to this exploration. The excellence of the work's construction gave it a quality which went beyond the common run. Its interest, however, only begins here. The contrast between the simplicity of its appearance and

3. R.W. SOUTHERN, *St. Anselm and his Biographer*, Cambridge 1963, p. 213-214. For sustaining my work on Honorius whilst at the same time saving me from many errors, I owe Dr. Southern a debt I cannot repay.

the complexity of the materials which went into its making is not to be explained simply by the perversities of its author. These, doubtless, played their
part; but the work as a whole was framed by considerations of a more general
importance. The *Elucidarius* was a catechetical handbook written in, or
shortly before, the year 1100, and in England. [1] I hope to prove that it
was formed by the special conditions which agitated the post-conquest English
church. The second part of this paper will, therefore, be devoted to an exploration of these conditions, and, particularly, to an effort to demonstrate how
well they account for the distinguishing features of the text. Finally, the
work was quite exceptionally popular, both in England and outside it. Forty-
one twelfth-century manuscripts of the whole Latin text survive now, and it
was turned into the vernacular with remarkable speed. [2] Honorius was never
to have quite such a success again. This popularity argues that the needs
which generated the production of the *Elucidarius* in England were not in all
their aspects exclusive to England. It argues too that any interpretation
of the part the *Elucidarius* played here is susceptible of a wide application.
In short, the *Elucidarius* is not only specially formed, but specially formative.

I. THE CONTENTS AND MANNER OF COMPOSITION OF THE « ELUCIDARIUS »

Honorius made the scope of the *Elucidarius* appear to be completely comprehensive. He called it a 'summa totius theologiae'. In most of the early
manuscripts it is divided into three books, roughly equal in length. The first
treats *De divinis rebus*, the second *De rebus ecclesiasticis* and the third *De futura
vita*. Book I deals with problems about man's knowledge of God and of the
persons of the trinity, about God's works of creation, the fall, the states of
angels and men before and after the fall, the redemption and the eucharist. In
Book II he turns to the problem of evil, the relations between evil men and
good men, between freedom and necessity, between original sin and baptism.
Different types of men are described and different remedies for sin are given.
Book III is concerned, as its title suggests, with paradise, purgatory and hell.
Honorius discusses the experience souls might have in each of these regions,
then disposes of the coming of Antichrist, the resurrection, the day of judgement, the fate of the world, and the joys of the just. There is a confident,
if optimistic, finality about the way in which he deals with the questions of
the *discipulus*. A few illustrations may serve to demonstrate this. Thus,
Book I, 21 :

    D. Sentiunt elementa Deum ?
    M. Nihilunquam fecit Deus quod insensibile sit. Quae enim sunt inanimata, nobis
       quidem sunt insensibilia et mortua; Deo autem omnia vivunt et omnia crea-

---

1. V.I.J. FLINT, *The Chronology of the Works of Honorius Augustodunensis,*
in *Rev. bénéd.* 82 (1972), p. 219-220.
2. The earliest translation into English is to be found in LONDON *British
Museum* Cotton Vespasian D XIV, and was perhaps made in 1125. On the
translations into French, cfr Y. LEFÈVRE, *L'Elucidarium et les Lucidaires,*
Paris 1954, p. 272 ff., and into Swedish, R. GEETE, *Svenska Kyrkobruk under
Medeltiden,* Stockholm 1957, and J. HELGASON, *Manuscripta Islandica* 4,
Copenhagen 1957. A recent article suggests that the translation into German took place earlier than was supposed : V. MERTENS, *Ein Lucidariusfrag-
ment des 12. Jahrhunderts,* in *Zeitschrift für deutsches Altertum und deutsche
Literatur* 97 (1968), p. 117-126.

torem sentiunt. Caelum quippe eum sentit, quia ob ejus jussum incessabili revolutione semper circuit ; unde dicitur : « Qui fecit caelos in intellectu. » Sol et luna et stellae eum sentiunt, quia loca sui cursus inerrabiliter servando repetunt. Terra eum sentit, quia semper certo tempore fructus et germina producit. Flumina eum sentiunt, quia ad loca unde fluunt semper redeunt. Mare et venti eum sentiunt, quia ei imperanti mox quiescendo obediunt. Mortui eum sentiunt, quia ad ejus imperium resurgunt. Infernus eum sentit, quia quos devorat eo jubente reddit. Omnia bruta annimalia Deum intelligunt, quia legem sibi ab eo insitam jugiter custodiunt.

Again, Book II, 31 :

D. Salvantur praedestinati, si non laborant ?
M. Praedestinatio taliter est instituta ut precibus vel laboribus obtineatur, ut dicitur : « Per multas tribulationes oportet nos introire in regnum Dei ». Parvulis itaque per mortis acerbitatem, provectis autem aetate datur praedestinatio per laborum exercitationem. Quia vero scriptum est : « In domo Patris mei mansiones multae sunt », unusquisque obtinebit mansionem secundum proprium laborem ; ita, prout quisque laboraverit plus, digniorem, qui minus, inferiorem possidebit. Nullus tamen plus laborare poterit quam eum divina gratia adjuverit nec aliam mansionem quis habiturus erit quam eam ad quam ante mundi praeordinatus fuit, quia « non volentis neque currentis, sed miserentis est Dei ». Ita nullus reproborum quidquam plus facere praevalet quam divina censura permittit nec aliam poenam habebit quam eum divinum judicium ante mundum secundum suum meritum habiturum praescivit, ut dicitur : « Antequam bonum vel malum facerent, dicitur : Esau odio habui, Jacob autem dilexi ». [1]

Something of the tone of the work may be gathered from its form and its contents, and from these passages in particular. The argument and the conclusions are didactic and simple; I have given only two examples out of very many. The materials from which these arguments and conclusions are drawn, however, are, for the most part, neither. They fall into two main categories. On the one hand Honorius employs sources currently in use in the exegesis of the bible; one can see, indeed, from these two quotations alone how ready he was to resort to it. On the other he plunders recent, and often very difficult, theological teaching.

The detailed analysis of Book I of the *Elucidarius* reveals that Honorius drew for it upon sources, and, more especially, selections from sources, which were clearly available to, and used by, compilers of the *Glossa ordinaria*. [2] This fact is at first concealed by the structure of the *Elucidarius*, which is not an exegetical work, and becomes evident only when the sources upon which Honorius relied are seen in separation from the text. The similarities are most evident in the case of the first three chapters of Genesis, but are there too for the Psalms, the Pauline Epistles and the Gospels, particularly the Gospels of St. Matthew and St. John. The implications of this correspondence may be important for the history of the Gloss itself. They are certainly a help in understanding the composition of the *Elucidarius*. The correspondence shews how very firmly rooted the *Elucidarius* was in discussions on the Sacred Page. It shows that Honorius was at this point involved in that intense exegetical activity which absorbed the best of scholarly effort in the late eleventh century, and that he was familiar with the materials from which its more monumental productions were constructed. This fact has not in general been noticed. This association is demonstrable in the sources Honorius uses.

---

1. The text of the *Elucidarius* is taken from the edition by Lefèvre, *ubi supra*.
2. A table showing this follows the paper.

In his choice of authorities he is comprehensive and orthodox: Ambrose, Jerome, Augustine, Cassiodorus, Gregory, Boethius, Macrobius. These were the authorities upon whom, for example Manegold of Lautenbach drew for his commentary on the psalter. [1] John Scotus Erigena is also a particularly important part of this picture. M. Cappuyns pointed to the fact that Anselm of Laon knew and used John Scotus's *De divisione naturae*, [2] and this is able to be seen clearly in those sections of the *Liber Pancrisis* which are Anselm's. [3] Honorius uses Erigena, not only in the *Clavis physicae*, which he says himself is nothing more than a rendering down of the *De divisione naturae*, [4] but also in the *Elucidarius*. He refers to him as Johannes Chrisostomus, and this surname is taken up in his *De luminaribus*. [5] The *Sententiae divinae paginae* both shew a knowledge of the *De divisione naturae* and refer to John Scotus as Chrisostomus. [6] We have here yet another link between the *Elucidarius* and a widely known system of biblical exposition. It is tempting, at this point, to speculate upon the method of the *Elucidarius's* composition. Many of its sources may be found in glosses, especially in glosses on Genesis, St. John and St. Matthew. The *Elucidarius* may, therefore, have been put together in part directly from glosses.

The second category of the materials from which the *Elucidarius* was made is even more interesting than the first. Honorius draws extensively upon the teaching of St. Anselm of Canterbury. In the *Elucidarius*, Honorius places St. Anselm firmly among those 'moderni magistri' whose opinions were worthy to be set beside, and occasionally even above, those of the early fathers. He seems on occasion to report St. Anselm's spoken word, and he certainly used a very early, and possibly spoken, version of St. Anselm's sermon *De beatitudine* in Book III. [7] In other places too his words reflect much of the spirit of St. Anselm though little of the written text. One suspects then either that his memory is at work, or that he is repeating a lesson given directly by St. Anselm. Sometimes there is a marginal reference in an important manuscript to Anselm, and yet the immediate source of the opinion stated cannot be traced. This may be a direct record of his teaching too. [8] Of the written works of St. Anselm, Honorius seems to have been most fond of the *Cur Deus Homo* and the *Monologion*. Of these two he made most use of the *Cur Deus Homo*. From it he seems to have gathered the opinion that the elect were made up of men and angels (ch. 26) and also his ideas on the necessity of the

1. G. Morin, *Le Pseudo-Bède sur les Psaumes et l'"Opus super Psalterium' de Maître Manégold de Lautenbach*, in *Rev. bénéd.* 28 (1911), p. 336. I have tried to defend Dom Morin's attribution in *Some Notes on the Early Twelfth-Century Commentaries on the Psalms*, in *Rech. de théol. anc. et méd.* 38 (1971), p. 86-88.
2. M. Cappuyns, *Jean Scot Érigène*, Louvain 1931, p. 245-246.
3. F. Bliemetzrieder, *Trente-trois pièces inédites de l'œuvre théologique d'Anselme de Laon*, in *Rech. de théol. anc. et méd.* 2 (1930), p. 55, n. 6.
4. J.-A. Endres, *Honorius Augustodunensis*, Kempten-Munich 1906, p. 140.
5. 'Joannes Scotus vel Chrysostomus, in scripturis insigniter eruditus' (Book III, chapter XII ; *PL* 172, col. 222).
6. F. Bliemetzrieder, *Anselms von Laon Systematische Sentenzen*, in *Beiträge zur Geschichte der Philosophie des Mittelalters* 18 (1919), p. 22.
7. V.I.J. Flint, *art. cit.* in *Rev. bénéd.* 82 (1972), p. 219, and, more fully, in the Note following this paper.
8. For example, *Elucidarius* I, 23, 170, 179.

X

incarnation and its application only to man (42-44). He takes from it too
his best demonstration of the horrors of sin and man's incompetence in the
face of it without God's help (95-120). It is interesting that he should do this.
From the point of view of Anselm, we have here another demonstration that
the *Cur Deus Homo* was suited to the needs of one working in the current
theological tradition. [1] From the point of view of Honorius, that he was
not afraid to make use of a treatise which was highly original, ready to criticise
and liable to be criticised. The *Sententiae divinae paginae* indeed criticise
explicitly some of the very arguments of the *Cur Deus Homo* for the necessity
of the incarnation that Honorius supports. [2] The *Elucidarius* seems to stand
at the junction between the *Cur Deus Homo* and the *Sententiae*, [3] but, on some
questions of striking importance, to prefer the views of St. Anselm.

The substance of the *Elucidarius* is clearly very weighty; but, if Honorius
moved towards St. Anselm's opinions with a firmness that amounted to fervour,
he moved with an equal vigour away from the saint's methods. He was not
interested in reflection, nor even in the reflective dialogue. He wholly esche-
wed subtleties. In book one, chapter 12, for example, he collapsed by the
use of such simple words as 'corporeus' and 'incorporeus', from which St. Anselm
shrank, a very long argument in the *Monologion* (xxii) about the whereabouts
of God. Anselm had taken five chapters of the *Monologion* (xx-xxiv inclusive)
to discuss the problem. He proceeded, characteristically, not by stating
verities but by dismissing absurdities. Here is how he began :

> ... summa essentia aut ubique et semper est ; aut tantum alicubi et aliquando,
> aut nusquam et numquam. Quod dico : aut in omni loco vel tempore, aut
> determinate in aliquo, aut in nullo. Sed quid videtur repugnantius, quam ut,
> quod verissime et summe est, id nusquam et numquam sit... At si determinate
> est in aliquo loco vel tempore : ibi et tunc tantum, ubi et quando ipsa est,
> potest aliquid esse ; ubi vero et quando ipsa non est, ibi et tunc penitus nulla
> est essentia, quia sine ea nihil est. Unde consequetur ut sit aliquis locus et
> aliquod tempus, ubi et quando nihil ommino est. Quod quoniam falsum est —
> ipse namque locus et ipsum tempus aliquid est —, non potest esse summa
> natura alicubi vel aliquando determinate. Quod si dicitur, quia determinate
> ipsa per se alicubi et aliquando est, sed per potentiam suam est ubicumque
> vel quandocunque aliquid est : non est verum. Quoniam enim potentiam
> eius nihil aliud quam ipsam esse manifestum est, nullo modo potentia eius
> sine ipsa est. Cum ergo non sit alicubi vel aliquando determinate, necesse
> est ut sit ubique et semper, id est in omni loco vel tempore. [4]

Honorius dealt with the problem in this way.

> D. Quomodo dicitur Deus in omni loco totus esse et simul et semper, et in nullo
> loco esse ?
> M. In omni loco esse totus ideo dicitur, quia in nullo loco impotentior est quam
> in alio ; ut enim in caelo, sic potens est in inferno. Simul esse dicitur, quia,
> eodem momento quo in Oriente, eodem cuncta disponit in Occidente. Semper
> autem in omni loco esse praedicatur, quia in omni tempore cuncta moderatur.
> In nullo loco esse dicitur, quia locus est corporeus, Deus autem incorporeus

1. R.W. SOUTHERN, *ubi supra*, p. 82-88, 357-361.
2. *Sententiae Divinae Paginae (SDP)* ; BLIEMETZRIEDER, *ubi supra*, p. 18 ;
Elucidarius I, 47.
3. There are, of course, enormous similarities between all three, for example :
Cur Deus Homo II, XXI ; *Elucidarius* I, 42-43 ; *SDP* 15-16. *Cur Deus Homo*
I, V, VIII, XII, XIX ; *Elucidarius* I, 115-118 ; *SDP* 41-42, 37-38. *Cur Deus
Homo* II, IX ; *Elucidarius* I, 119 ; *SDP* 39. For the *Cur Deus Homo*, see
F.S. SCHMITT, *Sancti Anselmi Opera Omnia* II, Edinburgh 1946, p. 39-133.
4. SCHMITT, *ibid.*, I, p. 35-36.

et ideo illocalis. Incirco in nullo loco continetur, cum ipse contineat omnia, in quo « vivimus, movemur et sumus. »

All that Honorius announces here as simple and obvious truths are conclusions reached only eventually by St. Anselm, and in the most painstaking possible manner. In chapter 61, the distinction between *imago* and *similitudo* disposed neatly and in a similar way of the difficulty St. Anselm had felt in the *Monologion* (xvi) about applying terms of quality and quantity to God, and Honorius made remarkably short work of St. Augustine's long discussion. Examples of this sort can be multiplied.

It is not easy to simplify St. Anselm's thoughts, but Honorius managed it. It is true that the glosses compress opinions, use extracts and overlook problems in the original works. However, the compression in the glosses hardly seems to have been undertaken on quite this scale, nor with quite this determination to render even the most unlikely of material into digestible fragments. Thus, if it is true to say that Honorius put into practice in this work certain skills which were practised commonly, in stricter justice one must add that he knew more about them, he pushed them to greater lengths, and he covered more ground than was common. He produced a work which was constructed on foundations as complex as, or more complex than, were, for example, the theological sentence collections, and which was, at the same time, more simple to read. In this we have a paradox. We see a man who displays the greatest mental acumen in the understanding and collecting of his material, at the same time firmly repressing any encouragement this material may have offered to its readers to think. He clearly revered St. Anselm yet he sought to express this reverence by removing from his works all the weight of contemplation the master had taken such care to put into them. He moved then with a theological lightness of step which has no parallel among his contemporaries. This deliberate refusal on the part of Honorius to allow his powers to be extended to the expounding of the arguments implicit in so many of his sources is perhaps the most important feature of the *Elucidarius*. It is not easy to understand the paradox. To try to do so it is necessary to look now a little more closely at the particular circumstances which, I hope to argue, caused the *Elucidarius* to be written.

II. THE « ELUCIDARIUS » AND THE POST-CONQUEST ENGLISH CHURCH

The late eleventh century was a time of exceptional difficulty for the pastoral clergy in general. It was one thing for the ecclesiastical reformers to try to remove the care of souls from the gift of laymen. It was quite another to ensure that this removal would produce the desired effect in the matter of a renewed and celibate clergy freed from the sin of simony. The regular life and common revenues were the best guarantees of celibacy and, similarly, the denial, with these, of individual gain was one of the best defences against simony. It was difficult, however, to persuade those who, as monks, had adopted the regular life to undertake pastoral cares themselves, [1] and it was difficult also to persuade those who would undertake them to adopt any firm

1. See the interesting remarks on the lack of evidence for parish work on the part of monks in this period by M. CHIBNALL, *Monks and Pastoral Work. A Problem in Anglo-Norman History*, in *Journal of Ecclesiastical History* 18 (1967), p. 165-172.

common rule. Furthermore, it fast became clear that some of the number of the bishops, on whom the task of procuring the desired effect was at first laid, might interpret their responsibilities to the reform in a highly curious way. Some actively denied monks any part in pastoral care at all, thus adding fuel to the flames and provoking an outcry in support of monastic rights which must have startled many of the holders of them. [1]

In England, these difficulties were both intensified and given a curious twist by the conquest. There, those who would support the principle of a renewed pastoral clergy had three particular difficulties to overcome if they were to make any headway at all. The first of these was made up, of course, of those who had no time for the clergy in any case, let alone for its renewal. Such people certainly existed before William arrived, but they were fortified at a crucial moment by men whose interest in material gain fell in happily with such an attitude. Some of these last acquired bishoprics. They had a redoubtable opponent from the first, in the shape of Archbishop Lanfranc; but they were much in evidence and not easy to quell. The second difficulty arose as a result of the prominence of the Benedictine Order in England, and the special nature of Anglo-Saxon monasticism. This was defensive, eccentric, inward-looking and profoundly un-intellectual; a state of affairs which was, if anything, fortified by Lanfranc's zeal for its correction. [2] In the third, and perhaps for our immediate purposes the most important, place stands the difficulty produced by the recent appearance in England of other, differently educated, monks and canons; men who were neither Anglo-Saxon nor Norman but Lotharingian in sympathy, and who were active in support of a renewal. Many of these occupied distinguished positions; for example Duduc and Giso of Wells, Walter and Robert of Hereford, Herman of Ramsbury and Sherborne, [3] Leofric of Exeter, Walcher of Malvern, Athelard of Waltham. [4] Some of them went so far as to introduce canons living a common regular life into their cathedrals. Walter, Robert's predecessor at Hereford (1061-1079) may have done so [5] and Leofric and Giso certainly did. [6]

One would have thought that these last reinforcements would greatly assist the reform of the pastoral clergy; such an ambition may even have brought the native Lotharingians to England. In the event, however, they did not, and therein lies the curious twist produced by the conquest. In the rapidly flowing tide of events which it stimulated, they were caught between the

---

1. There are valuable references to this outcry in U. BERLIÈRE, *L'exercice du ministère paroissial par les moines dans le haut Moyen Age*, in *Rev. bénéd.* 39 (1927), p. 246-247.

2. See, for example, R.W. SOUTHERN, *ubi supra*, p. 241-253, for the state of affairs in Canterbury.

3. Giso was born at St. Trond near Liège, and Walter was chaplain to Queen Edith. Cfr *Vita Aedwardi Regis*, ed. and transl. F. BARLOW (Nelson Medieval Texts), Edinburgh 1962, p. XLVII, 35, n. 3.

4. WILLIAM OF MALMESBURY, *De Gestis Pontificum Anglorum*, ed. N.E.S.A. HAMILTON, London 1870, p. 201. On the Lotharingians in England cfr also M.C. WELBORN, *Lotharingia as a Center of Arabic and Scientific Influence in the Eleventh Century*, in *Isis* 16 (1931), p. 197-198.

5. A.T. BANNISTER, *The Cathedral Church of Hereford*, London 1924, p. 25-26.

6. WILLIAM OF MALMESBURY, *ubi supra*, p. 201. *Historiola de primordiis Episcopatus Somersetensis*, ed. J. HUNTER in *Ecclesiastical Documents* (Camden Society), London 1840, p. 16-20.

Scylla of the conservative English Benedictines and the Charybdis of the secularising Norman bishops. Lanfranc foiled these last of much of their monastic prey, but had then a deal to attend to in the backward state of the prey itself. The seculars fell upon the efforts of the Lotharingians and especially upon the largely undefended sees of canons regular. An extreme example is John of Tours, Giso's successor, who destroyed Giso's reforms at Wells as soon as he became bishop in 1088, and persecuted the monks of the abbey of Bath when it was incorporated into his see. [1] Leofric's reforms at Exeter seem quietly to have been allowed to lapse. [2] Herman's monastic see of Sherborne was moved to Salisbury, and from 1089 the new Norman see was served by secular canons. Osmund, bishop of Salisbury and a gentler but not less decided supporter of the secular ideal, provided his cathedral with a written constitution, and York and the new Norman foundation at Lincoln seem to have adopted similar ones by 1090-91. Osmund's *Institution* provided for secular canons, holding separate prebends and able, under certain conditions, to live away from the see; [3] the antithesis of the arrangements of Giso, Leofric and perhaps of Walter. In this they had the ready support of the incumbent of the one Anglo-Saxon see which had remained undoubtedly secular, Maurice of London, who was himself no reformer. [4]

By the 1090s the only see sympathetic to the Lotharingians and the regular canons to survive this was Hereford. Robert, perhaps somewhat pugnaciously, tried to rebuild his cathedral on the model of that of Aix, [5] imported the *Chronicle* of Marianus from Mainz and struck up a friendship with the monk-bishop Wulfstan of Worcester which allowed, among other things, Marianus to be improved upon at Worcester in the famous *Worcester Chronicle*. [6] Perhaps it was this combination which saved him so long. Robert's successor at Hereford, however, Gerard (1096-1101) was himself a Norman and a secular, and under him the regular life at Hereford too seems, though more quietly, to have been consigned to oblivion.

We can, at best, trace to these years only the smallest beginnings of only three houses of those canons regular who were later to become such a support to the reform; perhaps not even as much as this. [7] We know little about the state at this time of the smaller houses of 'clerici' in England. The little we do know, however, suggests that they were neither able nor disposed to lend great strength to the cause of renewal. [8] All the onus for its support, if it

1. *Ibid.*, p. 21-22.
2. K. EDWARDS, *English Secular Cathedrals in the Middle Ages*, 2nd ed., Manchester 1967, p. 19.
3. *Institutio Osmundi* VI, in W.H. FRERE, *The Use of Sarum*, Cambridge 1898, p. 259.
4. C.N.L. BROOKE, in W.R. MATTHEWS and W.M. ATKINS, *A History of St. Paul's Cathedral and the Men associated with it*, London 1957, p. 18-22.
5. WILLIAM OF MALMESBURY, *ubi supra*, p. 300.
6. See my coming Note on the date of the *Worcester Chronicle*, in *Rev. bénéd.* 85 (1975), fasc. 3-4.
7. J.C. DICKINSON, *The Origins of the Austin Canons and their Introduction into England*, London 1950, p. 98-108. The three were St. Botolph's, Colchester, St. Mary's, Huntingdon, St. Gregory's, Canterbury. Dr. Dickinson is disinclined to allow them a history as regular houses until the reign of Henry I.
8. W. PAGE, *Some Remarks on the Churches of the Domesday Survey*, in *Archaeologia* 66 (1915), p. 61-102.

X

was to be supported at all, fell now with an extraordinary suddenness upon the
Benedictines. It is to this crisis and especially to the ill-prepared state in
which it found the Anglo-Saxon monks that we must ascribe the writing of the
Elucidarius.

Matters could hardly, in this last decade of the eleventh century, have
augured worse for the reform. First of all, there was the suddenness of the
demand coupled with the fact that almost nothing in the training of the English
Benedictines either inclined or equipped them to take on the burdens of the
pastorate. Secondly, they were confronted by strengthened secular bishops,
who had before them many examples of the refusal of such responsibilities to
monks. [1] Lastly there was the matter of their profound theological inade-
quacy. Never before, except perhaps in the aftermath of the first Viking
onslaught, had there been such a dearth of mental enterprise in this field as
there was in the Anglo-Saxon monasteries after the conquest. Many excuses
could be made for it and stern measures were taken to overcome it but the
fact was that, in the last decade of the eleventh century, there affairs stood. [2]
Furthermore, when Anglo-Saxon monks could be persuaded, usually by some
threat to cherished unreason, to take to food for the mind at all, and to write,
they wrote about miracles and saint's lives [3] and, if pressed, history. One
of the best examples, dating from these years, of Anglo-Saxon monastic composition we have is the *Worcester Chronicle*. [4] This was compiled with enormous

1. See the remarks on the bishops of these years and their, at best, indiffe-
rence to the reform, in V.H. GALBRAITH, *Notes on the Career of Samson, Bishop
of Worcester*, in *English Historical Review* 82 (1967), p. 86-87. The replacement
of Wulfstan by Samson in 1096 must have shown with a horrible clarity how
far episcopal office now was from the grasp of monks, and how difficult it would
be to regain it.

2. Perhaps in part because the stern measures came from men who were
not English and who had a sense of intellectual virtue quite alien from that
little to be found there. Much illumination upon this point is to be gained
from M.T. GIBSON, *The Place of Archbishop Lanfranc in Eleventh Century
Scholastic Development* (unpublished Oxford D. Phil. thesis). I am grateful
for her permission to read it. Dr. Gibson shews how the Normans, especially,
ignored what they found in England and set to work to provide for a more
demanding intellectual life, fortified by the virtues of clarity and order. Even
without the sense of alienation, of course, too much of such demands and
such virtues can be forbidding. The other half of this picture is filled by the
Lotharingians of whose precise effect we know so far distressingly little (cfr
M.C. WELBORN, *art. cit.*), and it may be that their extreme interests, for
instance in astronomy and mathematics, contributed to the depressed state
of Anglo-Saxon learning. This aspect of the problem would reward detailed
treatment. For some interesting remarks on the books Leofric gave to Exeter
and on the concerns of the eleventh century English scribes, see N.R. KER,
English Manuscripts in the Century after the Conquest, Oxford 1960, p. 7-8.

3. R.W. SOUTHERN, *The English Origins of the 'Miracles of the Virgin"*
in *Medieval and Renaissance Studies* 4 (1958), p. 176-216. Miracle stories
clearly formed an important part of St. Anselm's awn conversation. Cfr *Dicta
Anselmi*, ed. R.W. SOUTHERN, and F.S. SCHMITT, *Memorials of St. Anselm*
(The British Academy), London 1969, p. 196-268. The writing of saint's lives
presented frustrating and time-consuming difficulties. Cfr SOUTHERN, *ubi
supra*, p. 248-250.

4. See my coming Note on the date of the *Worcester Chronicle*, in *Rev.
bénéd.* 85 (1975), fasc. 3-4.

X

187

energy and skill and, with its consciousness of the strength of the sword and the injustices of taxation, [1] did, to a degree, articulate certain of the concerns of the outside world. It was not, however, penetrating in its analysis of these, nor was it creative in its remedies. There was certainly no suggestion that a correction to these evils might be found in a reformed understanding of the Christian message interpreted by an enlightened pastoral clergy.

It may be that we can assign the bringing of Anselm himself to Canterbury to this peculiarly necessitous situation. It is certain that the *Elucidarius* was written when this whole crisis, and especially the theological aspect of it, was at its height. It was devised as a means of resolving it. I have pointed out elsewhere that the interest of the *Elucidarius* in the reformed priesthood and its opposite distinguishes this earliest recension. [2] I have tried to shew here that it was to a quite extraordinary degree thorough yet, equally, extremely simple to read, and that it prized the views of St. Anselm. We may now explain these distinguishing features by this particular crisis. In one of the chapters of the earliest recension (1.200 d.) Honorius opposes the 'lignum scientiae bonae' to the evils of simony and the marriage of priests. This 'lignum' is, he says, knowledge of the divine scriptures and of the mysteries of God. The *Elucidarius* contains the questions which those who would work in the pastorate in pursuit of the reform must meet, and has, formed from the knowledge required, ready answers for them. It has, furthermore, the sort of answers which, but for Honorius's hard work, would have been remarkably hard to find, and furnished in a form startlingly easy to use. Finally, St. Anselm was above all things a Benedictine. The offering of answers from his works, although they were so difficult to render into the form required, must surely have been one of the most effective means available for encouraging other Benedictines in confidence and in support.

This way of looking at the *Elucidarius* explains, also, two further features of it. The early manuscripts have with the chapters, in the margins or in the text, lists of authorities. The lists certainly go back to Honorius, and are remarkably thorough and accurate. [3] They were obviously meant in part to serve the same function as the modern footnote and for a similar end; namely that the enquirer may, at need, find more solid support for the propositions. This was the Norman monastic library, perhaps even that built up by Lanfranc at Canterbury, made to work. Moreover, in some manuscripts (all of the earliest group) opinions clearly drawn from St. Anselm are ascribed to 'magister'. Such a title set St. Anselm firmly and, it seems, deliberately among the 'modern masters' whose contributions Honorius recommends so

1. One of the more interesting features of the *Worcester Chronicle* is its up-to-date denunciation of the Domesday Survey. Cfr W.H. STEVENSON, *A Contemporary Description of the Domesday Survey*, in *English Historical Review* 22 (1907), p. 72-84.
2. V.I.J. FLINT, *The Original Text of the Elucidarium of Honorius Augustodunensis from the Twelfth-Century English Manuscripts*, in *Scriptorium* 17 (1964), p. 91-94.
3. I have reproduced those in the English manuscripts for Book I in the Note following this paper, and I set against them, whenever I could find them, the references to the sources to which they appear to correspond. Many of these sources recall the Norman manuscripts brought to Christ Church by Lanfranc. I think especially of the works of Augustine, now Trinity College, Cambridge, B.3.31, B.4.2, B.5.26, B.5.28, and of Ambrose, now Cambridge University Library Kk.1.23.

strongly in his preface. [1] Again we may see in this one further aid to men who had to appear impressive but were ill-equipped to be so, and, in the inclusion of St. Anselm as 'magister', one further fortification for monks.

It is perhaps appropriate at this point to mention, also, a few small problems about Honorius's career as a whole upon which the *Elucidarius* throws light. He turned, it seems from canon into monk, and I have suggested that he did so at Worcester. [2] One important manuscript of Honorius's *Imago mundi* shews some connexion with Hereford. [3] Now Hereford was the last stronghold of Lotharingian endeavours for the reform, falling only, perhaps, in the late 1090s; just when the *Elucidarius* was conceived. The same manuscript contains the unique assertion that the author of the *Imago mundi* had been a canon at Mainz. [4] Honorius may then have been a canon of Lotharingian sympathies, [5] and have lived in this part of England at precisely this time. We should, I think, place his conversion to monasticism at about this point in his life, with the writing of the *Sigillum*, the *Speculum Ecclesiae* and, perhaps, the *Quod monachis liceat praedicare.* [6] We may even attribute to it a decision to serve the Benedictine Order in the cause of reform which dictated the rest of Honorius's career.

The context in which the *Elucidarius* was produced, then, is the wide one of the late eleventh century movement for the reform of the clergy, and the narrow one of the special conditions faced by this movement in England. The *Elucidarius* was written there at a time of quite extraordinary difficulty and bears, above all, the marks of this. It was a device to speed Anglo-Saxon monks into the task of serving and renewing the pastorate. Honorius was exposed to these agitations to an exceptional degree, and he confronted them with an exceptional document.

We learn more about the *Elucidarius* from these conditions, but we learn most about the conditions themselves. It seems that Honorius stood in the tradition of the Flemings, Folcard and Goscelin, in his efforts on behalf of the English Benedictines. Now, however, circumstances have changed. Their

---

1. Fr. Bliemetzrieder speaks eloquently about the importance of this respect for modern masters for the future of theology. He refers to Anselm of Laon and William of Champeaux but in so doing illuminates the task Honorius performed for St. Anselm and, especially, for the right of Benedictines to a place in this august company : « Jusqu'au temps d'Anselme de Laon les docteurs et les maîtres devaient s'effacer devant les grands docteurs canonisés par l'Église, se cacher modestement sous l'anonymat... Mais depuis le xiie siècle, à l'école de Laon, à la parole du 'Maître' acquiert elle aussi la valeur et le poids d'une autorité... C'est alors que prend naissance la scholastique, parce qu'alors débute la théologie d'école dont la compétence est reconnue ». *Art. cit.* in *Rech. de théol. anc. et méd.* 2 (1930), p. 78.

2. V.I.J. FLINT, *The Career of Honorius Augustodunensis. Some fresh Evidence,* in *Rev. bénéd.* 82 (1972), p. 75-80, 84-85.

3. Corpus Christi College, Cambridge, 66 (twelfth century, from Sawley), contains, as a frontispiece to Honorius's *Imago mundi,* a mappa mundi remarkably like the famous Hereford map.

4. Fol. 4 : « Iste Henricus, qui hunc librum edidit, fuit canonicus S. Mariae civitatis Maguntie, in qua ecclesia sunt canonici bis quater quaterdeni. »

5. In saying this I modify some remarks made in *Rev. bénéd.* 82 (1972), p. 85-86. In this I tried tentatively to connect this early part of Honorius's career with Lambach, but in doing so I overlooked the evidence of the Corpus manuscript.

6. V.I.J. FLINT, *art. cit.* in *Rev. bénéd.* 82 (1972), p. 232.

relics and their saints are not, even fortified by written lives, enough to guarantee the English monks a place of importance in the Anglo-Norman church. We know from hindsight that nothing was in the end enough to guarantee them this; yet it must have seemed, in the late 1090s just before the demise of Hereford, that there was a chance. This chance lay in the reform. The cause of the reform was, in the wide realm of general principle, both to William Rufus king of England and to Anselm archbishop of Canterbury an embarrassment; but in the more constricted one of practice, it was an opportunity. Here was a sphere in which monks, guarded as they should be from temptations to simony and from celibacy, might have a contribution to make. Above all, at a period when the public attitude of churchmen in general was confused, if not hostile, they might be seen to be making it. If only they could be provided with theological materials abstruse enough in their roots to satisfy persistent questioners yet simple enough in their exposition for the least learned to understand. If only the battle between hagiography and theology could be convincingly resolved in favour of a renewed theology, and if only this theology could be effectively served by catechesis. One can appreciate the enthusiasm with which the *Elucidarius* was received.

The matter does not, however, quite end here, for, once written, the *Elucidarius* took on a life of its own. This is not the moment at which to follow it into its independent existence, but two points may perhaps be made as a postscript. The first springs from the treatise's very success. It was seized upon with a vigour that has few contemporary parallels; and not merely by the clergy but by the laity too. There was clearly a demand for theological elucidation of this quality which spread far more widely, and was felt far more deeply, than that which first worked upon Honorius. The second point follows from this and leads to a question of a sinister kind. Of the forty-one twelfth century Latin manuscripts, the provenance of nineteen can be traced with some security. Of these nineteen, two come from Augustinian houses, two from Cistercian, one from the Grande Chartreuse. [1] The rest are from the Benedictines, and some from houses of particular age and intellectual distinction. [2] There is food for reflection here. The cost in terms of the original works Honorius so ruthlessly exploited for his conclusions, and especially in terms of the works of St. Anselm, was great. One may begin to wonder whether the price the movement for ecclesiastical reform levied upon the intellectual achievement of some Benedictine abbeys at the beginning of the twelfth century was not perhaps a little too high.

The University of Auckland
(New Zealand).

1. Augustinian houses : VIENNA NB 1180 (Klosterneuburg, fragments) ; OXFORD Bodley Lat. Th. e.9 (Flanesford, to Book II, 43). Cistercian houses : LONDON *British Museum* Royal 15.A.xx (Byland) ; DUBLIN *Trinity College* 279 (Rievaulx). Grande Chartreuse : GRENOBLE 272.
2. For example : Corbie (PARIS *B.N.* lat. 12315); St. Emmeram's, Regensburg (MUNICH clm 14348) and, of course, Worcester (CAMBRIDGE *University Library* Kk. IV.6).

THE SOURCES OF THE « ELUCIDARIUS »
OF HONORIUS AUGUSTODUNENSIS

This note sets out to demonstrate more clearly three points about the *Elucidarius* which have already been made. The first is that the earliest text contains careful and accurate references to authorities in the margins, and that St. Anselm is ranged among these authorities, sometimes as 'magister'. This is demonstrated by setting out the marginal references to Book I, the English manuscripts in which they appear and, where possible, the sources they indicate. The second is that the *Elucidarius* is closely linked with work upon the glossing of the Sacred Page. A list, again for Book I, is given of those sections of the earlier parts of the *Glossa Ordinaria* which use the same extracts from sources as Honorius does. This is singular and interesting. The third is that the *Elucidarius* is an especially early work. This is demonstrated by the closeness of the relationship between it and the earliest version of the *De beatitudine* of St. Anselm.

1

The manuscripts of the *Elucidarius* are denoted by letters of the alphabet :

A Corpus Christi College, Cambridge, 308
B British Museum, Royal 5.E.VI
C Lambeth 358
D British Museum, Royal 11 A VII
E MS. Bodley Lat. Th. c. 9. (32710)
F MS. Cambridge University Library Kk.IV.6
G British Museum, Royal 15 A XX
H Corpus Christi College, Cambridge, 439
I MS. Bodley Fairfax 26 (3906)
J MS. Glasgow University Library 244
K MS. Bodley Laud Misc. 237

B and C are the best texts of the earliest edition and B, it will be seen, refers very often to 'magister'. The numbering of the chapters is taken from M. Lefèvre's edition.

1 VIRGILIUS	BEGHIJ	
	Aeneid II, 708	
2 BEDA	BD	
	In Primam Epistolam Petri, PL 93, 45.	
3 PETRUS	BCDEGH	

The most likely explanation for this entry is that it refers to the quotation from *I Peter*, 12 in the preceding chapter. References to the Bible are included among the listed authorities in the manuscripts, although I have not noted the obvious ones. There is a similarity between the contents of chapter 3 and a passage in the *Introductio Theologia Scholarium* of PETER ABELARD ; cfr *Petri Abaelardi Opera*, ed. V. COUSIN (Paris 1859), ii.99. The date of this work, however, makes it far too late to have been known by Honorius, and it adds nothing to the passage from Augustine upon which it depends.

AUGUSTINUS	ABCGHJK	
	De Symbolo, PL 40, IX, 659.	
BOETIUS	K	
4 ANSELMUS	BCHIK	

Monologion, F.S. SCHMITT, *S. Anselmi Opera Omnia* i (Edinburgh 1946), (SCHMITT i), xlv, 62.

	AUGUSTINUS	AD
		De Beate Vita, *PL* 32, xxxiii, 975.
5	?	*Enarratio in Psalmum* LVIII i, *PL* 36, 704.
6	?	
7	?	
8	?	
9	?	
10	AUGUSTINUS	ABCHIK
		De Genesi ad Litteram, *PL* 34, XII, xxxiv, 483
11	?	
12	AUGUSTINUS	DJ
		Confessiones: Corpus Scriptorum Ecclesiasticorum Latinorum, xxxiii, VI iii, 118. *Sermones* cclxxvii et lii, *PL* 38, 1265, 367.
	ANSELMUS	ABC
		Monologion (SCHMITT i) xxii, 39-40.
13	BOETIUS	ABGHK
		De Consolatione Philosophiae I
14	AUGUSTINUS	ABCEGHK
		De Trinitate, *PL* 42, III xi, 881-82.
15	JOHANNES CRISOSTOMUS (JOHN SCOTUS ERIGENA)	CEGHIK
		De Divisione Naturae, *PL* 122, III, v, 635
		? (ch.16) *De Divinis Nominibus*, *PL* 122, IV, 1128-29.
	AUGUSTINUS	BCDEHK
		De Genesi ad Litteram, *PL* 34 I, ii, 174-75.
16	PLATO	ABCDEGHK
		AUGUSTINE, *De Civitate Dei*, *PL* 41, XI, xxi, 334-35. In this, Augustine refers by name to Plato.
17	?	
18	AUGUSTINUS	K
		De Genesi ad Litteram, *PL* 34, I, iv, 249.
19	YSIDORUS	J
20	YSIDORUS	B
		Quaestiones in Vetus Testamentum, *PL* 83, i, ii, 209-13.
	AUGUSTINUS	ABEGHK
		De Genesi ad Litteram, *PL* 34, IV xxxii, 318, V v 326.
21	JERONIMUS	ABCHK
	JOHANNES (C)	ABHJK
		De Divisione Naturae, *PL* 122, III, iii, 630-32.
22	AUGUSTINUS	ABCDEGH
		De Genesi ad Litteram, *PL* 34, I, xvii, 259-60.
23	AUGUSTINUS	EK
		De Genesi ad Litteram, *PL* 34 XI, xv, 437.
	MAGISTER	B
		De Humanis Moribus per Similitudines. R.W. SOUTHERN and F.S. SCHMITT, *Memorials of St. Anselm* (London 1969), (SOUTHERN and SCHMITT), p. 56-57.
		Cur Deus Homo (SCHMITT ii) I, xvii, 77-78.
24	DIONISIUS AREOPAGETICA	ABCEHIK
		PSEUDO DIONYSIUS. *Caelestis Ierarchia*, *PL* 122, 1049 (transl. John Scotus).
25	?	
26	DIONISIUS (A)	G
	ANSELMUS	ABCEHJ
		? *Cur Deus Homo* (SCHMITT ii) I, xviii, 77-78.
	AUGUSTINUS	DE
		De Genesi ad Litteram, *PL* 34, IV, xxxii, 317.
27	?	
28	?	
29	?	
30	GREGORIUS	K
		Homilia, *PL* 76, II, xxxiv, 1250-51.
31	JOHANNES (C)	ABEGHK
		Caelestis Ierarchia, *PL* 122, 1047.

32 MAGISTER   B
             ANSELM, *De Casu Diaboli* (SCHMITT i) IV, 242.

33 ?

34 AUGUSTINUS   BDEG

35 AUGUSTINUS   ABJK
             De Civitate Dei, PL 41, XI, xiii, 328-29.

36 ?

37 AUGUSTINUS   AGH
             De Genesi ad Litteram, PL 34, XI, xxiii, 41.

38 AUGUSTINUS   E
    ANSELMUS   AHK

39 ANSELMUS   E

40 ?

41 ?

42 ?

43 ?

44 GREGORIUS   E
             Moralia, PL 75, IV, iii, 642.

45 ?

46 GREGORIUS   ABDEGH
             Moralia, PL 76, XXXIII, xiv, 691.

47 MAGISTER   B
             ANSELM, *Cur Deus Homo* (SCHMITT ii) I, xvii, 75.

48 ?

48a AUGUSTINUS   K

49 ?

50 ?

51 ?

52 ?

53 ?

54 GREGORIUS   ABCGHK
             Homilia in Evangelium PL 76, II, xxxiv, 1250.

55 MAGISTER   B
             ? ANSELM, *Proslogion* (SCHMITT i) xvi, 112.

56 GREGORIUS   E

57 MAGISTER   B
             ANSELM, *Cur Deus Homo* (SCHMITT ii) I, xvi, 74-75.

58 GREGORIUS   AGHK
             Moralia, PL 75, IV, iii, 642.

59 MACROBIUS   ABDEGHIJK
             In. Somn. Scip. I, vi, 36, I xiv, 9.

    GREGORIUS   E
             Moralia, PL 75, VI, xvi, 740.
             This chapter draws upon a latin version of the Book of
             the Secrets of Enoch, cfr M. FORSTER, *Adams Erschaffung*
             und Namengebung, in *Archiv für Religionswissenschaft* 11
             (1908), 479-81. Christ Church Canterbury had a tenth
             century manuscript of this text, now Corpus Christi College,
             Cambridge, 326. It is not impossible that Anselm commen-
             ted upon this and that this is the reason for the reference
             to Magister in B here. The contents of chapter 64 (see
             below) seem to have been drawn from Anselm's teaching
             and are related to this text.

60 MAGISTER   B
             ? ANSELM, *Proslogion* (SCHMITT i) i, 100.

61 ?

62 AUGUSTINUS   BDEGHK
             De Civitate Dei, PL 41, XII, xxiii, 373.

    ANSELMUS   ABCEHJ
             Monologion (SCHMITT i) xi, 26.

63 ANSELMUS   ABHI
    AUGUSTINUS   GI

64 ANSELMUS   DIK
             There is clear evidence that Anselm furnished the material
             for this chapter, but it is to be found now not in his works
             but in a single manuscript of his *Dicta.* Honorius may

here, then, report the spoken word. The material is printed in SOUTHERN and SCHMITT, p. 318.

	AUGUSTINUS	ABHIK
		In Joannis Evangelium, PL 35, IX ii, 1465.
65	ANSELMUS	E
	AUGUSTINUS	D
		De Genesi ad Litteram, PL 34, III, xv, 239.
66	AUGUSTINUS	ABCFGHJK
		In Joannis Evangelium, PL 35, I, i, 1385-87.
	GREGORIUS	ABEH
67	GREGORIUS	CD
	AMBROSIUS	DEFHI
		Hexaemeron, PL 14, 123.
	ANSELMUS	K
68	AMBROSIUS	ADE
69	AMBROSIUS	AB²EH²
		De Paradiso, PL 14, I, i, 275-76.
	MAGISTER	B
	AUGUSTINUS	A
		De Civitate Dei, PL 41, XIV, xxvi, 434.
	ANSELMUS	C
70	?	
71	AMBROSIUS	GH
		De Paradiso, PL 14, I, x, 298.
	MACROBIUS	A
71a	JERONIMUS	K
72	?	
73	AUGUSTINUS	BDHK
		Enchiridion, PL 40, I, cv, 281.
74	AUGUSTINUS	ACEFGJ
		De Genesi ad Litteram, PL 34, IX, iii, 395.
75	MAGISTER	B
	(item)	ANSELM, *De Conceptu Virginali* (SCHMITT ii) xvi, 157.
76	AUGUSTINUS	C
77	MAGISTER	E
		ANSELM, *Cur Deus Homo* (SCHMITT ii) I, xviii, 80.
	AUGUSTINUS	K
78	AUGUSTINUS	ABGH
		De Genesi ad Litteram, PL 34, IX, vi, 397.
79	GREGORIUS	DE
80	?	
81	GREGORIUS	CE
82	?	
83	GREGORIUS	ABG
	AUGUSTINUS	K
		Enarratio in Psalmum CXXXIX, PL 37, 1807.
84	?	
85	AUGUSTINUS	J
		De Genesi ad Litteram, PL 34, XI, xxviii, 444, 445.
86	MAGISTER	E
87	?	
88	?	
89	?	
90	?	
91	YSIDORUS	ABDEGH
	AMBROSIUS	E
92	YSIDORUS	ABDEGH
		Quaestiones in Vetus Testamentum, PL 83, V, 222-23.
	AMBROSIUS	BEK
93	AMBROSIUS	A²BCDEGH²
		? *De Paradiso, PL* 14, IV, 283-84.
	JERONIMUS	DEG
		? *Liber Hebraic. quaest. in Gen., PL* 23, 862.
	ANSELMUS	K
94	AMBROSIUS	D
	MAGISTER	B
		Cur Deus Homo (SCHMITT ii) I, xxi, 88.

	ANSELMUS	E
95	ANSELMUS	A
		Ibid.
96	ANSELMUS	D
		Ibid.
97	ANSELMUS	AB
		Ibid.
98	AMBROSIUS	G
	ANSELMUS	CK
		Ibid.
99	?	
100	JOHANNES	BDEG

AUGUSTINE, *Tractatus in Joannem, PL* 35, IX, ii, 1461.

| 101 | YSIDORUS | ABCEGHK |
| 102 | ANSELMUS | ABCDEHK |

Cur Deus Homo (SCHMITT ii) I, xxiv, 92.

103	?
104	?
105	?
106	?
107	?
108	?
109	?
110	?
111	?
112	ANSELMUS	C

Cur Deus Homo (SCHMITT ii) I, xii, 69, xix, 84-86.

113	?
114	?
115	ANSELMUS	EI

Cur Deus Homo (SCHMITT ii) I, v, 52.

| | AUGUSTINUS | I |

De Trinitate, PL 42, XIII, xviii, 1032.

| 116 | ANSELMUS | ABCDH |

Cur Deus Homo (SCHMITT ii) II, viii, 102.

117	?
118	?
119	?
120	?
121	?
122	?
123	?
124	?
125	BOETIUS	ACEFIK

De Fide Catholica (STEWARD and RAND) 64-66.

126	AUGUSTINUS	BEIK
127	MAGISTER	D
128	?
129	AUGUSTINUS	D

Enarratio in Psalmum CXXXIV, PL 37, 1735.

130	MAGISTER	BE
131	MAGISTER	C
132	?
133	*Ecclesiastica*	ABCDE
	Historia	

OROSIUS, *Historiarum, PL* 31, VI, xx, 1053-54 ;
EUSEBIUS, *PG* 19, 519.

| 134 | ? |
| 135 | BEDA | ABCE |

In Matthaei Evangelium Expositio, PL 92, I, ii, 13.

136	?
137	?
138	YSIDORUS	K

Quaestiones in Vetus Testamentum, PL 83, 216.

139	?
140	?
141	?
142	?

X

143	?	
144	ANSELMUS	ABCHK
		Cur Deus Homo (SCHMITT ii) I, viii-ix, 59-61.
145	AMBROSIUS	CE
146	AMBROSIUS	ABHIK
	AUGUSTINUS	C
147	AUGUSTINUS	BDEK
		Enarratio in Psalmum LXV, PL 36, 793.
	MAGISTER	B
148	ANSELMUS	C
		Cur Deus Homo (SCHMITT ii) I, iii,51.
149	?	
150	?	
151	?	
152	?	
153	?	
154	ANSELMUS	D
155	?	
156	?	
157	AUGUSTINUS	EH
158	AUGUSTINUS	BC
	GREGORIUS	D
159	BEDA	BCE
		Expositio ir Lucae Evangelium, PL 92, vi, 724.
	GREGORIUS	ABCEK
		Moralia, PL 75, IV, xvi, 653.
160	YSIDORUS	ABCD
161	?	
162	MAGISTER	E
163	?	
164	?	
165	?	
166	?	
167	?	
168	?	
169	?	
170	*Ecclesiastica*	ABCHIJK
	Historia	
	YSIDORUS	BCH
	AUGUSTINUS	D²
		De Consensu Evangelistarum, PL 34, III, xxv, 1214.
171	?	
172	?	
173	?	
174	?	
175	?	
176	?	
177	AUGUSTINUS	BK
178	ORIGENIS	ABCJ
	MAGISTER	E
	AUGUSTINUS	EK
179	AUGUSTINUS	ABCDJK
		Sermo CXXXVII, *PL* 38, 754.
180	PASCHASIUS	BCDHJK
		Liber de Corpore et Sanguine Domini, PL 120, 1303-04.
	AUGUSTINUS	ADIJK
		Sermo CCLXXII, *PL* 38, 1247-48 ; *Tractatus in Joannem, PL* 35, XXVI, vi, 1614.
	AMBROSIUS	DE
181	ANSELMUS	JK
	SIMACHUS	E
	AMBROSIUS	BC
		De Sacramentis, PL 16, IV, iv, 443.
	AUGUSTINUS	K
182	?	
183	?	

184	ANSELMUS	AC
	AUGUSTINUS	E
185	?	
186	ANSELMUS	D
		Ep. 65 (SCHMITT iii) 183.
187	?	
188	?	
189	AUGUSTINUS	D
190	AUGUSTINUS	ABCEIJ
		Tractatus in Joannem, PL 35, VII, i, 1422.
	MAGISTER	BE
		ANSELM, *Ep.* 65 (SCHMITT iii) 182-83.
191	?	
192	?	
193	ANSELMUS	ABCHJK
		Ibid.
194	AMBROSIUS	BCEH
	PASCHASIUS	BEH
195	PASCHASIUS	BCHJ
	CYPRIANUS	E
		Liber de Lapsis, PL 4, xxv-xxvi, 500-501.
196	MAGISTER	C
197	MAGISTER	B
	AUGUSTINUS	D
198	AUGUSTINUS	ABCHJ
199	AUGUSTINUS	AIJK
		Contra Epistolam Parmeniani, PL 43, III, 94.
	AMBROSIUS	CE
	ANSELMUS	D
200	AMBROSIUS	B
	ANSELMUS	ABCEHIJK
201	?	
202	GREGORIUS	ABCEI
		Ep. lxix, *PL* 77, 1209.
203	?	

II

The *Elucidarius* and the *Glossa Ordinaria* use similar extracts from their sources in the following places. For the *Glossa Ordinaria* I refer to the text in *Biblia Sacra cum Glossa Ordinaria* (Antwerp 1617).

Elucidarius		*Glossa Ordinaria*	*Biblia Sacra*
Book I	2	*I Peter*, i	vi, 1311
«	11	*II Cor.* xii	vi, 447-48
«	12	*Acts* xvii	vi, 1175
«	15	*John* I	v, 1011
«	16/17/18	*Genesis* I, 8	i, 13
«	28	*Genesis* I, 8	i, 13
«	29	*Hebrews* I	vi, 801
«	31	*Matthew* xvi, ? *Luke* I	v, 283, v, 682
«	40	*Genesis* I	i, 26
«	48	*Matthew* viii	v, 168
«	49	*Apocalypse* xx	vi, 1659-60
«	55	*John* I, 9	iv, 1016
«	57	*Luke* xv	v, 895
«	59	*Genesis* I	i, 24
«	61	*Genesis* I	i, 30-31
«	65	*Genesis* I	i, 36
«	71a	*Genesis* II	i, 81
«	79/80	*Genesis* II	i, 81
«	84	*Genesis* III	i, 91
«	85	*Genesis* III	i, 89-90
«	86	*Genesis* III	i, 103

Elucidarius	Glossa Ordinaria	Biblia Sacra
Book I 87	Genesis II	i, 77
« 92	Genesis III	i, 110
« 93	Genesis v, IX	i, 133-34, 170
« 101	Romans v	vi, 68
« 124	Luke x	v, 833-34
« 126	Ezechiel xliv, Psalm XVIII	iv, 1436, iii, 571
« 130	? Colossians II, 3	vi, 618
« 135	Matthew ii	v, 57
« 136	Matthew ii	v, 65
« 137	Luke iii	v, 738
« 147	Romans viii	vi, 114
« 148/149	Mark xv	v, 645
« 157	I Machabees iii	iv, 2270-71
« 159	Luke xxiv	v, 988
« 161a	I Cor. xv	vi, 348
« 165	Ezechiel xliii, Psalm xxix	iv, 1434, iii, 641
« 172	Matthew xxvii	v, 462
« 173	Acts I	vi, 677
« 174	Acts I	vi, 969
« 176	Romans viii	vi, 115
« 180	John vi	v, 1121
« 181	I Cor. xi	vi, 293
« 182	I Cor. vi	vi, 240
« 196	Luke xxii	v, 959
« 201	Matthew vii	v, 146
« 202	Matthew xiii	v, 241-42

III

In Book III of the *Elucidarius*, Honorius used a version of the *De beatitudine* of St. Anselm. Manuscripts B and C refer to Anselm as the authority for this part of the text. The *De beatitudine* has been transmitted in two versions, one with additions. The first, drawn up by Eadmer in reply to a request, reports a sermon delivered by St. Anselm at Cluny 'and elsewhere' (SOUTHERN and SCHMITT, p. 273-91). Eadmer added twice to his original version. The second version is contained in the *Liber ex dictis beati Anselmi* of Alexander (*ibid*, p. 127-41). Alexander's version is the shorter of the two, and bears practically no formal or verbal relation to Eadmer's. They have certain quotations in common, and both list the seven glories of the body and the soul. In Alexander's version, however, the glories of the body follow those of the soul; in Eadmer's, the first appear at the beginning, the second in the middle of the narrative (ch. 7). Here the formal and verbal resemblances end. It is, then, exceedingly improbable that the two versions were copied the one from the other, and extremely unlikely too that the two reports were made at the same time. They must be treated as independent. There were at least two opportunities for the delivery of the sermon at Cluny, the one in 1100, when Eadmer may well have taken it down, the other during St. Anselm's stay at Lyons, 1104-1105, which may have fallen to the lot of Alexander.

When one compares Honorius's version with those of Eadmer and of Alexander, it becomes evident that it is nearest in spirit and in form to that of Eadmer. The ordering of Honorius's version follows that of Eadmer; for example, the description of the two 'beatitudines' and 'miseriae' (106) is included in the body of Eadmer's text (ch. 6) at the point in the development of the narrative at which Honorius reports it. It is included in the first section of Alexander's version. The following sections of Book III of the *Elucidarius* and Eadmer's version of the *De beatitudine* are closely related :

Elucidarius	Eadmer
87-89	Introduction, p. 274
106	1-4, 6-7
107-114	8
115	9-10
116	10
118	12-14
119	15

The wording of Honorius, although by no means copied slavishly, is more closely related to that of Eadmer than to that of Alexander. For example, Honorius 106 :

> Illorum vero talis est libertas, ut omnia obstantia penetrare valeant et nulla creatura eos retinere queat, sicut sepulcrum corpus Domini retinere non potuit quin inde resurgeret et januis clausis intraret.

Eadmer 4 :

> ... ita non erit obstaculum ullum quod nos retardaret, non clausura quae nos detineat, non elementum quod nobis ad velle pervium omnino non extet. Exempli causa: certe dominicum corpus, cui corpora nostra configuranda Paulus testatur ut supra meminimus, clauso sepulchro a mortuis surrexit, ac demum ad discipulos obseratis ianuis palpandum introiit, nobisque in hoc libertatis futurae documentum grande reliquit.

Alexander (p. 131) :

> Libere dominus clauso monumento exivit, libere infernum spoliavit, libere ad discipulos 'ianuis clausis' intravit. Libere sancti dei, si voluerint, infernum intrabunt, libere per ignem et ardentem picem transibunt, libere, quantum voluerint, ibi morabuntur absque laesione sui, quia in illa gehennali flamma nihil ardebit nisi tantum delicta.

Where the two versions differ in content, again Honorius appears to be more familiar with the content of Eadmer's. In chapter 106, for example, Honorius reports a discussion about the description of men as temples of God which appears in Eadmer's version, but not in Alexander's.

The dependence of Honorius upon the form, and some of the words and contents of Eadmer's version is, then, clear. It establishes also that Honorius refers to the very earliest form of the sermon. The original version of Eadmer ended at 'societatem daemoniorum' (SOUTHERN and SCHMITT, p. 287). The first addition went to 'praecipitati depereunt' (*ibid.*, p. 288), the second to the end of the printed text. Honorius uses neither of the additions but stops short at the end of the original. The association is not clear enough, however, for us to be able to conclude that he used Eadmer's written text. This is especially important. It seems that, here again, Honorius reports St. Anselm's spoken word and, in this case, a demonstrably early version of it. We have no reason to suppose that he ever went to Cluny. He must, then, have heard the sermon 'elsewhere', perhaps at Canterbury or at Worcester before 1097, the date of Anselm's first exile, or, at the latest, after St. Anselm's return in 1100 but before his last exile in 1103.

The University of Auckland
(New Zealand).

XI

THE COMMENTARIES
OF HONORIUS AUGUSTODUNENSIS
ON THE SONG OF SONGS

Honorius's active life, and most of his writings, occupied the first thirty three years of the twelfth century. Honorius himself moved about during these years, in space and, it seems, in religious affiliation. He certainly lived in England and in Germany, and he perhaps lived in Austria ; and he exchanged the vocation of a canon for that of a Benedictine monk. All the time he maintained his relentless output of treatises. These treatises deserve to be examined with some care for three reasons. First of all, they bear the mark of Honorius's travels and immediate enthusiasms. The mark is unmistakable, and gives substances to the outlines we have of his career and the chronology of his writings. [4] Secondly, Honorius's works were as a whole extremely popular in the twelfth century. They must, therefore, contain precious information about the concerns, and perhaps the abilities, of many twelfth century readers. Finally, and most important, they stand at the beginning of that larger movement of men and ideas often described as the twelfth century renaissance. We know little about the beginnings of this movement : but we do know that they, like it, were complex. These works may, therefore, help to unravel some of the complexities.

I have chosen to begin the examination (which must, in the end, be a long one, for he wrote so much), with two of Honorius's treatises, the *Sigillum* and the *In Cantica Canticorum*. In the *Sigillum* Honorius commented for the first time upon the Song of Songs ; and in the *In Cantica Canticorum* for the second and the last. The *Sigillum* was, it seems, written in England, perhaps at Worcester, and the *In Cantica Canticorum* in Germany, perhaps at Regens-

---

4. See my articles : *The Career of Honorius Augustodunensis. Some fresh Evidence*, in *Rev. bénéd.* 82 (1972), p. 63-86 ; *The Chronology of the Works of Honorius Augustodunensis*, *ibid.*, p. 215-242.

XI

burg. The *Sigillum* was the second work Honorius acknowledged as his, and was written immediately after the *Elucidarius*, perhaps in the year 1100. The *In Cantica Canticorum* was written immediately after the *Expositio Psalterii* and perhaps just before the lost commentary on the Gospels. It was dedicated to the successor of Cuno, probably Cuno of Regensburg (d. 1132). Both these works were popular, and, of course, they stand at the beginning of the renaissance. All the general reasons, in short, for an examination of Honorius's works apply especially well to these. There is one last reason for choosing these particular ones. This is that their place in the history of commentaries upon the Song of Songs has been a little distorted and, as a result, Honorius's contribution to these commentaries somewhat misunderstood. [1] Commentaries on the Songs of Songs are a vital source for the understanding of twelfth century thought, and it is therefore important that Honorius's own efforts be placed in their proper perspective.

1. *The place of the* Sigillum

Sixteen twelfth-century manuscripts of the *Sigillum* survive. Five of these are English manuscripts, and four of them come from the diocese of Worcester. The rest are from South Germany or Austria. The *Sigillum* was written to explain the lessons for the Feast of the Assumption. It was able to be incorporated into the *Speculum Ecclesiae* as part of the sermon for that feast. It is made up of commentaries on the Gospel and Epistle for the Assumption (*Luke* 10,34ff ; *Ecclesiastes* 24,11ff), and a commentary on the Canticle. This last commentary is treated briefly, and strictly within its liturgical context. [2] Honorius places a special emphasis in it on the place of Mary in the Song of Songs. Mary is accordingly described as the mediator between God and the church, and anything written about the church, says Honorius, is written about her. [3]

In his discussion of medieval commentaries on the Song of Songs, Dr Ohly suggested that at the beginning of the twelfth century there came about a marked change of emphasis. Origen, he pointed out, saw the Song of Songs as the expression of, on the one hand, the marriage between Christ and the church, and on the other, that between the christian soul and the Word. St. Ambrose followed him in this, although the latter did introduce the notion that the Virgin Mary's marriage to the Holy Spirit may be its object too, and in so doing identified the spouse with all consecrated women. Gregory the Great paid lip service to both views ; Augustine shewed enthusiasm for neither, preferring to use the Canticle as an argument in favour of the unity of the church against the Donatists. Bede offered little that was original. The first person really to break with tradition was Rupert of Deutz. He insisted that the Song had as its object the Divine Love manifested in the person of the son of God made man. He is incarnate in the Virgin Mary who is bride

---

1. F. OHLY, *Hohelied-Studien. Grundzüge einer Geschichte der Hoheliedauslegung des Abendlandes bis um 1200*, Wiesbaden, 1958.
2. *Spec. Eccl.* ; PL 172, 99 ff.
3. The titles he uses, 'Oratio Virginis pro conversis' (2, 17), 'Corpus de Virgine ad doctores' (3, 5), 'Laus Filii de Matre' (4, 1), 'Sequitur laus Filii exhibita Matri ad domum Patris sui advenienti' (4, 10), are not unlike those Dom Frenaud noted in liturgical manuscripts which contained the Song of Songs. G. FRÉNAUD, *Marie et l'Église d'après les liturgies latines du VIIᵉ au XIᵉ siècle*, in *Études Mariales* 9 (1951), p. 54-55.

of the Father, temple of the Holy Spirit and bride of Christ, and in her body the marriage of the love of God for humanity is celebrated. Thus the Song as it stands is a dialogue between Christ and Mary. Honorius, says Ohly, in his *Sigillum* followed Rupert in this Marian emphasis. After Honorius come the Cistercian commentaries, with that of St. Bernard foremost among them. St. Bernard was familiar especially with the works of St. Ambrose and, through florilegia, the ideas of the Greek Fathers. For St. Bernard the spouse is the church and, above all, the Christian soul. It is not Mary. St. Bernard returns to Origen. The Marian interpretation is followed by the Premonstratensians and by the Augustinian Canons ; the Cistercians on this part company with them.

This argument is, of course, full of importance for the history of commentaries upon the Song of Songs, and for the *Sigillum* in particular. If the revolution in thought in the early twelfth century is really as radical as Ohly would have us believe, then in supporting it Honorius played a most important part. The accuracy of Dr. Ohly's analysis of the contents of the commentaries he has examined is masterly, and the results most helpful ; but unfortunately the historical perspective he has advanced cannot now be accepted without question.

The revised chronology put forward for Honorius's works shews that Honorius did not follow Rupert, and did not imitate him. The *Sigillum* was not Honorius's most important attempt at a commentary upon the Canticle and cannot be accepted as a sure indication of his attitude towards it. Far more important even than this, however, is the fact that the emphasis upon Mary he puts forward in it was not a revolutionary one within the context in which he wrote. It is true that there is, as far as we know, no earlier commentary in which the Canticle is applied consistently to Mary. It is not true, however, that there was no earlier thought about it and no recognised need for one. Augustine inhibited the application of the Canticle to Mary, [1] but Bede certainly put it forward. Of *Canticle* 3,11 [2] he offered this interpretation :

hoc est aperte dicere : Videte Dominum in humanitate quam de Virgine Matre susceptam in maiestatis paternae dextera collocavit, Mater quippe sua illum diademate coronavit, quando Beata et intemerata Virgo de Spiritu Sancto concipiens, materiam illam illi sacrosanctae carnis de sua carne praebuit. [3]

Paschasius too expressed in his letter *Cogitis me* his belief that the Song of Songs bears primarily upon Mary, and his letter was extremely popular. [4]

---

1. A.-M. LA BONNARDIÈRE, *Le Cantique des Cantiques dans l'œuvre de saint Augustin*, in *Rev. des Études Augustiniennes* 1 (1955), p. 225-237. The early Fathers, however, who after Origen had been familiar with the concept of the church as the bride of Christ, found for the most part the parallelism between Mary and the church a helpful one. A. MÜLLER, *L'unité de l'Église et de la Sainte Vierge chez les Pères des IVe et Ve siècles*, in *Études Mariales* 9 (1951), p. 27-38.
2. 'Egredimini et videte, filiae Sion, regem Salomonem in diademate quo coronavit illum mater sua in die desponsationis illius et in die laetitiae cordis eius'.
3. *PL* 91, 1127. Other passages in Bede are in *PL* 91, 1077, 1102.
4. In his *Expositio in Mattheum* (*PL* 120, 106), too, he expresses this belief: When speaking of a wrong interpretation of the 'antequam convenirent inventa est in utero habens de Spiritu Sancto' he says : 'Non intellexerat ... quod de hac (Virgine) specialiter dictum sit in Canticis, quamvis generaliter de Ecclesia significatum intelligamus. Nimirum quia, quidquid in ea speciale narratur

One factor which played a major part in bringing this change about was the liturgy. [1] Liturgical excitement combined with a dearth of higher theological criticism (especially of criticism, as yet, of the vital doctrine of the Trinity) to provide exactly the conditions which were needed. For Mary to be accepted as the type of the church her position in the plan of salvation had to be assured, and so had the essential oneness of the Father, Son and Holy Ghost. The liturgy played a vital part in the first, and perhaps in the second. Especially important in the part played by the liturgy were the feasts of the Assumption and of the Birth of the Blessed Virgin. The feast of the Assumption, held on the 15th of August, goes back at least to the pontificate of Sergius and perhaps to that of Theodore (642-649). [2] In the west, by the end of the seventh century the general feast of St. Mary celebrated on the 18 January had been displaced by that of the Assumption, and in 813 the Council of Mainz confirmed that it was observed. [3] The offices for the Assumption and the Nativity incorporated as lessons several sections of the Song of Songs, and by the end of the eleventh century these offices had found a set form. [4] Paschasius's *Cogitis me* was written specifically for the feast of the Assumption and was used for the antiphons, responsories and lessons for the feast as early as the ninth century. [5]

Another factor which encouraged a Marian interpretation of the Song of Songs was that of the increased popular devotion to Mary, perhaps arising from the demands of the liturgy, perhaps contributing to them. Spiritual and psychological questions of the greatest complexity are, of course, involved in a true understanding of the springs of such a devotion, but in historical terms it is, crudely, measurable. It seems, or it did seem in the eleventh and twelfth centuries, to find its finest support in monasticism, and Benedictine Monasticism entered in the eleventh century upon what was perhaps the greatest period in its history. [6] For a people whose sympathies were aroused so much more easily by that which they could see than by that which they could not, a deep interest in a mystery such as that of the Assumption of the

---

affamine totum expressius monstratrum signatur in genere'. The reference to this passage is given by J.C. GORMAN, *William of Newburgh's 'Explanatio Sacri Epithalamii in Matrem Sponsi'* (Spicilegium Friburgense, 6), Friburg, 1960, p. 38. Bede was not interested in the bodily assumption of Mary. Of the mystery of the disappearance of the Virgin's body he says: 'sed a quo vel quando sit ablata nescitur' (*De locis sanctis*, 5 ; PL 94, 1183). Paschasius, however, was a little less sceptical, and shews in the wording of the passage on this in the *Cogitis me* that he at least had the possibility in mind : 'Quomodo autem, vel quo tempore, aut a quibus personis sanctissimum corpus eius inde ablatum fuerit vel ubi transpositum, utrumne resurrexit, nescitur' (*PL* 30, 123). He goes on piously to point out that nothing is impossible with God.

1. Ohly certainly mentions the liturgy and its importance but does so as though Honorius were one of the first to feel it. *Op. cit.*, p. 252-253.

2. A. CHAVASSE, *Les plus anciens types du lectionnaire et de l'antiphonaire romains de la Messe*, in *Rev. bénéd.* 62 (1952), p. 52.

3. J. BEUMER, *Die Marianische Deutung des Hohenliedes in der Frühscholastik*, in *Zeitschrift für Katholische Theologie* 76 (1954), p. 416, n. 17.

4. G. FRÉNAUD, art. cit., p. 51, 54.

5. B. CAPELLE, *La fête de l'Assomption dans l'histoire liturgique*, in *Ephem. Theol. Lovan.* 3 (1926), p. 37.

6. In an interesting article, E. Sabbe describes the tenth century as the turning point in that 'recul marial' which he says took place in the Europe of the Carolingians. E. SABBE, *Le culte marial et la genèse de la sculpture médiévale*, in *Rev. Belge d'Archéol. et d'Hist. de l'Art* 20 (1951), p. 107-108.

Blessed Virgin, the evidence for which had so uncompromisingly vanished, perhaps needed the additional strength of monastic example. ¹ In the eleventh century revived Benedictine Monasticism lent this strength, and devotion to Mary increased. In this century, English Benedictine abbeys began to celebrate, as well as the Assumption, the feast of the Conception of the Virgin, and from England the feast was taken back to Normandy. ² Dom Wilmart points to the collections made of homilies *De beata* to serve those parts of the Office given to these occasions. ³ Peter Damian and, above all, St. Anselm encouraged this Marian devotion and developed it. St. Anselm saw Mary as 'Mater restitutionis omnium' and pronounced of her 'Nihil aequale Mariae. Nihil, nisi Deus, maius Maria'. ⁴ Eadmer, perhaps inspired by his master, later wrote his *De Conceptione Sanctae Mariae.* ⁵ Stories of the miracles performed by the Virgin were especially popular in England, where the effects of the tenth-century monastic revival were still strongly felt, and where the emotional energies which revolted against the conquerors found an outlet in the fervent appreciation of all that was Anglo-Saxon. Collections of these miracle stories were made between about 1100 and 1140 by Anselm, nephew of St. Anselm, by Dominic of Evesham, by William of Malmesbury. ⁶

Honorius's *Sigillum*, far from being a revolutionary document, takes its place with ease in this development. It was a contribution made by him at an early and at, perhaps, a particularly sensitive point in his career, to an established liturgy. It was built upon orthodox sources. He uses Paschasius, Paul the Deacon, Bede, Haimo. ⁷ He also uses sources, and this fact is especially interesting, which were associated particularly with England. The section in the *Sigillum* which treats of the gospel for the assumption was taken largely from the sermon of Ralph of Escures on the same subject. ⁸ The next section, that on the Epistle (*Ecclesiastes* 24,11), was taken from the first of the homilies falsely attributed to St. Anselm. ⁹ This borrowing involved slightly more ingenuity than the first, for this homily was not written with

1. « La carence des reliques corporelles et la rareté des reliques vestimentaires rendaient l'initiation mariale par trop abstraite pour les moyenâgeux primitifs » (*Ibid.*, p. 109).

2. A.W. BURRIDGE, *L'Immaculée Conception dans la théologie de l'Angleterre médiévale*, in *Rev. d'Hist. Ecclés.* 32 (1936), p. 570-571.

3. A. WILMART, *Les homélies attribuées à S. Anselme*, in *Archives d'hist. doctr. et litt. du Moyen Age* 2 (1927), p. 14.

4. *Oratio VII* ; ed. F.S. SCHMITT, *Sancti Anselmi Opera Omnia* (Edinburgh, 1946-1961), III, 21. This is Anselm's great prayer to Mary, possibly written before 1077, and was one with which he took great pains. Cfr A.WILMART, *Les propres corrections de S. Anselme dans sa grande prière à la Vierge Marie*, in *Rech. de Théol. anc. et médiév.* 2 (1930), p. 189-204.

5. A. WILMART, *Les homélies...*, *art. cit.*, p. 9.

6. R.W. SOUTHERN, *The English Origins of the 'Miracles of the Virgin'*, in *Medieval and Renaissance Studies* 4 (1958), p. 176-216.

7. Paschasius (*PL* 30, 137-138, 140, 131-132) ; Honorius (*PL* 172, 517, 500, 506-507) ; Bede (*PL* 91, 1098-1099, 1102 ; *PL* 172, 501-502, 502) ; Paul (*PL* 95, 1567-1568 ; *PL* 172, 502, 511) ; Haimo (*PL* 117, 299-300 ; *PL* 172, 501 [Cant. 1, 11]).

8. See my article *The Chronology...*, *art. cit.*, p. 220.

9. *PL* 158, 585 (to 'Quasi myrrha electa'), 592. A. WILMART, *Les homélies...*, *art. cit.*, p. 6-7. The problem of the true author of this sermon is unsolved. The style is not unlike that of Ralph and it appears with his sermon in MS. Vallicelliana E.6.

XI

201

Mary in mind, but is about the relationship between Christ and the church. Honorius therefore substitutes Mary. The homily for instance explains that the 'tabernaculum' of Ecclesiastes is Christ's assumed body ; Honorius declares that it is the Blessed Virgin. [1] Both use, however, the same quotation from Psalms to give substance to the conclusion, and the plan of the homily can be followed very clearly throughout Honorius's exposition, although Honorius shortens it as ruthlessly as he did that of Ralph. The substitutions and also the borrowing of small pieces of information are quite blatant. [2] Honorius is here at his least attractive. In the section of the *Sigillum* in which Honorius explains the verse 'Oleum effusum nomen tuum' he uses, furthermore, four miracles of the Virgin. Mary overcomes all adversity as oil calms troubled waters, as she did in the case of the Jewish Boy whom she rescued from the fire into which his father had thrown him as a punishment for taking Christian Communion. She receives anyone who confides in her, although he is burdened with sin, and salves his weakness with the oil of Christ, as she did for Theophilus. A certain Mary obtained from the Virgin pardon for her misdeeds and the capacity to perform miracles. A man 'in extremis' was rescued from the devils who were coming to carry him off to hell, by the Virgin's cloak, and in return for his devotion to her. Theophilus and the Jewish Boy are old miracle stories and Honorius obviously knew that they would be familiar to his audience. The Jewish Boy appears in Gregory of Tours, [3] and again in Paschasius Radbert's *Liber de Corpore et Sanguine Domini*. [4] Honorius's report does not say that the miracle of the Jewish Boy was performed at Bourges, and so it is difficult to associate it on internal evidence alone with the early English collections of stories, [5] but Dominic of Evesham begins his account of the Miracles of the Virgin with the Jewish Boy, and goes on to the story of Theophilus, [6] and William of Malmesbury recounts both as well. [7] Two of Honorius's miracles, then, became an important part of a specifically English tradition. The third miracle is that of Mary of Egypt. This story was translated from the Greek by Paul the Deacon and is also used by Dominic and by William of Malmesbury. [8] This was known early in England. [9] I have not been able to find a clear source for the fourth miracle. It could be the 'drunken sacristan'. In William of Malmsbury's account of this, the Virgin

1. Homily ; *PL* 158, 586. Honorius ; *PL* 172, 498.
2. 'Jacob qui supplantator interpretatur'. *PL* 158, 587 ; *PL* 172, 498.
3. *Liber in Gloria Martyrum*, X ; *PL* 71, 714. The story is from a translation of Evagrius Scholasticus ; *PG* 86, 2nd part, 2769.
4. Chapter IX ; *PL* 120, 1298-1299.
5. The importance of the mention of Bourges in the early English collections is noted by RW. SOUTHERN, *art. cit.*, p. 192.
6. He probably compiled his collection after 1121, although he may have been collecting the material for it for many years. J.C. JENNINGS, *Prior Dominic of Evesham and the Survival of the English Tradition after the Norman Conquest* (Oxford B. Litt. thesis), 1958, p. 77.
7. His treatise was written after 1135, possibly even after 1138. I am greatly indebted to the kindness of Mr P.N. Carter who allowed me to read his unpublished thesis, *An Edition of William of Malmesbury's Treatise on the Miracles of the Virgin* (Oxford D. Phil. thesis), 1959.
8. CARTER, *op. cit.*, II, p. 551-558.
9. Anglo-Saxon references to it are reported, as Mr Carter points out, by W.W. SKEAT, *Aelfric's Lives of Saints* (Early English Text Society, 94), II, 1890, p. 447.

holds a 'manipula' not a 'capellana' to drive off the devil. [1] A little later in the *Sigillum*, Honorius tells of a fifth miracle, the miracle of the celestial music heard by a hermit on a certain night each year, which told him the date upon which the Nativity of the Virgin should be celebrated. [2] A source for this last miracle has not so far been found, but Honorius uses it again in his *Speculum Ecclesiae* and *Gemma Animae*, and St. Anselm uses it too. [3]

The attention Honorius paid in the *Sigillum* to evidence of the power of the Virgin which was popular in England is exciting. It is exciting not only because it fits into the general pattern of monastic interest in Mary, but also because it fits into the specific pattern proposed for Honorius's career. It brings him, in fact, back to the west of England. The miracles were not, of course, the exclusive property of England, but it is highly likely that Honorius found them there. I have already suggested that Honorius used the *Worcester Passionale* for his *Speculum Ecclesiae*. This seems to have been the source used by Dominic of Evesham for the stories of Theophilus and of Mary of Egypt. [4] It could also have been one of the sources used by Honorius for his *Sigillum*. [5] The *Worcester Passionale* contains, moreover, Paschasius's *Cogitis me*. [6] There are now, as I have mentioned, three twelfth-century Worcester manuscripts of the *Sigillum*, and one thirteenth-century one. [7] The two other English ones come from Malmesbury and from Evesham. Worcester was, of course, one of the oldest and proudest of the old English

---

1. CARTER, *op. cit.*, II, p. 413.
2. *PL* 172, 517.
3. Anselm used it in his long prayer to Mary (*Oratio* VII in Schmitt's edition). H.D.L. WARD, *Catalogue of Romances in the Department of Manuscripts in the British Museum*, II (London, 1893), p. 587-588. Ward did not mention the stories in the *Sigillum*.
4. JENNINGS, *op. cit.*, p. 80-81, 89.
5. One passage in the *Passionale* looks very much as though it provides the inspiration for a passage in the *Sigillum*. It is in the third sermon on the Purification :

Sermon (f. 141)	Sigillum (PL 172, 501).
Pulchra ut luna, electa ut sol, reparatio vitae, ianua celi, decus mulierum, caput virginum, fructifera sicut oliva in domo dei, virgo sancta, virgo prudens, virgo pulcherrima, virgo pudica, corpore decora, fide perspicua, mente praeclara, amore virginitatis devota, prophetis dei praedicta, a philosophis sanctis prenuntiata, ab archangelo salutata, ab spiritu sancto fecundata atque ab eodem obumbrata, cogitus virilis ignara, prole tamen fecunda, virgo innupta et tamen filio leta, fide concipiens et mundi gaudium pariens.	*Ecce tu pulchra es, amica mea ... ecce tu pulchra coram Deo in humilitate, ecce tu pulchra coram hominibus in castitate. Pulchra virginitate, pulchra fecunditate, pulchra in virtutibus, pulchra in operibus. Pulchra hic laude hominum, pulchra in coelis laude angelorum. Pulchra bis praedicatur, quia sine interiori et exteriori macula declaratur.*

Also another short one in the same sermon :

... nobis et hominem genuisti, et post partum virgo inviolata permansisti (f. 141v).	Ita Maria mater fuit Christum gignendo, virgo post partum clausa permanendo (499).

6. F. 285. This is concealed as the letter from Jerome In Eustochium.
7. The thirteenth century one is WORCESTER *Cathedral Library* F. 71.

monastic cathedrals, and was one of those most concerned for the preservation of the Anglo-Saxon devotion to Mary. Evesham was, according to report, founded as a result of a vision of the Blessed Virgin. At the end of the eleventh century this devotion was demonstrated by a singular revival in devotion to the feast of the Conception of the Blessed Virgin, and by the establishment of the cult of St. Anne.[1] The emphasis Honorius laid upon Mary in his first commentary on the Song of Songs was one which his English friends would have found welcome. We are not, then, called upon to witness any unusual spectacle through it ; only the rather familiar one wherein Honorius gauges with accuracy the interests of his public, and perhaps of himself. The *Sigillum* must be seen not as a fresh departure, but as part of a tradition already strong in the Benedictine Order, and in the West of England.

It is interesting that Honorius should become concerned with the place of the Blessed Virgin in the liturgy and in the church at this point in his life. There is a fresh departure, perhaps, of a kind here, but it affects not the history of literature upon the Song of Songs, but the history of Honorius's own development. The gospel for the Assumption, about which Honorius writes, is the section telling the story of Martha and Mary (*Luke* 10,38-42). Exactly why this text was originally chosen for this feast is not immediately easy to see, but it may be that the virgins Martha and Mary were seen to represent the two sides of life which the Blessed Virgin combined in one life to perfection, the active and the contemplative both at once.[2] This was, in any case, the reason given by Honorius.[3] It may be that Honorius had a particular reason for writing about this matter at this time. I have tried to suggest that Honorius became a Benedictine monk quite early in his life. The *Sigillum* perhaps bears the mark of this crisis and is additional evidence for it. The feast of the Assumption, further, was designed to strengthen belief in the connection between the incorruptibility of the physical body and that moral incorruptibility of which virginity is the sign,[4] and therefore in virginity itself. In his early works, works written just before and just after the *Sigillum*, Honorius was especially vehement in his opposition to priests of unchaste lives, and was particularly insistent upon the vocation to celibacy. It is hardly necessary to say how important a belief in the virginity of the Mother of God, and in her supreme position in the heavenly kingdom, is, not only if the monastic vocation is to be sustained but if it is to be thought about seriously at all. An emphasis upon Mary as the Bride of Christ leads too to reflections upon the nature of Christian marriage and the place of celibacy. Honorius may have been moved to write his *Sigillum* and to his declarations about the priesthood by these reflections.

The place of the *Sigillum* in the history of medieval commentaries upon the Song of Songs is not, then, quite the one Dr. Ohly gives to it. The *Sigillum*

---

1. A. WILMART, *Auteurs spirituels et textes dévôts du Moyen Age latin*, Paris, 1932, p. 264.
2. B. CAPELLE, *art. cit.*, p. 38-39.
3. 'Per Martham activa vita, per Mariam contemplativa designatur, quam utramque perpetua Virgo Maria in Christo excellentius excoluisse praedicatur' (*Sigillum* ; *PL* 172, 497).
4. This reason was advanced as early as the second century to explain the assumption of St. John. CAPELLE, *art. cit.*, p. 41-45. Paschasius Radbert in his *Cogitis me* speaks of the empty tomb of John in company with that of Mary.

was rooted in thought that was old, certainly to the Benedictine Order and to England. It should be seen first of all as further possible proof of Honorius's associations with this Order and with the West of England. It should be seen secondly as an effort to fulfil a need for a commentary on the Canticle in which the association between the church and Mary played a prominent part ; a need which was strongly and widely felt in the early years of the twelfth century.

2. *The place of the* In Cantica Canticorum

The long commentary was devised as a work of large scale biblical exegesis. This was not, however, specially adapted to explain the place of the Virgin Mary in the Canticle and the church. Indeed, she hardly appears at all. Instead, Honorius declares that the Canticle is throughout concerned with the marriage of Christ and his church :

materia libri est sponsus et sponsa, id est Christus et Ecclesia.

In format it follows the text of the Canticle strictly from beginning to end. Honorius applies with equal strictness the four methods of biblical exegesis to each section of the text. Suitable examples of weddings are set against each of these methods. Against the historical are set the marriage of Mary and Joseph and that of Solomon and the daughter of Pharaoh ; against the allegorical, the word of God made flesh and the binding of Christ to the church ; against the tropological, the union of the individual soul with Christ and the binding of the animal part of man to his spirit ; and against the anagogical, the association of the resurrected Christ with the angels and the union of the church with him in glory. The whole process of redemption, Honorius insists, is a fourfold one. There are four ages through which the marriage of Christ and his church must pass, 'ante legem', 'sub lege', 'sub gratia', 'sub Antichristo', and these ages correspond ingeniously both with the four parts of the world and with the four ages of man. [1] There are four biblical manifestations of the bride of Christ, with each of whom the Song is concerned. The manifestations are, the daughter of Pharaoh (*I Kings* 31 ; *Cant.* 1,8), the daughter of the king of Babylon (*I Kings* 10,2), the Sunamite (*Cant.* 6,12 ; *I Kings* 1,3), the Mandragora (*Cant.* 7,13). Honorius divides his work into four tractates to deal with each of the brides, and divides the text of the Canticle equally into four to fit the tractates. [2] Honorius shews in this work how skilful he had become in forcing well known frameworks to bear the burden of transmitting ill-known and difficult pieces of learning.

When one turns from the *Sigillum* to the longer commentary, one is confronted by an apparent difference and a real similarity between the two works. At a superficial level, it appears that the new departure comes about with this commentary. If one takes the framework prepared by Ohly, and sets this commentary against it, it seems that Honorius begins with it to move against the growing tide, for one of the most striking features of the longer commentary is the almost complete omission of the Virgin Mary. Nor does it describe with any enthusiasm the pilgrimage of the individual soul. These omissions appear to set Honorius's longer commentary apart. In fact, however, this commentary was not a new departure at all, but was as rooted as was the

---

1. *PL* 172, 351.
2. The divisions are at 2. 12, 6.9, 7.10.

Sigillum in an established approach to the Canticle : different, it is true, from those described by Ohly, but still strong in the twelfth century.

Honorius uses, in this longer commentary, accepted scholarly sources. Some of these cannot now be traced, for five at least of the commentaries known to have come from Germany are lost, and it is very likely that Honorius used some at least of these. [1] It is, however, possible, although painful, to discover some of the others. [2] One of the most striking things to emerge from the attempt to do this is the fact that Honorius certainly used work usually associated with the *Glossa Ordinaria*. The accessus in the first prologue to the longer commentary is very like that of Ralph of Laon to his commentary on St. Matthew. The divisions 'auctor', 'materia', 'intentio', 'finis' appear also in the commentary ascribed by Migne to Anselm, but probably in fact by Ralph too, on the Song of Songs. [3] This commentary is used by Honorius here, not exclusively but consistently. Honorius also used a series of passages of uncertain authorship which appear in the *Glossa Ordinaria*. [4] It is clear from the prologue that the longer commentary was written in close connection with the one Honorius wrote on the Psalter. This is an interesting juxtaposition. The little we know of the exegetical preoccupations of the late eleventh and early twelfth centuries, of those of Anselm and Ralph of Laon and of the early history of the *Glossa Ordinaria*, suggests that Honorius's biblical interests here coincided with those of his immediate predecessors and contemporaries. In the long commentary, quotations from the gospels of St. Matthew and St. John predominate in number over all other biblical references. [5] We know that the Gloss on these gospels was among the earliest parts of the *Glossa Ordinaria* to be compiled, [6] and that Anselm and Ralph were interested in them. It seems that in his choice of the Song of Songs as a text to expound, and in part of his exposition, Honorius was acting within a framework already built. The longer commentary seems to have been drawn from the work of glossing the Sacred Page, and, with Honorius's usual perspicacity, from the most fashionable of that work. The difficulties which beset all attempts completely to reconstruct his sources leads one to suspect that the true source may have been a copy of the Canticle already carefully glossed.

Honorius should have known Origen's commentary for South Germany was

---

1. Lost are the commentaries by Rabanus, by Ludbert of Fulda, his pupil, by Reinhard of Wurzburg, by Ludger of Luneberg, by Meinhard of Bamberg. F. STEGMÜLLER, *Repertorium Biblicum Medii Aevi* (Madrid, 1950-1961), n⁰ˢ 7051, 5419, 7180, 5421, 5572.

2. See Appendix.

3. J. LECLERCQ, *Le Commentaire du Cantique des Cantiques attribué à Anselme de Laon*, in *Rech. de Théol. anc. et médiév.* 16 (1949), p. 37.

4. Sections of this evidence are set out in Appendix V. In the 1617 edition of the *Glossa Ordinaria* (*BS*) the authorship of these passages is not acknowledged. I have been unable to find a manuscript which does acknowledge them. It is unlikely that Honorius used this system of extracts directly from the Gloss because he does not use others. It is more likely that the Gloss and Honorius used a common system.

5. I have counted thirty-six references to St. Mathew and twenty-seven to St. John.

6. B. SMALLEY, *Les commentaires bibliques de l'époque romane : glose ordinaire et gloses périmées*, in *Cahiers de Civilisation Médiévale* 4 (1961), p. 16.

rich in manuscripts of him. [1] He seems, however, hardly to have used him. In the first chapter, Honorius may take from Origen his description of the Canticle as drama. [2] Otherwise I have found no evidence of a direct dependence on Origen. The distinction between the interior and exterior man, for instance, comes from Genesis. Origen speaks of it in his prologue. Honorius in his exegesis of 'Quia meliora sunt ubera tua vino', [3] but Honorius takes nothing directly from Origen for this part of his exposition. In Rufinus's translation the breasts of the bridegroom are 'sapientia et scientia'. The wine is the Old Testament. Honorius uses the words 'sapientia et scientia' but says they are the breasts of his 'interior homo'. [4] Origen's exegesis of this section is far longer than Honorius's and greatly fortified with references to the Old and New Testaments. Apart from these two words which were to become common usage in the twelfth century, it is unlikely that Honorius took anything from this section. Honorius borrows in fact none of Origen's poetry for these first five chapters, and certainly none of his optimism. Here, for example, is Origen's application of the first verse of the first chapter to the soul :

> Osculetur me ab osculo oris sui. Dum enim incapax (anima) fuit, ut ipsius Verbi Dei caperet meram solidamque doctrinam, necessaria suscepit oscula, id est sensus ab ore doctorum ; ubi vero sponte jam coeperit obscura cernere, enodare perplexa, involuta dissolvere, parabolas et aenigmata, dictaque sapientum competentibus intelligentiae lineis explicare, tunc jam oscula ipsius sponsi sui, id est Verbi Dei, suscepisse se credat.

And here is Honorius's :

> Fidelis anima sponsa Christi cogitans ubi fuerit, ubi erit, ubi sit, ubi non sit, scilicet quod in originali et actuali peccato fuerit, quod in tremendo judicio Dei erit, quod in vanitatibus saeculi sit, quod in aeterna beatitudine non sit gemens et tremens dicit : Osculetur me osculo oris sui. Ac si dicat ; Ille qui in mea carne in dextera Patris sedet, meus advocatus, justus Judex me de peccatis dolentem, de judicio suo trementem, visitando osculetur, et pace signo amicitiae quam proprio ore poenitentibus promisit, me osculetur. [5]

The contrast here is a sharp one but is does well to illustrate the style and the approach which separates Honorius's commentary from that of Origen and from those which took Origen as their inspiration. Thus whilst I have found no point at which Honorius and Origen disagree, Honorius at many points chooses simply to pass over Origen's interest in explanations of the ways of God with the individual soul. Perhaps this interest was thought to breed insubordination. Certainly Origen believed that the soul could be enlightened without the help of human teaching. This is the interpretation he gives of verse 1 :

> Quoties ergo in corde nostro aliquid quod de divinis dogmatibus sensibusque quaeritur, absque monitoribus invenimus, toties oscula nobis data esse a sponso Dei verbo credamus. [6]

---

1. W.A. Baehrens, Die Überlieferung des Kommentars zum Hohenlied in Rufins Übersetzung, in Texte und Untersuchungen zur Geschichte der altchristlichen Literatur 42 (1916), p. 135-137.
2. PL 172, 349 ; PG 13, 83.
3. Genesis I, 26 ; II, 7. PL 172, 362 ; PG 13, 65.
4. PL 172, 363 ; PG 13, 87.
5. PL 172, 360-361 ; PG 13, 85.
6. PG 13, 86.

Honorius seems to have been writing for a community which he perhaps expected either never to have discovered, or to have put away from them, this capacity for independent thought. They were to 'drink' only the correct teachings.

In so far, then, as it is possible to assign the long commentary to a distinct tradition, it falls firmly into the 'scholastic' one.[1] Honorius shews nothing of the mystical vision of Origen, nor does he shew any of the 'Christian Socratism' of St. Augustine or St. Bernard. A profound difference of emphasis separates him from the more famous of the Cistercian commentaries. [2] With the help of the distance between Honorius and Origen, one can measure that between Honorius and these.

> Felix osculum, ac stupenda dignatione mirabile, in quo non os ori imprimitur, sed Deus homini unitur. [3]

Honorius never permits himself such an exclamation. It is, of course, artificial and to a large extent unjust to compare Honorius with St. Bernard ; they were men of a different stature, temporal and spiritual. There is, however, a distinction between the type of writing a follower of St. Bernard might allow himself and the type produced in the traditional milieux ; a distinction which can be especially well expressed in commentaries on the Canticle. William of St. Thierry, for instance, for the most part far more given to sobriety of thought than St. Bernard, nonetheless gives way to similar outbursts given the opportunities the Canticle provides :

> Osculetur, inquit, me osculo oris sui. O Amor, a quo omnis amor cognominatur, etiam carnalis ac degener. Amor sancte et sanctificans, caste et castificans, et vita vivificans, aperi nobis sanctum canticum tuum, revela osculi tui mysterium, venasque susurri tui quibus virtutem tuam et suavitatis tue delicias incantas cordibus filiorum tuorum. [4]

---

1. I take this terminology from Dom Jean Leclercq. He expresses splendidly these differences between 'scholastic' and 'monastic' commentaries : « ...le premier, peut-on dire, est écrit d'un point de vue collectif : il concerne les rapports de Dieu avec toute l'Église, le second est personnel: il traite des relations de Dieu avec chaque âme ; le premier insiste beaucoup sur la Révélation dont l'homme prend possession par la connaissance, par la foi ; le second parle surtout de l'union que réalise la charité ; le premier met l'accent sur la présence de Dieu dans son Église par l'Incarnation du Verbe, le second sur la présence du Christ en l'âme par son union mystique avec le Verbe incarné ; le premier enseigne l'amour qu'on doit à Dieu à cause de ce qu'Il fait pour nous, de tout ce qu'Il nous donne ; le second chante l'amour pur et désintéressé de l'épouse à cause de ce qu'il est pour lui-même et non en raison de ses œuvres et de ses bienfaits. Aussi le ton du commentaire monastique est-il plus ardent que celui du commentaire scolaire : il traduit, en effet, une ferveur, un rythme intérieur qui saisissent tout l'être, et non seulement une doctrine qui s'adresse à l'intelligence ». J. LECLERCQ, Le Commentaire de Gilbert de Stanford sur le Cantique des Cantiques, in Studia Anselmiana 20 (1948), p. 208-209.

2. De Bruyne has an illuminating passage on Cistercian commentaries in general. He insists upon their emphasis on the personal and points to three features which he thinks characteristic of them: their 'humanist' definitions of beauty and grace, corporal and spiritual ; their emphasis on self knowledge ; their 'musical' interest in order and proportion. E. DE BRUYNE, Études d'esthétique médiévale, II (Bruges, 1946), p. 37.

3. St. Bernard, Sermon 2 ; S. Bernardi Opera, éd. LECLERCQ-TALBOT-ROCHAIS (Rome, 1957), p. 10.

4. Guillaume de Saint-Thierry. Commentaire sur le Cantique des Cantiques, éd. M.-M. DAVY (Paris, 1958), p. 50.

Honorius stays firmly at the level of simple statement and patient explanation and lets opportunities for a deeper exploration pass him by :

> Fidelis anima est lectulus, in qua Christus per dilectionem habitat. Qui lectulus floret, dum anima se orando et legendo exercet. Lectulus etiam animae est bona conscientia, in qua, ut in lecto, secura quiescit anima. Qui lectus floret, dum aliis bonae vitae exemplum praebet. Ipsa est etiam domus Dei, in qua Christus habitat ut sponsus in thalamo. Cujus tigna sunt principales virtutes, scilicet prudentia, fortitudo, justitia, temperantia. [1]

Instruction there is ; enthusiasm and inspiration there most emphatically is not. His exegesis of chapter ii, verse 9 : 'similis est dilectus meus capreae hinnuloque cervorum' shews how willing he is to kill opportunities for a hopeful and humane exegesis :

> ideo similis capreae dicitur, quia sicut caprea velociter currit, et bonas herbas a noxiis eligit, sic Christus velociter obedientiam Patris explevit, bonos a malis in judicio segregabit.

There is not the shadow of a suggestion that the Song could be about human love.

In his bracing and didactic approach to the Canticle in his long commentary, therefore, Honorius again stayed within a soundly established tradition and tried to meet its needs. He was a 'scholasticus' and he wrote appropriately. Again, too, those needs were widely and it seems deeply felt. Twenty twelfth century manuscripts of the *In Cantica Canticorum* survive, two French, the property originally of Cistercian houses, and the rest from South Germany and Austria. In striking contrast with the surviving manuscripts of, for example, the *Elucidarius*, these exemplars are almost without exception beautifully written : Honorius's own admiration for his work [2] clearly found echoes among his contemporaries and many of his successors.

Conclusion

The contents and manner of composition of Honorius's two commentaries on the Song of Songs fit well into the outlines already proposed for his career ; and they are first and best to be understood as reflections of it. When set, furthermore, within a history of commentaries on the Song of Songs in general their place is not that generally ascribed to them. The interest the *Sigillum* shews in the place of Mary in the Song was not a new interest, nor was the *Sigillum* a particularly important treatise. It has been, in fact, a little over-rated. The significance of the longer commentary has, on the other hand, been underestimated. It has been made to appear quite unimportant in the development of thought upon the Canticle in the twelfth century, and yet it seems to have been closely involved with that work of glossing the scriptures which resulted in the *Glossa Ordinaria*, and it was copied by, not least, the Clairvaux of St. Bernard himself. A commentary of this kind still had clearly a rôle. This fact is an important one, and it is worth looking at it a little more closely.

It is possible to see in the difference between the longer commentary of Honorius and that of Origen, on the one hand, and that of Honorius and

1. *PL* 172, 381.
2. *PL* 172, 234.

St. Bernard on the other, the gulf which separates a christian to whom the good news of the redemption had become a little stale, perhaps over-ridden by the bad news of so much that had happened in time, and one to whom it was still fresh and exciting and full of hope. The commentaries of Origen and St. Bernard are full precisely with this sense of renewal and the Canticle provides a magnificent means for its expression. We are here on the edge of large issues. It may be that we have in his long commentary simply an index to Honorius's own frame of mind. This was his last long work ; he may have been an old man when he wrote it. He therefore merely used again but at greater length his talents for accumulating material and teaching from it clearly. He had retired now from the centre of activity and so his commentary is backward looking and notable for the ease with which it can be copied, even into stone, rather than for the inspiration it gives. Perhaps for him personally the good news had become a little tarnished by adversity and the 'invidia' of which he so often speaks. It may equally be, however, that the difference goes deeper than this, and that Honorius is here a spokesman not merely for himself but for a whole attitude to the christian message which embraced the message of the Song of Songs. To such an attitude the institution, not the individual, is the important thing, and prose is a safer vehicle for its defence than poetry.

If this attitude existed, it must have had the most profound effect upon the intellectual achievements of the twelfth century. The composition and popularity of Honorius's longer commentary suggests that it did exist. Honorius's own pride seems to have been strengthened by the knowledge that he spoke for a large section of the ecclesiastical community. This is of great importance in the understanding of twelfth-century learning. The bending of fine literature to practical purposes is not always intellectually an agreeable sight, and the action becomes a positively disagreeable one if by it the truth of the original is lost. The treatment meted out by Honorius to the Canticle in his long commentary comes dangerously near to this. The Song of Songs held a firm place in the liturgy and so in preaching and in devotion. It was an almost perfect vehicle for communication in general but, because of its nature, especially for the communication of that love of literature and that sensitivity to human and divine emotion which was one of the finest contributions of the renaissance. Honorius, however, was encouraged to apply his gifts for muscular scholarship and deft organisation to it. He reduced it, thereby, to the proportions of a didactic tract for the exaltation of an institution ; and this reduction was popular.

The study of Honorius's commentaries on the Song of Songs tells us a lot about what a not inconsiderable section of the articulate community of the first half of the twelfth century expected of their literature ; and, in good measure, received. The strength and effect of popularisers of Honorius's vigour, and of the institutions they served, has not yet been given its due weight in investigations of the twelfth century renaissance. A search for the origins of creative energy should not overlook the fact that it is often released by a reaction against cramping conditions. It is, ironically, possible that Honorius and some of his treatises helped to serve this purpose.

*
* *

This appendix sets out some suggested sources for the commentary *In Cantica Canticorum*. A section of the first book (verses 1-5) has been chosen for the reconstruction. The complexity of the reconstruction makes it appear likely that Honorius built his commentary upon a gloss or glosses upon the text ; one thinks immediately of the *Cantica Canticorum cum glosis* of the gift of Frater Heinricus.

Honorius, PL 172   *Source*

350 A-B   Glossa Ordinaria, *BS* III, 1817.
                Sicut enim in lege ... sacratiora.

359 B   Alcuin, *PL* 100, 642 B.
                Osculetur me ... non spernat.

360 B   Justin of Urgel, *PL* 67, 963 A.
                Tunc enim ... bonae voluntatis.

360 D   Glossa Ordinaria, *BS* III, 1821.
                Meliora sunt ... enecat parvulos.
                Alcuin, *PL* 100, 642 B.
                Osculetur me ... non spernat.
                ? Ralph of Laon, *PL* 162, 1189-90 D-A.
                Quia ubera tua ... tandem ad interitum.

361 A   Bede, *PL* 91, 1085 A.
                Aperuit ... adventum.

361 C   Robert of St. Vigor, *PL* 150, 1364-65 D-A.
                ... gustu suae ... osculum accendit.

361 D   Haimo, *PL* 117, 295 B.
                Per ubera ... peccatoris.

361-62, D-A   ? Ralph of Laon, *PL* 162, 1189-90 D-A.
                Quia ubera tua ... tandem ad interitum.

363 B   Robert of St. Vigor, *PL* 150, 1365 A.
                Ubera sponsi, dilectio Dei et proximi.

363 C   Haimo, *PL* 117, 295 B.
                Per ubera ... peccatoris.

363 D   ? Ralph of Laon, *PL* 162, 1190 B.
                Oleum quidem, dum in vase ... exposuit.

363-64 D-A   Haimo, *PL* 117, 295 C.
                Chrisma graece ... vocatum est.

364 B   Glossa Ordinaria, *BS* III, 1821.
                Nomen Jesu ... claudebatur angustiis.

365 B   Bede, *PL* 91, 1087 B.
                Trahe me ... adjuves.

365 C   Justin of Urgel, *PL* 67, 964 A-B.
                Trahe me post te ... sequendo proficiunt.

365 D   Haimo *PL* 117, 295 C.
                Adolescentulae dicuntur ... in Christo.
                Glossa Ordinaria, *BS* III, 1822.
                Universae ecclesiae ... per gratiam.

365-66 D-A	Gregory, *CCL* 144, 25 (460-471). Omnis qui trahitur ... unguentorum tuorum.
366 B	? Ralph of Laon, *PL* 162, 1190 C. Curremus in odorem ... coeleste bravium.
366 C	Glossa Ordinaria, *BS* III, 1823. Introduxit me ... nuntiat illis.
366 D	Robert of St. Vigor, *PL* 150, 1366 B-D. Introduxit me ... mox convalescimus. Recti diligunt te ...
367 B	Haimo, *PL* 117, 296 B. Memores uberum ... qui te diligit.
367 C	Robert of St. Vigor, *PL* 150, 1365 A. Quid autem per vinum ... temporalis exprimitur.
367 D	Bede, *PL* 91, 1087-88. Cellaria regis ... dignatus est.
368 B	Haimo, *PL* 117, 296 C. Nigra sum ... decora virtutum. Gregory, *CCL* 144, 35 (677-679). Ecclesia ex gentibus ... pacis dicitur.
368 D	? Ralph of Laon, *PL* 162, 1191 D. Exterius ... videtis.
368-69 D-A	Haimo, *PL* 117, 296-97 C-A. Formosam vero ... Christi inter angustias.
369 A	? Ralph of Laon, *PL* 162, 1192 B. Nolite considerare ... in carnalitate.
369 B	Justin of Urgel, *PL* 67, 965 C. Filii matris ... decrevit.
369 B	Haimo, *PL* 117, 297 C. Vox est primitivae ... regiones Samariae.
369 C-370 A	Gregory, *CCL* 144, 38-40 (735-771). Dicat ergo ... sollicitudinem amisi.
369 D	? Ralph of Laon, *PL* 162, 1192 A. Pelles quidem ... verus pacificus.
369 D	Glossa Ordinaria, *BS* III, 1824. Sicut pelles ... sit habitaculum.
370 B	Bede, *PL* 91, 1088 C, 1089 C. Nigra sum ... refulgeo. Nigra sum ... Salomonis.

*The University of Auckland
(New Zealand).*

XII

THE PLACE AND PURPOSE
OF THE WORKS
OF HONORIUS AUGUSTODUNENSIS

The aim of this paper is, despite its pretentious title, to introduce a provisional handlist of surviving twelfth century Honorius manuscripts. No firm analysis of Honorius's works can be made until they are edited afresh, and so no statement about their place and purpose can be definitive. The handlist is meant to serve as a beginning to this Herculean task. The search for the manuscripts, and the re-reading of the treatises they contain have, however, given rise to a suggestion which I have been encouraged to a limited extent to explore. The suggestion is an expansion of one already made. I have tried recently to argue that the *Elucidarius*, Honorius's first acknowledged treatise, was written as an answer to the special needs of the Benedictines in England in their support of the movement for ecclesiastical reform. [1] I now suspect that the serving of the Benedictine Order, in its pursuit of influence in the reformed church, formed the focus of Honorius's whole productive life. The bewildering scale and variety of his output, and even his changes of habitation from England to Bavaria, [2] were brought about, I would suggest, by the force and constancy of this single aim. The exploration of this suggestion has followed three separate routes : through the monastic background against which Honorius wrote, through the evidence of his writings, and through the evidence of the surviving twelfth century manuscripts of them. It seems sensible, therefore, to re-enact it under these three headings.

---

1. V.I.J. FLINT, *The 'Elucidarius' of Honorius Augustodunensis and Reform in late eleventh Century England*, in *Rev. bénéd.* 85 (1975), p. 178-198. On the deep concern shewn by Honorius for the monastic life see M.-O. GARRIGUES, *Bref témoignage sur la vie monastique du XIIᵉ siècle*, in *Studia monastica* 16 (1974), p. 45-53.

2. I have suggested that this change was made in about 1103 : V.I.J. FLINT, *The Chronology of the Works of Honorius Augustodunensis*, in *Rev. bénéd.* 82 (1972), p. 241. Splendid short accounts of the nature and contents of his works may be found in E.M. SANDFORD, *Honorius, Presbyter and Scholasticus*, in *Speculum* 23 (1948), p. 397-425, and, of course, in J.-A. ENDRES, *Honorius Augustodunensis*, Kempten-Munich 1906.

98

I. THE MONASTIC BACKGROUND

It is now a commonplace to observe that the last years of the eleventh century and the first decades of the twelfth saw a crisis in the history of Benedictine Monasticism in the West ; and that this crisis was intimately related to the reform. The monks most deeply affected by it were those who, without undergoing any radical reform themselves, were anxious to play a continuing rôle in the general movement. The crisis, although it took, of course, different forms at different times, [1] was compounded of certain basic ingredients. One of these was a developing inclination to pass public honours in the reformed church, appointments, that is, for the mediation of its newly fortified sacramental life, to men educated outside the old Benedictine tradition. Another was the drawing away of recruits by the reformed monastic orders ; another the urge towards the solitary devotional life. Yet one further ingredient was the denial of the rights of monks to tithes. Urban II went some way towards realising their worst fears on this score. [2] And if they were to have no tithes, it followed, for many, that they should have no 'cura animarum' and no public priesthood. [3] The two were necessarily very closely related. Such a denial was deeply damaging to those monks who found themselves in the situation I have described. It could serve such a variety of interests, from the most rabidly secular to the most radically monastic. [4] It was undoubtedly an attack

---

1. See N. CANTOR, The Crisis of Western Monasticism, in American Historical Review 66 (1960), p. 47-67, criticised by D. BETHELL, English black Monks and episcopal Elections in the 1120s', in English Historical Review, no. 333 (1969), p. 673-698.

2. Urban II ruled that monks may in future acquire tithes only with the consent of the bishop : G. CONSTABLE, Monastic Tithes from their Origins to the twelfth Century, Cambridge 1964, p. 92-93.

3. Cfr the ruling of the Lateran Council of 1123 : "Interdicimus abbatibus et monachis publicas poenitentias dare, et infirmos visitare, et unctiones facere, et missas publicas cantare. Chrisma et oleum, consecrationes altarium, ordinationes clericorum ab episcopis accipiunt in quorum parochiis manent" (J.D. MANSI, Sacrorum conciliorum nova et amplissima collectio 21, col. 285).

4. The severity of this challenge at precisely this time may be gauged by the fact that the problem of the monastic priesthood first finds a place, in the late eleventh and early twelfth centuries, in the theoretical literature of monastic spirituality. Cfr J. LECLERCQ, On monastic Priesthood according to the ancient medieval Tradition, in Studia monastica 3 (1961), p. 138. The literature on the rights of monks to pastoral care is immense, but for this period : R. FOREVILLE and J. LECLERCQ, Un débat sur le sacerdoce des moines au XIIe siècle, in Studia anselmiana 14 (1957), p. 8-118 ; U. BERLIÈRE, L'exercice du ministère paroissial par les moines dans le haut Moyen Age, in Rev. bénéd. 39 (1927), p. 227-250 ; Ph. HOFMEISTER, Mönchtum und Seelsorge bis zum 13. Jahrhundert, in Studien und Mitteilungen zur Geschichte des Benediktiner-Ordens 65 (1953-1954), p. 209-273, are helpful.

on the rights and economies of the unreformed Benedictines as they stood ; but it could very easily be disguised as a means to the true monastic vocation. Tithes could be seen as a reward for respectable spiritual services to the laity : but they could also be taken as a symptom of a type of secular involvement inimical to true monasticism. Persecutors of the old Benedictines and supporters of the new could, on this point, join forces, producing an almost intolerable situation ; for it was doubly hard for the Benedictines themselves to defy, in the name of the reform, men who denied them these rights for the highest of principles and in the same name. Finally, and perhaps worst of all, there appeared 'regular' competitors for the 'cura animarum' and its accompaniments. These were the Augustinian Canons. [1] They too appeared as a force in different places at different times, [2] but their rights were unassailable. [3]

The old Benedictines had their defenders, but there is a sense, even in the most generous of these, that time is running out. They have an air rather of comforting the victim than of vanquishing the foe. They adopt negative expedients. They vilify enemies, soften criticism, laud tradition for tradition's sake. [4] It

---

1. The position in which the canons found themselves at this time is beautifully set out by B. METZ. It is worth quoting in full here because it is so close to that which I have ascribed, at the beginning of this section, to the Benedictines and may serve more fully to illustrate their shared yet dangerously distinct vulnerabilities : « Ainsi l'ordo antiquus... se trouve finalement pris entre deux feux. Au même titre que le monachisme traditionnel, il est menacé dans son prestige, dans son statut d'arctior religio, par les réformateurs de tendance érémitique ... Inversement, face aux moines aussi bien qu'aux chanoines séculiers, l'ordo antiquus souffre, malgré sa prétention à remonter à S. Augustin et même aux apôtres, de sa position de nouveau venu dans l'Église, dépourvu de l'autorité et de la sécurité que confère une longue tradition. L'auteur du Libellus appartient donc à un groupe menacé — ce qui a pu l'inciter à prêcher la tolérance — et mal intégré à une Église qui vit encore sur l'opposition de l'ordo clericorum et de l'ordo monachorum — ce qui l'amène à se distancer de l'ecclésiologie traditionnelle » : A propos du 'Libellus de diversis ordinibus', in Revue d'histoire ecclésiastique 68 (1973), p. 820.

2. The literature on canons, too, is enormous, but an excellent bibliography may be found in M. PEUCHMAURD, Le prêtre ministre de la parole dans la théologie du XIIe siècle, in Recherches de théologie ancienne et médiévale 29 (1962), p. 52-53.

3. Ch. DEREINE, Vie commune, règle de Saint Augustin et chanoines réguliers au XIe siècle, in Revue d'histoire ecclésiastique 41 (1946), p. 403. Cfr the authorization granted to St. Botolph's Colchester by Pascal II (W. DUGDALE, Monasticon Anglicanum, ed. J. Caley, H. Ellis and B. Bandinel, VI, p. 106-107) and also HOFMEISTER, art. cit., p. 210.

4. Thus letter 192 of Ivo of Chartres for the consolation of the Benedictine community of Coulombs (PL 162, col. 196-202). Ivo encourages the Benedictines to object primarily to that arrogance and hypocrisy which will allow the attempted imposition of one man's view of spiritual poverty upon another.

is difficult to find any sober, coherent, positive advocacy of the part the Benedictines still have in the post-Gregorian church. [1] The reform, in short, had set afoot schemes of action and modes of contemplation which left the Benedictines with little ground on which to fight and, apparently, few means with which to join.

Honorius spent the greater part of his productive life in Germany, most probably in Regensburg. That part occupied the years approximately 1103-1140. I have said that it is difficult to find any positive advocacy on behalf of the Benedictines; but, interestingly, the most positive there is comes from Germany. Three major spokesmen undertook this advocacy before the middle of the century : Rupert of Deutz, Idung of St. Emmeram—and Honorius himself. Rupert, a monk of St. Laurence of Liège and of Siegburg, then as abbot of Deutz, was far removed from Honorius in space. He was in time, however, very near to him, and the gap in space was narrowed by the appointment of Cuno, Rupert's abbot at Siegburg, to the bishopric of Regensburg in 1126. [2] We have long been aware of certain striking similarities between the works of Rupert and Honorius. [3] Idung seems to have begun to write just after Honorius's active life had ended ; but he was directly associated with Regensburg, first as 'magister scolae' there, then as monk at Prüfening. [4] Rupert defended with ferocity the rights of monks to the priesthood, to preach, [5] and to

See also the defence of Orderic Vitalis : M. CHIBNALL, *The Ecclesiastical History of Orderic Vitalis* IV, Oxford 1972, p. 314-320.

1. Ivo was himself, of course, most inclined to support the canons regular ; cfr Ch. DEREINE, *Les coutumiers de Saint-Quentin de Beauvais et de Springiersbach*, in *Revue d'histoire ecclésiastique* 43 (1948), p. 418-419.

2. For Cuno, cfr R. BAUERREISS, *Honorius von Canterbury (Augustodunensis) und Kuno I, der Raitenbucher, Bischof von Regensburg 1126-1132*, in *Studien und Mitteilungen zur Geschichte des Benediktiner-Ordens* 67 (1956), p. 306-313, and below. For Rupert and Cuno, cfr R. BAUERREISS, *Regensburg als religiös-theologischer Mittelpunkt Süddeutschlands im XII. Jahrhundert*, in *Wahrheit und Verkündigung* (ed. L. Scheffczyk, W. Dettloff, R. Heinzmann) II, p. 1143.

3. M. MAGRASSI, *Teologia e storia nel pensiero di Ruperto di Deutz*, Rome 1959, p. 248 and 272-276.

4. Idung was *magister scolae* at Regensburg in 1133 and perhaps for some years afterwards. He became a monk at Prüfening in the diocese of Regensburg in about 1144 and, before he wrote his *Dialogus*, it seems, a Cistercian, possibly in Austria. The *Argumentum* was composed before 1145, and the *Dialogus* after 1153. Cfr R.B.C. HUYGENS, *Le moine Idung et ses deux ouvrages : 'Argumentum super quatuor questionibus' et 'Dialogus duorum monachorum'*, in *Studi medievali* 13 (1972), p. 296-298. Idung's memories of the persecution of monks under Bishop Hartwig, Cuno's predecessor, were vivid ; cfr *Argumentum, ibid.*, p. 362.

5. For him the two rights were intimately connected ; cfr *Altercatio monachi et clerici quod liceat monacho predicare* (PL 170, col. 542). Such a connexion

receive due reward. For him, the argument 'no "cura animarum" no tithes' could be turned with a compelling logic upon
its head to read 'if "cura animarum" then tithes'. [1] Idung's
arguments, set out in two of the four questions in his *Argumentum
super quattuor questionibus* are similar. [2] They shew some irritation but no doubts. One and the same person can be both 'clericus' and 'monachus' ; the latter office not only does not negate,
it actually improves, the former. [3] If a monk can receive clerical
orders he can preach ; if he preaches he deserves just rewards in
the form of tithes and offerings. If a monk-bishop can rule a large
parish, surely a monk-priest can rule a small. [4] There is more to
bring Rupert and Idung together, however, even than this. Rupert has a clear enemy in some of his diatribes : the Augustinian
Canons. They seem, according to him, to offer a severe challenge
to Benedictine preachers. [5] Idung does not single out the canons
for attack in the *Argumentum*. He objects to a broader world of
'clerici' and not, it seems, quite so violently as Rupert. [6] In the
Dialogue, however, his second work, the case is different. The
enemy is the same, and Idung is quite as fierce about it as Rupert.
It is worth quoting from this treatise, for Idung summarizes the
position very clearly, and gives a reason for the hostility with which
the Augustinians were regarded. The Cluniac of the dialogue
asks the Cistercian why it is that Augustinians claim the name
canon and refuse the name monk. The Cistercian replies :

> Aut imperitia aut vana gloria aut utrumque fecit eos errare. Glo-
> riantur enim se esse predicatores et doctores, dicendo : "Monachus non
> habet officium docentis", nos habemus, haec eadem verba Ieronimi
> nequaquam recte intelligentes nec adtendentes quod apostolus dicit ;
> "Quomodo predicabunt nisi mittantur ?" Itaque sola missio facit
> predicatorem. Et illi : "Nos", inquiunt, "quia clerici sumus, ex clericatu

seems to have been general at this period ; cfr M. PEUCHMAURD, *art. cit.*, p. 52-
77. Also Bernald of St. Blaise (*MGH Libelli de Lite* II, 98).

1. Letter to Everard (*PL* 170, col. 542-544).
2. HUYGENS, *art. cit.*, p. 343-370. The *Argumentum* is also printed in
E. DEMM, *Reformmönchtum und Slawenmission im 12. Jahrhundert*, Lübeck
and Hamburg 1970, p. 113-133.
3. HUYGENS, *art. cit.*, p. 347. It is difficult to sustain the view expressed
by Dom Jean Leclercq (*art. cit.*, p. 150) that Idung's position is merely an
elaboration of that of Hugh of St. Victor. Idung openly contradicts Hugh
at several points in the *Dialogus*, for example HUYGENS, p. 429-431, 433-434,
459.
4. *Ibid.*, p. 367-368.
5. Rupert describes the sharpness of the contention between Augustinians
and Benedictines in the *In Regulam S. Benedicti* IV, 1-2 (*PL* 170, col. 525-526).
6. *Argumentum, ibid.*, p. 362.

officium habemus". Quibus cum respondetur : "Ergo et monachi sacrum ordinem habentes, quia clerici sunt, ex clericatu officium predicandi habent", illi satis imperite respondent, dicentes : "Monachi habent clericatum ex indulgentia, nos ex debito." Errant enim in utroque, in hoc quod dicunt : "nos ex debito" et in hoc quod dicunt : "illi ex indulgentia". [1]

The Augustinians felt, it seems, that their very name gave them a standing both more secure than, and superior to, that of the Benedictines. This opinion asked for condemnation and received it. Honorius's views will be set out in the next section. For now, three points may be made about this polemic. The first is that the positive side of the advocacy lies in the stress all the spokesmen place on the contribution monks have still to make in the field of pastoral care. Secondly, all have an identifiable and assailable enemy : the Augustinian Canons. The fact that the enemy could be so identified perhaps helped the spirit of retaliation. [2] Thirdly, it appears that for some reason there was, in Regensburg, ground upon which to fight. All three are worth investigating closely, for they bear directly upon Honorius.

Those canons and monks who most wanted to be active in the reformed church came to South Germany and Austria in two main streams. One stream came by way of Passau, and one by way of Hirsau. [3] The Canons Regular were supported first in the diocese of Passau by Bishop Altman (1056-91). [4] St. Pölten and St. Florian stemmed from his early efforts. The archdiocese of

---

1. *Ibid.*, p. 428-429.
2. I should say here that the first two basic ingredients of the crisis I mentioned at the beginning, the competition of the schoolmen and the call of the solitary life, do not appear at this point to have been deeply important in this area. Gerhoh of Reichersberg maintained, in Regensburg in the 1130s, a furious independence of the teaching of the masters Anselm of Laon and William of Champeaux. Cfr P. CLASSEN, *Gerhoch von Reichersberg*, Wiesbaden 1960, p. 24 and 50-51. For the comparative lack of hermits see H. GRUNDMANN, *Deutsche Eremiten, Einsiedler und Klausner im Hochmittelalter (10.-12. Jahrhundert)*, in *Archiv für Kulturgeschichte* 45 (1963), p. 63-65.
3. H. JACOBS, *Die Hirsauer* (Kölner Historische Abhandlungen, IV), Köln 1961, p. 205. The diatribes of Boto of Prüfening against this pre-occupation on the part of his contemporaries perhaps serve to underline it : "Sed sicut iam supra dicere coepimus, neglecta communitate noxiam singularitatem induci in monasteria videmus, ab his qui in monastico ordine curam animarum susceperunt. Communem namque utilitatem Domus Dei postponentes, privatam singularitatem, quae humanis favoribus magis quam divinis iussionibus servire solet, sectantur" (*De Statu Domus Dei* III ; *Maxima Bibliotheca Veterum Patrum* 21, p. 501).
4. J.C. DICKINSON, *The Origins of the Austin Canons and their Introduction into England*, London 1950, p. 45-46.

Salzburg under Archbishop Conrad (1106-47) welcomed them enthusiastically. [1] They were fortified by the bitter memories of imperial persecution and the contrasting political attitudes of the Welf Dukes of Bavaria, and they spread within Conrad's diocese and outside it in the 1120s with remarkable rapidity. [2] The Hirsau reform, by way of the abbey of St. George in the Black Forest, [3] made great inroads at the same time. From St. George Hirsauer monks went to Ottobeuren, Benediktbeuern, Tegernsee, Admont, St. Ulrich in Augsburg, Prüfening. From Admont, under Abbots Wolfhold (1115-37) and Gottfried (1138-65) [4] the Hirsau reform reached Attl, Seeon, St. Peter's Salzburg, Ossiach, Prül, St. Emmeram's Regensburg, Melk, Weihenstephan, St. Lambrecht, Göttweig, Millstatt, Michelsberg, Biburg, Kremsmünster, St. George on the Langsee, Bergen, Odilienberg. [5] Prüfening was, of course, a Hirsauer house when Idung went there as a monk.

Regensburg, however, seems to have been a place apart ; this in two ways. First of all, it had a proud and independent monastic tradition. Regensburg was a centre of the Gorze-Trier reform in South Germany. [6] The city had a distinguished monastic history and provided, in St. Emmeram's and Weih St. Peter's, a haven for those scholarly 'inclusi' the Gorze reform favoured so highly. [7] It stood aside from Hirsau (William of Hirsau had originally been a monk of St. Emmeram's and had left it and St. Emmeram's did not receive Hirsauer customs until 1143) but was vul-

1. Ch. DEREINE, *Les chanoines réguliers dans l'ancienne province ecclésiastique de Salzbourg d'après les travaux récents*, in *Revue d'histoire ecclésiastique* 55 (1960), p. 909-915. Some valuable pages on both the tensions and common ground to be found between canons of the *ordo novus* and monks in the archdiocese of Salzburg may be found in P. JOHANEK, *Ein Mandat Papst Hadrian IV für die Mönche von Seeon und die Ordensreform in der Kirchenprovinz Salzburg*, in *Studien und Mitteilungen zur Geschichte des Benediktiner-Ordens* 83 (1972), p. 162-175.

2. J. MOIS, *Das Stift Rottenburg in der Kirchenreform des XI.-XII. Jahrhunderts*, Munich 1953, p. 146-148.

3. R. BAUERREISS, *St. Georgen im Schwarzwald, ein Reformmittelpunkt Südostdeutschlands im beginnenden 12. Jahrhundert*, in *Studien und Mitteilungen zur Geschichte des Benediktiner-Ordens* 51 (1933), p. 196-201, and 52 (1934), p. 47-56.

4. For an admirable summary cfr U. FAUST, *Gottfried von Admont*, in *Studien und Mitteilungen zur Geschichte des Benediktiner-Ordens* 75 (1964), p. 273-275.

5. H. JACOBS, *op. cit.*, p. 69ff.

6. R. BAUERREISS, *Kirchengeschichte Bayerns* II, St. Ottilien 1950, p. 53-87.

7. *Ibid.*, p. 168-171. The eleventh century St. Emmeram's manuscript of the chronicle of Hermannus Contractus (now clm 14613) has, in the margins, a pointing finger to indicate important facts about St. Emmeram's and about distinguished monks.

nerable to the impact of the Canons Regular, by way of Rottenbuch, relatively early. Certainly Bishop Hartwig, Cuno's predecessor, favoured them. [1] Secondly, under Bishop Cuno, Regensburg was a place in which great efforts were made to establish a
harmonious and working relationship between monks and canons.
The Siegburg reform had been devised to bridge this gap and Cuno,
when he left Siegburg and came to Regensburg, brought it to
Mondsee (1127), to Weltenburg (1127/28) and perhaps to St. Emmeram's. [2] Cuno was able to handle both canons and monks with
sympathy and tact, [3] so much so that he won the enthusiasm of
the redoubtable Gerhoh of Reichersberg. [4] This at last brings us
to Honorius.

Honorius and his writings appeared in South Germany exactly
where and exactly when the Benedictines were most involved,
both urgently and hopefully, in the battle for pastoral care. We
know that Honorius dedicated later works to Cuno, but he arrived
in fact before Cuno, before the Hirsau reform had begun to gain
strength and when the influx of the canons and the support given
to them by Hartwig was just beginning to be felt. He came, it
seems, to Weih St. Peter's. It would be too much to decide
that he was brought deliberately ; but it is not too much to claim
that he took an active and effective part. This battle, indeed,
later waged with success by Cuno and still later by the Hirsauer,
seems to provide, in its beginnings, the clue to Honorius's activities
we have needed for so long. As in England, so in Regensburg, the
underlying cause of monks and the reform, and the particular
tensions of the place in which he was called upon to serve it, provide the solution to the place and purpose of his works. In the
case of England I suggested that he was prompted to write by a
peculiar combination of political opposition and monastic opportunity ; a combination, moreover, given a special force by the pressure of time. The pressure of time remained a force in South
Germany, but the political opposition was replaced by a political

1. *Ibid.*, III, p. 32-37 ; Mois, *op. cit.*, p. 166-168 ; Huygens, *Idung, art. cit.*, p. 362.
2. J. Semmler, *Die Klosterreform von Siegburg. Ihre Ausbreitung und ihr Reformprogramm im 11. und 12. Jahrhundert*, Bonn 1959, p. 84-85.
3. Siegburg had maintained good relations with Rolduc and perhaps with Rottenbuch when Cuno was Siegburg's abbot and, of course, Norbert entered Siegburg while Cuno was in office. Cfr J. Mois, *op. cit.*, p. 130.
4. *Chronicon Magni Presbyteri Reichersbergensis (MGH SS* 17, p. 492) ; Gerhoh, *De Edificio Dei (MGH, Libelli de Lite* III, 137). Gerhoh was per-suaded to allow monks pastoral work as a justification of their collection of tithes ; cfr Classen, *op. cit.*, p. 42, 45, 177.

sympathy for which the Benedictines had competitors. In Regensburg there was ground on which the Benedictines could take a stand, but the whole was complicated, made both easier and harder by the pride of the local monastic tradition, by its distinctness and by the concentrated nature of the competition. He was met there by an even larger challenge and he confronted it with an even fiercer productive energy.

II. THE EVIDENCE OF THE WRITINGS

At those rare moments when Honorius stops being a compiler, he turns promptly to polemic. There is no mean between these two apparently very different activities. When he turns to polemic two pre-occupations above all stand out. One is with the dignities and responsibilities of the priesthood in general. The other is with the distinction of the monastic life and the rights, especially the rights to the priesthood, to which it can lay claim.

Honorius expresses his views on the priesthood most forcefully in the *Offendiculum*, in the *Elucidarius* and in the *Summa Gloria*. The position he takes up is that of the extreme reformer.

'Quantum differt lux a tenebris, tantum differt ordo sacerdotum a laicis.'
'Presbyteri ... qui speculum debent esse laicorum.' [1]

The priesthood is the power which rules the world, [2] and, indeed, controls its salvation. [3] It follows that priests must be men of blameless public life and, of course, celibate. [4] Anyone departing from these standards is worthy of the severest punishment. [5] The implication of these demands is strong, but there is a firm direct suggestion also that only monks and Regular Canons take the care required to furnish men suitable for such an office. [6]

If the priesthood is so vital to the renewal of the church, and

---

1. *Offendiculum*, chapters 38, 39 (*MGH Libelli de Lite* III, 51).
2. *Summa Gloria*, chapter 23 (*ibid.*, p. 73).
3. "Presbyter enim dicitur praebens iter ... scilicet populo de exsilio huius mundi ad patriam coelestis regni. Horum officium est missas celebrare, pro populo sacrificare, corpus Domini dispensare, praedicare, baptizare, poenitentes absolvere, infirmos ungere, mortuos sepelire, populum ad missam, vel nuptias, vel arma, vel peras, vel baculos, vel judicia ferre, et aquas, vel candelas, vel palmas, vel cineres, vel quaslibet res ad cibum pertinentes benedicere" (*Gemma Animae* I, 181 ; *PL* 172, col. 599).
4. *Offendiculum*, chapter 28 (*loc. cit.*, p. 47-48).
5. *Elucidarius* I, 185-189, 200a-200f ; ed. Y. LEFÈVRE, *L'Elucidarium et les lucidaires*, Paris 1954, p. 395-397, 401-402.
6. *Offendiculum*, chapter 28 (*loc. cit.*).

monks make good priests, perhaps the best available, then it
follows that monks must live up to their calling. [1] It follows, too,
that monk-priests must make themselves heard in the church.
This is the burden of Honorius's other polemical treatise, the *Quod
Monachis Liceat Predicare*. [2] Preaching, it should be said, is
only a part, though an important one, of those priestly activities
Honorius claims for monks. The treatise is written, as he says,
to counter those who :

> Sententias patrum, quas non intellegunt, pravo sensu ad errorem
> suum pervertunt, dicentes Christi sacerdotibus in monachica profes-
> sione constitutis non licere verbum dei populo predicare, pueros
> baptizare, penitentes suscipere, assumentes in patrocinium sui erroris
> sententiam Hieronimi eximii doctoris, quia dicit, quod monachis
> officium non habet ... docentis sed lugentis. [3]

These are the enemies Idung had to meet, and Honorius uses the
same weapons and makes the same claims. Monks are to have full
pastoral rights. He goes further, even, than this. He claims
that the rights of monks to a share in the pastoral priesthood are
not merely distinct from but superior to those of the Canons Regular.

> ... ecclesia habet duas professiones religionis, videlicet monachicam
> et regularem, hoc est communem vitam sub regula sancti benedicti
> vel sancti augustini ducentium ... Igitur sicut ecclesia de officio laicali
> aliquos ad clericale assumit, ita de utraque professione dignos ad cleri-
> cale officium elegit, quos in diversa ministeria distribuit. [4]

He goes on :

> Regularium itaque vita quanto a canonica est districtior, tanto a
> monachica remissior, et quanto ab illa altior, tanto ab ista inferior ac
> seculari vicinior ... Unde sicut a canonica licet cuique ascendere ad
> regularium vitam, ita licet a regulari cuique ascendere ad monachicam,
> nulli autem licet a monachica ad regularem sicut nec de regulari ad
> canonicam. Monachica etenim vita est arta et angusta via ... Per

---

1. This is the point forcibly made by the *De Apostatis*, attached, in the
early manuscripts, to the *Offendiculum*.
2. Printed by J.-A. ENDRES, *op. cit.*, p. 147-151.
3. *Ibid.*, p. 147.
4. *Ibid.*, p. 148. Also : "Nec episcopus aliter consecrat regularem presbyterum quam monachicum presbyterum, quia licet diversa sit professio, uterque
eodem fungitur officio. Nec aliter celebrat missam presbyter monachus, nec
aliis utitur vestibus in sacramentis quam regularis. Sicut ergo presbytero
regulari non ex regula sed ex officio suo licet missas celebrare, predicare,
baptizare, penitentes suscipere, ita nihilominus eodem modo presbytero
monacho non ex regula sed ex officio sacerdotali licet missas celebrare, predicare, baptizare, penitentes absolvere".

hanc artam viam summi viri gregorius, cassiodorus, ysidorus, martinus et alii innumerabiles ambulaverunt et per multas tribulationes regem glorie in gloria adierunt. Qui huic vite derogent, longe se a consortio illius alienant. [1]

These were fighting words, especially in view of the specific rulings of Urban II, later incorporated into the *Decretum*, against the transference of Regular Canons to the monastic life. [2]

If monks, then, were to win this battle, and it was a battle for no less than influence over the guiding principles of the reformed church, they must be supplied with suitable ammunition. When we turn from the polemic to the compilations, these last may be seen to provide the sort of ammunition which was needed. They fall into four main groups. Firstly there are works which bear upon the liturgy. These, the *Gemma Animae*, the *Sacramentarium*, the *Sigillum*, the *Eucharisticon*, go well beyond the purely monastic aspects of this. [3] Secondly, there are the works upon the Bible : the *Commentary on the Psalter*, that on the *Song of Songs*, the lost *Evangelia*, the exposition of the first chapters of Genesis known as the *Neocosmum* or *Hexaemeron*. These books of the Bible are surely among those most distinguished for their 'pastoral' bearing. Thirdly, there is a larger collection of works associated more generally with man's place in the world, his history and his moral purposes : the *Imago Mundi*, *Summa Totius*, *Libelli Quaestionum*, *Clavis Physicae*, *Cognitio Vitae*, *Elucidarius*, *Inevitabile*, *De Decem Plagis*, *Scala Coeli*, *De Animae Exilio et Patria*. Some of these are written in the form of simple catechisms and none of them is without pastoral application. Lastly there are the sermon collections. Two of these are lost but only one, the *Refectio Mentium*, was specifically confined to the brethren in chapter and one, the *Speculum Ecclesiae*, was certainly meant for popular audiences. [4]

When one turns to the contents of the compilations, the popular

1. *Ibid.*, p. 149-150.
2. Ch. DEREINE, *L'élaboration du statut canonique des chanoines réguliers, spécialement sous Urbain II*, in *Revue d'histoire ecclésiastique* 46 (1951), p. 552-553.
3. Dom Bauerreiss draws attention to the special stress Honorius lays upon the symbolic aspects of the liturgy. Cfr R. BAUERREISS, *Kirchengeschichte Bayerns* III, St. Ottilien 1951, p. 146-147.
4. The gift of frater Heinricus describes these as "sermones dulcissimi ad populum". Cfr T. GOTTLIEB, *Mittelalterliche Bibliothekskataloge Österreichs* I, Vienna 1915, p. 11. The sermons, for example *De Nativitate* (*PL* 172, col. 824-825), contain directives which certainly go far beyond the immediate needs of monks.

XII

108

intent becomes more evident. The *De Decem Plagis*, for instance, contains, in the setting of the infection of the plagues against the medicine of the commandments, vivid material for instruction and exhortation. The *Scala Coeli* encompasses *all* who would climb to heaven yet get lost on the way. [1] The *Elucidarius* asks and answers questions of a very broad scope indeed :

> Est grave peccatum ducere cognatam ?
> Quid sentis de militibus ?
> Quam spem habent mercatores ?
> Prodest Hierosolymam petere aut alia sacra loca invisere ?
> Peccant ministri qui a judicibus jussi damnatis mortis supplicium inferunt ? [2]

This treatise, although written in England, was, of course, widely copied, especially in the area with which we are concerned. The *Cognitio Vitae* was similarly unrestricted :

> Omnes ergo fideles ad lignum vitaeque fontem curramus, cuius gustu in aeternum beate vivamus. Libellus autem nomen, cognitio vitae, sortiatur : dum in eo vera vita tardioribus intellectu cognoscibilis reddi videatur. [3]

Many more examples could be given. Honorius may, in this, be contrasted with his near neighbour and contemporary, Boto of Prüfening, who was rigidly opposed to the pre-occupation of the Benedictine order with the pastorate. [4] The full contrast between them cannot be properly pursued until we know more about Boto's works, few of which can at the minute be identified. [5] The *De Statu Domus Dei*, however, is certainly more reflective, more suitable to the study and to the meditative turn of mind than anything Honorius wrote, and at least one of Boto's books is specifically described as 'legentibus satis gratum'. [6]

---

1. *E.g.* chapter 9 (*PL* 172, col. 1234).
2. II, 46, 54, 63, 77, 82 (LEFÈVRE, *op. cit.*, p. 425, 428-429, 434, 436).
3. *PL* 40, col. 1007.
4. See above, p. 102, n. 3.
5. Boto lived at Prüfening between the years approximately 1121-1168. Endres has set out extracts from his unpublished works ; cfr J.-A. ENDRES, *Boto von Prüfening und seine schriftstellerische Thätigkeit*, in *Neues Archiv* 30 (1904-1905), p. 634-640.
6. The works of Boto are set out in a chapter of the Passau test of the *De Scriptoribus Ecclesiasticis* of the so-called Anonymous of Melk : "Boto presbiter et monachus de cenobio bruviningerensi, ab adolescentia sua in scribendo et dictando occupatus, scripsit inter alia omelias super evangelia xxx et librum sermonum legentibus satis gratum ; scripsit etiam librum qui intitulatur de domo domini et alium de opere sancte trinitatis ; scripsit etiam commentum in ierarchiam Dyonisii ; scripsit quoque libellum qui vocatur 'Dominicus' de die dominica ; scripsit etiam librum grandiusculum super extremam partem

I do not mean to suggest that Honorius's treatises could not be read in the cloister : merely that it is extremely unlikely that it was for this end primarily that they were designed. This brings me finally to a consideration of the way in which the compilations as a whole were put together and presented. Honorius's works have two distinguishing features : complexity of composition and simplicity of exposition. The material he uses is often difficult, in some cases modern and sophisticated. It is drawn from an amazing variety of sources and encompasses a vast range of subjects. The really hard work, however, is directed to the end of giving the most reliable answers available ; never towards the asking of more questions and the furthering of discovery. One can find in the *Elucidarius* a multitude of instances wherein Honorius refuses to put his arduous reading at the service of further questioning. Many instances also are to be found in works less evidently catechetical. In the first book of the *Imago Mundi*, for example, for which Honorius consulted a quite bewildering number of authorities, he stops short again and again at the moment of doubt and deeper enquiry. [1] He does the same, perhaps more importantly, in his long commentary on the *Song of Songs*. [2] Whilst intellectual energy of a sort is clearly employed, it seems that intellectual enquiry is, even if this means injustice to the enquiries of the Fathers, to be ruthlessly suppressed.

The result is that complexity is always subordinated to simplicity ; and simplicity becomes therefore the outstanding characteristic and the all pervasive one. Yet Honorius does not let matters rest here. He seems to devote to the elaboration of simplicity all that solicitude he had refused to the elaboration of doubt. It becomes an art and with its aid he not merely gives

---

Ezechielis de edificio in monte ; scripsit quoque libellum de arte musica et alium de officio misse et super 'Te igitur'". Cfr P. LEHMANN, *Neue Textzeugen des Prüfeninger Liber de viris illustribus (Anonymous Mellicensis)*, in *Neues Archiv* 38 (1913), p. 555. The sermons on Ezechiel may also be meant rather for reading than for preaching ; cfr ENDRES, *art. cit.*, p. 633-634.

1. For example I, 6. Here Honorius refuses to follow the conflict between Macrobius and Bede over the question of the existence of the Antipodes though both sources were, quite clearly, open before him. Cfr *PL* 172, col. 122. MACROBIUS, *Commentariorum in Somnium Scipionis*, ed. F. EYSSENHARDT, Teubner-Leipzig 1892, II, 5, 1-4 ; BEDE, *De Temporum Ratione*, in C.W. JONES, *Bedae Opera de Temporibus*, Cambridge (Mass.) 1943, IX, p. 202-204. Again, I, 8-9 and 87, he suppresses St. Augustine's anxieties about the literal interpretation of Genesis 2, 4 and 24, although he clearly knew the relevant works. Cfr *PL* 172, col. 123, 141. AUGUSTINE, *De Civitate Dei* 13, 21 (*PL* 41, col. 394-395) ; *De Genesi ad Litteram* 10 (*PL* 34, col. 271-272).

2. V.I.J. FLINT, *The Commentaries of Honorius Augustodunensis on the Song of Songs*, in *Rev. bénéd.* 84 (1974), p. 207-208.

answers but positively injects them. This brings me to an aspect of Honorius's literary talent which has not, I think, previously been noticed. He displays an amazing sense of audience. There is a deal to be learnt from him in this field. He is fond of movements :

> Veterem cisternam relinquamus, ad fluenta novi fontis veniamus. [1]
> Ignea inferni loca inspeximus, ad refrigerium aquarum confugiamus. [2]

and a sudden change of view :

> Veni huc ad supercilium montis, unde cuncta aedificia conspicere possis damnatae civitatis. [3]

He has an instinct for when his readers flag which is rarely found in contemporary treatises, and a fine sense of when the threads of an argument are to be gathered together. This is the function of the discipulus in many of his works. [4] Honorius betrays, in fact, a considerable dramatic talent, with all the feeling for effect that that implies. He calculates the distance in communication between himself and the people he addresses with far more care than he ever calculates that in argument between one point and the next. The sheer charm of the tableaux he creates is so compelling that the most intractable of material is transferred almost without pain. For example, in the *Cognitio Vitae*, he sets up an argument he wishes to destroy in the form of ineffective siege engines :

> Fugatis tenebris de structura sacrae aedis, jam ad dissolvendas machinas contra eam erectas accingamur. Deum alicubi esse substantialiter, et ubique potentialiter, repugnat firmitati totius jam elaboratae disputationis, et subruitur impulsu evidentissimae rationis ... Hujus falsissimae opinionis machinamenta facile dissolvunt hujus sacrae turris instrumenta. [5]

In this way the battle is won before, on the grounds of argument, it has been fought. The discipulus continues good humouredly to advance these doomed constructions :

> Discipulus. Hujus ruinam non moleste ferimus, sed ad frangorem ejus potius fautores applaudimus, quia per hujus casum turris introitum speramus. Sed cum haec machina sit disjecta, ecce alia stat contra turrim erecta.

1. *Offendiculum*, chapter 21 (*loc. cit.*, p. 44).
2. *Imago Mundi* I, 37 ; *PL* 172, col. 133.
3. *Inevitabile* ; *PL* 172, col. 1220.
4. *Ibid.*, *PL* 172, col. 1202.
5. 28-29 ; *PL* 40, col. 1021-1022.

with the same result. Honorius is nearer in this to stage direction than he is to any other form of literary endeavour and stays so.

In sum, Honorius's compilations are prodigious efforts at covering ground. They succeed in covering an enormous amount of ground extremely thoroughly. They are not, however, devised for the furtherance of monastic meditation, nor even for purely monastic instruction. They are meant for projection on a very much larger scale. For this reason, the dramatic contriving within them is of a very high order, so high indeed that almost nothing remains to be done. In the *Speculum Ecclesiae*, to give a last, but particularly striking, example, Honorius 'produces' not merely the material but the speaker :

> Cum autem sermonem facis, non debes protenta manu quasi verba in faciem populi jaculare, nec clausis oculis vel in terram fixis, aut supino vultu stare ; nec caput ut insanus movere, vel os in diversa contorquere ; sed, ut rhetorica instruit, decenti gestu pronunciare, verba composite et humiliter formare, tristia tristi voce, laeta hylari, dura acri, humilia suppressa proferre. Ut magis auditoribus videatur ipsas res spectare quam te audire, verbis eas debes repraesentare. [1]

Honorius's compilations seem, in fact, to be very closely associated with his more directly expressed ambitions for the success of the reform and for that active monastic priesthood which he saw as essential to it. The distinction between polemic and compilation is itself, to this extent, artificial. It seems that we may find, both in his own stated views and in the nature of the labours to which he put himself, evidence of the tenacity of these ambitions.

III. THE EVIDENCE
OF THE SURVIVING TWELFTH CENTURY MANUSCRIPTS

This evidence falls into two classes: the surviving single treatises, of which a handlist is appended, and the codices in which one or more of Honorius's writings are found bound up with other works. The last class is the one which has the most immediate bearing upon the suggestion I have been attempting to pursue. This last class may be divided into a further two. The first of these divisions is made up of codices, often large and beautifully written, containing, together with Honorius's works, complete copies of long treatises. Examples of these are WORCESTER *Cathedral*

---

1. *PL* 172, col. 861-862.

Library Q. 66, and LONDON *British Museum* Royal 6.E. II. The second is made up of codices, for the most part smaller in size and not as carefully written, containing, with the work or works of Honorius, an enormous variety of selections and fragments. This second division is overwhelmingly the larger one and has in it a number of books which, in this context, seem to demand a careful examination.

Most of the codices containing the *Elucidarius* fall into this second division. The *Elucidarius* is, when it appears in a collection, almost always hidden in a confusion of theological fragments. Sometimes this confusion has tested the compilers of the relevant catalogues of manuscripts beyond endurance. A few examples may perhaps be enough to shew this. [1] One is *Bodley* Lat. Th. e 9 (32710). The *Elucidarius* in this codex is incomplete (ending at II, 43), the books have no headings and no attributions, and they are followed by a quite extraordinary miscellany. This includes the *Exaggeratio* of Heriger of Lobbes, part of a record of a council of Gregory VII, three pieces on the Lord's Prayer, the *Quindecim Signa*, a catechism on the creed, a passage 'De ordine clerici et quid sit clericus', a shortened version of Adso *De Antichristo*, extracts from a Bestiary, verses, extracts from the Fathers, part of a letter of Ivo of Chartres. [2] Another is *Bodley* Fairfax 26 (3908). Again, confusion and extreme fragmentation confront one. The *Elucidarius* (f. 38) is complete in this manuscript and is followed, though not immediately, by Augustine's *Enchiridion*. Before, between and after these two come excerpts and fragments. The codex begins with a part of the *Summa Sententiarum* and continues with short sermons and moral extracts. There follow sentences of the 'school of Laon', selections from the Fathers (Fulgentius, Augustine, Gregory, Isidore, Bede, Jerome), sections from a Bestiary, the *De Duodecim Abusivis*, *De Septem Principalibus Vitiis*, passages on sin, on vestments, on binding and loosing. After the *Elucidarius* come more 'sententiae', St. Bernard *De Laude Novae Militiae*, a sermon of Ivo of Chartres. After the *Enchiridion* we have more sermons and fragments of sermons. [3]

---

1. In numbering the contents of the codices I shall note only significant additions to the entries in the printed catalogues.

2. For the analysis of this part of the manuscript I am indebted to Miss A.C. de la Mare.

3. Ff. 1-8, *Summa Sententiarum* ; *PL* 176, col. 104 ff. Among the sermons and extracts (ff. 8v-16) are some from St. Bernard (f. 10 ; *PL* 183, col. 299) and Geoffrey Babion (ff. 10v, 11, 11v, 14, 14v ; *PL* 171, col. 728, 547, 535, 531, 463, 911). Ff. 16-16v, *sententiae* of the 'school of Laon' (cfr O. LOTTIN, *Psychologie et morale aux XII*e *et XIII*e *siècles* V, Louvain 1959, nos 229, 137). Ff. 17-

Many more codices containing the *Elucidarius*, trough not quite so complex in construction, display the same traits. *Bodley Laud Misc.* 237, for instance, has sermons, extracts from the *Verba Seniorum* and, perhaps, the *Vision of Wettin.* [1] *B.M.* Royal 5.E.VI has parts of the Pseudo-Isidore's *De Numero*, miscellaneous theological notes, a fragment from the 'school of Laon', [2] Gilbert Crispin's *Dialogue between a Jew and a Christian*, medicinal remedies in Old French. *B.M.* Royal 15.A.XX has Ciceronian tracts, notes, a letter of Ivo, Ghost Stories. *Corpus Christi College* CAMBRIDGE 439 has the *Liber Scintillarum*, theological extracts and the Pseudo-Isidore's *De Ortu et Obitu Prophetarum*. For the enormous compilation which is CAMBRIDGE *University Library* Kk.IV.6 it is perhaps best to refer directly to the catalogue entry, [3] but one may note the inclusion of the *De Arca Noe* of Hugh of St. Victor, enormous numbers of extracts and, again, the *De Ortu et Obitu Prophetarum*.

Two of the codices noticed above include items which bear directly upon the 'cura animarum'. The letter of Ivo of Chartres contained in *B.M.* Royal 15.A.XX is about the rights of canons regular to pastoral care and the ways in which these rights are to be defended. [4] *Corpus Christi College* CAMBRIDGE 439, has the conciliar decision ascribed to Pope Boniface IV ('Quod liceat monachis cum sacerdotali officio ubique ministrare'). [5] At least two more of the twelfth century codices known to me contain, with the *Elucidarius*, Pope Gregory the Great's *Cura Pastoralis*. [6] The books containing the *Elucidarius* seem, in short, to be for the most part 'pastoral' books, codices made up, that is, to serve the needs of a man or community with a care of souls.

It may be said that all this merely confirms that which has long

21[v], selections from the Fathers. F. 22, Bestiary. F. 23[v], *De Duodecim Abusivis.* F. 23[v], *De Septem Principalibus Vitiis.* Ff. 24-48, extracts on sin and the sacraments. Ff. 54[v]-59[v], *sententiae.* F. 59, *De Laude.* F. 63, sermon 5 of Ivo (*PL* 162, col. 535-553). Ff. 76-76[v], two fragments of sermons of St. Bernard : 87 and 59 (*PL* 183, col. 703, 682). F. 77, sermon of Ralph of Escures 'Intravit Ihesus' (*PL* 158, col. 644).

1. It is not certain that the *Vision of Wettin* was bound originally with the other two.
2. 'Tria sunt genera hominum Deo servientium' (cfr O. LOTTIN, *op. cit.*, n° 420).
3. *A Catalogue of the Manuscripts preserved in the Library of the University of Cambridge* III, 1858, p. 642-647.
4. F. 162 ; *PL* 162, col. 88.
5. F. 48 ; J.D. MANSI, *Sacrorum conciliorum nova et amplissima collectio* 10, col. 504-505.
6. KLOSTERNEUBURG 793, GÖTTWEIG 37.

been suspected about the place of the *Elucidarius*. We have not suspected it, however, of the other works ; and yet, when the codices containing them too are submitted to inspection of this sort, striking similarities emerge. Take, for example, codices containing the *Imago Mundi*, one of the least evidently 'pastoral' of Honorius's works. Among the earliest of these are MUNICH *Bayerische Staatsbibliothek* clm 536, 14348, 14731. All three of these contain, together with the *Imago Mundi*, the 'letters of Paul to Seneca', and identical passages from the Fathers on the moral interpretation of Genesis, Isaiah, Joel. [1] Clm 536 and 14348 have, in addition, a Bestiary and the *De Duodecim Abusivis*. The pattern begins to take on a familiar appearance. Clm 536 contains a lapidary and a fascinating series of mixed Latin and German charms, formule, aphorisms, miracle stories, the *Vision of Wettin*. It also has the same supposed pronouncement of Pope Boniface IV on the rights of monks to sacerdotal office. [2] Clm 14348 has sermons, extracts, Rupert of Deutz on the *Canticle*, a collection of miracles of the Virgin, an anonymous treatise on the Assumption, the *Elucidarius* and the *Visio Pauli*. Clm 14731 has more extracts attributed to Rupert, selections from the *De Concordia Evangelistarum*, notes on the liturgical year, the seven wonders of the world. PARIS *Bibliothèque Mazarine* 708 binds, with the *Imago Mundi*, the *Sententiae Divinae Paginae*, and the *Summa Sententiarum* of Otto of Lucca. One last codex containing the *Imago Mundi* which I have been able to examine with some care is ADMONT 400. We have the same pattern once again : questiones, a florilegium and sententiae of the style of the 'school of Laon' accompany Honorius's work. [3] The selections of the questiones made in this manuscript are particularly interesting, for they all bear upon the constitution of the church, the importance of its preachers, baptism, free will, sin—especially sexual sin—confession and renewal. These matters are pursued relentlessly, to the neglect of less unambiguously moral concerns. [4] The

1. Clm 536, ff. 57-65ᵛ ; clm 14348, ff. 242-246 ; clm 14731, ff. 51-59.
2. F. 85ᵛ. This is not noted in the catalogue.
3. Ff. 74ᵛ-118ᵛ, parts of the *Questiones super Genesim, super Exodum, super Leviticum, super Numeros, super Deuteronomium, super Ihesu Nave* printed in *PL* 93, also the *De Benedictionibus Patriarcharum* of Adrevaldus of Fleury. Ff. 118 on have a florilegium of passages from Jerome, Augustine, Ambrose Bede, interspersed with some *questiones* of the 'school of Laon' only one of which we have been able to identify : f. 135 (cfr O. LOTTIN, *op. cit.*, nº 109).
4. This can only be seen by taking the selections and setting them against the main text. Here, for example, are some of the selections from the Book of Genesis (in the manuscript they follow one another immediately) : "Planta-

florilegium is pre-occupied with these concerns as well, although the range is somewhat greater, including, as it does, tithe paying and usury. A quotation from the collection of 'sententiae' in the manuscript may help to make its pre-occupations clear. The 'sententiae' are attributed by the scribe to Jerome on Ezechiel :

> Item. Quamdiu anima in infancia est constituta peccato caret. Item. Ihierusalem in medio mundi sita est. Unde umbilicus terre dicitur. Iuxta illud operatus est salutem in medio terre. Item. Si vir cum muliere cɔcat dum menstruum patitur, concepti fetus vivium seminis trahit, ita ut leprosi et elephantici ex hac conceptione nascantur. Et feda in utroque sexu corpora parvitate et enormitate membrorum sanies corrupta denegetur. Item. Nec de rapinis et usuris et alieno malo panem quaesitum vertamus in miseriam, redemptio enim anime viri proprie divicie quod multos facere conspicimus qui divites et pauperes spoliant et agricolas. Ut taceam de militancium et iudicum violencia vel furta committunt, ut de multis parva pauperibus tribuant et in celeribus glorientur. Publiceque diacones in ecclesiis recitant offerentium nomina, tantum offert ille, ille tantum pollicitus est, placentque sibi ad plausum populi, torquente eos conscientia. Damusque miseris mannam ut gaudeant ad ea quae tribuunt et non lugeant ad ea quae rapiunt. [1]

It would be foolish, of course, to argue that these considerations were not proper to twelfth century Benedictines simply as Benedictines. Doubtless they would have been of assistance to all not yet proficient in the religious life and to all with casual contact with the outside world. But it seems foolish, too, to confine them to this rôle. The least that can be said of them is that they appeal to the least angelic and most human aspect of the monastic life ; that they blur the line between the monk and the christian living in the world. In company with the other contents of these manuscripts, however, it does seem that they were meant to serve a wider and more positive end than this.

It is not possible to analyse all the codices here, but certainly many of those containing other works by Honorius, works not, like the *Elucidarius* and *Speculum Ecclesiae*, so obviously pastoral in intent, yield similar results. Examples are ZWETTL 380, LINCOLN *Cathedral Library* 199, B.M. Royal 6.A.XI, containing

---

verat ... morte morietur" (*PL* 93, col. 269), "Quatuor esse ... mittatur eternum" (col. 270), "Serpens autem ... oculus obscuretur" (col. 278-279), "Quia seculum asperum ... amisit" (col. 279). The quotations on Genesis are also to be found in the *De Sex Dierum Creatione Liber* (*PL* 93, col. 207-234). Again, information purely instructive and not susceptible of a moral interpretation is omitted.

1. Ff. 119ᵛ-120. I have lately discovered a similar collection of 'sententiae' in another *Imago Mundi* manuscript : PARIS, *Bibl. Arsenal* 93, ff. 129-139ᵛ.

the *Gemma Animae*, KREMSMÜNSTER 114, VIENNA *National-bibliothek* 1959, ADMONT 579, containing the *Sigillum* and *Neocosmum*, VIENNA *Nationalbibliothek* 953, containing the *Cognitio Vitae*. Again we find sermons and fragments of sermons, exampla, sententiae of the 'school of Laon', treatises on virtues and vices, the *De Numero*, the *Bestiary*, the *De Antichristo* of Adso, excerpts from the *Enchiridion*, *Lapidaries*, *Passiones*, miracles of the Virgin, the *Liber Scintillarum*.

A word must be said, finally, about these codices which contain a large number of the works of Honorius bound together. The two most distinguished of these are *Bodley* Lyell 56, from the Benedictine abbey of Lambach, and clm 22225 from the Premonstratensian abbey of Windberg. The two contain similar, though not identical, collections of Honorius's writings arranged, for the most part, in the same order : that is (taking those acknowledged to be his), *Cognitio Vitae, De Libero Arbitrio, De Animae Exilio et Patria, De Duodecim Questionibus, De Decem Plagis, Quid Vasa Honoris, Quid sit Claustralis Vita, Quod Monachis Liceat Predicare, Questiones Octo de Angelo et Homine, Summa Gloria, Scala Coeli Major, Sententiae Patrum, Inevitabile, Sacramentarium*. [1] The Bodley manuscript adds the *Speculum Ecclesiae* to the beginning of its collection, clm 22225 adds the *Imago Mundi* to the end. KLOSTERNEUBURG 931, containing nine treatises certainly by Honorius follows these closely. [2] All these codices have bound with the works of Honorius 'questiones' of the style of the 'school of Laon' and a shortened version of the *De Arca Noe* of Hugh of St. Victor, and the first two contain the treatises of both Rupert and Honorius on the rights of monks to preach. It appears that the larger collections again, then, had at least some bearing on the pastorate. The pattern continues in the later larger collections, for instance in two fourteenth century codices, VIENNA *Nationalbibliothek* 1165 and ST. FLORIAN XI. 54 The first has seven works of Honorius bound up with the same shortened version of the *De Arca Noe* and the *De Miseria Conditionis Humanae* of Innocent III ; the second has five, bound with Gregory's *Cura Pastoralis*. One of the five is the *Utrum Monachis Liceat Predicare*.

---

    1. For *Bodley* Lyell 56 see the superb entry in Albinia DE LA MARE : *Catalogue of the Collection of Medieval Manuscripts bequeathed to the Bodleian Library, Oxford, by James P.R. Lyell*, Oxford 1971, p. 168-174.
    2. The *Cognitio Vitae, De Libero Arbitrio, Inevitabile, Scala Coeli Major, De Animae Exilio et Patria, Libellus Octo Quaestionum, Liber Duodecim Quaestionum, Quid Vasa Honoris, De Claustrali Vita*.

This discussion of the codices which have in them the works of Honorius has been undertaken in order to suggest that his writings fit, for the most part, into a genre of books made up to serve the needs of those involved in pastoral care. I have come to believe in this genre from an independent assessment of the purposes of the *Elucidarius* and from an examination of the codices in which the *Elucidarius* appears ; and, since there does not, to my knowledge, exist any agreed definition of a twelfth century 'pastoral' codex, I have undoubtedly to some extent conjured it into being. There is, however, it seems to me at least one other method of discovering whether this is mere conjury or has a more respectable basis. This method calls into service those codices, mostly of the late fourteenth and early fifteenth centuries, which contain 'artes predicandi'. It throws, as it were, the machinery into reverse. We may perhaps suppose that at least some of the codices which contain treatises on the art of preaching were directed to the problems of pastoral care. If, then, we find that these codices are, in their general features, similar to those I have been describing, we may, then, have a little more reason to suppose that the latter also had this concern primarily in view. It may be said immediately that the two classes of codices are similar. [1] Codices containing instructions on the art of preaching contain too, almost without exception, confused collections of 'sententiae', apparently confused fragments, exempla, moral precepts, histories, short works of instruction on the Bible, thoughts on the errors of the Jews, miracles and wonders, [2] medicinal remedies, [3] the *Cura Pastoralis*, [4] the *Liber Scintillarum*, [5] the *De Arca Noe*, [6] the *De Miseria Conditionis Humanae*. More, even, than this ; some of those containing 'artes predicandi' contain also, even at this late date, a work of Honorius. Examples of this are clm 3764, 13410, *B.M.* Harley 3244, all of which have the *Elucidarius* ; GRAZ *Universitätsbibliothek* 348, the *Sententiae Patrum* and *Inevitabile* ; *B.M.* Royal 6.E.,III, the *Cognitio Vitae* ; VIENNA *Schottenstiftsbibliothek* 311, an extract from the *Speculum Eccle-*

---

1. To establish this I took the list of manuscripts cited in Th.-M. CHARLAND, *Artes Praedicandi*, Paris-Ottawa 1936, p. 414-420, and examined, where the manuscripts were not accessible to me, the catalogue entries for the relevant codices. For the direction to Charland, as for so much else, I am indebted to Dr. R.W. Hunt.
2. Clm 4784, 5106.
3. *E.g.* clm 3580, 3590, 4760, 4784.
4. Clm 5983.
5. BASEL *Universitätsbibl.* B.X.9 ; clm 19130 ; *BM* Royal 7.C.I.
6. BASEL *Universitätsbibl.* B.IX.6.

118

siae ; clm 18957 Book I of the *Imago Mundi* ; clm 26691, the commentary on the *Song of Songs*.

CONCLUSION

The place of Honorius's writings may be defined within more stringent limits, and the writings themselves reflect a greater urgency of purpose than has previously been suspected. We may narrow his immediate activities most probably to the West of England, certainly to Regensburg. Honorius worked there within the confines of a certain section of the Benedictine Order : those who wanted, without great change and in the face of mounting challenge, to maintain their influence in the church. In that part of this influence had undoubtedly rested upon their rights to tithes, and in that these were inextricably bound with a claim at least to active priesthood, to maintain it the monks had to prove their ability to undertake the reformed priestly office. Deepening criticism and intensified competition put ever greater pressures upon them to do this. Honorius's purpose was to provide the Benedictines with the means to shew themselves fitted to undertake the care of souls just where and just when they were most urgently involved in the pursuit of it.

The handlist, finally, shews that the succeeded beyond his aspirations. The scale on which the works of Honorius were copied in the twelfth century is truly astounding. The list contains two hundred and sixty five separate items. One hundred and eighty nine of these can be traced with some certainty to their original libraries. Benedictine libraries predominate ; ninety four items come from Benedictine houses. Among these, the libraries of Hirsauer houses predominate. Houses of canons, however, Augustinian and Premonstratensian, run them a very close second with thirty seven items from Augustinian libraries and eighteen from Premonstratensian. Interestingly thirty four are of Cistercian origin. Only one comes from a Carthusian house. Honorius did his job so well that he was copied not merely by the Benedictines but by their rivals and their critics. The *Speculum Ecclesiae*, for instance, had a remarkable success with both. This is in one sense the ultimate accolade. Yet, was to be 'produced' so effectively an unmixed blessing for the Benedictines ? Was there not, in the field of learning, a good deal to be said for Boto's alarm ? The place and purposes of Honorius may be not merely more definable but also more sinister than we have supposed.

HANDLIST OF SURVIVING TWELFTH CENTURY MANUSCRIPTS
OF THE WORKS OF HONORIUS AUGUSTODUNENSIS

This is a list of surviving twelfth century manuscripts of Honorius's works together with their place of origin, where these can be found. An asterisk marks those I have seen and examined. I have indicated any hesitations I have felt about their dates. Interesting items and additions or corrections to the printed catalogues are noted. The manuscripts are listed first of all under works, then by order of the countries in which they are found now.

De Animae Exilio et Patria :

HEILIGENKREUZ *Stiftsbibl.* 77 ; Heiligenkreuz.
KLOSTERNEUBURG *Stiftsbibl.* 931 ; Klosterneuburg*.
OXFORD *Bodl. Libr.* Lyell 56 ; Lambach* [1].
MUNICH *Bayer. Staatsbibl.* clm 22225 ; Windberg* [2].

De Anima et de Deo :

OXFORD *Bodl. Libr.* Lyell 58 ; Melk* [3].

In Cantica Canticorum :

BALTIMORE *Walters Art Gall.* 387 ; Lambach [4].

---

1. *Bodley* Lyell 56. Items 2-22 of this manuscript are to be found in the same order in clm 22225 ; items 5, 6, 8, 10, 11, 15, 18, 20 in HEILIGENKREUZ 77 ; items 2, 3, 5, 6, 8, 10, 11, 15, 16, 18, 20 are in KLOSTERNEUBURG 931. These are the most important collections of Honorius's works which survive from the twelfth century. It is worth noting that they are all South German and Austrian, and shared between monks and canons. Items 2, 5, 10-14, 16, 17, 30 (1) are also in the fifteenth century manuscript PRAGUE XIII.G.15 (2382). The text in the Lyell manuscript of the *Speculum Ecclesiae* is similar to that in ST. FLORIAN XI.244. There is a marginal addition (f. 18) to the sermon on the Purification (*PL* 172, col. 852) which is similar to the account of the Feast of the Purification given in the *Gemma Animae* (III, 24). Items 17, 19, 21 differ slightly from the edition printed in Migne.
2. *Clm 22225.* This can be dated exactly, 1154-1159, the abbacy of Gebhard of Windberg :
   Pastor denotus Windbergensis Gebehardus
   Abbas existens virtutibus undique florens
   Hoc opus exiguum conscribere fecit in unum.
   Pro culpe venia rogo suscipe Virgo Maria (f. 1).
The important features of it are its similarity to Lyell 56 and its unique version of the *Imago Mundi.*
3. *Bodley* Lyell 58. Three *quaestiones* in this manuscript, which may be by Honorius, are printed by ENDRES, *op. cit.*, p. 150-154. This is the only example of them I have found.
4. This is described as nᵒ 144 in J. ROSENTHAL, *Bibliotheca Medii Aevi Manuscripta* II, Munich 1928, p. 48-51. De Ricci and Wilson attribute it to Seitenstetten near Linz, but the references they give for this attribution offer, in fact, no proof. In their description of the manuscript, however, they do note that it once bore the number 94 ; cfr S. DE RICCI and W.J. WILSON, *Census of Medieval and Renaissance Manuscripts in the United States and*

XII

ADMONT *Stiftsbibl.* 436 (two books) ; Admont*.
ADMONT *Stiftsbibl.* 255 ; Admont*.
INNSBRUCK *Universitätsbibl.* 300.
KLOSTERNEUBURG *Stiftsbibl.* 766 ; Klosterneuburg*.
VIENNA *Nationalbibl.* 1023*.
VIENNA *Nationalbibl.* 1059*.
ZWETTL *Stiftsbibl.* 345 ; Zwettl*.
OXFORD *Bodl. Libr.* Lyell 69*.
TROYES *Bibl. Mun.* 544 ; Clairvaux.
VITRY-LE-FRANÇOIS *Bibl. Mun.* 42 ; Trois-Fontaines.
ERLANGEN *Universitätsbibl.* 54 ; Heilsbronn.
MUNICH *Bayer. Staatsbibl.* clm 4550 ; Benediktbeuern.
MUNICH *Bayer. Staatsbibl.* clm 5118 ; Beuerberg.
MUNICH *Bayer. Staatsbibl.* clm 17091 ; Scheftlarn.
MUNICH *Bayer. Staatsbibl.* clm 18125 ; Tegernsee.
WOLFENBÜTTEL *Herz. Aug. Bibl.* Guelf. 511 Helmst. ; Lamspring.

De Claustrali Vita :

HEILIGENKREUZ *Stiftsbibl.* 77 ; Heiligenkreuz.
KLOSTERNEUBURG *Stiftsbibl.* 931 ; Klosterneuburg*.
OXFORD *Bodl. Libr.* Lyell 56 ; Lambach*.
MUNICH *Bayer. Staatsbibl.* clm 22225 ; Windberg*.

Clavis Physicae :

ADMONT *Stiftsbibl.* 579 (fragment).
VIENNA *Nationalbibl.* Ser. nova 3605 ; Lambach*.
ZWETTL *Stiftsbibl.* 298 ; Zwettl*.
PARIS *Bibl. Nat.* lat. 6734.
LONDON *Brit. Mus.* Harley 3851.

Cognitio Vitae :

KLOSTERNEUBURG *Stiftsbibl.* 931 ; Klosterneuburg*.
MELK *Stiftsbibl.* 532 ; Melk*.
VIENNA *Nationalbibl.* 953*.
OXFORD *Bodl. Libr.* Lyell 56 ; Lambach*.
OXFORD *Bodl. Libr.* Lyell 58 ; Melk*.
MUNICH *Bayer. Staatsbibl.* clm 22225 ; Windberg*.

De Decem Plagis :

OXFORD *Bodl. Libr.* Lyell 56 ; Lambach*.
MUNICH *Bayer. Staatsbibl.* clm 22225 ; Windberg*.

Elucidarius :

YALE *Univ. Libr.* 112.
GÖTTWEIG *Stiftsbibl.* 37 (R. 99) ; Göttweig.
GRAZ *Universitätsbibl.* 1002.
KLOSTERNEUBURG *Stiftsbibl.* 793 ; Klosterneuburg*.
KREMSMÜNSTER, *Stiftsbibl.* CXXXIII ; Kremsmünster*.

Canada II, New York 1935-1940, n° 2292. The 1863 catalogue of Lambach manuscripts, at present at the abbey, lists as n° 94 a codex with the same contents exactly as this.

MELK *Stiftsbibl.* 532 (fragment) ; Melk*.
VIENNA *Nationalbibl.* 757 (part)*.
VIENNA *Nationalbibl.* 807 ; ? Schottenkloster of St. Mary* [1].
VIENNA *Nationalbibl.* 864* [2].
VIENNA *Nationalbibl.* 1999 ; Neuss.
CAMBRIDGE *Univ. Libr.* Kk.IV.6 ; Worcester* [3].
CAMBRIDGE *Corp. Christi Coll.* 439*.
GLASGOW *Univ. Libr.* 244*.
LONDON *Brit. Mus.* Royal 5.E.VI*.
LONDON *Brit. Mus.* Royal 11.A.VII*.
LONDON *Brit. Mus.* Royal 15.A.XX ; Byland*.
LONDON *Dulwich Coll.* 22 (part).
LONDON *Lambeth Pal.* 358*.
OXFORD *Bodl. Libr.* Ashmole 1524 (fragment)*.
OXFORD *Bodl. Libr.* Fairfax 26*.
OXFORD *Bodl. Libr.* Lat. Th. e 9 (part) ; Flanesford*.
OXFORD *Bodl. Libr.* Laud Misc. 237 ; Eberbach*.
AMIENS *Bibl. Mun.* Lescalopier 31.
ANGERS *Bibl. Mun.* 213.
ANGERS *Bibl. Mun.* 296 ; Toussaints.
GRENOBLE *Bibl. Mun.* 272 ; Grande-Chartreuse.
LIÈGE *Bibl. Univ.* 164.
PARIS *Bibl. Arsenal* 371 ; Micy*.
PARIS *Bibl. Nat.* lat. 2155 and 3358 (one ms.) ; Moissac or Villencourt.
PARIS *Bibl. Nat.* lat. 2877 ; St. Martial of Limoges.
PARIS *Bibl. Nat.* lat. 2879.
PARIS *Bibl. Nat.* lat. 5134.
PARIS *Bibl. Nat.* lat. 10729.
PARIS *Bibl. Nat.* lat. 12315 ; Corbie.
PARIS *Bibl. Nat.* lat. 14985.
TOURS *Bibl. Mun.* 472 (fragment) ; Marmoutiers.
TROYES *Bibl. Mun.* 1429.
TROYES *Bibl. Mun.* 1547.
VERDUN *Bibl. Mun.* 54 ; St. Vanne.
BERLIN *Deutsche Staatsbibl.* Phill. 1695.
DRESDEN *Sächs. Landesbibl.* J.51 [4].
ERLANGEN *Universitätsbibl.* 216.
ERFURT *Wiss. Allgem. Bibl.* Amplon. 0-22.
KLAGENFURT *Studienbibl.* Perg. 3 ; Millstatt.
MUNICH *Bayer. Staatsbibl.* clm 13105 ; Prüfening* [5].

1. This manuscript, I have already tried to suggest, may have been the one mentioned as 'bene correctum' in the gift of Frater Heinricus. The text has the later variant for II, 7, and a series of marginal additions which are, without exception, drawn from the last recension of the *Elucidarius.* Cfr V.I.J. FLINT, *The Career of Honorius Augustodunensis. Some fresh Evidence,* in *Rev. bénéd.* 82 (1972), p. 68-69.
2. The *Elucidarius* was not originally bound with this collection.
3. The *Elucidarius* is followed in this manuscript by another set of questions and answers (ff. 60-62ᵛ). They are printed by J.-B. PITRA, *Analecta Sacra Spicilegio Solesmensi Parata* V, Paris 1888, p. 160.
4. War damage has rendered all but about thirty folios of this illegible.
5. This manuscript is discussed by A. BOECKLER, *Die Regensburg-Prüfeninger*

MUNICH *Bayer. Staatsbibl.* clm 14348 ; St. Emmeram's Regensburg*.
MUNICH *Bayer. Staatsbibl.* clm 16057.
DUBLIN *Trinity Coll.* 279 ; Rievaulx*.
PADUA *Bibl. Antoniana* Scaff. XXII.534.
BASEL *Universitätsbibl.* B.VIII.23 (fragment).

Eucharisticon :
HEILIGENKREUZ *Stiftsbibl.* 215 ; Heiligenkreuz.
VIENNA *Nationalbibl.* 863 ; ? St. Emmeram's Regensburg* [1].
ERLANGEN *Universitätsbibl.* 227 ; Heilsbronn.

Expositio Psalterii :
SALZBURG *St. Peter's Stiftsbibl.* a.IX.5 (second book)*.
VIENNA *Nationalbibl.* 910 (second book)*.
ERLANGEN *Universitätsbibl.* 51 ; Heilsbronn.
MUNICH *Bayer. Staatsbibl.* clm 4536 ; Benediktbeuern*.
MUNICH *Bayer Staatsbibl.* clm 5117 ; Beuerberg*.

Gemma Animae :
ADMONT *Stiftsbibl.* 366 ; Admont*.
GRAZ *Universitätsbibl.* 149 ; St. Lambrecht.
GRAZ *Universitätsbibl.* 768 ; Seckau.
GRAZ *Universitätsbibl.* 804 ; Millstatt.
GRAZ *Universitätsbibl.* 806 ; St. Lambrecht.
HOHENFURTH *Stiftsbibl.* 117 ; Hohenfurth.
KLOSTERNEUBURG *Stiftsbibl.* 580 (to I.CLV) ; Klosterneuburg*.
LINZ *Studienbibl.* 385.
LAMBACH *Stiftsbibl.* 35 ; Lambach*.
VIENNA *Nationalbibl.* 801* [2].
VIENNA *Nationalbibl.* 1025* [3].
VIENNA *Nationalbibl.* 1321 (to I.CIX)*.
ZWETTL *Stiftsbibl.* 380 ; Zwettl*.
PRAGUE *Univ. Bibl.* XIII.F.20 (2358)*.
CAMBRIDGE *Corp. Christi Coll.* 319 ; *Lessness*.
HEREFORD *Cathedral Libr.* O.I.V.
LINCOLN *Cathedral Libr.* 217*.

Buchmalerei des XII. und XIII. Jahrhunderts, Munich 1924, p. 125, 129. He marks the appearance of the *Inevitabile* and *Offendiculum* in the catalogue of 1140, and the *Elucidarius* in that of 1165. For later manuscripts of the *Elucidarius* see H. DÜWELL, *Noch nicht untersuchte Handschriften des 'Elucidarium' von Honorius Augustodunensis*, in *Scriptorium* 26 (1972), p. 337-342. I am indebted to Dr. Düwell, too, for some of the references to the twelfth century ones.

1. The first item in this collection, which is unidentified in the catalogue, is the *De Sacramento Altaris* of William of St. Thierry (*PL* 180, col. 341-366). This work is bound with the *Eucharisticon* in ERLANGEN 227 also.

2. This has (f. 67) the addition beginning 'Ecce filie hierusalem' noticed by ENDRES, *op. cit.*, p. 39-40. VIENNA *NB* 1025 and PARIS *BN* nouv. acq. lat. 363 have it also.

3. The last sentence of the *Gemma Animae* is written in a form very like that of the so-called anathema verse of manuscripts from Prüfening. Cfr BOECKLER, *op. cit.*, p. 10.

LINCOLN *Cathedral Libr.* 199 ; Heynings*.
LONDON *Brit. Mus.* Royal 6.A.XI ; Rochester*.
LONDON *Brit. Mus.* Royal 6.E.II*.
PARIS *Bibl. Nat.* nouv. acq. lat. 363.
PARIS *Bibl. Nat.* lat. 11579.
PARIS *Bibl. Nat.* lat. 13218.
ERLANGEN *Universitätsbibl.* 184 (extracts) ; Heilsbronn.
GOTHA *Forschungsbibl.* Membr. I.72.
MUNICH *Bayer. Staatsbibl.* clm 7974 ; Kaisheim*.
ROME *Bibl. Vat.* Reg. lat. 328.

Hexaemeron :

BALTIMORE *Walters Art Gall.* 387 ; Lambach.
ADMONT *Stiftsbibl.* 579 ; Admont*.
MELK *Stiftsbibl.* 532 ; Melk*.
Vienna *Nationalbibl.* 1023*.
MUNICH *Bayer. Staatsbibl.* clm 4550 ; Benediktbeuern*.
MUNICH *Bayer. Staatsbibl.* clm 4625 ; Benediktbeuern*.
MUNICH *Bayer. Staatsbibl.* clm 5118 ; Beuerberg*.
MUNICH *Bayer. Staatsbibl.* clm 17091 ; Scheftlarn*.

Imago Mundi :

NEW YORK *Pierpont Morgan Libr.* 81 (fragment) ; Radford* [1].
ADMONT *Stiftsbibl.* 400 ; Admont*.
GÖTTWEIG *Stiftsbibl.* 46 ; Göttweig*.
MELK *Stiftsbibl.* 248 ; Melk*.
SALZBURG *St. Peter's Stiftsbibl.* a.IX.1 ; St. Peter's*.
VIENNA *Nationalbibl.* 427 (book III).
VIENNA *Nationalbibl.* 507*.
VIENNA *Nationalbibl.* 539*.
VIENNA *Nationalbibl.* 818 ; ? Mondsee*.
VIENNA *Nationalbibl.* 2479*.
ZWETTL *Stiftsbibl.* 172 ; ? Zwettl*.
BRUSSELS *Bibl. Royale* 10862-5* [2].
CAMBRIDGE *Corp. Christi Coll.* 66 ; Sawley* (? early thirteenth cent.)
LONDON *Brit. Mus.* Add. 38665 ; Kenilworth*.
LONDON *Brit. Mus.* Royal 12.C.XIX (fragment)* [3].
LONDON *Brit. Mus.* Royal 13.A.XXI ; Hagneby*.
LONDON *Brit. Mus.* Harley 4348 ; St. Mary's-outside-the-walls Trier*.
LONDON *Brit. Mus.* Cotton Cleopatra B.IV ; Byland*.
OXFORD *Bodl. Libr.* Rawlinson B.434 (I, IV-XXXVI) ; Winchester*.
PARIS *Bibl. Arsenal* 93 (part) ; ? St. Victor*.
PARIS *Bibl. Mazarine* 708*.

---

1. This was given to the Augustinian Priory of Radford, near Worksop, by Philip, canon of Lincoln. It very closely resembles *BM* Royal 12.C.XIX.
2. According to the catalogue the *Imago Mundi* ends on f. 166ᵛ. It in fact ends at f. 139ᵛ and is followed by the *De Libero Arbitrio* and the *Inevitabile* (second recension).
3. See above, n. 1. I am indebted to Dr. M.-O. Garrigues for discovering for me two of the Paris manuscripts I mention, *Bibl. Arsenal* 93 and *BN* lat. 6560.

124

PARIS *Bibl. Nat.* lat. 6560*.
PARIS *Bibl. Nat.* lat. 11130 (books I-II)*.
PARIS *Bibl. Nat.* lat. 15009 ; St. Victor (? early thirteenth cent.)*.
BERLIN *Deutsche Staatsbibl. Preuss. Kult.* 956 (lat. fol. 307) (fragment) ;
    Havelberg.
FULDA *Hess. Landesbibl.* B.3 (book III) ; Weingarten*.
MUNICH *Bayer. Staatsbibl.* 536 ; Prül*.
MUNICH *Bayer. Staatsbibl.* 7793 ; Indersdorf*.
MUNICH *Bayer. Staatsbibl.* 7974 ; Kaisheim*.
MUNICH *Bayer. Staatsbibl.* 11336 ; Polling*.
MUNICH *Bayer. Staatsbibl.* 14348 ; St. Emmeram's Regensburg*.
MUNICH *Bayer. Staatsbibl.* 14731 ; St. Emmeram's Regensburg*.
MUNICH *Bayer. Staatsbibl.* 18918 (part of book III) ; Tegernsee*.
MUNICH *Bayer. Staatsbibl.* 22225 ; Windberg*.
STUTTGART *Württemb. Landesbibl.* Hist. Q155 ; Comburg*.
ROME *Bibl. Vat.* Reg. lat. 471 ; St. Mary's Stolp* [1].
ROME *Bibl. Vat.* Vat. lat. 1890*.
UPSALA *Universitetsbibl.* C. 699 ; St. Mary's Colbaz*.
VIENNA *Nationalbibl.* 1180.

Inevitabile :

HEILIGENKREUZ *Stiftsbibl.* 77 ; Heiligenkreuz*.
KREMSMÜNSTER *Stiftsbibl.* CXXXIII ; Kremsmünster*.
MELK *Stiftsbibl.* 532 (excerpts) ; Melk*.
BRUSSELS *Bibl. Royale* 10862-5*.
OXFORD *Bodl. Libr.* Laud Misc. 237 ; Eberbach*.
OXFORD *Bodl. Libr.* Lyell 56 ; Lambach*.
OXFORD *Bodl. Libr.* Lyell 58 (extracts) ; Melk*.
PARIS *Bibl. Nat.* lat. 2878.
ERLANGEN *Universitätsbibl.* 227 ; Heilsbronn.
MUNICH *Bayer. Staatsbibl.* clm 13105 ; Prüfening*.
MUNICH *Bayer. Staatsbibl.* clm 14348 ; St. Emmeram's Regensburg*.
MUNICH *Bayer. Staatsbibl.* clm 22225 ; Windberg*.
LEIDEN *Rijksbibl.* Vulc. 100 ; St. Pantaleon*.

De Libero Arbitrio :

HEILIGENKREUZ *Stiftsbibl.* 77 ; Heiligenkreuz*.
KLOSTERNEUBURG *Stiftsbibl.* 931 ; Klosterneuburg*.
ZWETTL *Stiftsbibl.* 298 ; Zwettl*.
BRUSSELS *Bibl. Royale* 10862-5*.
OXFORD *Bodl. Libr.* Lyell 56 ; Lambach*.
MUNICH *Bayer. Staatsbibl.* clm 22225 ; Windberg*.

De Luminaribus :

KLOSTERNEUBURG *Stiftsbibl.* 949 ; Klosterneuburg*.
ST. FLORIAN *Stiftsbibl.* XI.252 ; St. Florian.
ZWETTL *Stiftsbibl.* 225 ; Zwettl*.

1. In this manuscript the *Imago Mundi* is immediately followed by a passage beginning 'Eneas antenor Priamus fugerit de trois...'. Also bound with it are the *Libellus de VII miraculis mundi* and the *Adversus Paganos* of Orosius. In all this it is exactly like UPSALA C. 699.

Offendiculum :
KREMSMÜNSTER *Stiftsbibl.* CXXXIII ; Kremsmünster.*
MUNICH *Bayer. Staatsbibl.* 13105 ; Prüfening*.
LEIDEN *Rijksbibl.* Vulc. 100 ; St. Pantaleon*.

Questiones VIII & XII :
HEILIGENKREUZ *Stiftsbibl.* 77 ; Heiligenkreuz*.
KLOSTERNEUBURG *Stiftsbibl.* 931 ; Klosterneuburg*.
ZWETTL *Stiftsbibl.* 298 (fragment) ; Zwettl*.
OXFORD *Bodl. Libr.* Lyell 56 ; Lambach*.
DIJON *Bibl. Mun.* 42 (XII.Q) ; Cîteaux.
PARIS *Bibl. Nat.* lat. 15732.
MUNICH *Bayer. Staatsbibl.* clm 22225 ; Windberg*.

Questiones in Joannem, Mattheum, Proverbia, Ecclesiasten :
VIENNA *Nationalbibl.* 807 ; ? Schottenstift of St. Mary*.
ZWETTL *Stiftsbibl.* 73 ; Zwettl*.

Quid Vasa Honoris :
HEILIGENKREUZ *Stiftsbibl.* 77 ; Heiligenkreuz*.
KLOSTERNEUBURG *Stiftsbibl.* 931 ; Klosterneuburg*.
OXFORD *Bodl. Libr.* Lyell 56 ; Lambach*.
MUNICH *Bayer. Staatsbibl.* clm 22225 ; Windberg*.

Quod Monachis Liceat Predicare :
OXFORD *Bodl. Libr.* Lyell 56 ; Lambach*.
MUNICH *Bayer. Staatsbibl.* clm 22225 ; Windberg*.

Sacramentarium :
OXFORD *Bodl. Libr.* Lyell 56 ; Lambach*.
MUNICH *Bayer. Staatsbibl.* clm 22225 ; Windberg*.

Scala Coeli Major :
HEILIGENKREUZ *Stiftsbibl.* 77 ; Heiligenkreuz*.
KLOSTERNEUBURG *Stiftsbibl.* 931 ; Klosterneuburg*.
OXFORD *Bodl. Libr.* Lyell 56 ; Lambach*.
MUNICH *Bayer. Staatsbibl.* clm 22225 ; Windberg*.

Scala Coeli Minor :
OXFORD *Bodl. Libr.* Lyell 56 ; Lambach*.
MUNICH *Bayer. Staatsbibl.* clm 22225 ; Windberg*.

Sigillum :
BALTIMORE *Walters Art Gall.* 387 ; Lambach.
ADMONT *Stiftsbibl.* 579 ; Admont*.
INNSBRUCK *Universitätsbibl.* 300.
KREMSMÜNSTER *Stiftsbibl.* CXIV ; Kremsmünster*.
VIENNA *Nationalbibl.* 1023*.
VIENNA *Nationalbibl.* 1059*.
CAMBRIDGE *Univ. Libr.* Kk.IV.6 ; Worcester*.

LONDON *Brit. Mus.* Royal 4.C.XI (part) ; Worcester* [1].
OXFORD *Jesus Coll.* 54 ; Evesham* [2].
OXFORD *Merton Coll.* 181 ; Malmesbury*.
WORCESTER *Cathedral Libr.* Q.66 (part) ; Worcester* [3].
MUNICH *Bayer. Staatsbibl.* clm 4550 ; Benediktbeuern*.
MUNICH *Bayer. Staatsbibl.* clm 5118 ; Beuerberg*.
MUNICH *Bayer. Staatsbibl.* clm 17091 ; Scheftlarn*.
MUNICH *Bayer. Staatsbibl.* clm 18125 ; Tegernsee*.

Speculum Ecclesiae :
ADMONT *Stiftsbibl.* 131 ; Admont*.
GÖTTWEIG *Stiftsbibl.* 47 (R.104) ; Göttweig*.
KLOSTERNEUBURG *Stiftsbibl.* 478 ; Klosterneuburg*.
KLOSTERNEUBURG *Stiftsbibl.* 480 ; Klosterneuburg*.
KLOSTERNEUBURG *Stiftsbibl.* 1118 (extracts) ; Klosterneuburg*.
KREMSMÜNSTER *Stiftsbibl.* CXXII ; Kremsmünster*.
ST. FLORIAN *Stiftsbibl.* 244 ; St. Florian.
ST. FLORIAN *Stiftsbibl.* 251 ; St. Florian.
SALZBURG *Universitätsbibl.* M.I.34*.
VIENNA *Nationalbibl.* 880* [4].
VIENNA *Nationalbibl.* 950*.
VORAU *Stiftsbibl.* 167 ; Vorau.
VORAU *Stiftsbibl.* 179 ; Vorau.
OXFORD *Bodl. Libr.* Lyell 56 ; Lambach*.
PARIS *Bibl. Arsenal* 518*.
AUGSBURG *Bischöffl. Ordinariatsbibl.* 11 (excerpts).
ERLANGEN *Universitätsbibl.* 279 ; Heilsbronn.
ERLANGEN *Universitätsbibl.* 280 (part I) ; Heilsbronn.
ERLANGEN *Universitätsbibl.* 281 (part II) ; Heilsbronn.
MUNICH *Bayer. Staatsbibl.* clm 4580 ; Benediktbeuern*.
MUNICH *Bayer. Staatsbibl.* clm 4590*.
MUNICH *Bayer. Staatsbibl.* clm 5515 ; Diessen*.
MUNICH *Bayer. Staatsbibl.* clm 7700 ; Indersdorf*.
MUNICH *Bayer. Staatsbibl.* clm 16022*.
MUNICH *Bayer. Staatsbibl.* clm 18698 ; Tegernsee*.
WÜRZBURG *Universitätsbibl.* Mp. th. f. 76.
LENINGRAD *Publ. Libr.* Irm. lat. 22.

---

1. The two Worcester copies of the *Sigillum*, this one and WORCESTER Q. 66, are practically complementary. The first ends at 'consecrat' (f. 240 ; *PL* 172, col. 499), the second begins at 'Gloriosa virginis' (f. 145 ; *PL* 172, col. 499). Both are inserted later into the last folios of the codices in which they appear.
2. This is the earliest extant copy of the *Sigillum* and was once in the collection of Sir John Prise ; cfr N.R. KER, *Sir John Prise*, in *The Library* 10, (1955), p. 9. On f. 1 is written, in an early twelfth century hand, 'Nobilis henrici cuius pereunt inimici'.
3. See above, n. 1.
4. This manuscript, and VIENNA 950, supply the lack in Migne noticed by J. KELLE, *Untersuchungen über das 'Speculum Ecclesiae' des Honorius und die 'Libri Deflorationum' des Abtes Werner*, in *Sitzungsberichte der Kaiserlichen Akademie der Wissenschaften* 145 (1902), p. 2 ff.

St. Gall *Stiftsbibl.* 1075 ; St. Gall.
Zurich *Zentralbibl.* Rh. 33 ; Rheinau.

   Summa Gloria :

Oxford *Bodl Libr.* Lyell 56 ; Lambach*.
Paris *Bibl. Arsenal* 93 ; ? St. Victor*.
Munich *Bayer. Staatsbibl.* clm 22225 ; Windberg*.

   Summa Totius :

Vienna *Nationalbibl.* 382 ; Lambach*.

The University of Auckland
(New Zealand).

XIII

World history in the early twelfth century; the 'Imago Mundi' of Honorius Augustodunensis

I

THE *Imago Mundi* of Honorius Augustodunensis was, in the twelfth century, enormously popular. Twenty surviving twelfth-century manuscripts of the whole text are known to me now; a further nineteen of parts and fragments may be added to that number.[1] The whole was issued, I think, in 1110, and was revised by its author three times, in 1123, 1133, and 1139 respectively.[2] The work was written in South Germany, most probably at St. Emmeramm's in Regensburg, and the most important of the surviving manuscripts come from the areas of South Germany and Austria.[3] An early

[1] A provisional list of the surviving twelfth-century manuscripts of the *Imago Mundi*, both complete and incomplete texts, is set out in the appendix to V. I. J. Flint, 'The place and purpose of the works of Honorius Augustodunensis', *Rev. bén.*, 87 (1977), pp. 123–4. The present paper was completed with the help of the Humanities Research Centre, A.N.U., Canberra, and the Research Committee of the University of Auckland. I am grateful to both, and, once again, to the care and advice of my colleague, Philip Rousseau.

[2] Here I differ from Wilmanns, *MGH, Scriptores*, x. pp. 127–8. A part of the material which has led me to the conclusion that the work was written in 1110 and reissued in only three recensions ascribable to Honorius himself will be set out below. I hope to set out the rest more fully in my forthcoming edition. Wilmanns printed that section of Book III which dealt with the sixth age and had items of German interest. The whole text of the *Imago Mundi* was last printed in *PL* 172, cols 115–88. All detailed references will be to the chapters and pages of this edition.

[3] The suspicion that it was written in Regensburg comes from the specific entry (of a kind which is rare) in the section dealing with Bavaria (Book I, xxiv) 'in qua est civitas Ratispona'. It is supported in general by the distribution of the surviving twelfth-century manuscripts.

World history in the early twelfth century; the 'Imago Mundi'

form of the text, however, circulated in England, where Honorius may also have spent an early part of his career.[1]

The plan was not unambitious; the work covers space and time and the history of man. It was meant, furthermore, to be consulted easily and to save its readers time and effort. This fact its author drives home.[2] He insists too that he saves his readers time in order to direct them to truth; a truth that is firmly traditional and equally firmly Christian.[3] Ease of consultation implies, indeed requires, the sacrifice of questioning, of novelty, and, above all, of non-Christian criticism. This once accepted, the rewards appear to be great. The information supplied is most carefully compiled and most easy to assimilate in detail; and one may be sure that it will not lead one into deep and difficult waters.

The treatise is composed of three books. It is subdivided, in the best manuscripts, into some three hundred carefully headed chapters. Book I deals with the constitution and geography of the known world, with some confident glimpses into the unknown, then the composition and disposition of the further elements of water, air, and fire. The planets, zodiac, and constellations claim attention next. The geography, beginning with the four rivers of paradise, is underlaid by biblical geography. The discussion of the elements owes much to the work of biblical scholars—Isidore, Bede, and Rabanus. Book II describes the time of the world and of the heavens with its liturgical and secular measurements. It adds practical advice on the computus and guides to the major ecclesiastical feasts. The same three scholars, with Helpericus, are here in evidence again. Book III is a world history, and it is with this that we shall be chiefly here

[1] V. I. J. Flint, 'The career of Honorius Augustodunensis', *Rev. bén.*, 82 (1972), pp. 75–80.

[2] The short passage dilating upon Honorius's labours, beginning 'Rogo te lector' and printed by Migne (*PL* 172, col. 197) as a preface to the *De Luminaribus* is in fact attached, in fifteen of the thirty-nine surviving twelfth-century manuscripts I have mentioned, to the *Imago Mundi*.

[3] The first prefatory letter begins with tributes to the sevenfold spirit and the Trinity. The second ends with a tribute to tradition. 'Nihil autem in eo pono, nisi quod majorum commendat traditio.' *PL* 172, col. 120.

XIII

concerned. It was an integral part of the treatise from the beginning.[1] It recounts, in the briefest outline, the pre-history and history of the human race. It begins with the fall of the angels, and proceeds with the creation and the fall of man. It extends the story through the kingdoms of antiquity and the Old Testament, to the Roman Empire, then the German, the direct successor to the Roman.

Book III is constructed in accordance with a highly traditional Christian plan, the plan, that is, of the six ages of the world, and it uses sources upon which, within a structure of this kind, one would expect Honorius to draw. Genesis, Numbers, Orosius, Eusebius-Jerome, Isidore, Cassiodorus, Bede, the *Historia Miscella*, Frutolf of Michelsberg provide in their chronicles almost all the material Honorius needs for his account of the first five ages. For the sixth he supplements this by drawing upon Hermannus Contractus, both the *Chronicon* and the *Compendium Bernoldi*, and perhaps upon an early text of the *Chronicon Wirziburgense*.

The annexation of an historical section to a geographical and computistical treatise seems to have no surprises to offer. The composition of Easter Tables involved, after all, so often the addition of historical information in the convenient spaces provided. Examples of this are legion. The *Annales Majores* of St. Emmeramm's are themselves to be found in a ninth-century codex containing computistical information, and a more famous Munich compu-tistical collection, also from St. Emmeramm's, contains (ff. 1–7) a short chronicle and the *Annales Minores* of the abbey.[2] Special stimuli towards the compiling of histories of the deeds of men as an extension

[1] I have found the whole or parts of Books I and II without any part of Book III in only four of the thirty-nine twelfth-century texts I have examined that is, in MSS BL, London, Royal 12 C xix, Pierpont Morgan Library, New York, 107, BN, Paris, Lat. 11130, Bibl. Vat., Rome, Lat. 1890.

[2] Bayerische Staatsbibliothek, Munich, clm. 14456 and 210. Famous English examples of such a combination in manuscripts of the eleventh and twelfth centuries are to be found in MS St. John's College, Oxford, 17, in MSS BL, London, Cotton Caligula A xv, Cotton Nero C v, Harley 3667, 3859, in MSS St. John's College, Cambridge, 22, Trinity College, Cambridge, 884, 1369. For a discussion of the first and of some other examples see C. Hart, 'The Ramsey Computus', *EHR*, 85 (1970), pp. 29–44.

[213]

XIII

World history in the early twelfth century; the 'Imago Mundi'

of exegesis of the Bible were to the fore, furthermore, just when
Honorius was writing. The great master Anselm of Laon (d. 1117)
gave particular attention to the book of Genesis[1] and Hugh of St.
Victor singled out the literal/historical interpretation both of the
historical books of the Bible and of the others, for special emphasis in
his *Didascalicon*.[2] These attentions were accompanied by an enormous
increase in that type of historical writing which took the form, on
the model of Orosius, of a world chronicle *ab initio peccati hominis*.
This form was especially prevalent in Germany[3] and Honorius
contributed to it in his own *Summa Totius*, a treatise which begins
with a disquisition on the books of Holy Scripture and proceeds
with the history of man from the fall. Wilmanns rightly thought
that Book III of the *Imago Mundi* was in part an epitome of this.
An interesting outcrop of historical writing of this kind was to be
found in the West of England, in that version of the *Universal
Chronicle* of Marianus Scotus of Mainz which Robert bishop of
Hereford (1079–95) had imported and which John of Worcester
extended. Marianus constructed his history within a revised computistical framework. One of the most important manuscripts of
the *Imago Mundi*, furthermore, MS Corpus Christi College,
Cambridge, 66, both shows asssociations with Hereford and connects the author of the text with Mainz.[4] We seem to have in all

[1] Many of the *sentences* attributed to him have reference to this book, for
example, those printed by Lottin; O. Lottin, *Psychologie et morale aux xii*e
*et xiii*e *siècles*, v (Louvain, 1959), pp. 30, 36–41, 44–5.
[2] C. H. Buttimer (ed.), *Hugonis de Sancto Victore Didascalicon de Studio
Legendi* (Washington, 1939), VI, iii.
[3] M. Manitius, *Geschichte der Lateinischen Literatur des Mittelalters*, iii (Munich,
1931), p. 320. An admirable study of the history of the world chronicle is
provided in A. von den Brincken, *Studien zur Lateinischen Weltchronistik bis
in das Zeitalter Ottos von Freising* (Dusseldorf, 1957).
[4] The Mappa Mundi which prefaces the text of the *Imago Mundi* in Corpus
66 has long been known to be related to the Hereford Map. W. L. Bevan
and H. W. Phillott, *Medieval Geography. An Essay in Illustration of the Hereford
Mappa Mundi* (London, 1874), pp. xxxvi–xxxix. The relevant passage reads
as follows: 'Iste Henricus qui hunc librum edidit fuit canonicus ecclesiae sancte
marie civitatis Magontie, in qua ecclesia sunt canonici seculares bis quater
quaterdeni.' Henricus was perhaps Honorius's real name; V. I. J. Flint, 'The
Career of Honorius', pp. 63–75.

[214]

this an apotheosis of that tradition within which the historical section of the *Imago Mundi* was formed.

We know, finally, that the computus was, in the twelfth century, considered essential equipment for a priest.[1] It is possible that the historical notes which went with it so often were intended to serve as a *philacterium* for a longer story; one suitably edifying for an audience.[2] Honorius was deeply concerned for the office and the efficacy of the priest. The addition of a history to a computus and a Christian geography makes excellent sense within the context we may reconstruct for the *Imago Mundi*, and one of the functions of Book III may have been as a *recapitulatio*, most probably of the *Summa Totius*, for the use of the priest in the movement for ecclesiastical reform.

Book III appears, then, a somewhat unremarkable piece of work. The project was a grand one, but it had been tried before. The realization of it was meticulous; but meticulousness of detail and simplicity of expression are characteristics of all of Honorius's works. It was not the most ambitious of historical enterprises, even of those of Honorius, and it was a part of a tradition we can readily describe. One may well ask, then, by what right it claims attention here. The rights, I would contend, are very many, and their discussion forms the substance of this paper. Book III was not the largest effort of Honorius at history, but it was by far the most popular.[3] There may be something to be learnt from this. The text of the *Imago Mundi*, Book III as well, appears quite unexceptional; the context of Book III completely suitable. There is very much more to be learnt, I

[1] Gratian numbers a computus among the books without which a priest is scarcely worthy of the name. E. Friedberg, *Decretum Magistri Gratiani* (Leipsig, 1879), Prima Pars, Dist. xxxviii, c. 5, pp. 141-2.
[2] Bede says of his own chronological recapitulation that it was written 'ob memoriam conservandam'. B. Colgrave and R. A. B. Mynors (ed.), *Bede's Ecclesiastical History of the English People* (Oxford, 1969), v, 24, p. 560. The close relationship between this *recapitulatio* and Easter Annals is discussed by C. W. Jones, *Saints Lives and Chronicles* (Ithaca, 1947), pp. 31-8.
[3] Only one twelfth-century copy of the *Summa Totius* survives, MS Österreichische Nationalbibliothek, Vienna, 382, and this is incomplete.

think, than this. There is certainly more to be learnt about the text, to which we will turn in the next section. There may then be more to be seen in the context, to which we will turn in sections 3 and 4. Book III, I will contend, fits into the whole so snugly now because our knowledge of the whole is incomplete. There are gaps in our present understanding of this context, and there are traps in that simplicity so characteristic of Honorius's work. The place of Book III of the *Imago Mundi* may emerge as almost the opposite of that which I have so far described for it. Far from being a mere historical annex, and to be dismissed as such, it may be treated as a source for the illumination of our understanding of a whole genre of medieval historical writing. This is a large claim to make; but it may prompt further enquiry, not least by myself.

2

The changes between the original text of the *Imago Mundi* and the three recensions which cover the period 1110 to 1139 are marked by, among other things, internal variants to the text. The variants are distributed throughout the books but fall by subject into the following simple categories. There are variants dealing with alternative computistical methods, variants giving information about wells to which certain extraordinary characteristics are attached, variants telling of remarkable stones and metals and animals, variant mythical stories about the constellations, variants dealing with weather forecasting and the horizon, and, in the historical section, variants dealing with the deaths of emperors. The original text was gradually expanded by the addition of information concerned exclusively with these matters. A few examples of these preoccupations may be given.[1] To Book I xiii the recension of 1123 adds the following sentence:

India quoque magnetem lapidem gignit, qui ferum rapit, adamantem etiam, qui non nisi hircino sanguine frangi poterit.

---

[1] I omit, for reasons of space, the computistical variants, the weather signs, and II xxv De Orizonte (added in 1133).

To I xiv this:

Persida lapidem pyrrhitem mittit, qui manum prementis urit, et sinelitem cuius candor cum luna crescit et deficit.

To I xix this:

in hac equae a vento concipiunt sed foetus non amplius triennio vivunt.

To I xxvii this:

Arcadia arbeston lapidem mittit, qui semel accensus extingui non potest. In Epiro est fons in quo faces accessae extinguuntur, et interum extinctae accenduntur . . .

To I cxxvi it adds to the sentence on Anticanis:

qui canis Orionis fertur, et ob insigne meritum inter sidera locatur.

In I xxxiii, to the section on the Garamantes we have added:

Apud quos est fons tam frigidus diebus ut non bibatur, tam frigidus noctibus ut non tangatur.[1]

The same recension varies the information given in the original text about the signs of the zodiac Cancer and Scorpio and about the star Delphinus. The original text of I xcv (as opposed to that which Migne prints and the 1123 recension adopts), for example, reads, for its first sentence:

Quartum est cancer, qui maximum a neptuno hominibus inmissus a perseo interemptus, ob insigne inter sidera est translatus.

Of I xcix:

Octavum est scorpius, qui maximus Orionem percussit dum bestias terrae occidit, et ob terrae gratiam astra meruit.

Of I cxix:

Cui coniungitur Delfinus, qui arionem chicaristam de piratis eripuit.[2]

---

[1] I take the text of this recension from one of the best manuscripts containing it, that is MS BL, London, Cotton Cleopatra B iv.

[2] For these variants I rely on one of the best copies of the original text, MS Corpus Christi College, Cambridge, 66.

World history in the early twelfth century; the 'Imago Mundi'

The variant passages are carried into the successive recensions. One variant which distinguishes two later copies of that which I take to be the earliest form of the text (MS Corpus Christi College, Cambridge, 66 and MS BL, London, Royal 13 A xxi) concerns the signs of the zodiac. Seven of these, in the Royal manuscript, are given a consciously Christian and, in some cases, a consciously natural explanation. They begin on folio 20 of the text, immediately after I xcviii, and read:

Primum signum est aries, eo quod Abraham optulit arietem pro Ysaac filio sui. Vel quia aries habet longa cornua de capite procedentia, ita sol in illo mense extendit radios suos. Vel sicut sol vadit ad dextrum maris ionium, ita aries iacet super latus dextrum in marcio, ut dicit Beda.

Secundun signum est taurus, eo quod Iacob sicut taurus luctavit cum angelo usque mane dum benediceret ipsum.

Tercius est gemini, eo quod Adam et Eva de uno corpore facti sunt.

Quartum est Cancrus, pro eo quod Iacob cancerius sum librum pensavit.

Quintum est leo, pro eo quod Daniel in lacu leonum fuit.

Sextum est virgo, pro eo quod tempus illud est sterile sicut virgo intacta.

Septimum est libra, eo quod Iudas Scarioth pretium sanguinis accepit. Vel quod in illo mensium est equinoctium.

After the seven intrusions the text continues with I xcix.

A still later recension, dateable tentatively to 1133, maintains the interest in stones and wells and stars, adds computistical material and adds material of a far more grisly kind. In the short accounts of reigns of Roman emperors, given in Book III, there appears, sometimes above the written text, sometimes incorporated within it, specific information about the ways in which the emperors met their ends. Excellent examples of this type of addition are to be found in MS Stiftsbibliothek Zwettl, 172. Thus, for example, to the record of the reign of Antoninus Pius it adds the information 'morbo obiit' and 'similiter id est morbo' to that of Marcus Antoninus Verus. Again, to the records of Constantius, Constantine and Constans are added respectively the legends, 'dolore periit',

'occiditur a fratre Constante', and 'hic in Hispania occiditur'.
Similarly, to the entries for Constantius and Galerius Maximus we
have added 'In Anglia moritur' and 'seipsum interfecit'.[1] This
attention to the deaths of emperors is to be found in the *Summa
Totius* too.[2]

A close examination of the manuscripts has revealed one other
feature which, whilst not distinguishing the recensions, is none the
less striking enough to be worthy of note. The chapter on the planet
Saturn (I lxxvi) is the object of a great deal of attention. The
sentence 'In cuius exortu post triginta annos qui imaginem de aere
fuderit, loqui ut hominem probabit', is very frequently displaced.

We may, of course, attribute many of these additions and attentions to the discovery of new material[3] or to the chance vagaries of
scribes. There is more to be said, however, than this. For one thing,
much of the added information is readily to be found in the *De
Civitate Dei* of St. Augustine,[4] a text Honorius knew well in 1100
and one upon which he can hardly therefore be supposed to have
fallen accidentally in 1123. Secondly, and far more importantly, the
material is linked by nature. We are in a world of calculation by the
sun and by the moon, a world which looks to the stars and, with

---

[1] *PL* 172, col. 181. There is much more interpolated information of this
kind.

[2] In the one surviving twelfth-century manuscript of this such information
is often inserted, once again, between the lines as though it had been added.
The insertions here, however, are less startling, for this manuscript contains
much marginal information which would reward close examination.

[3] In MS Österreichische Nationalbibliothek, Vienna, 1180 (late twelfth
century), there is (fo. 188) a treatise *De Septem Lapidibus* which contains
together all the material on stones Honorius scatters through his own. I have
not found a source for the Christian interpretation of the zodiac but parts of
it are clearly related to the *Livre des Créatures* of Philip of Thaon. T. Wright
(ed.), *Popular Treatises on Science written during the Middle Ages* (London, 1841),
pp. 35–6. In its emphasis on Jacob, too, it may reflect that astrological pre-
occupation with the twins, Esau and Jacob, which characterized the late
twelfth century. M.-Th. d'Alverny, 'Astrologues et théologiens au xiie siècle',
in *Mélanges offerts a M.-D. Chenu* (Paris, 1967), pp. 38–41. The Royal copy is
of the early thirteenth century.

[4] *De Civitate Dei*, XXI, v.

World history in the early twelfth century; the 'Imago Mundi'

careful reference to their demonic origins, amends its star myths.[1]
This world expects exceptional qualities to be attached to springs
and wells and stones and animals, and is prepared to ascribe, though
perhaps with some misgivings, qualities to the planet Saturn which
bear a remarkable resemblance to pre-Christian stories of a kind
one may find, for example, in the *Asclepius*.[2] It is concerned, lastly,
about fate; especially about the fates of pagan rulers. We have, in
the *Imago Mundi*, in short, a geography, cosmology, and history
consciously Christian, and yet one which through its various
recensions betrays a consistent interest in material from a quite
different world. The material is related to the world of primitive
magic[3] and astrology.[4]

3

The historical section of the *Imago Mundi*, then, is an integral part
of a treatise which displays, throughout its recensions, one consistent concern. This concern is for the repeated inclusion of material
whose unifying characteristic is its relevance to the worlds of
astrology and magic. In the light of this concern we may think
again about the function in the treatise of Book III, and again about
the various contexts within which historical writing in the Middle
Ages may have been produced. It may be that there is a connection

[1] The condemnation is to be found in I cxxxvii, after Honorius has drawn
on Hyginus's *Fabulae* and *Astronomicon* for these myths.

[2] A. D. Nock and A.-J. Festugière (ed.), *Corpus Hermeticum*, ii *Asclepius*
(Paris, 1946), chapters viii and xiii, pp. 326, 347–9.

[3] The *Indiculus Superstitionum*, for example, *MGH*, *Leges*, I. i. 19–20,
condemns superstitions associated with stones and wells, and auguries from
beasts including, interestingly enough, horses. The making of gifts to stones
and wells was a preoccupation of early Christian penitentials in the Germanic
world; J. Raith, *Die Altenglische Version des Halitgarischen Bussbuches* (Hamburg,
1933) p. 29.

[4] The capacity of adamant to attract iron is often cited in astrological works.
It is, for example, one of the instances used by Alkindi to illustrate his own
astrological beliefs. Planets, signs of the zodiac, and stars with their representations form a preoccupation of the *Liber Introductorius* of Albumasar in its Latin
translation. M.-Th. d'Alverny and F. Hudry, 'Alkindi. De Radiis', *Archives
d'histoire doctrinale et littéraire du moyen âge*, 41 (1974), pp. 142, 144.

not merely between Book III and the magical preoccupations of
the *Imago Mundi* itself but between the writing of world history and
that half attractive, half feared magical dimension of thought and
action by which Christian society in the West was at times both
served and beset. To examine this possibility we may look a little
more closely at the constitution of this dimension and the quality
of the attention it received.

It is hard to know how widely in the early Middle Ages the
magical arts were practised, and it is hard to know how well the
science of astrology was understood. Certain assertions may, however, be made with comparative safety. Astrology the science could
never be separated far from that science of astronomy by which the
computus was supported;[1] nor, on the other hand, was it at all easy
to divorce it from that magic the Christian liturgy must in part
reject. The problem was compounded by the fact that, for certain
sorts of magic, Christianity had a use. It had a use, for example, for
that magic which inspired a fear of demons, for that divination
which could put dreams to Christian moral purposes, and for that
kind of supernatural intervention which, called miraculous, could
be ascribed to prayer and grace.[2] The wholesale censure, then, which
would embrace both astrology the science and the soothsaying,
oracles, divination, incantation, wonders, and all the paraphernalia
of augury by birds and beasts, objects and dreams, it so often brought

[1] A. Van de Vyver, 'Les plus anciennes traductions latines médiévales
(x–xi siècles) de traités d'astronomie et d'astrologie', *Osiris*, i (1936), pp. 655–91,
shews how closely linked astronomical and astrological translations were to
computistical collections.

[2] In a seminal article to which I am deeply indebted M.-Th. d'Alverny drew
attention to the relationship manifest in a late twelfth-century French manuscript between magical incantation and Christian prayer. M.-Th. d'Alverny,
'Récréations monastiques. Les couteaux a manche d'ivoire', in *Recueil de
travaux offert a M. Clovis Brunel* (Paris, 1955), pp. 11–12. The line between
grace and erotic magic was very hard to draw, see, for example, the remarks
on Ficino in F. Yates, *Giordano Bruno and the Hermetic Tradition* (London,
1964), p. 127. The need for careful distinction in the cause of preserving belief
in Christian miracles was felt by Augustine, *De Civitate Dei*, x. 9, but in
practice the distinction was, even to him, a very fine one.

in its train[1] could not be maintained. Patristic condemnation weighed upon it[2] but astrology and its magical accompaniments remained an object of attention in the early Middle Ages, and conspicuously so in the areas with which we are here concerned. In one of the chief feasts of the liturgy, even, the feast of the Epiphany, there was provided a recurrent occasion for reactions of a complicated kind. There was room for the condemnation of alarming magical and astrological practices,[3] but also for more sober reflection upon the respectably supernatural. Thus, behind the somewhat theatrical repetition of fiercely hostile views,[4] there remained a deeper current of receptive thought. Here astronomy, astrology, and some even of their more dubious adjuncts could be received[5]

[1] A. Bouché-Leclercq, *Histoire de la divination dans l'antiquité*, i (Paris, 1879), pp. 92–104.

[2] Some further helpful references to these condemnations are to be found in H. Bober, 'The zodiacal miniature of the Très Riches Heures of the Duke of Berry—its sources and meaning', *Journal of the Warburg and Courtauld Institute*, ii (1948), pp. 4–5.

[3] Thus Gregory the Great uses a sermon on the Feast of the Epiphany to attack astrologers; *Homiliae in Evangelium. In Die Epiphania, PL* 76, cols 1110–12.

[4] Caspari found in a ninth-century Einsiedeln manuscript the heading 'et qui fatum malum aut bonum in hominibus esse credunt, transgressores et pagani sunt'. This and other condemnations of astrology and astral magic in Latin sources in the early Middle Ages may be found in F. Boll, C. Bezold, W. Gundel, *Sternglaube und Sterndeutung* (Leipsig, Berlin, 1931), pp. 173–87.

[5] Besides the Latin *Asclepius*, astrological material was transmitted through the *Astronomicon* of Manilius and the *Mathesis* of Firmicus Maternus. It came to the north-west, too, through translations (A. Van de Vyver, 'Les plus anciennes . . .') and was by some eagerly sought. R. Latouche (ed.), *Richer: Histoire de France*, ii (Paris, 1937), iii. 43, 50–3, pp. 50–1, 58–63. E. Svenberg, *Lunaria et Zodiologica Latina* (Gothenberg, 1963), adds to the sources mentioned above by editing nine texts of lunar and zodiacal prognostications taken from manuscripts of the ninth to the twelfth centuries, and refers to another three manuscripts from these centuries with such texts. As early as 1916 Cumont drew attention to two ninth-century manuscripts, one then at Dresden (MS 183), and one at Paris (BN, Nouv. Acq. lat. 1614), and to a further tenth-century one from Notre Dame (BN, Lat. 17868), which showed a clear interest in astrology; F. Cumont, 'Astrologica', *Revue archéologique*, 3 (1916), 11–16. In 1941 M. L. W. Laistner drew together valuable references to the reception of astrological material in the West in the early Middle Ages;

and even welcomed.[1] It is within this deeper current that, if I am right, the *Imago Mundi* as a whole is to be placed.

As in general with deep currents, so in particular with this one, the overwhelming need was, on the part of the thoughtful, for understanding tempered by care. This need was recognized early, and led to definition and distinction. Thus Isidore, Bede, Hermannus Contractus[2] (to name only a few, and those few well known to Honorius) allowed the claims of astrology to the attention of certain Christians, by insisting on a division. Some parts, the *naturales* could be pursued. Others, the *superstitiosas*, were to be rejected. The pursuit remained 'natural' provided that no attempt was made to determine through it human destinies and mores. Such an attempt plunged one into the superstitious,[3] for human destinies and mores

M. L. W. Laistner, 'The Western church and astrology during the early middle ages', *Harvard Theological Review*, 34 (1941), pp. 251–75, reprinted in his *The Intellectual Heritage of the Early Middle Ages* (New York, 1957), pp. 57–82.

[1] A form of astrological medicine was often employed to help in the practice of blood-letting. Practitioners allowed themselves to be guided towards and away from certain days in certain months, and relevant information was often provided in computistical collections. The Ramsey Computus (MS St. John's College, Oxford, 17) contains much information of this kind; for example on fos. 4, 16–21ᵛ. See also E. Wickersheimer, 'Figures Medico—Astrologiques des ixᵉ, xᵉ et xiᵉ siècles', *Janus* (*Archives internationales pour l'histoire de la medecine*), 19 (1914), pp. 157–77. 'Egyptian Days', days especially unlucky not only for blood-letting but for numerous other activities as well, are often listed in early manuscripts; see, for example, the list in L. Thorndike, *A History of Magic and Experimental Science*, i (New York and London, 1923), pp. 695–6. Valuable references to such concerns in early English manuscripts are to be found in H. Henel, 'Altenglischer Mönchsaberglaube', *Englischer Studien*, 69 (1934/5), pp. 329–49.

[2] Hermannus Contractus wrote works on the astrolabe. J. Drecker, 'Hermannus Contractus über das Astrolab', *Isis*, 16 (1931), pp. 200–19.

[3] W. M. Lindsay (ed.), *Isidori Hispalensis Episcopi Etymologiarum Sive Originum Libri XX* (Oxford, 1911), III, xxvii. In his *De Natura Rerum* he allows influence over man and under providence to the moon and to comets; xix. 2, xxvi. 13, *PL* 83, cols 992, 1000. Bede condemns astrologers in his *De Temporum Ratione*, iii; C. W. Jones (ed.), *Bedae Opera De Temporibus* (Cambridge, Mass., 1943), pp. 183–4. In his own *De Natura Rerum*, xxiv, however, he accepts Isidore's position on the influence of comets, and in his *Expositio in Actus Apostolorum*, i, he allows lot casting under apostolic conditions; *PL* 90,

World history in the early twelfth century; the 'Imago Mundi'

had to remain firmly within the scope of divine creation and the hope of divine providence and grace. To maintain this complex distinction a deal of common ambiguous ground between astronomy and astrology on the one hand, and astrology and magic on the other, had, for the Christian scholar, continually to be traversed, reviewed, demarcated, and the perspectives and purposes of the knowledge so acquired continually adjusted. The essence of the exercise lay in the devising of a means of acceding to that which was good and of service without danger of contamination by that which was harmful. This exercise, for its success, required great subtlety and intricate checks and balances.

It is hard, too, to know the place of magic and astrology in the twelfth century; but again some few things may be said with certainty. We do know that some of the magical arts which were practised were feared and condemned.[1] We know too that the complex distinction between the respectable 'natural' and the un-respectable 'superstitious' was repeated and sustained.[2] A third fact

cols 243–4, *PL* 92, col. 945. The distinction between 'natural' and 'super-stitious' may to some extent correspond with our distinction between the scientific and the non-scientific. But, in default of contemporary remark, one may not assume this.

[1] Gratian showed great concern about the place in Christianity of magic and divination, and quoted a deal of Augustine and Jerome and a number of conciliar decrees condemning both. E. Friedberg, ed. cit., Part II, Causa xxvi, Questiones i–v, vii (13–18), pp. 1020–36, 1044–6. In England, the Council of London 1125 included the canon: 'Sortilogos, ariolos et auguria quaeque sectantes eisque consentientes, excommunicari precipimus, perpetuaque notamus infamia'. *Chron. John*, 21. And see the *Policraticus* of John of Salisbury, l. 12; C. C. J. Webb (ed.), *Policraticus Sive De Nugiis Curialium et Vestigiis Philosophorum Libri viii*, 1 (Oxford, 1909), p. 50; William of Malmesbury on Gerbert and the witch of Berkeley; *GR*, i (RS, 1887), pp. 193–203, 253–5, and Marbod of Rennes, *Liber Decem Capitulorum*, *PL* 171, cols 1704–5.

[2] In his *Didascalicon* ii. 10, written before 1130, Hugh of St. Victor again divided the respectable 'natural' part of astrology from the 'superstitious'. As he revised his *Didascalicon* Hugh added a further condemnation of magic and the corruption of morals divination brings with it, C. H. Buttimer, ed. cit., VI, xv. Notable among the others are William of Conches, *De Philosophia Mundi*, II, v, *PL* 172, col. 59 (wrongly attributed to Honorius), and Abelard, *Expositio in Hexaemeron*, V. Cousin (ed.), *Opera Hactenus Seorsim Edita*, i (Paris, 1849), pp. 647–51.

is, at first sight, more surprising, though for these purposes, as I think, revealing. Some magical and astrological interests were maintained[1] and others were pursued in the Christian West with a vigour which has no previous parallel. Early and important evidence of the maintenance and pursuit of this further knowledge comes from Bavaria and from England; from, in short, those very areas with which the *Imago Mundi* shows some clear early connection. Later and striking evidence comes from the period 1123–39 within which, if I am right, the text was revised. The early Bavarian evidence is indicative.[2] The later, and partly English, evidence is of a more concentrated kind than is generally made clear. This fact deserves to be stressed.

The corpus of knowledge about astronomy, astrology, and divination received an enormous reinforcement in the late eleventh and early twelfth centuries. To put the matter a little more strongly, it is, in truth, remarkable how large a proportion of the energies of the most distinguished scholars and of the most famous translators of this period was devoted to astronomical, to astrological, and to magical material. Devotion of this gravity raised the status of the subject and was, most probably, designed to do so. More remarkable still, for the purpose of this discussion, is the fact that some of the

---

[1] Five of the best manuscripts of the Latin *Asclepius* are twelfth-century ones. A. D. Nock and A.-J. Festugière, *Corpus Hermeticum*, ii *Asclepius* (Paris, 1946), pp. 259–60. Knowledge of Firmicus Maternus seems, too, to have undergone a revival. Marbod of Rennes finds him worthy of attack; *Liber Decem Capitulorum*, PL 171, col. 1704; Bernard Silvestris, of imitation; B. Stock, *Myth and Science in the Twelfth Century, a Study of Bernard Silvester* (Princeton, 1972), pp. 82–6. He is known, too, to William of Malmesbury, see below, p. 236, n. 1.

[2] St. Emmeramm's Regensburg had an important eleventh-century copy of some of the writings of Hermannus Contractus on the astrolabe, now MS, Bay. Staatsbibl., Munich, clm. 14836. St. Peter's, Salzburg, has a twelfth-century copy; MS Stiftsbibliothek St. Peter's Salzburg, a V 7. Clm. 560, seemingly a Bavarian manuscript, contains an eleventh-century copy of the *Mathesis* of Firmicus Maternus, Books I and II, and MS Bay. Staatsbibl., Munich, clm. 22307, an eleventh-century manuscript from Windberg, has the Letter of Petosiris. A. Van de Vyver, art. cit., pp. 674–6. For Lorraine and England see M. C. Welborn, 'Lotharingia as a centre of Arabic and scientific influence in the eleventh century', *Isis*, 16 (1931), pp. 188–99.

best of the evidence for the influx of this material into Europe comes from the West of England, not far in time and place from Robert of Hereford's importation of the computistical method and world chronicle of Marianus Scotus. In England, for instance, Walcher, prior of Malvern from *c.* 1091, paraphrased the *De Dracone* of Petrus Alphonsus, and, between 1108 and 1112 and then again before 1120, produced two astronomical treatises. The astronomical work of Petrus Alphonsus himself was well enough known in England by 1120 to influence Walcher's second treatise.[1] Passages in Petrus's *Disciplina Clericalis* (1, 9) are, if we are to take them seriously, of especial interest, for he seems to admit divination and even necromancy to the company of the liberal arts.[2] Peter also wrote a *Letter to the Peripatetics* in which he was especially concerned to defend the science of astronomy.[3] Adelard of Bath, working seemingly a little later than Peter, translated in 1126 the tables of Al Khwarismi (a compilation especially useful in the casting of horoscopes), and translated also the *Liber Prestigiorum* of Thabit ben Qurra and the *Isagoge Minor* of Albumasar. In his *De Eodem et Diverso* (written before 1115, just possibly in England) Adelard claims for celestial bodies power over the sublunary world, and, for men learned in astronomy, powers of prediction.[4] Though he

---

[1] For Walcher and Petrus Alphonsus see C. H. Haskins, 'The introduction of Arabic science into England', in *Studies in the History of Medieval Science* (Harvard U.P., 1924), pp. 113–18. References to the two treatises and to the paraphrase of the *De Dracone* are to be found together with another by Walcher in MS Bodleian Library, Oxford, Auct. F.1.9, fos 86–99. They precede the *Khorasmian Tables* of Adelard of Bath. This manuscript comes from Worcester and also contains a copy of Robert of Hereford's revision of Marianus.

[2] L. Thorndike, op. cit., ii. pp. 72–3.

[3] This letter is to be found in a single manuscript of the late twelfth century, MS BL, London, Arundel 270, fos 40ᵛ–44ᵛ. This treatise contains references to astrological medicine, suited perhaps to Petrus in his capacity as doctor to Henry I; Thorndike, op. cit., pp. 70–1. It contains, fos 23ᵛ–33ᵛ, a copy of the historical section of the *Imago Mundi*. See below.

[4] H. Willner, 'Des Adelard von Bath de Eodem et Diverso', *Beiträge zur Geschichte der Philosophie des Mittelalters*, 4 (1903), pp. 31–2.

travelled widely Adelard was certainly in the West of England in
1130, and perhaps made his translation of the tables of Al Khwarismi
there.[1] Both Walcher and Adelard were familiar with the use of the
astrolabe, and the latter wrote a treatise on it also.[2] The chronicler
John of Worcester knew of Adelard's version of the Khorasmian
Tables.[3]

This interest in 'scientific' astrology became especially intense in
the third and fourth decades of the twelfth century. Compilations
and translations very largely astrological and divinatory occupied
the energies of John of Spain, Plato of Tivoli, Robert of Chester,
Herman of Carinthia, Hugh of Santalla. Some of the more striking
of their works may be named and on occasion dated.[4] The abridgement of Ptolemy's great astrological treatise the *Quadripartitum*, an
abridgement known as the *Centiloquium* or *Fructus*, was translated
possibly as early as 1136 by John of Spain, and then again by Hugh

[1] One early manuscript of a version of these, MS Corpus Christi College,
Oxford, 283, a twelfth-century manuscript from St. Augustine's, Canterbury,
has bound with it some material by Petrus Alphonsus. In this (fo. 142ᵛ)
Petrus is described as the 'translator' of Adelard's work. This may mean that
Adelard used Petrus as an interpreter; Haskins, 'The introduction of Arabic
Science', p. 118.

[2] The astrolabe, together with other early medieval astronomical instruments, seems primarily to have been used for calculation, especially for
astrological purposes. E. Poulle, 'Les instruments astronomiques de l'occident
latin aux xiᵉ et xiiᵉ siècles', *Cahiers de civilisation médiévale*, 15 (1972), p. 40.
For Adelard see C. H. Haskins, 'Adelard of Bath', in *Studies*, pp. 20–42. If
Adelard was indeed the author of a *Mappe Clavicula*, he was also interested in
alchemy. Adelard was employed for a time in the exchequer of Henry I. In
that he employed such men as Petrus and Adelard in such important practical
positions Henry I may himself have been more sympathetic towards astrology
than we have supposed.

[3] J. H. R. Weaver, ed. cit., p. 53.

[4] For these see Haskins, *Studies*, pp. 9–14, 43–66, 67–81. See also Francis
Carmody's caveats on some of the attributions; F. J. Carmody, *Arabic
Astronomical and Astrological Sciences in Latin Translation. A Critical Bibliography*
(Berkeley, Los Angeles, 1956), p. 5. This is a helpful compilation but erratic
in its description of manuscripts. I use for convenience here the latinized forms
of names to be found in this.

World history in the early twelfth century; the 'Imago Mundi'

of Santalla.[1] The whole *Quadripartitum* was translated by Plato of Tivoli in 1138, in a version which was widely popular, and Plato may have been the translator of yet another version of Ptolemy's hundred aphorisms on astrology. The majority of the other translations by John of Spain was astrological,[2] including the rudiments of the science (*De scientia astrorum*) by Alfraganus (translated 1135–7), the *Liber Introductorius*, to the mystery of judgements by the stars, by Alcabitius, and the *Introductorius*, containing a detailed defence of astrology, by Albumasar. Many of the astrological works of Messehalla were transmitted to the West by John. Then, in 1142, John compiled his own *Epitome Totius Astrologiae*. To the two translations by Plato of Tivoli already mentioned may be added the *De Motu Stellarum* of Albategni (1134–8), the *Capitùla Stellarum* of Almansor and the *De Nativitatibus* of Albohali (both seemingly in 1136),[3] and Robert of Chester's contribution to the growing astrological and quasi-magical corpus included the *De Iudiciis Astrorum* of Alkindi, and treatises on alchemy and the astrolabe. Robert's friend, Herman of Carinthia, with whom he was in 1141 involved in the translation of the Koran for Peter the Venerable, added a

[1] Hugh was asked for his translation by Bishop Michael of Tarazone (1119–51) especially to provide a guide through the growing forest of astrological material. Between these years Hugh produced at least five other related translations including the *De Motibus Planetarum* (a commentary on Alfraganus) and a *De Nativitatibus*, possibly of Messehalla. A version of the *Compendium Aureum* on gems, magic, and alchemy, ascribed to Hugh, is to be found in the twelfth-century MS BN, Paris, 13951, fos 1–31.

[2] A fuller list than that provided by Haskins of John's translations from the Arabic is to be found in M. Steinschneider, 'Die Europäischen Übersetzungen aus dem Arabischen bis Mitte des 17 Jahrhunderts. A. Schriften bekannter Übersetzer', *Situngsberichte der Kaiserliche Academie der Wissenschaften in Wien, Philosophisch-historische Klasse*, 149 (1904), no. 68.

[3] For other undateable astrological works by Plato, for example the *De Revolutionibus Nativitatum* of Alkasan, see Steinschneider, 'Die Europäischen', no. 98. He may also have translated a geomancy, to be found now in a very late copy from Polling, MS Bay. Staatsbibl. Munich, clm. 11998. Attention is drawn to the learned nature of Plato's work on geomancy and that of some of his near contemporaries by T. Charmasson, 'Les premiers traités latins de geomancy', *Cahiers de civilisation médiévale*, 21 (1978), 121–136.

translation of the *Fatidica* or *Prognostica de Revolutionibus* of Saul ben Bischr (1138), another translation of the *Introductorius* of Albumasar (*c.* 1140) and perhaps one of his *De Occultis*, and a translation of Ptolemy's *Planisphere* in 1143. Herman's own *De Essentiis* (1143) contains a deal of astrological information. The effect of these translations on the West was not, perhaps, immediately widespread; but the concern which led to their being commissioned was undeniable. The energy with which the 'natural' aspects of astrology and divination was pursued suggests that the danger from the darker side of these arts may have been a lot more pressing than we have been inclined so far to suspect.

I have said that the response such interests demanded of thoughtful Christians was a complex one. The material required both concession and containment; the variants to Book I and II of the *Imago Mundi* provide again, I think, some indication of the quality of the response these concerns received. One striking feature of the variants is the orthodox source of some of them; the *De Civitate Dei* of Augustine. Now this text was itself designed both to concede to its own source and to contain those implications in it which were threatening to Christians.[1] Another characteristic shown by the variants, and this characteristic extends to other sections of the treatise, is Honorius's tendency to stop short at the possibly 'superstitious'.[2] He is even wary of concessions made by Isidore.[3] There

---

[1] For two of the stones Augustine mentioned, for example, adamant and pyrrhites, he drew upon the *Natural History* of Pliny, xxxvii. 61 and 144. Pliny, however, ascribed to the former power to drive fear from the mind of man, and to the latter the power (attested by the Magi) of subduing human violence. Augustine omits both these remarks. Some limited commentary on the constellations, too, was permitted by Gregory the Great, *Moralia in Job*, IX, ix, *PL* 75, cols 865–9.

[2] Honorius's treatment of the planets is an obvious example of this tendency. He ascribes to them colours (I lxxviii) in the manner of Bede's *De Natura Rerum* xv, *PL* 90, cols 230–1, but, with the exception of the curious passage on Saturn I have mentioned, no part in the government of human affairs. This is in marked contrast to, for instance, the *De Essentiis* of Herman of Carinthia, Thorndike, op. cit., ii. p. 42. It is also in contrast to the *De Philosophia Mundi* of William of Conches, II, xvii–xix, *PL* 172, cols 62–3, although Honorius makes use in other parts of William's source for these passages, Macrobius.

seems to be in this a clear consciousness of that common ambiguous ground of which I spoke; a realization of the need to pay attention to, but show reserve about, that material upon which the 'natural' and the 'superstitious' may make common cause. The secret of safety lay in knowing when to venture upon the natural, and when to draw back and fend away the clearly superstitious by a christianized semblance of it. Yet even when such distinctions had been made, and even when the status of the subject had been so raised, some underlying problems of emphasis, attitude, and perspective may still remain. Even when the respectable aspects of astronomy, astrology, and magic were known and so controlled, and even when their superstitious concomitants had been so conjured away as to make it all seem quite innocuous, there could be something about the whole which still would threaten Christian morality. To abandon subjects to which such serious attention had been so consciously devoted was clearly beyond question: a further control had to be found. This brings us, lastly, to Book III. We may look again at the function of historical writing, both within the *Imago Mundi* and outside it.

4

A fundamental source of opposition between magic and astrology, and the Christian view of man, lay in the attitudes of each to free

---

J. Willis (ed.), *Ambrosii Theodosii Macrobii Commentarii in Somnium Scipionis*, i (Teubner-Leipzig, 1970), 18–20, pp. 76–7. This belief in the harmful qualities of, for example, Saturn and Mars, and the contrasting benevolence of Jupiter, was almost a commonplace when Honorius wrote. It is to be found, in the Pseudo-Clementine *Recognitions*, which were well known (Laistner, 'The Western Church', pp. 78–80), and also in the *Liber Alchandreus*. Honorius's reserve is perhaps all the more marked in that we have a surviving important eleventh-century text of this; MS Bay. Staatsbibl., clm. 560, apparently from Bavaria (this same codex also contains a copy of Firmicus Maternus).

[3] In Book I, lxviii, Honorius describes the planets as *erraticae* because of their wandering courses, a description drawn from Isidore's *Etymologies*, III, lxiii. In his *De Natura Rerum*, however, Isidore described the planets as *errantia* because they induced men to err; xxiii. 3, *PL* 83, col. 996. Although he used this work Honorius again stopped short at this addition. In I cxxxvii, and unlike Isidore again, Honorius allows only that comets *portend* events.

will.[1] Magic and astronomy, even at their most respectable, would still submit the will of man to the power of the stars, and the future to the future of the horoscope and determinings of particular acts and objects. The Christian would submit it ultimately only to hope in the providence of God, to that power of choice which allowed man to reject this, to that grace which would restore to man the means of responding once again in time. One way of demonstrating the Christian perspective, its attitude to providence and its emphasis on hope, became very early clear to Christian apologists. It lay in the writing of world history. The demonstration of God's fore-knowledge, his part in creation and in its subsequent passage under the direction of man through time, was a formidable weapon against a narrow fatalism, and was recognized as such.[2] The Bible, especially the historical books, and treatises on providence and free will themselves were, of course, valuable assistants in the cause. The writing of history, especially of history from the fall, gave a further strength. If astrology and magic were ways of foretelling the future in such a way as to uphold its submission to the stars and dreams and particular natural objects, the writing of Christian history was a way of recounting the past in such a way as to hope to submit that future to the control of Christian man.

This particular means of combating magic and those aspects even of the science of astrology which threatened Christian morality

[1] One of the clearest expositions of this opposition is to be found in the *Homiliae in Hexaemeron* of St. Basil, VI, 5–7, *PG* 29, pp. 127–34. Many expressions of it are to be found, of course, in the works of St. Augustine, for example *De Genesi ad Litteram*, II, xvii, *PL* 34, cols 278–9. Thorndike points to the acknowledgement in the *Questiones Naturales* of Adelard of Bath of a possible conflict between independent scientific observation and the expression of orthodox beliefs about the nature of God and the divine will. Op. cit., ii.28.

[2] *De Civitate Dei*, V, i–xi. C. Zangemeister (ed.), *Pauli Orosii Historiarum adversum Paganos Libri VII* (Teubner, Leipsig, 1889), Preface, pp. 6–7. In the *De Doctrina Christiana*, II, xxviii, Augustine opposes books of history to 'libri ... haruspicum'. J. Martin (ed.), *Sancti Aurelii Augustini De Doctrina Christiana* (Corpus Christianorum, Turnholt, 1962), II, xxviii. pp. 44, 63. Cassiodorus advances a similar view in his *Institutes*, in the chapter 'De Historicis Christianis'. R. A. B. Mynors (ed.), *Cassiodori Senatoris Institutiones* (Oxford, 1937), I, xvii. p. 55.

was recognized, if I am right, early in the Middle Ages.[1] It may not be mere coincidence that those scholars, of whose accommodating attitudes to astrology I have spoken, wrote histories and chronicles *ab initio peccati hominis* on the model of Orosius, and included in them miracles, Christian dreams and prophecies, and promptings to Christian ethical behaviour.[2] This particular aspect of this enquiry, unhappily, may not be followed here. My purpose in this last section is to make claims simply for Book III. The claims I would make are these. The first four decades of the twelfth century were, I have tried to show, again preoccupied to a striking degree with the problems of magic and astrology, and with the need for Christian morality to triumph. Book III of the *Imago Mundi* was related to these needs in the same way as the non-historical sections of the text were related to them, and as earlier historical writing was related to such preoccupations. Book III, that is, like the non-historical material, tried to concede an interest in the strange and supernatural, and then, in company with the earlier historical treatises, many of which it used, to contain its more dangerous effects within a Christian perspective. This process is reflected in the contents of the early codices which contain the text. Lastly, we may assign to Book III the role of guide. It may be that other twelfth-century historical treatises were, in part at least, compiled to

---

[1] Ælfric, for example, condemns the taking of auguries from horses in that same part of his sermon on auguries in which he speaks of the goodness of God's creation in seven days, and refers too to the power against the superstitions he had mentioned of free will and the command 'Declina a malo et fac bonum'. W. W. Skeat, *Aelfric's Lives of the Saints*, EETS, 82 (London, 1885), pp. 370–5, 379–83. I owe these references to Dr Audrey Meaney.

[2] The *Chronicles* both of Isidore and of Bede follow, in the *De Natura Rerum* and the *De Temporum Ratione* respectively, chapters on the Christian Easter, PL 84, cols 86–107, PL 90, cols 516–79, as if to demonstrate the association between the redemption and Christian history and responsibility. That the connection between early Christian historical writing and ethical purpose was a deep one has long been observed; C. W. Jones, 'Bede as early medieval historian', *Medievalia et humanistica*, 4 (1946), pp. 31–2. See also some illuminating passages in R. W. Hanning, *The Vision of History in Early Britain* (New York, 1966), pp. 75 ff.

countermand that fatalism which the most respectable interest in astrology might involve. We may take these claims in order.

Five of the number of manuscripts of the *Imago Mundi* I have already mentioned have in them interpolations to Book III. These illustrate the first claim I would make; that of the effort to concede and contain. Four have a short addition at the very beginning, after the birth of Cain and Abel:

Occiso autem a Caym Abel, Adam centum annos duxit in luctu et merore, et deinceps conjugali thoro uti noluit. Post hoc divino iussu ammonetur a sancto angelo, ut denuo uxorali fruatur contubernio, quatinus maledictio Caym excludatur benedictione nascentis. Post hec genuit filium nomine Seth.[1]

The curse of Cain is overthrown through the intervention of a divinely directed angel. One manuscript has six far longer interpolations of which I can here only recount the contents. Four of the interpolations, all from Book VIII of Cassian's *Collations* ('De principatibus seu potestatibus'), are, again, about moral choice assisted by divine and angelic intervention, and about the power of man to triumph over evil.[2] The last of the four refers directly to the danger presented to this power by indulgence in the magical arts.[3] I have not been able to find a source for two of the interpolations but they are preoccupied again with this same subject. One is given over to a discussion of the sentence 'In principio fecit deus celum et terram'. The principles of God's control over creation are re-asserted. The power given both to angels and men is stressed, and so

[1] MS BL, Cotton Cleopatra B iv, fo. 22ᵛ. The other three manuscripts are MSS Paris, BN, 15009, and Bibliothèque Mazarine, 708; London, BL, Add. MS 38665.

[2] MS Bay. Staatsbibl., Munich, clm. 22225, fos 150ᵛ–152ᵛ, 152ᵛ–153, 154–6, 157ᵛ–158, *Collatio* VIII, vi–xii, xvii, xxiii–xxv, xxii–xxiii, PL 49, cols 730–4, 750, 761–70, 758–60. *Collatio* VIII is, of all Cassian's *Collations*, the one most preoccupied with magic arts. It is singular that it is from this that the extracts are made.

[3] 'Hanc ergo scientiam . . . aereos daemones venerarentur et colerent'. PL 49, col. 758. This reference to the successive vulnerability of the seed of Seth connects well with the interpolation common to the previous four manuscripts, and may perhaps reflect contemporary discussion.

is the fall of both, the resulting vulnerability of man to sin and to the devil, and the effects in the struggle of redeeming grace. The second interpolation is a tissue of biblical legends. There are wonder stories about the burial of Adam, the hill of Calvary, the wood of the tree of paradise, and the signs foretelling the day of judgement. Portents, high places, and wood are prominent; but again man is lifted above the determined by his capacity to respond to angelic and divine intervention manifested in a profoundly, but to the compiler respectably, supernatural way.[1] In all these interpolations, in fact, the emphasis is placed upon Christian responsibility and susceptibility, their direction through time and protection against ill by divine intervention.

This effort to show interest in, but to contain the effects of, the magical and fatalistic is echoed by the contents of many of the collections with which the *Imago Mundi* was early bound. The very best text of the 1139 recension, for example,[2] is bound with traditional and Christian wonder stories (the seven wonders of the world, the seven miracles associated with the birth of Christ), visions, charms, cures, the *Liber Proverbiorum* of Otloh of St. Emmeramm's, the Bestiary, and extracts which in part bear directly upon the reception of superstitious belief.[3] In other words, that need for wonder and for signs of supernatural intervention which could so easily choose a doubtful path was fed, as it was in the *Imago*

[1] Fos 153–4, inc. 'In principio fecit deus celum et terram', fos 156–7 inc. 'Secundum dicta dominica terra es et in terram ibis. Erat autem adam xxx cubitorum altitudinis.'

[2] MS Bay, Staatsbibl., Munich, clm. 536, from Prül.

[3] For instance fo. 62ᵛ contains the following entry upon lucky and unlucky days. 'Tres dies sunt et noctes in quibus si virilis fuerit genitus sine dubio corpus eius integrum manet usque in diem iudicii. Hoc est in vi et in iii idus et in iii kalendas februarii et est mirabile misterium. Quot in anno sunt dies, tot uniuscuisque membra mulieris, id est ccclxvi, et tot elemosinis peccata hominum sunt redemenda. Tres dies maledicti dicuntur. Non in his tribus diebus sanguinem minuas, aut de ansere manduces, vel potionem sumas. Hoc est viiii kalendae aprilis, die lune, intrante augusto, die lune, exeunte decembre, die lune. Hi tres dies maledicti dicuntur.' Honorius, in the *Imago Mundi* II cix, re-echoed that belief in the Egyptian Days which was early accepted as respectable.

Mundi itself, by material to confine it within accepted boundaries. Similar items are to be found bound with other important early manuscripts.[1] Two very slightly later codices (of the late twelfth or early thirteenth centuries) fulfil this need in a different but related way. They bind parts of Book III, and, in the second case, Book III alone, with astrological and magical texts defensibly 'natural'. MS Preussische Staatsbibliothek, Berlin, lat. 956, has, with parts of the *Imago Mundi*, the translation of Alfraganus's *De Aggregationibus Scientia Stellarum* by Gerard of Cremona, a treatise on alchemy, three lapidaries, and one of the fullest available accounts of astrological practice and of the materials astrology required, the *Liber Introductorius* of Alcabitius, translated by John of Spain.[2] The second codex, BL, London, Arundel 270, which has Book III alone, binds with it a treatise 'De Utilitatibus Astrolabii' and the only copy we have of the *Letter to the Peripatetics* of Petrus Alphonsus.[3] In these two codices we have, actually in the same collection as parts of the *Imago Mundi*, rare copies of 'scientific' and acceptable works upon astrology and magic of precisely the sort to which, in its own way, Book III as well was related.

We may turn lastly to the role of Book III as a guide. It may be that more Christian writers than we have so far suspected turned to history with both the attraction and the threats of magic and astrology very much in mind. This idea may not be explored far here; but there are signs to which we may point. Long ago Thorndike drew attention to the consciously christianized cosmology and astrology of the chronicle of Raoul Glaber.[4] The early twelfth-century evidence is, so far, less striking. But it is there. William of Malmesbury was, for example, one of the most distinguished of Honorius's

---

[1] For example MSS Bay. Staatsbibl., Munich, clm. 14348 and 14731, both from St. Emmeramm's Regensburg, contain the same extracts. The first manuscript has the Bestiary too.

[2] A very full description of this codex is given in V. Rose, *Die Handschriften— Verzeichnisse der Königlichen Bibliothek zu Berlin*, II, iii (Berlin, 1905).

[3] Thorndike, op. cit., ii. pp. 70–2.

[4] Ibid. i. 674–6. More recently M.-Th. d'Alverny has drawn attention to the fact that Helinard of Froidmont attacked astrologers in his *Chronicle*. M.-Th. d'Alverny, 'Astrologues', pp. 39–49.

World history in the early twelfth century; the 'Imago Mundi'

contemporaries in the writing of history. William wrote within easy reach in time and space of that area of England in which the revival of interest in astronomy and astrology was so vigorous, and he was himself involved in it.[1] His ambiguous attitude to the subjects is a striking aspect of his historical writing. He both condemned and reverenced them.[2] We may have in William's interest in history, in conscious succession to Bede, that same desire to distinguish, accommodate, and, above all, to contain. I have mentioned the *Didascalicon* of Hugh of St. Victor, its firm condemnation of the superstitious and of harmful magic, but its defence, in Book II, 10, of the 'natural' aspects of astrology. In this same chapter Hugh again defined and condemned the superstitious by its incompatibility with man's free choice. Hugh's attitude to, and illustration of, the guidance of free choice has been proved, most convincingly, to be an historical one.[3] A third person, well worthy of attention in this context, is Otto bishop of Freising (1137–58). Otto, once a pupil of Hugh, devoted his own life to the writing of

---

[1] MS Bodleian Library, Oxford, Auct. F. 3. 14, a computistical, astronomical, and astrological collection, was probably drawn up for him. N. R. Ker, 'William of Malmesbury's Handwriting', *EHR*, 59 (1944), p. 374.

[2] William made much of Gerbert's nefarious reputation for dabbling in the occult, and told with some disapprobation of how Archbishop Gerard of York was suspected of reading Firmicus Maternus in secret. He spoke of the results of Robert of Hereford's successful divination from the stars, however, with respect and, in the *Historia Novella*, showed deference to prognostications from the stars and sun and weather. *GR*, i. pp. 193–203; *GP*, p. 259, n. 6; K. R. Potter (ed.), *The Historia Novella by William of Malmesbury* (NMT, 1955), pp. 43, 50.

[3] R. W. Southern, 'Aspects of the European Tradition of Historical Writing: 2. Hugh of St. Victor and the idea of Historical Development', *TRHS*, 5th series, 21 (1971), p. 164. Hugh, like William, was interested in, and knowledgeable about, astronomy and astrology. He knew the *Asclepius* and the Pseudo-Hermetic *Liber Hermetis Mercurii Triplicis de VII Rerum Principiis*; J. Taylor, *The Didascalicon of Hugh St. Victor* (New York, 1961), p. 20. MS BN, Paris, lat. 14754, an early twelfth-century codex of astronomical texts from St. Victor, may also have been his own: A. Van de Vyver, 'Les plus anciennes', p. 685. It seems, too, that he wrote a world chronicle; R. Baron, 'La Chronique de Hugues de St. Victor', *Studia Gratiana*, xii (1967), 167–79. This is bound with a copy of the *Imago Mundi* in MS BN, Paris, lat. 15009.

history. In his own *Chronicle* (written between 1143 and 1146/7) he
consciously set himself within the tradition of Augustine and
Orosius[1] and subscribed with an equal vigour to their view of the
associations between history, the guidance of divine providence,
and Christian morality.[2] We may even detect signs in Otto's work
of that 'naturalizing' of myth and wonder which, I have suggested,
was so conspicuous a part of the recensions of the *Imago Mundi*.[3]
Finally, it is a commonplace to observe that medieval chroniclers
were alive to the influence in human affairs of comets and aerial
phenomena. Less commonly observed is the possibility that this too
had a context. Comets and aerial phenomena of this kind lay on the
common ground between the natural and the superstitious in
astrology. We may have, in the admission of their influence, not
evidence of the credulous superstitions to which medieval writers
of history were prey, but evidence instead of a far from credulous
concern for that proper accommodation of astrological knowledge
in which historical writing played so important a part.[4]

I have looked, in this discussion, at only one of the many possible
motives for the medieval writing of history. I have looked at history
as a counterpoise in a balance of very great delicacy; and I have

[1] Transl. C. C. Mierow, *The Two Cities* (Columbia University Press, 1928,
reprint 1966), p. 95.

[2] Ibid. pp. 94, 402–3. This same purpose is evident in the very first sentence
of his *Gesta Frederici*; F.-J. Schmale (ed.), *Ottonis Episcopi Frisingensis et
Rahewini Gesta Frederici seu rectius Chronica* (Darmstadt, 1965), p. 114.

[3] Otto's tendency to find, where possible, 'natural' or 'historical' interpretations for Greek myths was noticed by Mierow in his introduction to *The Two
Cities*, p. 56. Interestingly, the feast to which Otto paid the most marked attention in his historical writing was the feast of the Epiphany. L. Arbusow,
Liturgie und Geschichtsschreibung im Mittelalter (Bonn, 1951), pp. 20–1.

[4] Weaver, for instance, sums up the work of John of Worcester; 'Where he
deviates from his task as an annalist, it is that he may record an edifying vision
or miracle, the last hours of a fellow monk or some remarkable natural
phenomenon.' J. R. H. Weaver, ed. cit., p. 11. John's interest in comets,
aerial phenomena, and the demonstration of the just judgement of God in
history is very striking. He too, of course, knew of the contemporary interest
in astrology and mentions that of Adelard of Bath; ibid. p. 53.

suggested that some kinds of medieval historical writing, especially the world chronicle, may have been undertaken less for themselves than as responses to a particular demand. This demand was generated in its turn by a particular kind of enquiry; enquiry legitimate, even desirable; but enquiry of a type which, if left to itself, could constitute a threat to the basis of Christian society. This type of enquiry I have defined as broadly magical and astrological. It gained especial currency in the first four decades of the twelfth century. In the form of a distinction between the 'natural' and the 'superstitious' it carried from the first some counterpoise within it; but at a time of increased interest, Christian society may, I have argued, be expected to feel the need of more constraints upon it. These constraints historical writing could, in certain forms, supply. Through the preoccupations of the early twelfth-century recensions of the *Imago Mundi*, and the involvement in them of its historical book, Book III, I have tried to suggest that in the twelfth century the world chronicle did supply these needs and was designed to do so. Here there is an irony. Though astrology was early encouraged by that same concern for the computus which fostered the beginnings of Christian history, the first made, with time, an enemy of the second. This irony the *Imago Mundi* encapsulates too.

In laying so much stress upon world history as a counterpoise, I do not mean to suggest that this was the only, or even, perhaps, the chief part that it had to play. I mean still less to imply that history was the most forceful opponent of astrology and magic the Christian world could devise. But as the disparity in object between the world chronicle and that determinism which denies a place to human choice is at all times so very striking, so too, at certain periods, is the concurrent appearance of the two so different types of interest. This concurrence deserves some thought. We may have, in the world chronicle, work of a far more complex order, and signs of threats to Christianity far more frightening, than we have previously suspected.

Anti-Jewish Literature and Attitudes
in the Twelfth Century

In a recent paper, I attempted to use the text of the *Imago Mundi* of Honorius Augustodunensis in a particular way. I employed it as an echo-sounder into the still murky depths of early twelfth-century monastic learning. Through an examination of the variants which help to distinguish the various recensions of the work, and of the company the *Imago Mundi* kept in twelfth-century codices as a whole, I tried to suggest that Honorius, in writing it, responded to an interest in astrology and magic which was more widespread in the twelfth century than we had previously realised, and which pressed, therefore, upon the pastorate with a greater strength than we had hitherto suspected.[1] It became possible to extend our understanding of Honorius's task, and to probe more deeply into the character of the man himself. Complications, even contradictions, began to emerge. On the one hand, Honorius was a proven and enthusiastic proponent of the movement for ecclesiastical reform, one who may very well have suffered severely in its cause;[2] on the other, he was a venturer away from the respectable and open pastures of patristic orthodoxy into the dubious undergrowth of popular belief and superstition.

In the present paper I should like to pursue this last aspect of Honorius's involvement, as it is reflected in the *Imago Mundi*, a little further. I propose to use the *Imago Mundi* as an echo-sounder once again, but this time into a different, though still murky, depth. It may enable us to look into a world quite as important as that of astrology and magic to the pastorate and to the aims of the reform; the world of Jewish–Christian relations at the time of the early crusades. The exploration of this second world is the main preoccupation of this particular paper. This exploration is, I should make clear at the outset, extremely tentative, and its first aim is to direct attention to an aspect of twelfth-century thought and learning about which we badly need to know more. This being said, some relatively firm preliminary statements may be made. Firstly, Rabbinic exegesis, especially exegesis of the *Book of Genesis*,

---

[1] V. I. J. Flint, 'World History in the Early Twelfth Century: The *Imago Mundi* of Honorius Augustodunensis', in *edit.* R. H. C. Davis and J. M. Wallace-Hadrill, *The Writing of History in the Middle Ages* (Oxford 1981), pp. 211–238. The preparation of the present paper was made possible by the award of a membership at the Institute for Advanced Study, Princeton, and the support of the Auckland University Research Committee, to each of which I am grateful. For all my work on Honorius my greatest debt is to Sir Richard Southern.
[2] V. I. J. Flint, 'Heinricus of Augsburg and Honorius Augustodunensis. Are they the same person?', *Revue Bénédictine* 92 (1982), 148–158.

XIV

40

affected the approach to the Bible of the ecclesiastical reformers more profoundly than many of us have in general supposed. Its effects can be seen in the text of the *Imago Mundi* and, especially, in certain interpolated twelfth-century manuscripts of this text. Secondly, the shadow (and the threat) of Rabbinic exegesis stands behind certain legends of the cross and Moses which, though in part extremely well known to students of medieval literature, have not yet been seen against this background. The placing of these legends within this context promises to be very rewarding indeed. Thirdly, Honorius was himself quite as conscious of the claims of contemporary Jewish teaching, particularly of the teaching of the Jewish communities of South Germany and Austria, as he was of the claims of popular magical beliefs.

The evidence which forms the basis of this discussion is drawn from the mid-twelfth-century manuscript Ms. Bayerische Staatsbibliothek, Munich, clm. 22225. Clm. 22225 comes from the Premonstratensian abbey of Windberg, in the diocese of Regensburg. A dedication and verse at the beginning shews that it was written for Abbot Gebhard of Windberg between the years 1154 and 1159.[3] The codex as a whole contains one of the most important of the surviving collections of Honorius's works, one which may, indeed, be not far removed from the collection of the author himself.[4] The text of the *Imago Mundi* to be found in this codex is a remarkable one. It is not in detail a particularly good scribal effort. Its remarkable feature is to be found in the fact that it has placed in it, often without distinguishing heading or change of hand, a series of interpolations unique, so far as I have been able to determine, to this manuscript. Some of the interpolations can be identified; some can not (not, at least, by me). All look at first sight random, and only when they are detached from the text and examined for themselves does light begin to dawn. The interpolations are linked, I shall attempt to shew, by a single but strong thread. Each one is preoccupied with Jewish teaching upon matters crucial both to Jewish and to Christian thought.

To demonstrate this, and before venturing upon the wider scene, it is necessary both to print the interpolations as a whole, and to discuss them one by one. The interpolations—there are seven of them—are printed, therefore, in the appendix to this paper, together with references to those sections of the *Imago Mundi* into which they are intruded. They are given in the order in which they appear, and are numbered accordingly, 1–7. For the initial exploration, however, I have chosen a slightly different arrangement. The

---

[3] For a description of this manuscript see *edit.*, V. I. J. Flint, 'The Imago Mundi of Honorius Augustodunensis', *Archives d'Histoire Doctrinale et Littéraire du Moyen Age* 49 (1982), 28.

[4] The collection, which may be close to, or may even have been, that of Honorius himself, is to be found in Ms. Bodleian Library, Oxford, Lyell 56. It is described in A. C. de la Mare, *Catalogue of the Collection of medieval manuscripts bequeathed to the Bodleian Library Oxford by James P. R. Lyell* (Oxford 1971), pp. 168–174. Dr de la Mare remarks upon the similarity between Lyell 56 and clm. 22225.

interpolations fall into three main groups. There are, firstly, four drawn from the *Collationes* of Cassian (numbers 1, 2, 4 and 6); secondly, two containing the legends (numbers 5 and 7);[5] lastly one which reports 'theological' teachings similar in style and manner to that generally associated with the school of Laon (number 3). The main groups will be treated in this order. To save constant appeal to the appendix a short summary of each extract will preface each treatment.

I. *The Extracts from Cassian*

All four of these extracts are from Book VIII of the *Collationes*. We may take them in their own internal order, giving them the numbers they have in the appendix.

(a) No. 1. Ff. 150v–152v. This interpolation is taken from Book VIII, chapters vi–xii.[6] It is concerned with the problem of the fallen angels, and especially with the passages in Ezechiel and Isaiah about the fall of Lucifer and the Prince of Tyre, passages upon which Christian teaching about the devil and the Fall was so largely based.[7] Cassian begins by asserting that, since all that God created was good (*Genesis* I, 31), then he cannot have created demons as such; nor did he begin by creating our world. Cassian proceeds, interestingly, to report the literal Jewish account of the process of the creation through time—making specific reference to the Christian view that Christ is the beginning of all things (*John* I, 3) and drawing the conclusion, based on *Colossians* I, 16, that the original angelic powers were created in Christ at this beginning. He then concentrates upon the problem of whether Lucifer fell through envy—which led him eventually to seduce Adam and Eve—or through pride. In the original of this dialogue, Germanus, a worthy forerunner of Honorius's own willing *discipulus*, sets up the proposition to be denied by his master Serenus (although the names are here omitted). Until now, says Germanus, it had been believed that Lucifer fell through envy. Not so, says Serenus. The devil had become a serpent before he ever seduced Adam and Eve (*Genesis* III, i). He was thus far removed from the angelic and full of envy before this encounter. Pride was his first sin; envy only the second.

We cannot enter here into Cassian's own purpose in writing these particular chapters and those later drawn by the interpolator from him, although we may observe in passing that Jewish settlement in Southern France is attested from

---

[5] A part of the interpolation to clm. 22225 containing the legends of the cross was printed by W. Meyer, 'Die Geschichte des Kreuzholzes vor Christus', *Abhandlungen der Philosophisch-Philologischen Classe der Königlich Bayerischen Academie der Wissenschaften* 16 (1882), 103–165. The legends of Moses from the same manuscript have not, to my knowledge, previously been printed.

[6] *Edit.* M. Petschenig, *Johannis Cassiani Collationes XXIIII* (C. S. E. L. Vienna 1886), pp. 222–228.

[7] *Ezechiel* XXVIII, 11–18; *Isaiah* XIV, 12–15.

the fourth century A.D.,[8] and that there was a sufficiently large population there in the fifth century to excite the alarms of Evagrius.[9] Certainly this first passage is relevant to Jewish teaching upon the subject of the creation of angels and demons and upon the Fall in the form in which it reached twelfth-century Germany. Christian teaching is here measured against Jewish on two counts: firstly in the matter of the place of angels and demons in the chronology of creation (an issue to which Cassian draws specific attention); and secondly in that of the original cause of the Fall.

In regard to the creation of angels and demons, literal Jewish exegesis of *Genesis* had it that the angels were created on the second day, or on the fifth, not, in general, on the first day, that stressed by Christians.[10] Christian understandings of Rabbinic teaching, too, could lead to the conviction that they taught that God created demons. This was certainly what Agobard of Lyons believed in the early ninth century,[11] and a suggestion of it is to be found in the Midrash on *Genesis*.[12] In the matter of the Fall the Rabbis had it that jealousy was the original cause of the lapse of the angels from grace. The *Pirke de Rabbi Eliezer*, a compilation of Rabbinic teaching credibly dated to the mid-ninth century[13] and widely circulated in North-Western Europe, explains that the angels were jealous of man's capacity to name God's creatures, a capacity which far exceeded theirs.[14] Sammael, their leader, brought about the destruction of Adam and Eve accordingly, using the serpent as his tool. The Jewish story goes further. Sammael proceeded to seduce Eve herself, to cause her, as a result, to conceive and bear Cain. Cain inherited the violent and evil nature of his sire, and his own offspring were accordingly degenerate.[15] The women among them seduced the remnants of the lapsing angels, and giants were born of their intercourse.

This account springs primarily from extended thought about the *Book of Genesis*. The story of the seduction of Eve by Sammael is an expansion of

[8] B. Blumenkranz, *Auteurs Juifs en France Médiévale* (Toulouse 1975), p. v, and 'Les premières implantations de Juifs en France: du Ier au début du Ve siècle', *Academie des Inscriptions et Belles-Lettres. Comptes rendus des séances de l'année* 1969, 162–174.

[9] B. Blumenkranz, *Juifs et Chrétiens dans le Monde Occidental 430–1096* (Paris 1960), p. 11.

[10] *Midrash Rabbah. Genesis* I, 3, transl. H. Freedman, *The Midrash* I (London 1939), pp. 5, 24–25. *Pirke de Rabbi Eliezer* iv, transl. G. Friedlander, *Pirke de Rabbi Eliezer* (London 1916), pp. 20–21. They were created on the first day, however, according to the *Book of Jubilees*. See M. Th. d'Alverny, 'Les anges et les jours', *Cahiers Archéologiques* 9 (1957), 271–300, especially 283. I owe this reference and many other suggestions to Mlle. d'Alverny and to colleagues she has been kind enough to consult on my behalf. Neither she, nor they, are of course responsible for the propositions I set out as a result.

[11] B. Blumenkranz, *Les Auteurs Chrétiens Latins du Moyen Age sur les Juifs et le Judaïsme* (Paris 1963), p. 165. Agobard too reports the Jewish belief that the Law was given before the creation of the world.

[12] *Transl. cit.*, pp. 52–53.

[13] *Transl. cit.*, pp. liii–lv.

[14] *Ibid.*, ch. xxi, p. 150. See also L. Ginzberg, *The Legends of the Jews* (Philadelphia 1909–1946), I, p. 105, V, pp. 133–134.

[15] *Pirke de Rabbi Eliezer* xii, *transl. cit.*, pp. 158–60.

Genesis IV, 1, 'and Adam knew Eve, his wife, and she conceived and bare Cain, and she said I have acquired a man child from the Lord', and the development is an expansion of *Genesis* VI, 1–6.[16] All these expansions were a normative part of Rabbinic exegesis, and Jewish teaching here is, in both chronology and emphasis, widely different from the Christian on this peculiarly sensitive and pastorally vital subject. According to Jewish chronology, the fall of the angels as a whole did not precede the seduction of Adam and Eve, but followed it. Adam and Eve, and especially one line of the offspring of Eve, that of Cain, bear a very heavy burden of responsibility for the fallen state of God's creation brought about by jealousy and lust. These, therefore, take pride of place as the deadliest of sins.

This chronology and this emphasis was a very old bone of contention for Christians. Origen, for example, tackled the problem in his *Contra Celsum*.[17] Commenting on the same sections of Ezechiel and Isaiah, he insisted, as does Cassian here, that the fall of the angels preceded that of Adam and Eve, and that it sprang not from lust but from pride. Old the problem may have been, but this particular interpolation shews that it remained relevant, and particularly so to a state of affairs in which the Jewish view was alive and currently expressed.

(b) 2. Ff. 152v–153. This interpolation, again taken from a later section of the *Collationes*,[18] is still concerned with angels, but this time with the good and bad angels attached, according to Cassian, to each individual human being. He depends upon *Matthew*, the *Psalms*, the *Acts of the Apostles* and the *Shepherd of Hermas* to support him in his conviction that these two angels are indeed attached to man, and in his conclusion that divine protection is always at hand against the onslaughts of the evil angel.

We know that medieval German Jewish mysticism was especially rich in angelology. Eleazar of Worms, for example, wrote a *Book of the Angels* expressing views upon the guardian angels of each man which are very close to those uttered by Cassian here, and these, interestingly, passed into the teachings of Berthold of Regensburg in the thirteenth century.[19] Jews and Christians could, indeed, grow close on this subject.[20] Nevertheless, there is once more a difference of emphasis to which, again, this passage from Cassian draws attention.

Jewish teaching gave more power and independence to the evil angel than did Christian, and evidence of this may actually be found in twelfth-century Regensburg. It is attributable to the school of Judah ben Samuel He-Hasid of

---

[16] R. H. Charles, *The Apocrypha and Pseudepigrapha of the Old Testament. ii. Pseudepigrapha* (Oxford 1913), *Book of Enoch* V–VI, pp. 191–192 (and notes), *Book of Jubilees*, V, i, p. 20.

[17] VI, 44; PG 11, 1367.

[18] VIII, xvii; *edit. cit.*, pp. 233–234.

[19] M. Güdemann, *Geschichte des Erziehungswesens und der Cultur der Juden in Frankreich und Deutschland* (Vienna 1880), I, pp. 162–163; II, pp. 165, 180.

[20] Ginzberg, *op. cit.*, V, p. 76.

Regensburg (d. 1217) and may be seen in the *Book of Raziel* and in the *Sefer Hasidim* (*Book of the Pious*) springing from that school.[21] Moreover the corrective to the power of the evil angel was not, according to the Rabbis, to be found in that form of divine care of which Matthew speaks, but in the Law. The passages from the *New Testament* which Cassian cites, and the interpolator includes, are ones which directly counteract this emphasis on the Law and offer a different view of the ways in which evil inclinations are to be countered. We are still, we may remark, dealing with subjects particularly relevant to the problems of pastoral care.

(c) 4. Ff. 154–156.[22] We return here to that concern with the Law which underlay the choice of the previous interpolation. The first part of this passage concerns the giving of the Law. The view expressed here by Serenus is that, at his creation, man had a natural knowledge of the law, and that if he had continued to observe it, no written law would have been necessary. The habit of sin having however corrupted his vision of this law, the Mosaic Law had to be given him, so that at least the fear of punishment would keep some of the original knowledge alive. Before the written law, though, Cassian repeats, man certainly had infused knowledge of it. We have abundant proof of this fact from the lives of holy men; Abel, for example, knew about making offerings, Noah could distinguish between clean and unclean animals, and Enoch learnt to walk with God. Cassian devotes considerable space to giving Old Testament examples to reinforce his double proposition that the law was thoroughly known before it was given to Moses, and that, at the outset, the creation was perfect. God was therefore justly angered by those who sinned before the giving of the written law, indeed, before the flood, and so they thoroughly deserved punishment. There is nothing to be said, he insists, on behalf of those who mock at the God of the Old Testament for leaving it so long before he produced a law—as though God learnt through his mistakes. Cassian quotes from *Ecclesiastes* III, 14, and from I *Timothy* I, 9, 'The law is not made for a righteous man but for the lawless and disobedient, for the ungodly and for sinners' in support of his argument. It therefore follows, he continues, that the written law was not given at the beginning, because it would have been superfluous had the natural law remained in observance. But equally, the doctrines of evangelical perfection could not be revealed until the law had been given. Precepts such as 'turn the other cheek' need to be measured against those of the old law, some of which required excessive revenge.

Cassian goes on then to discuss a text from *John* VIII, 44: 'for he is a liar and father of it'. He treats of the fatherhood of man in the production of the human body, adding that man's fatherhood is to be seen only as an instrument of God's. The production of man's soul is entirely God's work.

[21] K. Kohler, 'Demonology', *Jewish Encyclopedia* IV (New York and London 1901–1905), pp. 514–520.

[22] VIII, xxiii–xxv; *edit. cit.*, pp. 241–247.

The birth of man is essentially the work of God, but the parts are separate, the flesh returning to the dust and the soul returning to God. Only God can be said to be the father of spirits. In that the devil is a spirit, God is his father. Thus, when the pride of the devil prompted him to think he could be the equal of God, he became a liar and the father of deception and death.

Here we tackle the problem of Jewish attitudes to the Law head on. Reverence for the Law as it was given to Moses, recorded in the *Pentateuch* and extended so enormously in the Talmud, stands at the basis of Jewish teaching and practice. The Law was, moreover, considered by Jews to have stood at the basis of creation: 'Thus God consulted the Torah and created the world, while the Torah declared "In the beginning God created", "beginning" referring to the Torah, as in the verse "The Lord made me as the beginning of His way" (*Prov.* VIII, 22).'[23] The *Pirke de Rabbi Eliezer* makes the message of this passage especially clear: 'Seven things were created before the world was created. They are: the Torah, Gehinnom, the Garden of Eden, the throne of Glory, the Temple, Repentance, and the Name of the Messiah.'[24] The diminishment of the place of the Law in the story of the creation, fall and redemption of man which Cassian undertakes in this section thus flies in the face of some of the fundamental precepts of Judaism. It also contradicts much that we know was being taught just when clm. 22225 was being put together. Talmudic Law was the object of a great deal of devoted attention in the eleventh and twelfth centuries, from Rabenu Gershom ben Judah, through Rashi and the Tosafists (especially Eliezer ben Nathan of Mainz) to Maimonides.[25] The insistence on the superiority of New Testament precepts is, of course, an especially direct Christian challenge to the Jewish position.

(d) 6. Ff. 157v–158.[26] Here we come upon the lines of Seth, Cain and Ham. That of Seth, we are told, devoted its original great skill and learning to the worship of God, and to the needs of life, until its alliance with the line of Cain. Thereafter, this knowledge, learnt in piety, was turned to profane uses with demonic aid. Thus were discovered the magic and malefic arts, and this generation abandoned the worship of God and turned to that of the elements and fire and demons. These occult practices survived the flood because, says Cassian, Ham, according to ancient tradition, was initiated into them. He knew he must not bring such knowledge into the ark and so, to proof it against water, he engraved it upon metal and stone. He found his records after the flood and so transmitted an everlasting sacrilege to posterity. To that extent, Cassian adds, there is truth in the popular belief that angels taught the occult arts to men, and in the story that the sons of Seth and the daughters of Cain begat children who were worse than they were. So mighty were they, indeed, and so evil, that they became known as

[23] *Transl.* H. Freedman, *The Midrash*, I (London 1939), p. 1.
[24] *Transl. cit.*, pp. 11–12; see also *The Midrash, ubi supra*, pp. 6–7.
[25] A. Eckstein, 'Ratisbon', *Jewish Encyclopedia* X, p. 332.
[26] VIII, xxi–xxii; *edit. cit.*, pp. 239–241.

giants. They lived by thieving and violence rather than by the work of their own hands. Hence it was that nothing short of the flood could purify the world. This transgression on the part of the sons of Seth, whereby they violated through lust a law which had always been instinctually observed, made it necessary to introduce written laws prohibiting marriage between members of hostile races and religions (*Deuteronomy* VII, 3; *Exodus* XXXIV, 16; III *Kings* XI, 2). Cassian's willing 'discipulus', Germanus, is then allowed to confess that he finds this punishment unfair, since marriages of this type were not forbidden before the promulgation of the Law.

Germanus's dilemma is answered in fact in the passage discussed immediately before this one, for though it precedes the present one in this series, the order is reversed in Cassian. The change here seems to have been dictated by the needs of this section of the *Imago Mundi*. The present passage passes on to consider further points of chronology; the matter of the 'misalliance' of the lines of Seth and Cain; the origins of magic and profane knowledge; and the relative responsibility for the transmission of this of Seth and Ham.

We come back yet again here to Jewish and Christian exegesis of the *Book of Genesis*. In paying lip service to popular belief, Cassian in fact refers back to the story given in the *Book of Enoch* VI–VII, and partly attended to in the first interpolation, wherein the fallen angels taught men magic when they indulged in lustful intercourse with the daughters of men. His own view is widely different, and clearly expresses the Christian position. In the first place, he expressly refers to the Christian interpretation of *Genesis* VI, 1–6, whereby the daughters of men have intercourse not with angels but with the sons of Seth. Giants are born indeed, but they are not the semi-demonic giants of apocryphal literature, but degenerate human being for whom the Mosaic Law eventually became necessary because their profanities survived the flood. Again, both Judaic chronology and moral emphasis are subverted by the Christian account. Demons become less overpowering, lust less fatally destructive, the Law more a response to human need than divine command. The changes are subtle but fundamental. Seth, too, is rehabilitated. According to Jewish legend, he was most learned and even given to writing his learning down upon tablets,[27] but here the responsibility for its eventual profanation is firmly removed from him. Ham is the true culprit.[28] By making this change, Cassian and the interpolator both join a strong stream

[27] Rabbinic legend has it that Seth inherited the *Book of Raziel* from Adam, and also that he knew astronomy, invented Hebrew characters and divided time into weeks, months and years. He and his children made tablets of this knowledge, which survived. Ginzberg, *op. cit.*, V, p. 118, pp. 149–50.

[28] The most recent translator of this section of the *Collations* has been unable to find a source for this tradition; E. Pichéry, *Jean Cassien Conférences* ii (Paris 1958), p. 30.

of tradition, both Jewish and Christian, by which Ham is condemned,[29] and rescue Seth from indignity as the ancestor of Christ. That magic, too, which survives the flood, is clearly to be associated in this passage with Hebrew writing, thus feeding the somewhat sinister reputation as magicians possessed by Jews in the middle ages.[30]

All of the extracts from Cassian seem to have been chosen for their bearing on the specifically Jewish teaching on *Genesis*. We shall return to this. For the moment one more general observation may be made, one which springs in particular from the first extract and its context and concerns our approach to the treatment of sin and the Fall in medieval literature. A long time ago now Professor Morton Bloomfield led the way into this complex subject.[31] In a discussion which was largely chronological, he pointed to the Christian emphasis on pride (one that he thought may have begun with Cassian) and to its survival as the most important sin until the later middle ages. He contrasted this emphasis with an earlier stress on gluttony and lust which that of Cassian seemed to have replaced.[32] The present passage gives some substance to this account but may expand our appreciation of it. Such changes may not now need to be explained primarily by the force of time, but by that of social tension. It seems probable, indeed, in this case, that far from disappearing from the scene, the 'earlier' emphasis on gluttony and lust persisted among Jewish communities and became at times so threatening that it impelled the development of a clear contrast on the part of Christians. The incidence of this 'later' Christian emphasis may perhaps best be understood not in chronological terms but in those of the relative strength of its Jewish rival. A large part of that Christian tradition of which Professor Bloomfield speaks may have been forged far more forcefully than we have realised by a need to respond to the teaching of the Jews.

II. *The Collections of Legends*

Two of the interpolated extracts contain legendary material. Unlike the earlier interpolations, I have been unable to find a direct written source for these. They may, in fact, record stories whose currency was primarily oral. They are extremely valuable, both for this reason and because, like the Cassian extracts, they give rise to more general reflections, this time about the form and development of legend in medieval literature.

---

[29] According to Jewish legend the sexes were to be separate in the ark, but Ham ignored this prohibition and was punished by becoming black. Ginzberg, *op. cit.*, V, pp. 55–56. The Midrash on *Genesis* speaks of Ham's degradation, his abuse of his father's nakedness and his copulating with a dog in the ark, which, again, was the cause of his becoming black; *transl. cit.*, I, pp. 289, 292, 293.

[30] For the reputation of Jews as magicians see Güdemann, *op. cit.*, III, 233.

[31] M. Bloomfield, *The Seven Deadly Sins* (Michigan State College Press 1952).

[32] *Ibid.*, pp. XIV, 69–74.

(a) 5. Ff. 156–157. This extract contains, in essence, a set of legends about the coming and death of Christ. It begins with the burial of Adam at Calvary, the provision of a coffin suited to his extraordinary stature by an angel, the planting of a kernel from the tree of the forbidden fruit within his mouth. It continues through a number of Old Testament events and associates Calvary with each one of them. Noah planted his vineyard on Calvary, and it was there that Ham saw his father naked. It was on Calvary that Abraham offered up Isaac, that Jeptha sacrificed his daughter, that Manoah sacrificed the kid on hearing of the conception of Samson, that Josiah killed the priests and the dogs licked up the blood. Christ offered himself there for the salvation of the world, there where Abel had been the first sacrificial victim to honour God when he was killed by Cain.

We proceed from legends about Calvary to legends about the cross.[33] The original kernel, we are told, grew into a tree under which King Solomon was accustomed to sit in judgement and where he gave his first judgement between the women. Sheba, queen of Ethiopia, also known as the Sibyl, a creature with goose feet and bright and shining eyes, came to listen to the wisdom of Solomon, but when she saw him beneath the tree, she venerated the tree instead of him. Solomon was understandably surprised by this, but his half-brother managed to extract an explanation from the queen. She told him, and wrote in verse to the king himself, that she had venerated the tree because it would bring about the redemption of the world. On the reception of this prophecy and the verses, Solomon ordered the tree to be cut down and made into the table of the shewbread in the Temple. There it stayed until the destruction of Jerusalem by Nebuchadnezzar, when it was made into a bridge. However, Jeremiah, brother of Susannah, discovered its true nature, and in the time of Ezra it became, in turn, a part of the portico of the Temple sanctuary. Then, finally, it was cast into the pool at Solomon's gate, where an angel visited it daily to worship it. In the time of Christ it cured the sick who came to the pool for healing, among them Judas, who is seen here as the object of Christ's reproach in John V, 14. Then Simon, Joseph's nephew, father of Alexander and Rufus, and himself a carpenter, took it out of the pool to make it into the cross. This is the wood celebrated in the Mass and the wood collected by the widow of Zareptha. The passage ends, significantly, with the statement that this is the wood upon which Pilate affixed the inscription 'This is the King of the Jews'.

This particular interpolation is perhaps the most interesting and complex of them all, and the references to the alternative Jewish traditions are here at their most evident.

[33] The section of this interpolation containing legends on the cross was printed by W. Meyer, 'Die Geschichte des Kreuzholzes vor Christus', *Abhandlungen der Philosophisch-Philologischen Classe der Königlich Bayerischen Akademie der Wissenschaften* 16 (1882), 110–111, but without the accompanying material. For this reason, and because Meyer is hard to come by, I have reprinted this section with the rest in the appendix.

First of all, with the story of the planting of the kernel from the tree into the mouth of the dead Adam, we join the stream of legends about Seth, Adam's third-born son, conceived after the murder of Abel and to replace him (*Genesis* IV, 25). Stories of Seth's care of Adam, and of Seth's efforts to undo the evils of the Fall by returning to paradise for the mercy of God and for help from the tree of life were widely popular in the twelfth and thirteenth centuries, and notably so in Germany. Stemming originally from expansions of the apocryphal lives of Adam and Eve,[34] these stories have their roots in Hebrew tradition,[35] as have, of course, so many of the legends of the wood of the tree of life. In this passage we have both clear concern with this strong Hebrew tradition and an equally clear Christianisation of it.

Stories of Adam and Eve and Seth and of early recourse to the tree of paradise may to some extent be shared by Jews and Christians without offence to the divisions between them. The story of the extraordinary height of Adam with which the passage begins, for instance, comes from Jewish tradition,[36] and so does the legend that Adam was buried by angels.[37] Stories of the eventual fate of the tree, however, may not be so shared. The idea that the wood of the tree of paradise which precipitated the Fall could be used again in the cross upon which the atonement was made was, understandably, a beautiful one in Christian eyes, but once seized upon was naturally antipathetic to Judaism. Judaism had its own legends about the fate of the tree, legends which, understandably, stressed the central features of the Jewish faith. Thus one tradition, and apparently a very old one, has it that the wood taken from the tree of paradise eventually became the rod of Moses,[38] another that it provided a writing reed for the torah.[39] Without entering at this point into the tangled problem of the chronological development and relationships of such legends, it is easy to see how the Christian stories could be used as polemic against the Jews, one rendered all the more forceful by its resemblance at certain points to Jewish tradition. The

---

[34] See on this E. C. Quinn, *The Quest of Seth for the Oil of Life* (Chicago 1962), pp. 15–46. My debt to this learned study is very great. On German interest in the story of Adam and Eve, Seth, and the tree of paradise, in the thirteenth century and later, see A. C. Dunstan, 'The Middle High German "Adam und Eva" by Lutwin and the latin "Vita Adae et Evae"', *Modern Language Review* 24 (1929), 191–199, and B. Murdoch, 'Genesis and Pseudo-Genesis in late Medieval German Poetry', *Medium Aevum* 45 (1976), pp. 70–77.

[35] W. Meyer, 'Vita Adae et Evae', *Abhandlungen der Philosophisch-Philologischen Classe der Königlich Bayerischen Akademie der Wissenschaften* 14 (1878), p. 207.

[36] J. A. Fabricius, *Codicis Pseudepigraphi Veteris Testamenti, Volumen Alterum* (Hamburg 1741), pp. 41–42. Also *Pirke de Rabbi Eliezer, transl. cit.*, p. 100. The Midrash on *Genesis* tells how Adam's height, which originally filled the whole world, was reduced to 100 cubits after his sin. *Transl. cit.*, pp. 91, 155.

[37] Ginzberg, *op. cit.*, I, 100. The tradition that Adam was buried by three archangels is also to be found in Jewish apocryphal literature, for example in the so-called Apocalypse of Moses; R. H. Charles, *The Apocrypha and Pseudepigrapha of the Old Testament* ii (Oxford 1913), p. 151.

[38] Ginzberg, *op. cit.*, VI, 14 n. 82; A. Rappaport, *The Folklore of the Jews* (London 1937), p. 127; *Pirke de Rabbi Eliezer* x, *transl. cit.*, pp. 312–313.

[39] Ginzberg, *op. cit.*, III, p. 477.

Christian legends could, furthermore, be used to bring into question once again Jewish reliance upon the Old Testament alone, to diminish the stature of the great Old Testament figures against the stature of the Redeemer, and to stress Christian belief in the fulfilment of Old Testament prophecy in Christ.

They are used in precisely this way here. The immediate association of the shared legends about Adam, and commonly known Old Testament events, with Calvary (an association not made sufficiently clear by those who have concentrated only upon the rood legends to be found in this passage)[40] leaves us in no doubt that the Christianisation of Jewish tradition is this passage's ultimate purpose. It is the purpose too of the inclusion in this text of legends about the cross, and this fact may give us a greater understanding of the origins of these last.

The beginning assertion that Adam was buried at Calvary is in direct opposition to that Jewish tradition which had him buried at Hebron,[41] and to a second tradition, also Jewish, which had him buried on the site of the Temple.[42] The opposing Christian view which placed his grave on Calvary is clearly to be found in Origen and in some of the later Fathers.[43] I have found no source for the further associations with Calvary but their purport is evident enough, especially as the next of the associations in line—Calvary as the site of Noah's vineyard, in which Ham saw his father naked (*Genesis* IX, 22)—actually compares this event with Christ's crucifixion by the Jews. Calvary is then, as we saw, described as the site of four Old Testament sacrifices and two bloodstained encounters. The references to these Old Testament sacrifices and slaughters are soundly based (they are, respectively, to *Genesis* XXII, 9; *Judges* XI, 34–39; *Judges* XIII, 19–20; II *Kings* xxiii, 20; III *Kings* xxi, 19; *Genesis* IV, 4), but the association of them with Calvary in biblical terms, of course, is not. In this way, however, the place of Christ's death is seen as a place of death central in the history of Israel.

This process of Christianisation becomes particularly striking when we turn to the legends of the cross. King Solomon, for all his wisdom and greatness, is no proof against the message of the queen, who was also a prophet. No amount of Old Testament misuse of it, its utilisation in buildings or as a bridge, for example, or its eventually being cast away, can destroy the redemptive and healing power of the wood. In the story of the pool, indeed, we are taken straight from the Old Testament to the New, for the pool of healing is the pool of John V, 2–4:

---

[40] See for example E. C. Quinn, *op. cit.*, pp. 72–84 where, in an otherwise most interesting discussion, the polemical element of these legends has been quite lost.

[41] For the tradition of Adam's burial at Hebron see Jerome, *Liber de Situ et Nominibus Locorum Hebraicorum*, PL 23, 906; Ginzberg, *op. cit.*, I, p. 289, V, p. 256 n. 263; *Pirke de Rabbi Eliezer*, xx, *transl. cit.*, p. 148.

[42] F. Piper, 'Adams Grab auf Golgotha', *Evangelisches Jahrbuch* (1861), 19; Ginzberg, *op. cit.*, V, p. 137.

[43] PG 13, 1777; Ambrose, *Expositio Evangelii Secundum Lucam*, edit. M. Adriaen, *Sancti Ambrosii Mediolanensis Opera* IV (Turnholt 1957), p. 378.

Now there is at Jerusalem by the sheep market a pool which is called in the Hebrew tongue Bethesda, having five porches. In these lay a great multitude of impotent folk, of blind, halt, withered, waiting for the moving of the water. For an angel went down at a certain season into the pool, and troubled the water: whosoever then first after the troubling of the water stepped in was made whole of whatsoever disease he had.

The pool of Bethesda is sometimes associated with the pool of Siloe, to be found in *Nehemiah* III, 15. This part of the interpolation, indeed, pays special attention to Old Testament prophets, and it becomes easy to see why. All of those included seem to have been chosen in order that they may be detached from their association with the Jewish Messiah and attached instead to the Christian one. Thus, after the making of the wood into the table of the shewbread,[44] and the re-making of it into a bridge, Jeremiah makes an appearance; and the facts that Susannah was his sister and that both were the children of the High Priest Hilcias are especially mentioned. In this way the Book of *Daniel* becomes involved in the story,[45] and so, in particular, do specifically Jewish anxieties about false and true prophecies of the Messiah.[46] With the widow of Zareptha and her two sticks (III *Kings* xvii, 12) we touch upon that Jewish legend which would see the widow's son, the prophet Jonah (resuscitated by Elias in this chapter of the *Book of Kings*) as a possible Messiah.[47] Here, of course, the widow is drawn instead into the fate of Christ, as her son, in the Gospels, was seen as Christ's precursor.[48] The echoes here for Jews and Christians would have been resounding.

Those Gospel passages which would see Jonah as a precursor of Christ do not merely diminish the stature of Jonah against that of his greater successor; they also diminish in the same breath Solomon against Christ, and they associate the 'Queen of the South' with their demonstration that Solomon's wisdom had its limits. This context makes the treatment of the Queen of Sheba and King Solomon in the present passage doubly interesting. Again we see the compiler of the legends reaching back from the New Testament to a radical re-working of some well worn stories in the Old.

The first point of interest in this rendering of the tale of Solomon and the queen is the identification of the queen with the Sibyl. Jewish teaching had long attempted to focus upon itself the reverence anciently given to the Sibyls, and had even taken the step of ascribing to them verse teachings which were in fact Jewish. Christians were not slow to follow this example,

---

[44] This is itself an intrusion into, and a veiled criticism of, the Hebrew legend which would have it that the table of the shewbread descended directly from the time of Moses; Ginzberg, *op. cit.*, III, p. 160.

[45] The story of Susannah and the Elders is in *Daniel* XIII, 2–69.

[46] Jewish legend, reported by Jerome, maintained that elders of the kind who attempted to seduce Susannah supported such attempts with the claim that such conjunctions might produce the Messiah; Ginzberg, *op. cit.*, VI, p. 426.

[47] Ginzberg, *op. cit.*, VI, p. 351.

[48] *Matthew* XII, 40–42; Luke XI, 29–32.

though using this time the Sibyl as a witness to the coming of Christ.[49] The Sibyl here stands clearly within this latter tradition. The verses quoted may indeed be taken from the *Contra Iudeos* of Quodvultdeus.[50] The initial Greek letters of the twenty-seven lines spell out the Greek for 'Jesus Christ, the son of God, the Saviour'. The merging of the Sibyl with the Queen of Sheba drives the point home. The queen held a firm place in Jewish tradition too as a prophet, and one who, as here, wrote down her prophecies.[51] She did not, however, then prophesy, as here, the coming of Christ. The Sibyl and the queen became identified in Greek sources at least as early as the ninth century[52] and there, as here, they point firmly to the New Testament[53] and to Christ. By the ninth century in Germany the visit of the Queen of Sheba to Solomon could be seen as a prefiguration of the journey of the Magi to the Christ child.[54] This particular part of the story set out here thus sprang again from a strong tradition of Christian polemic.[55] It has, moreover, an extra touch which is very evidently German. The goose feet and bright and shining eyes make the Sibyl and the Queen of Sheba at once a familiar figure to German mythology[56]—further proof, if such were needed, that this interpolation sprang from and was directed to German concerns, and an

[49] H. C. Lanchester, 'Sibylline Oracles', *Encyclopedia of Religion and Ethics* XI (New York 1921), pp. 497–498.

[50] Edit. R. Braun, *Opera Quodvultdeo Carthaginiensi Episcopo Tributa* (Turnholt 1976), pp. 248–249. They are to be found also, of course, in St Augustine's *City of God*. Edit. E. M. Sanford and W. M. Green, *Saint Augustine, the City of God against the Pagans* v (Loeb, Harvard U.P. and London 1965), pp. 442–444. See also *edit.* J. Geffcken, *Die Oracula Sibyllina bearbeitet im Auftrage der Kirchenväterkommission* (Leipzig 1902), pp. 153 ff.

[51] The story of Solomon's sending a message to the queen and her writing a reply is in the *Targum Sheni*; Ginzberg, *op. cit.*, IV, 143–144.

[52] J. L. Herr, 'La reine de Saba et le bois de la croix', *Revue Archéologique* 23 (1914), pp. 18–19.

[53] The New Testament passage to which they point is to be found in *Matthew* XII, 42: 'The Queen of the South shall rise up in the judgement with this generation, and shall condemn it; for she came from the uttermost parts of the earth to hear the wisdom of Solomon; and behold a greater than Solomon is here.' Also *Luke*, XI, 31. This involves an adaptation of III *Kings*, 10.

[54] Rabanus Maurus, *Commentaria in Libro II Paralipomenon*, PL 109, 472–473.

[55] Although this interpolation is a polemical one there are also signs of appeasement. The treatment of Solomon, for instance, though again a part of a long tradition, shews more subtlety than is usually associated with efforts to supersede Jewish teachings, for he and Ezra are allowed to betray at least some reverence for the wood of the cross, for both place it in the Temple. This is an adaptation of that tradition which would have Solomon throwing the wood crossly away, and may have been an adaptation intended to suggest that Solomon could be seen as a precursor of Christ. Quinn, *ubi supra*, p. 82. The treatment of Solomon is here kinder than that in the *Historia*; Meyer, 'Die Geschichte . . .' *art. cit.*, p. 107. It is an adaptation which shews a certain respect for Jewish teaching, for in this there is a strain of legend which would have the tree of paradise used in the construction of the tabernacle. Ginzberg, *op. cit.*, II, pp. 291–293; V, p. 105; VI, p. 66.

[56] The queen with goose feet has long been associated with the splay-footed spinning-woman of Germany mythology, Berhte, and both, in turn, with the Queen of Sheba; K. Simrock, *Handbuch der deutschen Mythologie* (Bonn 1878), pp. 391–393. The bright and sparkling eyes may perhaps have been developed from the fact that Berhte in Old High German is Perahta, bright. These observations and references come from Quinn, *op. cit.*, pp. 78–79.

indication of the lengths to which polemic in a particular cause could be allowed to go.

Towards the end of the passage, we are taken, furthermore, firmly into the land of dramatised legend and popular apocryphal gospel literature. I have found no source for the idea that the paralytic cured by Christ at the pool of Bethesda was in fact Judas, and that it was to Judas that Christ addressed the words of *John* V, 14: 'Behold thou art made whole: sin no more less some worse thing happen to thee', but the phrase is reminiscent of that addressed to Mary Magdalen in *John* VIII, 11. Since the development of the treachery of Judas was linked in the gospel with the later story of Mary Magdalen (*John* XII, 3–8), and since the contrast between the careers of the two became a favourite subject for dramatic exposition, this may be the origin of this singular exposition of *John* V, 14. If so, there is illumination to be gained from the dramatised contrast. According to this, Judas's complaint in *John* XII, that the ointment lavished by Mary upon Christ should have been sold in aid of the poor, was grounded in greed for his lost commission on the sale—in this case thirty pieces of silver. The tragedy to which this lost thirty pieces of silver led, and the involvement of the Jews in this particular aspect of it, was central to the story. We may have in this passage a reference to this association and an attempt to awaken these ideas. With Simon we turn to the apocryphal *History of Joseph the Carpenter* (though here Simon appears as a son of Joseph himself and not as Joseph's nephew). Alexander and Rufus are described as kinsmen of Evodius in the apocryphal *Assumption of the Virgin*, and as companions of Andrew, Peter and Matthias in the *Acts of Peter and Andrew*.[57] All of these figures are popularly known and prominent characters in stories of the life and fate of Christ and serve to lead us into the broadest possible dimensions of New Testament enthusiasm. The anxiety to lead the reader from the Old to the New Testament, and to make the journey attractive to a wide audience, seems to admit, indeed, of great licence in this cause.

(b) 7. Ff. 159–159v. We turn here from legends about Adam, Calvary and the cross to legends about Moses. Moses, we are told, was born in the time of King 'Ceneres', by whose edict the children of the Jews were to be put to death by their midwives. The child Moses was so beautiful, however, that he was set upon the water in a basket of rushes, where he was discovered by the daughter of the king as she went to bathe. Moved by his plight and his beauty, she decided to adopt him. Fortunately his aunt was close by, and was able to induce the unknowing princess to employ Moses's mother as his nurse. Moses, as he grew up, became the king's cup-bearer and then his military commander.

War broke out between Egypt and Ethiopia. Moses was required, through the machinations of persons at court envious of him, to lead the king's army

---

[57] On the dramatised stories of Judas and Mary see C. Gauvin, *Un Cycle du Théâtre Religieuse Anglais au Moyen Age* (Paris 1973), pp. 173, 226, 346. For Simon, Alexander and Rufus see M. R. James, *The Apocryphal New Testament* (Oxford 1924), pp. 79, 84, 194, 458.

54

into Ethiopia, a terrifying prospect because of the renowned dragons and serpents and wild beasts of Ethiopia. Moses protected his army by a combination of goats and storks, which consumed the serpents. He then besieged the capital city. The queen of Ethiopia so admired Moses that she offered to surrender it if he would marry her. He did so and took her back to Egypt, where they remained until the smiting of the Egyptians. They then took refuge with Jethro. Moses shortly afterwards married Jethro's daughter, causing his sister Miriam to protest at his having two wives, and to declare that this was why the disease of elephantiasis ravaged the people. The reader is then referred to the 'historia' for further details. The passage ends by crediting Moses with the rediscovery of the letters of the Hebrew alphabet, which had been burnt when Abraham was banished to Ur and the 'ignis chaldeorum'—a rediscovery Moses shared with Ezra.

This is an extraordinary mixture, based partly upon *Exodus* II, 1–10, 15–25 (the story of Pharaoh's daughter and the marriage of Moses to the daughter of Jethro) and *Numbers* XII, 1–2 (the mention of the Ethiopian woman) but largely on the *Antiquities* of Josephus,[58] on Artabanus[59] and on Midrashic exegesis of *Exodus*. The story follows Josephus, with intrusions and omissions of a kind which suggest that either an interpolated and abbreviated text or the memory of the compiler is at work,[60] until (and including) the marriage of Moses with the daughter of Jethro. We seem then to turn to legend from a different source, and to Jerome and Augustine for the story of the origin of Hebrew letters.[61]

Again, at first sight we seem simply to be confronted with a confused tissue of partly biblical, partly historical, partly legendary material about a distinguished Old Testament figure. Only when we look more closely does the bias of these stories become evident. The central part of the story, the double marriage of Moses, reveals it. This double marriage has no place in ancient Rabbinic legend.[62] Jewish teaching does not, indeed, treat of the Ethiopian marriage as a separate one,[63] but only with the marriage with

[58] F. Blatt, *The Latin Josephus* (Aarhus 1958), pp. 196–204.

[59] Artabanus was known largely through the *Praeparatio Evangelica* of Eusebius. For these passages see *Praeparatio Evangelica* IX, 27; PG 21, 730.

[60] Artabanus names the king, Cenephres, for instance, as Josephus does not. Josephus confines the edict to male Hebrew children, and he names Pharaoh's daughter, Thermutis, the Ethiopian city, Meroe, the Ethiopian queen, Tharbis. Moses also employs stags and ibises, not goats and storks, against the serpents according to Josephus. Storks are to be found in Jewish accounts; Ginzberg, *op. cit.*, II, p. 287. For interesting observations on the ultimate sources of Artabanus and Josephus see I. Levy, 'Moïse en Ethiopie', *Revue des Etudes Juives* 53 (1907) 201–211; T. Rajak, 'Moses in Ethiopia: Legend and Literature', JJS 29 (1978), pp. 111–122.

[61] Jerome refers to the Hebrew tradition of the 'ignis Chaldeorum' in his *Hebraicae Quaestiones in Libro Geneseos. Edit.* P. Antin, *S. Hieronymi Presbyteri Opera* i (Turnholt 1959) 15. For the parts of Abraham, Moses and Ezra in the history of the Hebrew language according to Jewish legend see Ginzberg, *op. cit.*, VI, pp. 443–444. Also *transl.* R. H. Charles, *The Book of Jubilees* (London 1902), pp. 95–96. For the reference to Augustine see below.

[62] Ginzberg, *op. cit.*, V, p. 409.

[63] *Pirke de Rabbi Eliezer* xl, *trans. cit.*, p. 313.

Zipporah, Jethro's daughter, which it equates with the marriage to the Cushite woman of *Numbers* XII, 1–2. The description here, then, of Moses as an acknowledged bigamist, is drawn from selected sources to which Rabbinic exegesis was, on this point, opposed. So is the description of Moses as the king of Egypt's favourite, the general who acted on Egypt's behalf. The Midrash knows of a campaign in Ethiopia, but one in which Moses plays a very different role. Here he is the defender of the Nubians against a usurper, Balaam, who had seized their capital and throne. His single marriage to the princess Zipporah is his reward for this noble defence.[64]

On all these issues the stories about Moses diminish him, and run counter to the way in which certain Jewish traditions wished him to be seen. The final section of the passage compounds this: the bigamy of Moses is made responsible for the scourge of elephantiasis. Artabanus/Eusebius find the origin of the disease of elephantiasis in the reign of Cenephres, and we have seen that the present compiler, or his source, had some knowledge of Artabanus. Artabanus, however, makes Cenephres himself responsible for the onset of the disease. It sprang not from the bigamous marriage of Moses, but was Cenephres's punishment for the edict by which he made Jews wear clothes which distinguished them from Egyptians.[65] I have not found a source for the account of the disease given here, but it is clear that it is a source prejudiced against Moses, and it appears to have been selected in preference to the account more sympathetic to the Jews which Artabanus gives. In the last word of the passage even Moses's place in the history of Hebrew is contested. He, Abraham and Ezra share this pride of place in Jewish legend.[66] This last section contains, however, a reference to Augustine. This reference appears to be to the *City of God*, XVIII, xxxix. Here Augustine objects to the idea that Moses and Abraham were at all prominent in the rediscovery of Hebrew letters.[67]

Instead of that Rabbinic tradition, then, which sees Moses as the mediator between God and Israel,[68] the saviour of Israel from Egypt, the means by which the Torah was at last given to the chosen people, the deliverer of Israel from the plagues,[69] we have a servant of Egypt's king and the perpetrator of an illicit marriage which actually caused the appearance on earth of a previously unknown disease. A hero figure central not merely to Jewish

[64] See on this D. J. Silver, 'Moses and the hungry birds', *Jewish Quarterly Review* 64 (1973), pp. 124–125.

[65] *Praeparatio Evangelica* IX, 26; PG 21, 731.

[66] Ginzberg, *op. cit.*, VI, pp. 443–444.

[67] W. C. Greene, *Saint Augustine, The City of God Against the Pagans* VI (Loeb, London and Harvard U.P. 1960), p. 12.

[68] 'Mediateur entre Dieu et Israël, il est au point de départ de toutes les institutions divinement données à Israël.' R. Bloch, 'Quelques aspects de la figure de Moïse dans la tradition Rabbinique', in *edit.* H. Cazelles et al., *Moïse, l'Homme de l'Alliance* (Paris 1955), p. 93.

[69] *Ibid.*, pp. 119–149. Note that the murder of the Egyptian maltreating the Hebrew of *Exodus* II, 11–12, is omitted here.

history but to the contemporary Jewish liturgy[70] becomes very nearly a villain. Further, as Moses is robbed of his distinguished role in the history of Hebrew, so his sister Miriam is robbed of hers as prophetess of the salvation of Israel through Moses.[71] Miriam here is not a prophet but a critic. She speaks of disaster, and that as a result of Moses's sexual licence. There is absolutely no sign of that Christian tradition which, far from diminishing Moses, would see him as the type and precursor of Christ.[72] The attitude is consciously of the most negative.[73]

Again, these interpolations give rise to reflections of a more general sort. The sight of rood legends, for instance, placed within this particular context may lead us to look rather differently upon their origins and history. Meyer saw them as a product of the crusading movement.[74] The discovery of an eleventh-century fragment containing them[75] prompts perhaps some revision of this view. One such is provided by this context. Stories of this sort about the cross sprang primarily from a need to counter Judaism. Legends about the cross seem originally to have been attached to apocryphal Jewish works, and to have continued to be so.[76] We are back at the *Book of Genesis* and at expansions of it of Jewish and Christian origin, and at that Jewish and Christian moral teaching which sprang from this book and these expansions. The rood legends developed as a result of a wish to find in all this distinctive Christian moral teachings and prefigurations of Christ, and fulfilments, in the crucifixion, of Old Testament prophecies.[77]

When we look at the problem in this way, we might even venture a little more thought about the style and nature of the various other legends which sprang from *Genesis* and the apocrypha. It has, for instance, been most ably shewn that Seth is early, often but not invariably, associated with the rescue from paradise for the world of a part of the living tree of life.[78] He does not appear here. Instead, an angel performs that task which is so often his. Dr Quinn explains Seth's rather variable popularity as the central figure partly

---

[70] K. Hruby, 'Moïse dans la liturgie synagogale', *ibid.*, pp. 317–343.

[71] Bloch, *art. cit.*, pp. 107–109.

[72] *Ibid.*, pp. 161–166.

[73] It is possible that this negative attitude was directed not merely to the Moses of the Jews but to the great dignity given to Moses by the *Koran* as well. See Y. Moubarac, 'Moïse dans le Coran', in *ibid.*, pp. 373–391.

[74] Meyer, 'Die Geschichte . . .', *art. cit.*, pp. 105–106.

[75] N. R. Ker, 'An eleventh century old English legend of the cross before Christ', *Medium Aevum* 9 (1940), pp. 84–85; A. S. Napier, *History of the Holy Rood Tree* (EETS 103, London 1894), pp. 2–35.

[76] E. C. Quinn, *The Penitence of Adam. A Study of the Andrius Manuscript* (U. Mississippi Press 1980), p. 33.

[77] Here I differ from Quinn, *The Quest of Seth . . . op. cit.* pp. 3–4, where she proposes that the rood legends sprang from a desire to understand the previous history of the cross discovered by St Helena. She does, however, draw attention to the interesting possibility that the image of the tree growing from Adam's mouth may be based upon *Isaiah* XI, 4: 'and he shall smite the earth with the rod of his mouth'. *Ibid.*, p. 77.

[78] *Ibid.*, pp. 8–12.

by his failure completely to fulfil the requirements of a medieval hero, partly by the chronology and accidents of oral and textual transmission. There are, however, other possible explanations. The particular requirements of polemic at particular periods may well have dictated the conscious introduction or omission of particular persons and objects. In this case it may well be that an angel seemed more suitable as an agent of salvation for Christians than Seth; especially as good angels form so large a preoccupation in the related interpolations. Seth, after all, clearly springs from Jewish tradition, and stories of the safe entry of human beings into paradise come from the Old Testament, not the New.[79] In short, the state of contemporary Christian–Jewish relations played a large part in the elements and persons stressed in legends of this kind. We might note that the process of Christianisation does not involve a stress on baptism (as for instance in the *Gospel of Nicodemus*) or on the Trinity (as in the early English rood legends), but on Calvary and the cross. Here we may well have an example of anti-Jewish polemic fitted to the period of the crusades; to this extent Meyer's analysis was an accurate one. The 'ways of tradition' may in general be more influenced by contemporary social pressures and by propaganda than we have cared to believe.[80]

(To be continued)

---

[79] Ginzberg, *op. cit.*, II, p. 313.
[80] The phrase 'the ways of tradition' is borrowed from the discussion of these ways found in R. S. Loomis, *Arthurian Tradition and Chrétien de Troyes* (New York 1948) pp. 38–58. Propaganda and polemic do not appear among the sixteen forces active upon the transmission of tradition he describes. A fascinating discussion, however, of the possible influence of the Jewish *Seder* ritual upon certain sections of Chrétien de Troyes's Story of the Grail is to be found in E. J. Weinraub, *Chrétien's Jewish Grail* (Chapel Hill 1976), pp. 50–77 and especially pp. 102–108 which suggest that direct exhortation to the Jewish people may have been a part of Chrétien's purpose.

XIV

III. *Theological Questions and Answers*

3. Ff. 153–154. I described these, in the edition of the *Imago Mundi*, as 'questions and answers on *Genesis* in the style of the school of Laon', and so they are. They seem, at first sight, to be efforts simply to resolve difficulties arising in the course of the Christian exegesis of the Scriptures; but they are more than this. They are efforts to resolve those difficulties which arise when the Christian exegesis of the Scriptures is measured specifically against the Jewish.

The passage begins with a discussion of *Genesis* I, 1: 'In the beginning God created heaven and earth', and an effort to shew how this can be reconciled with the statement in *Ecclesiasticus* XVIII, 1: 'He that liveth forever created all things together'. We are offered, in the process, biblical and patristic (Jerome and Augustine) examples of the concept 'In the beginning', one of which is taken to mean 'in the Son'. We are then taken through the course of creation, first heaven and earth, the angels and the human soul, then the rest of the work: earth, water, air, fire. The idea that the angels were created at the very beginning is doubly stressed and is reinforced with quotations from the Old Testament and Paterius. That the fall of the angels happened also at this very beginning, on, indeed, this first day, is also stressed, and the separation of good from bad angels is in fact held to be the burden of *Genesis* I, 4: 'and he divided the light from the darkness'. Heaven and earth and the creation of the human soul become then the work of the second day. The third day sees the separation of the waters from the dry land, the fourth the creation of the sun, moon and stars, the fifth that of birds and fish, the sixth that of the beasts. Then, with the help of the Trinity, God makes Adam and, sending him into a deep sleep in the care of angels, he takes a rib and makes Eve.

The question arises as to why God makes Eve from Adam's rib and not from earth, as he did Adam. The answer is immediate: in order that she may realise her subjection to man. We proceed to the forbidden fruit and to the refusal to mankind of the knowledge of good and evil. We are told that knowledge of evil may be equated with breaking the commandments, knowledge of good, with keeping them. The original nakedness of the pair, too, means that they were originally clothed in the grace of God. There follows the story of the temptation, dramatised (as in *Genesis* III, 1–5) as a

XIV

184

dialogue between Eve and the serpent—here equated with the devil. Two reasons are given for the involvement of Adam. Firstly, he ate because when she had eaten the fruit the woman did not die after all. Secondly, Adam did not wish to hurt her. The subsequent mutual knowledge of their nakedness is explained allegorically as a knowledge of their loss of grace; the fig leaves are seen as symbols of the addition of sin.

Adam, the interpolation continues, was guilty of six sins: of pride, sacrilege, homicide, fornication, theft and greed. This is what is meant by the reign of death of *Romans* I, 14. Without the cross and the redemption, man, sinful and just alike, would have remained subject to this reign. But man has been redeemed.

The references to the words of Jerome and Augustine on *Genesis* I, 1 give us our first clue to the direction of this discussion. The reference to Augustine seems in fact to be less to his *De Genesi ad Litteram* than to the *Sermo ad populum* I, in which he stresses that passage from the gospel of John which condemns the Jews for their unbelief.[81] This passage is worth quoting in full, for its message is so clear:

> Ait enim Dominus incredulis Judaeis: 'si crederitis Moysi, crederetis et mihi: ille enim de me scripsit' (*John* V, 46). Cur ergo non ipsum Dominum intelligam, in quo principio fecit Deus Pater coelum et terram? Nam 'In principio fecit Deus coelum et terram', Moyses utique scripsit, quem de Domino scripsisse, ipsius Domini voce firmatur. An forte non est etiam ipse principium? Neque hinc dubitare oportebit, loquente Evangelio, ubi Judaei cum a Domino quaesissent quis esset, ipse respondit: 'Principium, quia et loquar vobis' (*John* VIII, 25). Ecce in quo principio fecit Deus coelum et terram. Coelum ergo et terram fecit Deus in Filio, per quem facta sunt omnia, et sine quo factum est nihil: ut etiam Evangelio concordante cum Genesi, secundum Testamenti utriusque consensum teneamus haereditatem, litigiosasque calumnias exhaereditatis haereticis relinquamus.

The burden of Augustine's criticism concerns the failure of the Jews to accept that Christ, the son, is the 'principium' of which this verse of *Genesis* speaks, and their refusal, too, to accept that this part of the Old Testament is fulfilled in the New. Indeed, this whole first section of the passage is preoccupied once again with the fulfilment of the Old Testament, especially the utterances of Solomon and the Prophets, by the New. The reference to Jerome is, furthermore, to his *Hebraicae Questiones in Libro Geneseos* and to his discussion in this of Aquila's translation of the Hebrew word 'bresith' by 'in capitulo'.[82] Jerome's translations from the Hebrew were, of course, frequently challenged by advocates of the Jewish position.[83] Here Jerome's authority is firmly upheld.

[81] *Sermones ad populum* I, 2; PL 38, 24–5.
[82] *Edit.* P. Antin, *S. Hieronymi Presbyteri Opera* i (*Corpus Christianorum* 72, Turnholt 1959), p. 3.
[83] See, for example, the attitude of Bodo-Eleazar, convert-deacon of Louis the Pious; PL 121, 486.

Besides this, this section is full of reference to those other Jewish-Christian anxieties made now so familiar, especially through the interpolations from Cassian. Thus, the idea that the angels were created on the first day is again in direct contravention of the Midrash. As we saw, according to this, the angels were created on the second day, or on the fifth—but certainly not on the first. The fact that the Christian position is supported here by Old Testament quotations—quotations from, moreover, *Job* and *Proverbs*—drives the distinction and the polemical aspect of it home. The idea that the fall of the angels happened at this very beginning is, again as we saw above, inimical to Jewish teaching, and so is the idea that the devil and the serpent were one and the same.[84] Jewish legend, too, held that the soul of Adam could have been created after his body.[85] The point is nowhere in the passage expressly made, but the form followed by the discussion and the sources invoked ensure that special emphasis is placed upon those points at which Jewish and Christian teachings diverge most sharply. It is perhaps for this reason that the Trinity is singled out as God's helper in the creation of Adam and angelic help relegated to the creation of Eve.[86] It is worth noticing that in his anxiety to stress the priority of the fall of the angels, and to find biblical support for this, the compiler of this passage acts in defiance of a warning given by Augustine himself.[87]

At other points, however, Christian and Jewish teaching is in accord, and where it is so it seems that at least some effort is made to emphasise this too. Thus the six sins of Adam seem to be a direct echo of the six precepts given to Adam in Rabbinic exegesis.[88] The sleep of Adam and the care taken to save him pain when his rib is made into Eve is stressed by the *Pirke de Rabbi*

[84] On all this see the discussion of the first extract from Cassian; cf. *JJS* 37 (1986), pp. 41–3. The reference to Paterius is to his *Expositio Veteris ac Novi Testamenti* I, i–ii; PL 79, 685–6.

[85] Ginzberg, *op. cit.*, V, 79.

[86] Insistence upon the Trinity was early a central part of polemic against the Jews. R. M. Ames, *The Debate between the Church and the Synagogue* (unpubl. Ph.D. dissertation, Columbia University 1950), p. 441, quoted in E. C. Quinn, *The Quest of Seth*, p. 149, n. 27. The Trinity is taken as the explanation of the 'Faciamus' of *Genesis* I, 26 by the Fathers of the church in contradistinction to the Jewish explanation which held that 'Faciamus' applied to the angels. See on this M.-Th. d'Alverny, 'Comment les théologiens et les philosophes voient la femme', in *La Femme dans les Civilisations des Xe–XIIIe Siècles* (C.E.S.C.M. Poitiers 1977), p. 15. The patristic position on 'Faciamus' is to be found in the *Sententiae Divinae Paginae* of the 'school of Laon'. *Edit.*, F. Bliemetzrieder, 'Anselms von Laon systematische Sentenzen', *Beiträge zur Geschichte der Philosophie des Mittelalters* 18 (1919), 20. The ultimate source seems to be the *De Genesi ad Litteram* I, vi, of Augustine; PL 34, 250–1.

[87] Commenting on *Genesis* I, 4, 'and he divided the light from the darkness', Augustine warns against reading such an allegory into this passage; *De Genesi ad Litteram* I, xvii; PL 34, 258–9.

[88] See the Midrash on *Genesis* II, 16; *transl. cit.*, p. 131—also p. 91 for the frequent association of the number six with the fate of Adam. The six sins of Adam are to be found too in Honorius's *Elucidarius* and the *Sententiae Anselmi*; Y. Lefèvre, *L'Eludicarium et les Lucidaires* (Paris 1954), pp. 378–9; F. Bliemetzrieder, *art. cit.*, pp. 65–6. They are also in the *Enchiridion* of Augustine; PL 40, 254. They passed, possibly from the *Elucidarius*, into the late twelfth century German work *Anegenge*; B. O. Murdoch, *The Recapitulated Fall* (Amsterdam 1974), pp. 86–7.

Eliezer.[89] The position taken on the guilt of Eve seems to be closer to Jewish views than to those of some of the Fathers,[90] and the idea that Adam was tempted because Eve had not immediately died on eating the fruit appears to have an echo in the *Targum Pseudo-Jonathan*.[91] The similarities are not allowed simply to be stated though. In the first two cases care is taken to shew how the shared teaching has its justification in the New Testament, in this case with the help of quotations from the gospel of John and the epistles of Paul. Such similarities were, I suspect, allowed to emerge only when they could be so contained. I have found, for example, in the anonymous *De Sex Dierum Creatione Liber* a context for the second reason given in the present passage for Adam's submission to Eve: that is, that he did not wish to hurt her. This same reason is advanced in the *De Sex Dierum*, but it has a rider:

> Sicut legimus quod fecit Salomon, quia propter dilectionem mulierum Deum suum contra se irritavit.[92]

We seem to have a shadow here of further discussions bearing upon the limitations of Solomon.

Although I have nowhere found a passage identical with this among the published fragments of the 'school of Laon' there are many similarities between them. I have already drawn attention in the footnotes to some of those between the present passage and the *Sententiae Divinae Paginae* and the *Sententiae Anselmi*. There are many more between it and these,[93] between it and other treatises and fragments known to be associated in some way with the 'school', and between it and treatises whose association, though not yet proved, is likely. Thus, the *Glossa Ordinaria* on *Genesis* carefully includes the four elements in the scheme of creation, and uses similar quotations in the discussion of 'In principio'.[94] The clothing of Adam in grace and the reasons for the subjection of Eve are to be found in fragments of teaching associated with Anselm of Laon.[95] Especially striking is the connection between this passage and the anonymous *Quaestiones Super Genesin* printed among the spurious works of Bede. This, alone among the possible sources I have examined, gives, for example, the same allegorical explanation of *Genesis* I, 4: that is, that the division of light from darkness signifies the division of the good angels from the bad.[96]

Some years ago now I advanced tentatively the suggestion that the teaching of the so-called 'school of Laon' was preoccupied with and directed

[89] *Pirke de Rabbi Eliezer* xii; *transl. cit.*, p. 87. It is also stressed in the *Sententiae Anselmi*; Bliemetzrieder, *art. cit.*, pp. 57–8.
[90] Augustine, for example, was not nearly so severe; M.-Th. d'Alverny, *art. cit.*, p. 20.
[91] E. G. Hirsch, 'Eve', *The Jewish Encyclopedia* V (New York and London 1905–), 275.
[92] PL 93, 231.
[93] Bliemetzrieder, *art. cit.*, pp. 13, 20, 52, 57–62.
[94] PL 113, 67–70.
[95] O. Lottin, *Psychologie et Morale aux XIIᵉ et XIIIᵉ Siècles* (Gembloux 1959), no. 133, p. 104, no. 169, p. 123.
[96] PL 93, 247.

towards Jewish beliefs with a greater urgency of purpose than we have previously imagined.[97] The context and associations of the present passage give a little more substance to that suggestion.

IV. *The Context of the Interpolated Imago Mundi and of the Text Itself*

The idea that the clm. 22225 interpolations to the *Imago Mundi* were directed towards the Jews came as a bolt from the blue to me. It should, however, have been an idea shattering only in its obviousness. The *Imago Mundi* was meant, after all, to be of service to the movement for ecclesiastical reform, and to have wide reference. It was written at Regensburg, and the presence of a Jewish community at Regensburg is exceptionally well attested. Regensburg had, in fact, the oldest German ghetto for which there is evidence; a ghetto which was, furthermore, bounded closely to the north, west and south by Christian settlements.[98] The Jews there were influential, educated and vocal. By the close of the eleventh century Menachem ben Machir, a noted Jewish liturgist and cousin of Isaac ben Judah, Rashi's teacher, was among them,[99] and by the second half of the twelfth century Regensburg was perhaps the main German Jewish cultural and talmudic centre. Rabbi Ephraim ben Isaac of Regensburg (*c.* 1110–1175) was one of the most distinguished members of an active group of tosaphists there, a group which included Isaac ben Mordecai and Judah ben Samuel He-Hasid.[100] He may well have been teaching whilst Honorius was writing.

The Abbey of St. Emmeramm of Regensburg, where, if I am correct, Honorius put together the greater part of his *Imago Mundi*, is especially prominent in the early history of the Regensburg Jewry. The earliest historical reference, indeed, to a Jew in Regensburg is to be found in a document of 981, whereby St. Emmeramm's purchased a piece of property from the Jew Samuel.[101] Two eleventh century monks of St. Emmeramm's speak of Regensburg Jews. Arnold of Vohlburg tells of discussions between Jews and Christians on the subject of miraculous cures,[102] and the more famous Otloh of St. Emmeramm's speaks of a dream a fellow monk had wherein a Jew of Regensburg was consigned to hell, a fate which Otloh seems to have thought both probable and deserved.[103] It seems with hindsight, therefore, to be the most natural thing in the world to expect a compilation

[97] V. I. J. Flint, 'The "School of Laon": A Reconsideration', *Recherches de Théologie Ancienne et Médiévale* 43 (1976), 106–7.
[98] R. Straus (*transl.* F. Gerson), *A History of the Jews in Regensburg and Augsburg* (Philadelphia 1939), pp. 1–7.
[99] L. Zunz, *Literaturgeschichte der Synagogalen Poesie* (Berlin 1865–7), pp. 158, 250.
[100] Article 'Ratisbon' by A. Eckstein, *The Jewish Encyclopedia* X (New York and London 1905–), 330–3.
[101] J. Aronius, *Regesten zur Geschichte der Juden im frankischen und deutschen Reiche bis zum Jahre 1273* (Berlin 1902), p. 135.
[102] *De Miraculis S. Emmerammi* I, 15; PL 141, 1013–14.
[103] *Liber Visionum*; MGH, SS, XI, 383.

coming from the diocese of Regensburg, such as clm. 22225, and the works of popular reforming Regensburg Christian writers of the period of the crusades, such as Honorius, to reflect contemporary discussions and differences between Christians and Jews.

Natural it may be but, to my knowledge and, it must be said, shame, this line of approach to the works of Honorius and the codices which contain them has not so far been taken. When it is, we may expect, I think, some startling revelations and some exciting new perspectives to open out before us. In the short compass of an article these revelations and perspectives cannot be pursued very far. It is, however, possible to make a few preliminary observations on the basis of the text of the *Imago Mundi* itself and the codices which contain it.

Book III of the *Imago Mundi* gives evidence of Honorius's own concern for Jewish tradition. This concern is especially clear in chapter I of this book (which chapter, of course, gave rise to the first six of the seven interpolations discussed so far). Chapter I begins with the fall of the first angel and ends with the foundation of Babylon,[104] and reference to Jewish teaching is rife throughout it. Honorius stresses immediately, for example, that the first angel fell through pride, as does interpolation I. Interestingly, he calls this angel Sathahel, not Satan. Satan, according to the Midrash on *Genesis*, was created with Eve—a chronology of the Fall which counters the Christian one.[105] Satanel, in the *Book of Enoch*, on the other hand, seduced Eve.[106] Honorius perhaps used the name Sathahel in order to maintain the Christian distinction but to reconcile it where possible with apocryphal literature. Immediately after the first four of the interpolations we proceed to the statements that Adam was formed in Hebron and stayed in paradise with Eve for seven hours, that they were both cast into exile for their disobedience to God's command and that in addition to the births of Abel and Cain they had thirty sons and thirty daughters. This is an extraordinary mixture. In the formation in Hebron and in the production of the sons and daughters Honorius adds, again, apocrypha to the *Genesis* account, some of it clearly Jewish.[107] The next section is equally mixed. Honorius deals with the death of Adam, his burial at Calvary and the return of his body then to Hebron. Like interpolation 5, which follows it in clm. 22225, this section betrays yet again a consciousness of both Jewish and Christian tradition and, as in that particular interpolation, a desire to incorporate that in the Jewish which seems harmless to the Christian. Immediately afterwards, Honorius retires sharply from the possibly harmful. We come again to Seth and the giants. Giants are mentioned here in the text, but no account is given of their birth,

[104] *Edit. cit.*, pp. 123–6.
[105] *Transl. cit.*, p. 137.
[106] *Transl. cit.*, pp. 191–2.
[107] Ginzberg, *op. cit.*, I, 289, V, 256 n. 263.

and certain reliable and early manuscripts omit them altogether.[108] This same selective care is seen in the statement, which follows closely, that Lamech killed Cain. This statement is itself an expansion of *Genesis* IV, 23–24. The text of the *Imago Mundi* found in clm. 22225 expands upon this again, and gives the additional information that Lamech was blind, and killed Cain when hunting, mistaking him for a wild beast. This expansion of *Genesis*, in both the short and longer form, is purely Rabbinic.[109] It seems that Rabbinic teaching here was acceptable; certainly there was an acute consciousness of it.

The final part of chapter I shews a great and constantly stressed awareness of the differences between the *Septuagint* and that which Honorius calls 'Hebraica veritas' in the reckoning of time. Honorius scrupulously records both reckonings. It shews to the end, too, the exceptionally delicate path Honorius trod between literal adherence to *Genesis* and the incorporation of legend which is Jewish. No deviation is allowed in the case of Noah, about whom legend abounded; but Shem and Melchisedech are identified, and King Shem is said to be the founder of Salem. These positions are not biblical but Jewish. Clm. 22225 even incorporates the purely Jewish tradition that Shem began the building of Salem, later called Jerusalem.[110] This concern for, and openness to, Jewish tradition about the founding of Jerusalem is particularly interesting when set within the context of the crusades.

Book III chapter I has lastly one more piece of evidence to contribute to the growing picture. In the appendix to my edition of the *Imago Mundi* I drew attention to one interpolation to this chapter found in early manuscripts (though not in clm. 22225). I thought then, and still think, that this particular interpolation shews the sure mark of Honorius himself. It is to be found in four twelfth century manuscripts of the text, all of them, interestingly, either English or with associations plausibly English. They are: London B.L. Cotton Cleopatra B IV (from Byland), B.L. Add. 38665 (from Kenilworth), Paris B.N. 15009 (from St. Victor but of possibly English origin), and Paris Bibl. Maz. 708 (of unknown provenance but very closely related to the English manuscript B.L. Add. 38665).[111] This interpolation follows the 'Abel et Cain genuit' of the text[112] and reads:

> Occiso autem a Caym Abel, Adam c. annos duxit in luctu et in merore, et
> deinceps coniugali thoro uti noluit. Post hoc divino iussu ammonita a sancto

---

[108] *Edit. cit.*, p. 125.

[109] It was a tradition known to St. Jerome, who refers to it in a letter to Damasus. Ep. XXXVI; PL 22, 455. See also Ginzberg, *op. cit.*, I, 116–17.

[110] Jerome, *Hebraicae Quaestiones in Libro Geneseos, edit. cit.*, p. 19. See also Ginzberg, *op. cit.*, V, 255 ff., n. 102 for the view that Jewish tradition identified Melchisedech with Shem to counter the Christian emphasis on him as a prototype of Christ. The notion that Shem began the construction of Salem is stated as a fact in the *Imago Mundi* Book I, 15; *edit. cit.*, p. 56.

[111] These manuscripts are described in the edition, pp. 24, 30, 32.

[112] *Edit. cit.*, p. 124.

190

angelo, ut denuo uxorali fruatur contubernio, quatinus maledictio Caym excludatur benedictione nascentis. Post hec genuit filium nomine Seth.

This passage, dealing as it does with the troubled questions of the line of Cain and the line of Seth (from which line Christ, of course, sprang), leads us directly back once more to problems preoccupying Jews and Christians as they struggled to interpret *Genesis* IV–VI, and with which, as we saw above, certain of the interpolations to clm. 22225 were preoccupied.[113] The tradition of the withdrawal of Adam from Eve after the murder of Abel by Cain is a Jewish one, although Jewish sources generally give one hundred and thirty years as the measure of the period of abstinence (in deference to *Genesis* V, 3) and not one hundred as here.[114] The tradition of the total rescue of Adam's line through Eve by the birth of Seth, however, is Christian. The story of the seduction of Eve by Sammael, the greatest of the falling angels, meant that by Jewish tradition the procreative powers of Eve could always be suspect, having been so corrupted from the start. Rabbinic teaching would have it too that Adam became reconciled to the idea of procreation after the Fall not because he was ordered to be so by God, through an angel, as here, but because he learnt that by this means the Torah would eventually be given to the world. He heard of this through Lamech, Cain's grandson. Jewish tradition thus gives an account of the circumstances leading up to the birth of Seth which is very much less centred upon Seth, the ancestor of Christ, than the one in this small intrusion, and one less to the credit of Adam and, especially, Eve. This interpolation appears to be an effort to reinforce the Christian view.

The connection of these four interpolated manuscripts with England is especially interesting, because the story of Adam's abstinence from Eve before the birth of Seth appears, apart that is from sources dealing specifically with Jewish teachings,[115] earliest to be found in an English manuscript of legends of the cross.[116] My conviction that this intrusion was made by Honorius himself sprang from the fact that there is a passage similar to this in the *Elucidarius*:

D. Quo ivit tunc Adam?
M. In Hebron est reversus, ubi est creatus; ibique filios procreavit. Occisum autem Abel a Cain, centum annos luxit et Evae amplius copulari noluit. Sed, quia Christus a maledicto semine Cain nasci noluit, per angelum admonitus Evae est iterum sociatus et pro Abel est Seth genitus, de cuius stirpe est Christus natus.[117]

---

[113] See above pp. 187–8.

[114] Midrash on *Genesis*, *transl. cit.*, p. 203.

[115] For example, in certain texts of the *Revelations* of Pseudo-Methodius. On this see P. Meyer, 'Notice du Ms. A 454 de la Bibliothèque de Rouen', *Bulletin de la Société des Anciens Textes Français* (1883), 95–6.

[116] R. Morris, *Legends of the Holy Rood* (E.E.T.S. 46, London 1871), p. 21. There the period of abstinence is two hundred years.

[117] I, 93; Y. Lefèvre, *L'Elucidarium et les Lucidaires* (Paris 1954), p. 377 and notes pp. 116, 120.

This work, of course, was written in England. A further, though much later, English codex containing the *Imago Mundi*, Corpus Christi College, Cambridge, 66 (the Bury St. Edmund's section) has, immediately following Honorius's treatise in the collection, a set of legends of the cross, again with a reference to the two hundred year period spent by Adam in mourning and abstinence before the birth of Seth.[118] There was perhaps more anxiety about, and more effort to find a reconciliation with, certain elements of Jewish belief in England in the middle ages than we have previously believed. This possibility may lead to yet further thought about the social context of certain of the motifs of early English literature.

A great deal more could be said about the text of the *Imago Mundi*, especially about that of Book III. Book III chapter 6, for instance, the chapter which in clm. 22225 incorporates the last of the interpolations, the legends of Moses (number 7), is full of reference and accommodation to Rabbinic tradition.[119] There are signs, too, in the other two books; the chapters on the sea, and on sweet and salt water (I, 51, 52) seem to be related, for example, to discussions of the same questions in Genesis Rabbah. The reduction of the heavens to three in I, 145–147, counters popular (though not necessarily learned) Jewish belief in the seven.[120]

Finally, it is perhaps worth pointing, very tentatively, to some of the features of those twelfth century codices in which I have found the *Imago Mundi*. The fact that Ms. Paris, Bibliotheque Nationale Lat. 15009 binds with it a very early copy of the *Contra Iudeos* of Petrus Alfonsus of course leaps to the eye. Less striking but still perhaps significant are these few facts. Works with very clear, and sometimes allegorized, Old Testament reference seem to loom largely,[121] and so do histories taking us from the years *sub lege* to the years of grace.[122] Some of the extracts from the 'School of Laon' deal clearly with Jewish concerns.[123] Sermons and treatises on the Assumption, William of Malmesbury's work on the miracles of the Virgin and extracts

[118] Ms. Corpus Christi College, Cambridge, 66, ff. 221v–224r. This is discussed by M. Laza, 'La Legende de "l'Arbre de Paradis" ou "Bois de la Croix"', *Zeitschrift für Romanische Philologie* 76 (1960), 34–63.
[119] *Edit. cit.*, pp. 128–9 and notes. There are also occasions in Book III where clm. 22225 makes additions which, though less spectacular than the interpolations, clearly refer also to Jewish belief, e.g. III, 2, p. 126 n. 6.
[120] Ginzberg, *op. cit.*, V, 10.
[121] Ms. Stiftsbibliothek Admont 400, for example, binds with the *Imago Mundi* a series of *Quaestiones* on the Pentateuch, Ms. Bayerische Staatsbibliothek, Munich clm. 14731 has moralised comments on Genesis, Isaiah, Joel, Stuttgart, Landesbibliothek Hist. Q.155 has Hugh of St. Victor on *Ecclesiastes*, Ms. Stiftsbibliothek Göttweig 103 has the *Commentarius in Genesim* of Remigius of Auxerre, Ms. Osterreichisches Nationalbibliothek Vienna 1180 has a great deal of the Old Testament itself.
[122] For example Ms. Corpus Christi College, Cambridge, 66, Ms. Paris, Bibliothèque Nationale Lat. 15009.
[123] Cf. ms. clm. 14348, ff. 243–5.

and treatises on free will are widely to be found.[124] Here we enter deep waters indeed, but it may be said that the periodic revivals of interest in the cult of the Virgin and the problem of free will are phenomena for which not all the explanations have been exhausted. In the matters both of distinguishing the Christian religion from the Jewish and of drawing the two together each occupied a central place.[125] There is of course a danger of exploiting this particular vein of ore beyond its legitimate yield and arguing that anything stridently Christian is ipso facto equally stridently anti-Jewish. These deposits do seem, however, carefully used, to be capable of yielding some novel and unexpected returns.

Conclusion

The possible lessons to be drawn from this discussion appear to me to be these. In the first place, it seems likely that Honorius himself had a hand in the choice and composition of the intrusions to ms. clm. 22225. The tenor of the intrusions and that of Book III of the text of the *Imago Mundi* itself are, in the reference each has to Jewish tradition, remarkably similar. Text and interpolation flow one into the other smoothly and without artifice. Some of the interpolations, moreover, bear signs which seem recognisable to habitual readers of Honorius. The legends, for example, are very ingeniously constructed, and weave stories of a questionable lineage with material whose authority is not in doubt in a markedly familiar way. Elements of them are to be found in works known to be Honorius's own.[126] Wide appeal and suitability for this particular purpose seem to be the criteria which guide the choice of the selector of the interpolations; they are criteria paramount in Honorius's writings too. If these interpolations were in fact made by the author of the *Imago Mundi*, then the case for the importance of clm. 22225 in the transmission of Honorius's works is very greatly strengthened, and our understanding of his own preoccupations immeasurably increased. The need to consider the teaching of the Jews, especially that of the Jews of

---

[124] For example in Mss. Paris, Bibliothèque Nationale Lat. 6560, clm. 14348, Stiftsbibliothek Melk 248, Brussels Bibliothèque Royale 10862–5.

[125] The denial of the virginity and power of Mary was important to Jewish polemic, see Ratherius of Verona, *Qualitatis Coniectura*; PL 136, 535–7. See also B. Blumenkranz, 'Vie et survie de la polèmique anti-juive', *Studia Patristica* I, i, *Texte und Untersuchungen zur Geschichte der altchristliche Literatur* 63 (1957) 469. For interesting remarks on the Jewish and Christian attitudes to election and divine revelation, as opposed to rational freedom of choice, see A. Grabois, 'Un chapitre de tolérance intellectuelle dans la société occidentale ou XII⁰ siècle: le "Dialogus" de Piérre Abelard et le "Kuzari" d'Yehudah Halévi', in *Piérre Abélard Pierre le Vénérable* (Colloques Internationaux du Centre Nationale de la Recherche Scientifique, Paris 1975), pp. 645–52.

[126] Meyer pointed to the fact that Honorius reported the story that the wood of the cross was cast into the temple pool and was visited by the angel in his *Speculum Ecclesiae*; 'Geschichte des Kreuzholzes . . .', *art. cit.*, p. 108.

Regensburg and England, is of outstanding importance to an appreciation of Honorius and this need may re-direct our attitude to him.

The second lesson is this. A very long time ago now, Miss Beryl Smalley pointed to the interest shewn by the twelfth century school of St. Victor in Jewish teaching on the Bible.[127] A few years later, Sir Richard Southern observed that nearby Jewish settlements must have had an influence on the teaching of St. Anselm of Canterbury.[128] He said than that the Jews had been 'too much overlooked as a source of criticism and an incentive to enquiry'.[129] This is still so. There has been no concerted effort to look from this particular perspective at *any* of the major intellectual and social problems which confront historians of the early twelfth century. Yet it is probable that it is of the utmost importance to very nearly all of them: the 'Investiture Contest', the 'School of Laon', the concerns central to theological, legal and cosmological studies, the rise and form of the universities.[130]

Lastly, we may with the help of clm. 22225 re-think some of our approaches to the history of medieval legend. The establishment of a chronological textual tradition is, of course, important, but perhaps not quite so important as we have allowed it to become. Textual tradition should now perhaps absorb a little less attention; the impact of contemporary social pressure—competitive social pressure especially—should attract a great deal more. Clm. 22225 shews, I think, quite clearly that anxieties about the Jews stood behind the Latin legends of the cross contained by it. These same anxieties may have stood behind many such legends, in Latin and in English. There are implications here for the history of medieval literature itself. The teaching of the Jews may have had a deeper impact upon the traditions, teachings and writings of medieval society than we have even begun to recognise. These may all seem rather large claims to make on the basis of a single somewhat carelessly copied twelfth century manuscript of a single twelfth century text. The message of clm. 22225 is, however, a remarkably direct one. The teachings of the Jews reverberate in it through the work of an ecclesiastical reformer, through exegesis of the Old Testament, incipient theology, the material of monastic meditation, the most popular of popular literature. They deserve our serious concern.

---

[127] B. Smalley, *The Study of the Bible in the Middle Ages* (Oxford 1952), pp. 149–72.

[128] R. W. Southern, *St. Anselm and his Biographer* (Cambridge 1963), pp. 88–91.

[129] *Ibid.*, p. 89.

[130] Attention should be drawn here to the recent contribution by M. L. Arduini, *Ruperto di Deutz e la controversia tra Cristiani ed Ebrei nel secolo XII* (Rome 1979). This, containing an excellent bibliography and edition of Rupert's *Anulus seu Dialogus inter Christianum et Iudeum* (*c.* 1125-7), provides the kind of preparatory material most needed. Rupert, of course, was a younger contemporary of Honorius and in many ways indebted to Honorius for the direction of his own work.

XIV

194

Appendix: The Interpolations to clm. 22225

In printing the interpolations I have decided to retain the sometimes rather curious orthography of the manuscript, merely modernising the punctuation and adding capitals for proper nouns. The extracts from Cassian and a part of that containing legends of the cross are, of course, available in print. I give here, however, the manuscript readings, only drawing attention to glaring discrepancies.

1. *150–152v*

This interpolation begins immediately after 'eternum exsilium incidit' of Book III, i, of the *Imago Mundi* (*edit. cit.* p. 124). Cassian *Collationes* VIII, vi–xii, *edit. cit.* pp. 222–8. *Serenus de principatibus.*

Absit ergo ut deum quicquam creasse confiteamur quod substantialiter nequam seu malum sit, dicente scriptura: 'Omnia que fecit deus valde bona' [*Genesis* I, 31]. Si enim apostate angeli a deo creati sunt, vel ad hoc facti, ut hos malicie gradus teneant, ac semper deceptionibus et ruinis hominum vacent, contra predicte scripture sententiam infamabimus deum velut creatorem atque inventorem malorum, quod scilicet pessimas voluntates ac naturas ipse condiderit, ad hoc eas creans ut semper in nequicia perseverantes numquam transire possunt in bone voluntatis affectum. Hanc igitur rationem diversitatis huius traditione patrum de sanctarum scripturarum fonte percepimus. Ante conditionem visibilis creature huius spiritales celestesque virtutes deum fecisse, que propter hoc quod scirent se ad tantam beatitudinis gloriam beneficio creatoris ex nichilo fuisse productas perpetuas ei gratias referentes indesinenter eius laudibus inhererent nemo fidelium dubitat. Nec enim existimare debemus creationis et opificii sui principia ab huius mundi constitutione deum primitus inchoasse, quasi anterioribus atque innumeris seculis ab omni providentia et dispensatione divina fuerit ociosus, ac tamquam non habens in quos bonitatis sue exerceret beneficia, solitarius atque ab omni munificentia alienus fuisse credatur, quod de illa inmensa ac sine principio et incomprehensibili maiestate sati inutile[1] est incongruumque sentire ipso domino de illis potestatibus hec dicente: 'Quando facta sunt simul sydera laudaverunt me voce magna omnes angeli mei' [*Job* XXXVIII, 7 Sept.]. Qui ergo intersunt creationi syderum ante illud principium in quo factum dicitur celum et terra creati fuisse manifestissime conprobamus, quippe qui pro istis omnibus visibilibus creaturis quas videbant ex nichilo processisse creatorem magna voce referuntur et admiratione laudasse. Ante illud ergo temporale principium, quod a Moyse dicitur quodque mundi huius secundum hystoricum immo Iudaicum sensum signat etatem, salvo scilicet nostro sensu, quo nos interpretamur omnium rerum Christum esse principium in quo omnia creaverit pater secundum illud: 'Omnia per ipsum facta sunt et sine ipso factum est nichil' [*John* I, 3], ante illud Geneseos inquam temporale principium omnes illas potestates celestesque virtutes deum creasse non dubium est, quas apostolus per ordinem dinumerans ita describit: 'Quia in Christo condita sunt omnia in celis et in terra, visibilia et invisibilia, sive angeli, sive archangeli, sive throni, sive dominationes, sive principatus, sive potestates. Omnia per ipsum et in ipso creata sunt.' [*Col.* I, 16.] De illorum itaque

---

[1] *Edit. cit.*, p. 223 'satis humile'.

numero nonnullos principes fuisse collapsos, lamentatio Ezechielis sive Esaye manifestissime docent. In quibus principem Tiri, vel illum Luciferum qui mane oriebatur, flebili planctu cognoscimus lamentari, et de illo quidem ita dominus ad Ezechiel: 'Fili hominis, leva planctum super principem Tyri; et dices ei, hec dicit dominus deus. Tu signaculum similitudinis, plenus sapientia, perfectus in decore in deliciis paradysi dei fuisti. Omnis lapis preciosus operimentum tuum. Sardis, topazius et iaspis, crisolitus et onix et berillus, saphirus et carbunculus et smaragdus. Aurum opus decoris tui, et foramina tua in die qua conditus es preparata sunt. Tu cherub extensus et protegens posui te in monte sancto dei, in medio igniturum lapidum ambulasti, perfectus in viis tuis a die conditionis tue inventa est iniquitas in te. In multitudine negociationis tue repleta sunt interiora tua iniquitate et peccasti. Et eieci te de monte dei et perdidi te. O cherub protegens in medio lapidum igneorum, elevatum est cor tuum in decore tuo. Perdidisti sapientiam tuam a decore tuo, in terra proieci te, ante faciem regum dedi te, ut cernerent te. In multitudine iniquitatum tuarum et iniquitate negociationis tue polluisti sanctificationem tuam.' [*Ezechiel* XXVIII, 11–18.] Esaias quoque de alio: 'Quomodo cecidisti de celo Lucifer, qui mane oriebaris? Corruisti in terram qui vulnerabas gentes; qui dicebas in corde tuo. In celum conscendam super astra dei ponam solium meum. Sedebo in monte testamenti in lateribus aquilonis ascendam super altitudinem nubium ero similis altissimo.' [*Isaiah* XIV, 12–14.] Quos tamen non solos ex illo beatissime stationis apice corruisse scriptura commemorat, dicens terciam partem stellarum draconem illum secum pariter pertraxisse, unus quoque apostolorum evidentius docet: 'Angelos vero qui non servaverunt suum principatum, sed relinquerunt suum domicilium, in iudicium magni diei vinculis eternis sub caligine reservavit' [*Ep. to Jude*, 6]. Illud etiam quod ad nos dicitur: 'Vos autem sicut homines moriemini et sicut unus de principibus cadetis' [*Psalms* LXXXI, 7], quid aliud quam multos principes cecidisse significat? Quibus indiciis ratio diversitatis huius ista colligitur. Has differentias ordinum, quas instar sanctarum celestiumque virtutum adverse potestates habere dicuntur, vel ex illius anterioris ordinis gradu in qua unaquaque creatura fuerat nunc etiam retentare, vel certe de celestibus devolutas ad similitudinem illarum virtutum que ibidem perseverant, pro nequicie sue merito, in qua unaquaque malum crevit, hos inter se gradus et ordinum vocabula in parte contraria vindicasse. Nos hactenus credebamus causam atque inicium ruine seu prevaricationis diabolice qua de angelica statione deiectus est, invidia specialiter extitisse, quando Adam et Evam livida calliditate decepit. Non esse illud prevaricationis illius seu deiectionis inicium Geneseos lectio manifestat, que anti illorum deceptionem serpentini nominis nota eum credit inurendum ita dicens: 'Serpens autem erat sapientior' sive ut Hebraici exprimunt libri 'Callidior cunctis bestiis terre quas fecit dominus deus' [*Genesis* III, 1]. Intelligitis ergo quod ante illam circumventionem primi hominis de angelica discesserat sanctitate, ita ut non solum nominis huius insigniri mereretur infamia, sed etiam in nequicie tergiversatione ceteris preferetur bestiis terre. Non enim vocabulo scriptura bonum angelum designasset nisi[2] de his qui in illa beatitudine perseverant diceret: 'Serpens autem erat sapientior omnibus bestiis terre.' Nam hoc cognomen non solum Gabrieli vel Michaheli nullo modo posset aptari sed ne bono quidem cuiquam homini conveniret. Apertissime itaque et

---

[2] *Ibid.*, p. 226 'nec'.

serpentis vocabulum et comparatio bestiarum non sonat angeli dignitatem, sed prevaricatoris infamiam. Denique livoris ac seductionis materia qua ut hominem deciperet instigatus est. De anterioris ruine causa extitit, quos scilicet de limo terre nuperrime figuratum ad illam eum gloriam cerneret evocandum, unde cum esset unus de principibus se meminerat corruisse. Et idcirco priorem eius lapsum quo superbiendo corruerat, quo etiam serpens meruerat nuncupari, secunda ruina per invidiam subsecuta est. Que inveniens cum adhuc aliquid in se rectum habentem,[3] ita ut etiam cuiusdam colloquii cum homine possit habere consortium, sententia domini in ima utiliter deiectus est, ut non iam sicut ante sublime aliquid intuens et excelsus incederet, sed ut solo coherens reperet et humiliatus super ventrem terrenis escis et operibus pasceretur, occultum deinceps publicans inimicum ac ponens inter ipsum et hominem utiles inimicicias salutaremque discordiam, ut dum cavetur tamquam hostis noxius amiciciis fraudulentis ulterius homini non possit. In quo tamen et illud nos precipue debet ut a malis consiliis declinemus quod licet deceptionis auctor congrua pena et condempnatione plectatur, nec ille per seductionem[4] supplicio careat. Licet aliquando leviore quam ille qui auctor deceptionis extiterit, quod hic expressum plenissime cernimus. Adam namque qui seductus est, immo ut apostoli verbis eloquar qui 'seductus non est' [*I Tim.* II, 14], sed seducte adquiescens in exiciabilem videtur accessisse consensum, sudore vultus ac labore tantummodo condempnatur. Qui tamen illi non per suam sed per terre maledictionem sterilitatemque decernitur. Mulier vero que huius rei persuasor extitit, multiplicationem gemitum ac dolorum atque tristicie promeretur, perpetuo pariter iugo subiectionis addicta. Serpens autem primus qui incentorum huius offense est, perenni maledictione multatur. Quam ob rem summa sollicitudine et circumspectione cavendum est a consiliis pravis, quia sicut auctorem puniunt, ita deceptum nec peccato faciunt carere nec pena. Tanta vero spirituum densitate constipatus est aer iste, qui inter celum et terram diffunditur in quo non quieti ociosique pervolitant, ut satis utiliter humanis aspectibus eos providentia divina subtraxerit. Aut enim terrore concursus eorum vel horrore vultuum, in quos se pro voluntate sua cum libitum fuerit transformant atque convertunt, intolerabili formidine homines consternarentur atque deficerent, nequaquam valentes hec carnalibus oculis intueri, aut certe nequiores cottidie redderentur exemplis eorum iugibus et imitatione viciati, et per hoc inter homines et immundas atque aerias potestates fieret noxia quedam familiaritas ac perniciosa coniunctio, quia hec flagicia que nunc inter homines admittuntur, vel parietum septis vel locorum intervallo et quedam verecundie confusione celantur. Que si aperta iugiter visione conspicerent, ad maiorem furoris incitarentur insaniam, nullo scilicet interveniente temporis puncto, quo ab istis sceleribus eas cernerent desinentes, quippe quas nulla lassitudo carnalis seu occupatio familiaris rei, ac sollicitudo cottidiani victus quemadmodum nos a ceptis intentionibus etiam invitissimos nonnumquam cessare compellunt.

---

[3] *Ibid.*, p. 226 'in sese erectum'.
[4] *Ibid.*, p. 227 'quidem qui seducitur'.

2. *152v–153*

This continues without a break in the text. Cassian *Collationes* VIII, xvii; *edit. cit.*, pp. 233–4.

Nam quod unicuique nostrum duo cohereant angeli, id est bonus et malus, scriptura testatur. Et de bonis quidem salvatur. 'Ne contempnatis unum' inquiens 'ex minimis istis pusillis; dico enim vobis quod angeli eorum in celis semper vident faciem patris mei qui in celis est' [*Matthew* XVIII, 10]. Illud quoque 'inmittet angelus domini[5] in circuitu timentium eum et eripiet eos' [*Psalm* XXXIII, 8]. Necnon etiam quod in Actibus Apostolorum de Petro legitur, quia 'angelus eius est' [*Acts* XII, 15]. De utrisque vero Liber Pastoris plenissime docet. Si autem consideremus et illum qui beatum Iob expeciit, apertissime instruemur illum fuisse, qui semper insidiatus est ei numquam eum ad peccandum potuerit incitare, et idcirco potestatem a domino poposcisse velut qui non virtute illius, sed domini defensione qui illum semper protexerit vinceretur. De Iuda quoque dicitur 'et diabolus stet a dextris eius' [*Psalm* CVIII, 6].

3. *Ff. 153–154*

This is distinguished from the foregoing passage only by beginning on a fresh line and with a larger than usual capital letter.

Oportet ergo inquirere, vel intelligere, quomodo dicit Moyses 'In principio fecit Deus celum et terram' [*Genesis* I, 1], vel quomodo hic de preterito narrat, id est per spiritum sanctum ad fidem nostram roborandam ut cognoscamus quomodo iniciate sunt creature et alibi dicitur 'qui manet in eternum omnia creavit insimul' [*Eccl.* XVIII, 1]. Si tantum dixisset et amplius non ostendisset poteramus credere, non poteramus intelligere. More materno dominus per spacio dierum voluit nobis ostendere ut essent in re et permanerent, sed hic inquirendum est dum dicit 'In principio fecit deus celum et terram' [*Genesis* I, 1]. De quali principio dicit dum multa principia legamus? Iohannes evangelista dicit 'In principio erat verbum' [*John* I, 1]. Et dominus ait 'Ego sum principium qui et loquor vobis' [*John* VIII, 25]. Et iterum, 'Inicium sapientie timor domini' [*Psalms* CX, 10]. Et alibi, 'Inicio domine terram fundasti' [*Psalms* CI, 26]. Sanctus Hieronimus et Augustinus sic dicunt, 'In principio' secundum hebraicam veritatem hoc est in capitulo facere deus celum et terram, id est in breviarium in momentum et ad sensum. 'In principio fecit deus celum et terram', hoc est in filium. Et aliter, 'In principio' inicio creaturarum quatuor creaturas ex nichilo creavit deus, celum et terram, angelos et animam humanam, relique vero creature ex ipsis procedunt, id est terra, aqua, aer et ignis. Dixit deus 'Fiat lux' [*Genesis* I, 3] et est, sed ista dictio nec per litteras nec per sillabas nec per personas nec per ullam creaturam potest intelligere, sed dixit hoc est verbum quod est filius ut Iohannes dixit, 'In principium erat verbum' [*John* I, 1]. 'Fiat lux' [*Genesis* I, 3], hoc est angeli qui prima creatura intelligitur, ut propheta dixit, 'Cum fecisset celum et terram laudaverunt me angeli mei' [*Job* XXXVIII, 7]. Et in proverbiis Salemonis legimus 'Ante quam quicquam a principio faceret, ego iam concepta erat, ludens coram eo omni tempore' [*Proverbs*

---

[5] Ms. has 'dominos'.

VIII, 22, 24, 30], hoc est sapientia que data est angelis et hominibus non sapientia divinitatis. Ergo prima dies ipsa lux, scilicet angeli. Sic autem angeli creati sunt, testante Paterio in excerptionibus beati Gregorii de creatione celorum ac firmamenti, ut si vellent in stabilitate lucis permanerent, sin autem nollent labi possent. Unde et Satan qui seorsum fluens interpretatur cum sequacibus legionibus circuit. Post lapsum vero, 'divisit deus lucem a tenebris, appellavitque lucem diem' [*Genesis* I, 4], hoc est angelos qui in veritate permanserunt priusque celi vocati et post lapsum adeo firmati, nec amodo casuri firmamenti sunt dicti. Tenebras vero noctem, hoc est apostatas angelos quorum casus est inreparabilis. Secundam dies celum et terram et animam humanam. Tercia die quando segregata est aqua ab arida id est a terra. Quarta die luminaria in celo, sol et luna et stelle. Quinta die volatilia celi pisces de aqua fecit. Sexta die quadrupedia omnia de terra facta sunt. Postea consilium trinitatis fecit hominem ut dicitur 'Faciamus hominem ad imaginem et similitudinem nostram' [*Genesis* I, 26], id est in eternitatem et immortalitatem. 'Inmisit ergo dominus soporem in Adam' [*Genesis* II, 21] id est in exstasin mentis in curia angelorum et 'tulit una de costis eius et replevit pro ea carne' [*ibid.*] id est non permisit angelum nichil facere, sed 'omnia per ipsum facta sunt et sine ipso facta est nichil' [*John* I, 3], ut cognoscamus quod unus creator tantummodo est. Queritur cur non de limo sed de costa edificavit Adam mulierem, id est ut non superbiret contra virum et diceret se simile esse viro quia dominus sic dixit, 'Sub viri potestate sis et ipse dominabitur tui' [*Genesis* III, 16]. Et acceperunt mandatum de domino ut de ligno scientie boni et mali non comederent. Lignum scientie boni id est custodia mandati. Lignum scientie mali, hoc transgressio mandati. 'Erant autem utique nudi' [*Genesis* II, 25] id est quia vestiti erant de gratia dei propterea non erubescebant quia nullam concupiscentiam habebant. 'Sed serpens erat callidior cunctis animantibus terre' [*Genesis* III, 1], et quod diabolus per ipsum loqueretur. Qui dixit ad mulierem 'Cur precepit vobis deus ne comederetis?' [*Genesis* III, 1]. De hoc ligno non dixit aliud nisi ipsum preceptum prius commemoverit ut excusationem mulier non haberet. Et ipsa mulier ad serpentem preceptum dixit. Dixit autem serpens ad mulierem 'nequaquam morte moriemini' [*Genesis* III, 4], id est quia sciebat quod ipsa immortalis erat, ita et anima sed mentitus est, quia mortalitatem [sic] quam habuit perdidit. 'Aperientur oculi vestri', hoc est in malum, 'et eritis sicut dii' [*Genesis* III, 5], id est transgressores sicut ipsi demones ut propheta dicit 'Omnes dii gentium demonia' [*Psalms* Gk., XC, 6]. Queritur cur comederit lignum vetidum Adam. Due enim cause fuerunt. Prima eo quod mulier comederit, et statim mortua non fuerit, in corpore, alia ut non contristaret eam. 'Aperti sunt oculi amborum' [*Genesis* III, 7], in malum. 'Cumque se cognovissent esse nudos' [*Genesis* III, 7], hoc est de gratia dei, 'consuerunt folia fici' [*ibid.*], id est addiderunt peccatum super peccatum quando se excusaverunt 'post meridiem' [*Genesis* III, 8], quia de luce ad tenebras declinaverunt, hoc est de immortalitate ad mortalitatem. Sex peccata habuit Adam, superbia, sacrilegium, homicidium, fornicationem, furtum et avariciam. Nam superbia est quia homo in sua esse voluit potestate, et in deo sacrilegium quia deum non credidit. Homicidium quia se ipsum precipitavit in mortem. Fornicationem spiritalem quia integritas mentis humane serpentina suasione corrupta est. Furtum quia cibos prohibitos usurpavit. Avariciam, quia plusquam sibi sufficeret appetivit. Per ista sex peccata omnes homines iustos et peccatores diabolus habuit in potestate. Unde apostolus ait 'Regnavit mors ab Adam usque ad Moysen, etiam in eos qui non peccaverunt' [*Romans* I, 14]. Nisi enim christus venisset et formam

servi accepisset, sanguineque suo nos redemisset nullus poterat in regnum dei
introire, sed in cruce alligavit diabolum principem demoniorum, et posuit eum in
infernum, liberans inde animas iustorum testante scripture quia momordit
infernum, iustos eripiens impios inibi relinquens, quia quod mordemus, partem
abstrahimus, partem dimittimus. Resurgens autem die tercia a mortuis non solum
ille sed etiam multa corpora sanctorum qui dormierant surrexerunt cum eo, et visi
sunt in sancta civitate.

4. *Ff. 154–156*

This continues without a break in the text. Cassian *Collationes* XVIII, xxiii–xxv;
edit. cit. pp. 241–7.

Serenus. Deus hominem creans omnem naturaliter ei scientiam legis inseruit. Que
si fuisset ab homine secundum propositum domini ut ceperat custodita, non
utique necessarium fuisset aliam dari, quam litteris postea promulgavit. Erat
superfluum enim extrinsecus offerri[6] remedium, quod adhuc intrinsecus vigebat
inscriptum. Sed quia hec ut diximus penitus corrupta iam fuerat libertate usuque
peccandi, velut huius exsecutor an vindex, et ut ipsis scripture verbis eloquar
adiutrix apposita est moysaice legis severa districtio, ut vel metu pene presentis,
non penitus bone scientie naturalis extinguerent, secundum prophete sententiam
dicentis 'legem dedit in adiutorium' [*Isaiah* VIII, 20 Sept.]. Que etiam secundum
apostolum pedagogus velut parvulis data fuisse describitur, erudiens scilicet eos
atque custodiens, ne ab illa disciplina in qua naturaliter fuerant instituti, quadam
oblivione discederet. Nam quia sit homini omnis scientia legis ab inicio creationis
infusa, hinc manifeste probatur, quod mandata legis absque littere lectione ante
legem, immo ante diluvium omnes sanctos observasse cogniscimus. Quem
admodum enim scire poterat Abel necdum lege mandante, quod de primiciis
ovium suarum et de adipe ipsarum sacrificium deo deberet offerre, nisi per insitam
legem sibi naturaliter fuisset edoctus? Quem admodum Noe quod mundum vel
immundum esset animal discrevisset, non dum hec legali distinguente mandato,
nisi scientia naturali fuisset instructus? Unde Enoch didicit ambulare cum deo,
cum nullam legis illuminationem ab aliquo consecutus? Ubi Sem et Iafeth legerant
'turpitudinem patris tui, non revelabis' [*Genesis* IX, 23], ut incedentes retrorsum
patris verenda velarent? Unde monitus Abraham spoliis hostium que sibi
offerebantur, ne retributione laboris consequeretur abstinuit, vel decimas sacer-
doti Melchisedech que moysayca lege precipiuntur exsolvit? Unde idem ipse
Abraham, unde Loth transeuntibus atque peregrinis humanitatis iura et ablutio-
nem pedum nec dum evangelico coruscante mandato suppliciter obtulerunt? Unde
Iob tantam devotionem fidei, tantam castimonie puritatem, tantam humilitatis,
mansuetudinis, misericordie, humanitatis conscientiam consecutus est, quantam
nunc ne ab illis quidem qui evangelia memoriter tenent videmus impleri? Quem
sanctorum legimus ante legem ullum legis non observasse mandatum? Quis illorum
non custodivit: 'Audi Israel dominus deus tuus unus est' [*Deuteronomy* VI, 4]?
Quis non implevit illud: 'Non facies tibi sculptile neque ullam similitudinem eorum
que in celo sunt sive in terra, vel eorum que in aquis sub terra' [*Exodus* XX, 4]?

---

[6] Ms. has 'offorri'.

Quis eorum non observavit: 'Honora patrem tuum et matrem' [*ibid.*, 12] vel illa que in decalogo subsecuntur: 'Non occides, non adulterabis, non facies furtum, non falsum testimonium dices, non concupisces uxorem proximi tui' [*ibid.*, 13–17] aliaque his multo maiora quibus non solum legis sed etiam evangelii prevenere mandata? Ita ergo intelligimus ab inicio deum omnia creasse perfecta, nec fuisse quod ordinationi eius principali velut inprovide et inperfecte necesse esset adiungi, si in illo statu ac dispositione que ab ipso creata sunt universa mansissent. Et idcirco in eos qui ante legem, immo diluvium, peccaverunt, iusto iudicio animadvertisse deum probamus, quia transgressi legem naturalem meruerunt sine excusatione puniri. Nec in illorum incidemus blasphemiam calumpniam, qui ignorantes hanc rationem derogant deo veteris testamenti ac detrahentes nostre fidei subsannantesque respondent, quid ergo placuit deo vestro ut post tot annorum milia legem voluerit promulgare, tanta secula passus sine lege transire? Quod si postea melius aliquid adinvenit, apparet enim in primordio mundi inferiora vel deteriora sapuisse, et post hec velut experimentis edoctum cepisse [sic] rectiora prospicere ac principales ordinationes suas in melius emendare. Quod inmense praescientie dei penitus convenire non poterit nec sine ingenti plasphemia hec de ipso ab heretica insania proferuntur dicente Ecclesiaste: 'Cognovi quoniam omnia que fecit deus ab inicio ipsa erunt in eternum. Super illa non est quod addatur, et ab illis quod auferatur.' [*Ecclesiastes* III, 14 Sept.] Et idcirco 'Iustis non est lex posita, iniustis autem et non subditis, impiis et peccatoribus, sceleratis et contaminatis' [*I Tim.* I, 9]. Illi namque habentes naturalis atque insite legis sanam atque integram disciplinam nequaquam lege hac extrinsecus adhibita litterisque descripta quoque in adiutorium illi naturali data est indigebant. Ex quibus apertissima ratione colligitur, nec legem istam per scriptam litteris dari ab inicio debuisse. Erat enim hoc superfluum fieri, stante adhuc naturali lege, nec ad integrum violata, nec evangelicam perfectionem tradi ante legis potuisse custodiam. Non enim poteram audire: 'Qui te percusserit in dexteram maxillam, prebe illi et alteram' [*Matthew* V, 39], qui contenti non erant talionis equalitate iniurias proprias vindicare, sed letales calces ac telorum vulnera pro alapa levissima rependebant et pro uno dente percutientium animas expetebant. Sed nec dici illis poterat: 'Diligite inimicos vestros' [*ibid.*, 44], in quibus magnus fructus et utilitas ducebatur, ut amicos eius diligerent, declinarent vero ab inimicis et solo ab eius odio dissiderant, nec opprimerent illos et interficere festinarent. Illud vero quod vos de diabulo moverat 'Quia mendax est et pater eius' [*John* VIII, 44], quod videlicet tam ipse quam pater suus mendax pronunciari videtur a domino, satis absurdum est hoc vel leviter oppinari. Ut enim Paulo ante diximus spiritus spiritum non generat, sicut nec anima, quidem potest animam procreare, licet concretionem carnis non dubitemus humano nos semine coalescere, itaque de utraque substantia, id est carnis et anime, que cui ascribatur auctori apostolo manifestius distinguente 'Deinde patres', inquit 'carnis nostre habuimus eruditores et reverebamur, non multo magis subiciemur patri spirituum et vivemus?' [*Hebrews* XII, 9]. Quid hac divisione clarius[7] potuit diffiniri, ut carnis quidem nostre patres homines pronunciaret, animarum vero deum solum esse patrem constanter exprimeret? Quamquam et in ipsa corporis huius concretionis ministerium tantummodo sit hominibus ascribendum, summa vero deo omnium creatori dicente David, 'Manus tue fecerunt me et plasmaverunt me' [*Psalms*

---

[7] Ms. has 'claruit'.

CXVIII, 73]. Et beatus Iob, 'Nonne sicut lac', inquit[8] 'mulxisti coagulasti me ut caseum ossibus et nervis inseruisti me' [*Job* X, 10–11 Sept.]. Et dominus ad Hieremiam, 'Priusquam te in utero formavi novi te' [*Jeremiah* I, 5]. Ecclesiastes vero utriusque substantiam nature atque originem examinatione ortus atque inicii, ex quo videlicet unaquaque processit, et consideratione finis ad quem unaqueque contendit, satis evidenter ac proprie colligens pariterque de huius corporis atque anime separatione disceptans ita disseruit, 'Priusquam convertatur pulvis in terram sicut fuit, et spiritus revertatur ad deum qui dedit eum' [*Ecclesiastes* XII, 7 Sept.]. Quid apertius dici potuit, quam ut materiam carnis quam pulverem nominavit, quia de hominis semine sumit exordium, eiusque videtur ministerium seminari, velut e terra[9] sumptam iterum reverti pronunciaret ad terram. Spiritum vero qui non per commixtionem sexus utriusque generatur, sed peculiariter a deo solo tribuitur ad auctorem suum redire signaret. Quod etiam per illam dei insufflationem que Adam primitus animavit, evidenter exprimitur. Itaque his testimoniis manifeste colligimus patrem spirituum dici neminem posse nisi deum, qui eos cum voluerit facit, homines vero carnis nostre tantummodo nominari patres. Igitur et diabolus secundum hoc quod vel spiritus vel angelus bonus creatus est patrem neminem habuit nisi deum conditorem suum. Qui cum superbia fuisset elatus et dixisset in corde suo, 'Ascendam super altitudinem nubium, ero[10] similis altissimo'[11] [*Isaiah* XIV, 14], factus est mendax 'Et in veritate non stetit' [*John* VIII, 44], sed de proprio nequicie thesauro mendacium proferens non solum mendax, sed etiam pater ipsius mendacii factus est, quo deitatem homini repromittens ac dicens 'Eritis sicut dii' [*Genesis* III, 5], in veritate non stetit, sed ab inicio factus est homicida, vel Adam in conditionem mortalitatis inducens, vel Abel instigatione sua per manum fratris interimens. Sed iam disputationem nostram duorum ferme dierum lugubratione confectam subsequens aurora concludit, ac de profundissimo questionum pelago cimbam collationis huisce ad tutissimum portum conpendium nostre rusticitatis adtraxit. In quo quidem profundo quanto nos interius divini spiritus introduxerit flatus, tanto diffusior precedens oculorum aciem semper aperietur, inmensitas ac secundum sententiam Salemonis, 'longius' fiet a nobis 'magis quam erat. Et alta profunditas, quis inveniet eam?' [*Ecclesiastes* VII, 24–5 Sept.] Quam ob rem deum deprecemur, ut in nobis vel timor eius vel caritas que nescit cadere immobilis perseveret, que nos et sapientes in omnibus faciat et a diaboli telis protegat semper illesos. Paterius.

The *Imago Mundi* then begins again at 'Adam primus homo' (III, i, p. 124) and continues to 'assumptus est rediit', when the next interpolation begins.

5. *Ff. 156–157*

Secundum dicta dominica 'terra es et in terram ibis' [*Genesis* III, 19]. Erat autem Adam .xxx. cubitorum altitudinis. Mortuo autem eo, apparuit angelus domini ferens ostrum eiusdem longitudinis, expanditque illud super eum ac nucleum vetiti ligni ori eius inponens et sic sepultus est ut supra scriptum est. In eodem etiam

---

[8] Ms. has 'in quid'.
[9] Ms. has 'econtra'.
[10] Ms. omits 'nubium ero'.
[11] Ms. omits 'altissimo'.

colliculo Calvarie plantaverat Noe vineam, delusque est in ibi a Cham, virilia patris cernentis, sicut Christus crucifigentibus eum Iudeis. Ibi Abraham optulit Ysaac filium suum. Eodem in loco Iepte dux Israel post victoriam sacrificavit filiam suam. Voverat enim, iturus in proelium, si victoria potiretur quod primum occurreret ei in reversione in domo sua illi offerret in sacrificium. Ergo reversus cum triumpho occurrit ei filia salutans eum, quam mox vivam obtulit in holocaustam. Ibidem etiam angelus domini nunciavit uxori Manue conceptum Samsonis. Statimque Manue eodem in loco vitulum sacrificavit, ac iure eiusdem carnis perfusum flamma est consumptum coram angelo. Ibi sub Helia super eundem lapidem Iarahel sacerdotes occidit, unde a canibus eadem in vinea est commesta. Christus vero se ipsum ibi etiam optulit patri pro salute mundi. Abel quoque ibi primo cum sacrificio deum honoravit, unde a fratre Cain occisus est. Igitur de prefato nucleo crevit arbor, sub quo rex Salomon solebat examinare populum, ibique primum iudicium peregit inter meretrices. Saba quoque Ethiopissa et regina quoque, que et Sibilla, habens pedes anserinos et oculos lucentes ut stelle. Hec enim nobilissima veniens e finibus terre audire sapientiam Salemonis, eum sub arbore residentem repperit, faciemque regis sprevit ac adorando honorem arbori exhibuit. Salemon vero, ut hoc vidit, intra se miratus obstupuit. Habebat autem Salemon fratrem omunciolum ex patre haut uterinum. Postquam autem Saba regina locuta est Salemoni que habebat in corde suo, flagitabat recessura pro munere quod acceptura erat ab ipso donari sibi omunciolum. Quod rex letabundus complevit, hac de causa que post patuit. Nam proficiscente illa Selomon fratriolum seorsum tulit dicens: 'Cum regina propriam repedaverit regionem, sciscitare ab ea quare me spreto arborem sit adorata.' Quod ita actum est. Nam cum regina quadam die iocaretur cum eo, ait ad eam: 'O domina, mi dic queso, quare adorando arborem praetuleris domino meo rege?' At illa ait: 'Sapientia apud dominum tuum latet non ignoratur. Arbor de qua interrogas redemptionem feret seculi futuri. Gemina enim ex ea ligna conficientur in quibus salus credentium suspendetur. At tamen versibus istis per te intimabo Salomoni, quantus rex iste fuerit tanti obprobrii. Hoc enim novi eum scire desiderare, cum te mecum iussit proficiscere. Nam de nativitate Christi ut profitetur sermo 'Vos inquam convenio iudei.' Sic est vaticinata, ut testantur ista metra.
Iudicii signum tellus sudore madescit.
E celo rex veniet per secla futurus.
Scilicet in carne presens, ut iudicet orbem.
Unde deum cernent incredulus atque fidelis.
Celsum cum sanctis evi iam termino in ipso.
Sic anime cum carne aderunt, quas iudicat ipse.
Cum iacet incultus densis in vepribus orbis.
Reicient simulachra viri, cunctam quoque gazam.
Exuret terras ignis pontumque polumque.
Inquirens, tetri portas effringet averni.
Sanctorum sed enim cuncte lux libera carni.
Tradetur, sontes eternaque flamma cremabit.
Occultos actus retegens tunc quisque loquetur.
Secreta atque deus reserabit pectora luci.
Tunc erit et luctus, stridebunt dentibus omnes.
Eripitur solis iubar et chorus interit orbis.
Volvetur celum, lunaris splendor obibit.

Deiciet colles, valles extollet ab imo.
Non erit in rebus hominum sublime vel altum.
Iam equantur campis montes et cerula ponti.
Omnia cessabunt, tellus confracta peribit.
Sic pariter fontes torrentur fluminaque igni.
Et tuba dum sonitum tristem dimittet ab alto.
Orbe, gemens facinus miserum variosque labores,
Tartarumque chaos monstrabit terra dehiscens.
Et coram hic domino reges sistentur ad unum.
E celo recidet ignisque et suffhuris amnis.

Ergo ista metra a Sabilla Salemoni sunt destinata. Que cum perlegisset, arborem precidi precepit, mensamque propositionis in domo dei formari constituit. Que permansit dum ad tempus eversionis Hierusalem, que acta est a Nabuchodonosor qui et Cambises rege Babilon sub Ioachim rege Israel, qui captus cecatus et abductus est. Interim eadem mensa a quodam trans locum lutulentum est posita, ad iter transeuntium, sed postea ab Hieremia propheta filio Helchie fratre Susanne uxoris Ioachim idem lignum est revelatum atque sub Esdra propheta, qui renovavit legem post transmigrationem Babilonis, est posticio sanctuarii innexum. Denuo inde sublatum pro nichilo est putatum, piscineque in porticu Salomonis est iniectum, et inibi ab angelo cottidie visitatum et adoratum usque ad tempus domini testantur debiles cubantes in prefato porticu prestolantes atque motum necnon Iudas, qui unus probatur ex ipsis domino ad eum dicente: 'Ecce sanus factus es, vide ne deterius tibi aliquid contingat' [*John* V, 14] signans quomodo eum esset traditurus. Post vero Simon pater Alexandri et Rufi qui erat faber lignorum filiusque fratris Ioseph nutritoris domini momento passionis illud aqua evellens, utilitati sue volens aptare, a ministris Pilati scilicet paganis angariatus est, ut tolleret illud ad crucem Ihesu. Hic est lignum illud quod memoratur diebus singulis in celebratione missarum quia qui in ligno vincebat eodem subauditur ligno revinceretur. Hec sunt etiam illa duo ligna que collegit vidua Sarepthena ad quam missus est Helyas. Quarta nempe particula seorsum caput erecta ut Lucas testatur, Pilatus apposuit propter inscriptas litteras hic est rex Iudeorum.

The *Imago Mundi* now begins again at 'Abel filius Adae' and continues to 'servi de Cham' (*edit. cit.* III, i, pp. 124–5).

6. *Ff. 157v–158*

Cassian *Collationes* VIII, xxi–xxii, *edit. cit.* pp. 239–41.

Serenus. Igitur[12] scientiam omnium naturarum per successionem generationum semen Seth paterna traditione suscipiens, donec divisum a sacrilega propagine perduravit, quemadmodum sancte perceperat, ita etiam vel ad dei cultum ad utilitatem vite communis exercuit. Cum vero impie generationi fuisset admixtum, ad res prophanas ac noxias que pie didicerat instinctu quoque demonum derivavit, curiosasque ex ea maleficiorum artes atque prestigias ac magicas superstitiones audacter instituit, docens posteros suos ut sacro illo cultu divini numinis derelicto,

---

[12] *Edit. cit.*, p. 239 'hanc ergo'.

vel elemento huic,[13] vel ignem, vel aerios demones venerarentur et colerent. Hec igitur quam diximus curiosarum rerum noticia quomodo in diluvio non perierit ac supervenientibus[14] seculis innotuerit, licet hoc minime absolutio proposite questionis exposcat, tamen quia occasio huius expositionis admonuit, prestringendum breviter puto. Quantum itaque antique traditiones ferunt, Cham filius Noe, qui superstitionibus istis et sacrilegis et prophanis erat artibus institutus, sciens nullum se posse super his memorialem librum in archam prorsus inferre, in qua erat una cum patre iusto ac sanctis fratribus ingressurus, scelestas artes ac prophana commenta diversorum metallorum laminis, que scilicet aquarum corrumpi inundatione non possent, et durissimis lapidibus insculpsit. Que peracto diluvio eadem qua, celaverat curiositate perquirens sacrilegiorum ac perpetue nequicie seminarium transmisit in posteros. Hac itaque ratione illa vulgi opinio, qua credunt angelos vel maleficia vel diversas artes hominibus tradidisse, in veritate completa est. De illis ergo quemadmodum diximus filiis[15] Seth et filiabus Cain nequiores filii procreati sunt, qui fuerunt robustissimi venatores violentissimi, ac crudelissimi[16] viri, qui pro enormitate corporum vel crudelitatis atque malicie gigantes nuncupati sunt. Hi namque finitimos populari ac rapinas inter homines exercere primi ceperunt, preda pocius exigentes vitam suam quam sudore operis ac labore contenti, et quorum usque eo scelera supercreverant, ut expiari mundus alias nisi diluvii inundatione non posset. Ita ergo filiis Seth libidinis instigatione transgressis illud mandatum, quod exordio mundi huius naturali instinctu diutissime fuerat custoditum, necesse fuit per litteram legis postea reparari. 'Filiam tuam non dabis filio eius uxorem nec de filiabus eorum accipies filio tuo, quia seducent corda vestra, ut discedatis a deo vestro et sequamini deos earum ac serviatis eis' [*Deuteronomy* VII, 3; *Exodus* XXXIV, 16; *III Kings* XI, 2]. Germanus. Merito potuisset illis ex hac presumptione coniugii crimen transgressionis ascribi, si data fuisset illis ista preceptio. At cum seiunctionis istius observantia necdum aliqua fuisset constitutione prefixa, quemadmodum illis permixtio generis ad noxam debuit inpugnari, que nullo fuerat interdicta mandato? Lex enim non preterita solet crimina, sed future dampnare.

The *Imago Mundi* now begins again at 'Arfaxat filius Sem' (III, 1) and goes on to 'et templum Delphicum' (III, 6, *edit. cit.*, pp. 125–9.

7. *Ff. 159–159v*

Hic idem Moyses natus secundum edictum regis Ceneretis ut ceteri infantes Hebreorum ab obstetricibus iussus est interimi. Sed cum adeo pulcher visus esset, in aquam cirpeo in vase est iniuctus, sicque periculum mortis evasit. Contigit autem ut filia regis prefati ad balneandum progrederetur, ad stagnum vagientemque puerum ut audivit mota miseratione ait: 'Hic ex infantibus Hebreorum.' Iussitque eum elevari ex aqua. Et ut vidit eum elegantem ac decorum aspectu dixit puellis suis: 'Iste puer adoptimus, mihi erit filius. Quis enim mihi enutrietur?' Aderat tunc forte matertera Moysi que ait ad eam: 'Est domina mihi mulier

---

[13] *Ibid.*, p. 239 'elementa haec'.
[14] Ms. has 'superbientibus'.
[15] Ms. has 'filii'—perhaps a sign that the text was being read aloud.
[16] *Edit. cit.*, p. 240 'truculentissimi'.

quedam domui mee quam apertam novi ad educandum puerum. Hanc si placet vocabo.' Currensque celerius adduxit sororem suam, matrem scilicet Moysi, traditusque est ignoranter matri proprie ad alendum, datis ferculis regiis diebus singulis ex aula iussu filie regis. Completisque itaque lustris .v. annorum, recepit eum mater adoptiva scilicet filia regis in aulam, atque sic quindennis inter pincernas regis est deputatus. Demumque sublimando dux militum est profectus. Interea exortum est bellum inter Egyptios et Ethiopes. Sed in regionem Ethiopum nullus intrare quierat pro multitudine serpentium, draconum ceterarumque bestiarum. Iussu ergo regis, Moyses dux milicie cum exercitu illinc est directus consilio primatum, quorum invidia opprimebatur eo quod agilis ad omnia videretur, quatinus illic in itinere aput prefatis feris vita privaretur. At Moyses congregata multitudine caprarum et cyconiorum preire fecit exercitum, ut multitudo serpentium ab ipsis consumpta, illesus transiret exercitus. Cum ergo intrasset terram Ethiopum, obsedit civitatem metropolitanam regionis illius, in qua erat regina Ethiopum. Igitur obpugnatis muris plurimis diebus, Ethiopissa ascenso muro sic fertur dixisse Moysi: 'Vir decorus videris sapientia sustentaris, urbs est inexpugnabilis sed ne sine honore laborasse inveniaris, tibi libens trado civitatem si me iure coniugii tecum revertens abduxeris.' Quod et factum est. Nam abduxit eam, remeans in Egyptum acceptam uxorem. Mansit autem post victoria in aula usque ad interfectionem Egyptii. Deinde non ferens inimiciam Pharaonis, ad Ietro sacerdotem se cum Ethiopissa contulit. Cuius etiam filiam accepit uxorem, unde postea Maria soror eius murmor incurrit, dicens eum duas habere uxores pro quo morbo elefantino per multata describitur. Reliqua si quis vult scire historiam persequatur. Ipse etiam primum reinvenit litteras hebraicas, que erant conbuste cum Abraham a paganis deiectus est in ur, quod est ignis qui fuit deus Chaldeorum, de quo eum eripuit dominus et ab Hesdra, qui et Malachias, post civitatem sunt renovate, quarum elementa figurarum fiunt xxii. Augustinus. Tempora iudicum. dccxviii anni.

The text of the *Imago Mundi* now continues at 'Iosue qui et Ihesus' (III, 6, *edit. cit.*, p. 129).

HONORIUS AUGUSTODUNENSIS
Bibliographical addendum

The best recent summary bibliography is that by R. Haacke and M. L. Arduini in the *Theologische Realenzyclopädie* xv (De Gruyter, New York/Berlin 1985) 576–578, (hereafter TR). Dr Arduini is herself an energetic contributor to Honorius studies and matters closely related and her writings (most listed) should be read with care and attention. TR, though good, is not, of course exhaustive. The excellent work of Henning Düwell has been omitted, although his 'Noch nicht untersuchte Handschriften des Elucidarium von Honorius Augustodunensis', *Scriptorium* 26 (1972), 337–342 and *Eine altfranzösische Übersetzung des Elucidarium* (Munich 1974) contribute greatly to our understanding of this text. So do R. P. Kinkade, *Los Lucidarios españoles* (Madrid 1968) and M. Dando 'L'adaptation provençal de l'"Elucidarium" d'Honoré d'Autun et le catharisme', *Cahiers d'Etudes Cathares* 28 (1977), 3–34. The readiness with which some of Honorius's treatises were translated into the vernacular is very striking. I have hardly touched upon this subject in my own work on him, but I believe it to be of the first importance, especially to the history of certain of the themes of medieval vernacular literature and drama. Thus F. Chiovaro, *L'Ymagine del Mondo (Firenze, Bibl. naz., cod. Palat. 703)* (Naples 1977) should be noted. I have reviewed this last, not altogether kindly, in *Cahiers de Civilisation Médiévale* 24 (1981), 70–71.

The writings of M-O. Garrigues deserve particular attention. Most of these are listed in TR (although her surname is mis-spelt). Further items are:

'La tradition manuscrite de la Summa Totius', *Acta Classica* 17 (1974), 121–137.

'Utrum Honorius ubique sit totus?', *Abhandlungen des Braunschweigischen Wissenschaftlichen Gesellschaft* 35 (1983), 31–64.

'Honorius Augustodunensis. De Esu Volatilium', *Studia Monastica* 28 (1986), 75–130.

'Utrum Honorius...' is a spirited attack on some of my efforts on Honorius which are reprinted here. It might with profit be read with them. Some of our disagreements are paleographical and scribal, which only the most determined investigator will follow to the end, one or two of them concern positions about which I had myself earlier expressed doubts, and for some (I would indicate pp. 37–38 and their accompanying notes, and p. 40 n. 60, especially) the counter evidence, frankly, will not bear the weight here placed upon it. The reader, however, must judge, and for the most part he or she may do so on the basis of the material included in this collection, although I might perhaps draw attention here to some work on Honorius I published after 'Utrum Honorius...' had gone to press; V. I. J. Flint, 'Honorius Augustodunensis. Imago Mundi', *Archives d'Histoire Doctrinale et Littéraire du Moyen Age* 49 (1982), 7–153. This does, I think, reinforce certain of my earlier conclusions, especially those which concern the chronology of Honorius's career and works. If I am thus largely unrepentant (and, through a splendid talent for caricature, perhaps a little mis-reported into the bargain) this does not diminish my gratitude to Dr Garrigues for views which are as stimulating as they are provoking, and for a great deal of helpful and generous correspondence. The battle serves too to emphasise the need for more careful work on all our parts if Honorius is to be given the position in the history of medieval ideas his voluminous output deserves. Here some present news is heartening. R. D. Crouse will shortly bring out a collection of essays and full bibliography on him (to be published by *Storia e Letteratura*) and the editors of *Corpus Christianorum* propose to include the works of Honorius in their series. These undertakings hold much promise.

INDEX

I. INDEX OF PERSONS AND PLACES

(The names of biblical personages and of regions are omitted.)

II. INDEX OF MANUSCRIPTS

(This is arranged alphabetically in accordance with the countries in which the manuscripts are now found.)